ANCIENT CHRISTIAN APOCRYPHA

THE BIBLE AND WOMEN

An Encyclopaedia of Exegesis and Cultural History

Edited by Mary Ann Beavis, Irmtraud Fischer,
Mercedes Navarro Puerto, and Adriana Valerio

Volume 3.2: Ancient Christian Apocrypha:
Marginalized Texts in Early Christianity

ANCIENT CHRISTIAN APOCRYPHA

Marginalized Texts in Early Christianity

Edited by
Outi Lehtipuu and Silke Petersen

SBL PRESS

Atlanta

Copyright © 2022 by SBL Press

All rights reserved. No part of this work may be reproduced or transmitted in any form or by any means, electronic or mechanical, including photocopying and recording, or by means of any information storage or retrieval system, except as may be expressly permitted by the 1976 Copyright Act or in writing from the publisher. Requests for permission should be addressed in writing to the Rights and Permissions Office, SBL Press, 825 Houston Mill Road, Atlanta, GA 30329 USA.

Library of Congress Control Number: 2022941820

Contents

Acknowledgments ix
Abbreviations xi

Introduction
    Outi Lehtipuu and Silke Petersen 1

No Longer Marginalized: From Orthodoxy and
    Heresy Discourse to Category Critique and Beyond
    Karen L. King 13

Part 1. Newly Discovered Texts: Nag Hammadi and Related Writings

Female Disciples of Jesus in Early Christian Gospels:
    Gospel of Mary, Wisdom of Jesus Christ, and Other
    Gospels in Dialogue Form
    Judith Hartenstein 33

Rewritten Eve Traditions in the Nature of the Rulers (NHC II 4)
    Antti Marjanen 45

Sophia and Her Sisters: Norea, Protennoia, Brontē
    Uwe-Karsten Plisch 57

Becoming Male and the Annulment of Gender Difference:
    Return to Paradise?
    Silke Petersen 69

Part 2. Texts in Continuous Use: Infancy Gospels and Apocryphal Acts of Apostles

Birth and Virginity in the Protevangelium of James
  Silvia Pellegrini 91

Gender Roles in the Infancy Gospel of Thomas
  Ursula Ulrike Kaiser 111

Ways of Life in the Apocryphal Acts of Apostles:
  Chastity as Autonomy?
  Carmen Bernabé Ubieta..127

Apostolic Authority in the Acts of Thecla
  Outi Lehtipuu 147

Gender and Slavery in the Acts of Andrew
  Bernadette J. Brooten..165

Gender and Disability in the Acts of Peter:
  Apostolic Power to Paralyze
  Anna Rebecca Solevåg...187

Part 3. Female Voices in Ancient Texts?

Perpetua, Her Martyrdom, and Holy Scriptures
  Anna Carfora 207

Genesis according to Proba and Eudocia
  María José Cabezas Cabello..221

Pilgrim of the Word: The Bible and Women in
  Egeria's *Itinerarium*
  M. Dolores Martin Trutet 239

Mixed Doubles: The Epithalamium of Paulinus and Therasia
  Cristina Simonelli..263

Early Christian Female Theologians in Profile:
 Maximilla's and Quintilla's Visions for the Church
 Heidrun Mader 277

Early Christian Women in Leadership Positions:
 The Testimony of Grave Inscriptions
 Ute E. Eisen 295

Bibliography 317

Contributors 357
Ancient Sources Index 361

Acknowledgments

In preparation for this volume, an international colloquium, Scritti di donne e scritti apocrifi tra primo cristianesimo e tardo antico, was organized at the Monastero dei Bendettini Coro de note in Catania, Sicily, on September 11–13, 2014. Most contributors to this volume took part in this gathering. We would like to thank all participants for the active and progressive discussions and particularly the organizers of the colloquium, Arianna Rotondo and Adriana Valerio. We also express our thanks to the University of Catania (Dipartimento di Scienze Umanistiche), the center FRIB–Futuro in ricera 2012 (La percezione dello spazio e del tempo nella trasmissione di identità collettive. Polarizzazioni e/o coabitazioni religiose nel mondo antico [I–VI secolo d.C.]), and the University of Graz for their financial support for the colloquium.

In addition, we would like to acknowledge the translators of the German, Italian, and Spanish chapters, Dennis Slabaugh (Uwe-Karsten Plisch, Silke Petersen, Ursula Ulrike Kaiser, Heidrun Mader, Ute Eva Eisen) and Liisa Laakso-Tammisto (Silvia Pellegrini, Anna Carfora, Christina Simonelli), and the translators of LBS Scandinavia (Carmen Bernabé Ubieta, Maria José Cabezas Cabello, M. Dolores Martin Trutet). Judith Hartenstein translated her contribution herself. In addition, Heli Ala-Maunu has helped with the translation of this introduction (originally written in German) and, together with Johanna Salovaara, with the compilation of the bibliography. Special thanks are due to Brian Duvick, who generously shared his yet-unpublished English translation of Eudocia's *Homerocento*.

Last, we want to thank Mary Ann Beavis, the English editor for the series Bible and Women, and Nicole Tilford, SBL Press Production Manager, for their support and help in the publication process.

Abbreviations

1 Apol.	Justin, *Apologia i*
1 Clem.	1 Clement
2 Clem.	2 Clement
Ab. urb. cond.	Livy, *Ab urbe condita*
AC	Antigüedad y Cristianismo: Monografías históricas sobre la Antigüedad tardía
AC	*Antiquité classique*
AcApAp	Acta Apostolorum Apocrypha
ACLS	American Council of Learned Societies
AcT	*Acta Theologica*
Act. Verc.	Actus Vercellenses
Acts Andr.	Acts of Andrew
Acts John	Acts of John
Acts Pet.	Acts of Peter
Acts. Phil.	Acts of Philip
Acts Thecla	Acts of Thecla
Acts Xanth.	Acts of Xanthippe and Polyxena
ACW	Ancient Christian Writers
Aen.	Virgil, *Aeneid*
Aeth.	Heliodorus, *Aethiopica*
Aev	*Aevum: Rassegna de scienze, storiche, linguistiche, e filologiche*
AFLF	*Annali della facoltà di lettere e filosofia dell'Università di Macerata*
AHR	*American Historical Review*
AIL	Ancient Israel and Its Literature
ALGHJ	Arbeiten zur Literatur und Geschichte des hellenistichen Judentums
Am.	Ovid, *Amores*
An.	Tertullian, *De anima*

ANF	*Ante-Nicene Fathers*
Ann.	Tacitus, *Annales*
Ap. John	Secret Book of John (NHC II 1, III 1, IV 1, BG 2) (Apocryphon of John)
Apoc. Pet.	(Greek) Apocalypse of Peter
Ars	Ovid, *Ars amatoria*
Ascen. Isa.	Martyrdom and Ascension of Isaiah 6–11
Aug	*Augustinianum*
Autol.	Theophilus, *Ad Autolycum*
b.	Babylonian Talmud
BAC	Biblioteca de autores cristianos
Bapt.	Tertullian, *De baptismo*
Barn.	Barnabas
BBA	Berliner byzantinistische Arbeiten
BCNH	Bibliothèque copte de Nag Hammadi
BETL	Bibliotheca Ephemeridum Theologicarum Lovaniensium
BF	Die Bibel und die Frauen
BG	Berlin Gnostic Papyrus
BHM	*Bulletin of the History of Medicine*
Bib	*Biblica*
BibInt	Biblical Interpretation Series
BibInt	*Biblical Interpretation*
BibRef	Biblical Refigurations
BJS	Brown Judaic Studies
BK	*Bibel und Kirche*
Bk. Thom.	Book of Thomas (NHC II 7)
BLS	Bible and Literature Series
BP	Biblioteca patristica
BSGRT	Bibliotheca scriptorum Graecorum et Romanorum Teubneriana
BW	Bible and Women
BZNW	Beihefte zur Zeitschrift für die neutestamentliche Wissenschaft
C. du. ep. Pelag.	Augustine, *Contra duas epistulas Pelagianorum ad Bonifatium*
ca.	circa
Cant. Pauli Cor.	Origen, *Cantanae in sancti Pauli epistolas ad Corinthios*

Carm.	Paulinus of Nola, *Carmina*
Catech.	Cyril, *Catechetical Lectures*
CCSA	Corpus Christianorum: Series Apocryphorum. Turnhout: Brepols, 1983–
CCSL	Corpus Christianorum: Series Latina. Turnhout: Brepols, 1953–
Cent. verg.	Proba, *Cento vergilianus de laudibus Christi*
CH	*Church History*
Cher.	Philo, *Cherubim*
ClQ	*Classical Quarterly*
Cod. justin.	Codex justinianus
Cod. theod.	Codex theodosianus
Congr.	Philo, *De congressu eruditionis gratia*
CPE	*Connaissance des Péres de l'Eglise*
CRAI	*Comptes rendus de l'Académie des inscriptions et Belles-Lettres*
CS	*Cistercian Studies*
CSEL	Corpus Scriptorum Ecclesiasticorum Latinorum
CSHG	Cambridge Studies in Historical Geography
CSPFF	Convegno di Studio promosso dalla Fondazione Franceschini
CT	Codex Tchacos
Cult. fem.	Tertullian, *De cultu feminarum*
Curios.	Plutarch, *De curiositate*
d.	died
Daphn.	Longus, *Daphnis and Chloe*
DH	Denzinger, Heinrich, and Peter Hünermann. *Enchiridion symbolorum definitionum et declarationum de rebus fidei et morum*. 45th ed. Freiburg: Herder, 2017.
Dial.	Justin, *Dialogus cum Tryphone*
Did.	Didache
Did. Apost.	Didascalia apostolorum
Dig.	Digesta
EC	Escriptors Cristians
ECCA	Early Christianity in the Context of Antiquity
Ecl.	Virgil, *Eclogae*
EDNT	Balz, Horst, and Gerhard Schneider. *Exegetical Dictionary of the New Testament*. ET. 3 vols. Grand Rapids: Eerdmans, 1990–1993.

EHO	Estudios históricos la Olmeda
EJL	Early Judaism and Its Literature
EKKNT	Evangelisch-katholischer Kommentar zum Neuen Testament
Ep.	*Epistula(e)*
Eph.	Xenophon of Ephesus, *Ephesian Tale*
Epigr.	Martial, *Epigrams*
Erat.	Lysias, *On the Murder of Eratosthenes*
EstBib	*Estudios bíblicos*
EstCl	*Estudios clasicos*
ET	English translation
Eth. nic.	Aristotle, *Ethica nicomachea*
EUZ	Exegese in unserer Zeit
Exeg. Soul.	Exegesis on the Soul (NHC II 6)
Exc.	Clement of Alexandria, *Excerpta et Theodoto*
FC	Fathers of the Church
FCNTECW	Feminist Companion to the New Testament and Early Christian Writings
FKDG	Forschungen zur Kirchen und Dogmengeschichte
FKG	Frauen–Kultur–Geschichte
Fr. Ps.	Origen, *Fragmenta in Psalmos 1–150*
Garr.	Plutarch, *De garrulitate*
GCS	Die griechischen christlichen Schriftsteller der ersten [drei] Jahrhunderte
GG	Geschichte und Geschlechter
GIBBENS	Guides et inventaires bibliographiques de la Bibliothèque de l'École normale supérieure
Git.	Gittin
Gos. Jud.	Gospel of Judas (CT 3)
Gos. Mary	Gospel of Mary
Gos. Pet.	Gospel of Peter
Gos. Phil.	Gospel of Philip (NHC II 3)
Gos. Thom.	Gospel of Thomas
Hab. virg.	Cyprian, *De habitu virginum*
Haer.	Irenaeus, *Adversus haereses*
Helv.	Jerome, *Adversus Helvidium de Mariae virginitate perpetua*
Herm. Mand.	Shepherd of Hermas, Mandate(s)
Herm. Vis.	Shepherd of Hermas, Vision(s)

HI	Historia Incógnita
HispSac	*Hispania Sacra*
Hist. eccl.	Eusebius, *Historia ecclesiastica*
Hist. pag.	Paulus Orosius, *Historiarum adversus paganos*
HNT	Handbuch zum Neuen Testament
Hom. Josh.	Origen, *Homiliae in Josuam*
Hom. Luc.	Origen, *Homiliae in Lucam*
HTR	Harvard Theological Review
ICIS	Inscriptiones Christianae Italiae Subsidia
Ign. *Eph.*	Ignatius, *To the Ephesians*
Ign. *Phld.*	Ignatius, *To the Philadelphians*
Ign. *Smyrn.*	Ignatius, *To the Smyrnaeans*
Ign. *Trall.*	Ignatius, *To the Trallians*
IJerusalem	Thomsen, Peter, ed. *Die lateinischen und griechischen Inschriften der Stadt Jerusalem und ihrer Umgebung.* Leipzig: Hinrichs, 1922.
Il.	Homer, *Iliad*
Inst.	Gaius, *Institutiones*
Iter. conj.	John Chrysostom, *De non iterando conjugio*
Itin.	Egeria, *Itinerarium*
JAAR	*Journal of the American Academy of Religion*
JBL	*Journal of Biblical Literature*
JECS	*Journal of Early Christian Studies*
JFSR	*Journal of Feminist Studies in Religion*
JR	*Journal of Religion*
JRS	*Journal of Roman Studies*
JSNT	*Journal for the Study of the New Testament*
JSNTSup	Journal for the Study of the New Testament Supplement Series
JSOTSup	Journal for the Study of the Old Testament Supplement Series
JSPSSup	Peleponnesica: Journal of the Society of Peloponnesian Studies Supplement
Ketub.	Ketubbot
l(l).	line(s)
LCC	Library of Christian Classics
LCL	Loeb Classical Library
Leuc. Clit.	Achilles Tatius, *Leucippe and Clitophon*
LHBOTS	The Library of Hebrew Bible/Old Testament Studies

LXX	Septuagint
m.	Mishnah
Marc.	Tertullian, *Adversus Marcionem*
Mart. Pet.	Martyrdom of Peter
MDATC	*Materiali e discussioni per l'analisi dei testi classici*
Melch.	Melchizedek (NHC IX 1)
Metam.	Ovid, *Metamorphoses*
MLC	*Miscellània Liturgica Catalana*
MScRel	*Melanges de science religieuse*
MST	Mittellateinische Studien und Texte
MT	Masoretic Text
MTS	Marburger theologische Studien
MTSR	*Method and Theory in the Study of Religion*
Nat. Rulers	Nature of the Rulers (NHC II 4) (Hypostasis of the Archons)
NETS	Pietersma, Albert, and Benjamin G. Wright, eds. *A New English Translation of the Septuagint*. New York: Oxford University Press, 2007.
NewDocs	Horsley, Greg H. R., and Stephen Llewelyn, eds. *New Documents Illustrating Early Christianity*. North Ryde, NSW: The Ancient History Documentary Research Centre, Macquarie University, 1981–.
NHC	Nag Hammadi Codices
NHMS	Nag Hammadi and Manichaean Studies
NHS	Nag Hammadi Studies
NKJV	New King James Version
Norea	Thought of Norea (NHC IX 2)
NovT	*Novum Testamentum*
NovTSup	Supplements to Novum Testamentum
NPNF2	*Nicene and Post-Nicene Fathers*, series 2
NS	new series
NT	New Testament
NTAbh	Neutestamentliche Abhandlungen
NTD	Das Neue Testament Deutsch
NTOA	Novum Testamentum et Orbis Antiquus
NTP	Novum Testamentum Patristicum
NTS	*New Testament Studies*
Od.	Homer, *Odyssey*
Odes Sol.	Odes of Solomon

Ol.	Pindar, *Olympionikai*
Orig. World	On the Origin of the World (NHC II 5)
OT	Old Testament
OTP	Charlesworth, James H., ed. *Old Testament Pseudepigrapha*. 2 vols. New York: Doubleday, 1983, 1985.
Paed.	Clement of Alexandria, *Paedagogus*
Pan.	Epiphanius, *Panarion*
Paraph.	Nonnus of Panopolis, *Paraphrasis S. secundum Ioannem euangelii*
Paraph. Shem.	Paraphrase of Shem (NHC VII 1)
par(r).	parallel(s)
Pass. Andr.	Passion of Andrew
Pass. Perpet. Felicit.	Passio Perpetuae et Felicitatis
Pelag.	Jerome, *Adversus Pelagianos dialogi III*
Per.	Prudentius, *Peristephanon*
Phil.	Polycarp, *To the Philippians*
PG	Patrologia Graeca [= Patrologiae Cursus Completus: Series Graeca]. Edited by Jacques-Paul Migne. 162 vols. Paris, 1857–1886.
PL	Patrologia Latina [= Patrologiae Cursus Completus: Series Latina]. Edited by Jacques-Paul Migne. 217 vols. Paris, 1844–1864.
Pol.	Aristotle, *Politica*
prol.	prologue
Prot. Jas.	Protevangelium of James
PW	*Paulys Real-Encylopädie der classischen Altertumswissenschaft*. New edition by Georg Wissowa and Wilhelm Kroll. 50 vols. in 84 parts. Stuttgart: Metzler and Druckenmüller, 1894–1980.
QE	Philo, *Quaestiones et solutiones in Exodum*
RAC	Klauser, Theodor, et al., eds. *Reallexikon für Antike und Christentum*. Stuttgart: Hiersemann, 1950–.
RBén	*Revue Bénédictine*
RCT	*Revista Catalana de Teologia*
Res. Gest.	Ammianus Marcellinus, *Res Gestae*
RGG	Dieter Betz, Hans, ed. *Religion in Geschichte und Gegenwart*. 4th ed. Tübingen: Mohr Siebeck, 1998–2007.
Rhet.	Aristotle, *Rhetorica*
RIDA	*Revue International des droits de l'Antiquité*

RPP	Betz, Hans Dieter, et al., eds. *Religion Past and Present: Encyclopedia of Theology and Religion*. 14 vols. Leiden: Brill, 2007–2013.
SAC	Studies in Antiquity and Christianity
SC	Sources chrétiennes
SEAug	Studia ephemeridis Augustinianum
SECA	Studies in Early Christian Apocrypha
SEJ	Studier i exegetik och judaistik utgivna av Teologiska fakulteten vid Åbo Akademi
SemeiaSt	Semeia Studies
Sib. Or.	Sibylline Oracles
SIDS	Società Italiana Delle Storiche
Sir	Sirach or Ecclesiasticus
SJLA	Studies in Judaism in Late Antiquity
SJPJA	Studies in Jungian Psychology by Jungian Analysts
Sod.	Pseudo-Cyprian, *De Sodoma*
ST	*Studia Theologica*
Strom.	Clement of Alexandria, *Stromateis*
STT	Studi e testi tardoantichi
SubEp	Subsidia epigraphica
SUNT	Studien zur Umwelt des Neuen Testaments
SWR	Studies in Women and Religion
T. Ab.	Testament of Abraham
TA	Transformationen der Antike
Teach. Silv.	Teachings of Silvanus (NHC VII 4)
TENTS	Texts and Editions for New Testament Study
Testim. Truth	Testimony of Truth (NHC IX 3)
TFE	Theologische Frauenforschung in Europa
TRE	Krause, Gerhard, and Gerhard Müller, eds. *Theologische Realenzyklopädie*. Berlin: de Gruyter, 1977–.
Tri. Trac.	Tripartite Tractate (NHC I 5)
Trin.	(Pseudo-)Didymus, *De Trinitate*
True Doctr.	Celsus, *True Doctrine*
TS	Texts and Studies
TS	*Theological Studies*
TTCLBS	T&T Clark Library of Biblical Studies
TU	Texte und Untersuchungen
TV	*Teología y vida*

TWNT	Kittel, Gerhard, and Gerhard Friedrich, eds. *Theologische Wörterbuch zum Neuen Testament*. Stuttgart: Kohlhammer, 1932–1979.
US	*Una Sancta*
VC	*Vigiliae Christianae*
VCSup	Supplements to Vigiliae Christianae
Virg.	Ambrose, *De virginitate*
Virginit.	John Chrysostom, *De virginitate*
Virt. vit.	(Pseudo-)Aristotle, *De virtutibus et vitiis*
Vis. Paul	Vision of Paul
Vit. Sanct. Mel.	Gerontius, *Vita Sanctae Melaniae*
Wis. Jes. Chr.	Wisdom of Jesus Christ
WMANT	Wissenschaftliche Monographien zum Alten und Neuen Testament
WUNT	Wissenschaftliche Untersuchungen zum Neuen Testament
ZNW	*Zeitschrift für die neutestamentliche Wissenschaft und die Kunde der älteren Kirche*
Zost.	Zostrianos (NHC VIII 1)
ZSS	*Zeitschrift der Savigny-Stiftung für Rechtsgeschichte*

Introduction

Outi Lehtipuu and Silke Petersen

The present volume in the international series The Bible and Women: An Encyclopaedia of Exegesis and Cultural History deals with early Christian apocryphal texts, in other words, texts that are not included in the New Testament canon of Scripture. Before we turn to the structure and contents of the volume, it is useful to take a closer look at the concept of apocrypha.

1. Ancient Christian Apocrypha

The expression *ancient Christian Apocrypha*, used in the title of this volume, is coined to replace the older term *New Testament Apocrypha* and is used, for example, in the leading text collection of the German-speaking world.[1] In English, an equivalent modification, *early Christian Apocrypha*,

---

1. Christoph Markschies and Jens Schröter, eds., *Evangelien und Verwandtes*, vol. 1 of *Antike Christliche Apokryphen in deutscher Übersetzung* (Tübingen: Mohr Siebeck, 2012). This is a thoroughly revised version of the older collection *Neutestamentliche Apokryphen in deutscher Übersetzung*, vol. 1, *Evangelien*, vol. 2, *Apostolisches, Apokalypsen und Verwandtes*, ed. Edgar Hennecke and Wilhelm Schneemelcher (Tübingen: Mohr Siebeck, 1997). Schneemelcher's edition was a reworked and enlarged version of the collection of Edgar Hennecke (originally published in 1904) and hence often referred to as Hennecke-Schneemelcher. The collection was translated into English by R. McLeod Wilson as *New Testament Apocrypha*, vol. 1, *Gospels and Related Writings*, vol. 2, *Writings Relating to the Apostles, Apocalypses and Related Subjects* (Louisville: Westminster John Knox, 2003), also known as Hennecke-Schneemelcher-Wilson. In the English-speaking world, a major contribution has also been the collection of Montague R. James, *The Apocryphal New Testament Being the Apocryphal Gospels, Acts, Epistles, and Apocalypses, with Other Narratives and Fragments* (Oxford: Clarendon, 1975). This collection has been reworked by J. Keith Elliott, *The Apocryphal New Testament: A Collection of Apocryphal Christian Literature in an English Translation* (Oxford: Clarendon, 1993).

is also used.² The older term, with the New Testament defining the scope, is too limited and even anachronistic, as some of the apocryphal texts were written at a time when the New Testament canon did not yet exist.³ Thus, some recent publications prefer expressions such as "gospels that *became* apocryphal" to make it clear that the distinction between canonical and apocryphal was not unambiguous and fully fixed at the time these texts were written but was the result of a long process.⁴ At the end of the second century, Irenaeus of Lyon prioritized the Gospels of Matthew, Mark, Luke, and John, which later *became* canonical, and justified his claim why there need to be exactly four gospels (*Haer.* 3.11.8–9).⁵ Around the same time, Clement of Alexandria quoted from the Gospel of the Egyptians, commenting that the quote is not "in the four gospels that have been handed down to us" (*Strom.* 3.93.1). These examples show the openness of the situation; the intensity of Irenaeus's justification of the fourfold gospel implies that this was not unquestioningly accepted. Clement, on the other hand, did not totally reject the Gospel of the Egyptians and was willing to use it, albeit interpreting it differently from other early Christians.

A further example of this kind appears in the church history of Eusebius of Caesarea (*Hist. eccl.* 6.12.3–6) and relates to Serapion, the patriarch of Antioch around 200 CE. A church nearby had asked Serapion for permission to use the Gospel of Peter, which he first approved, but then, after hearing that it contained heretical teachings, he wrote a letter to withdraw his approval. From this we may conclude that, around 200 CE, there was a church that had access to the Gospel of Peter and was willing to use it and that there was a patriarch who at first did not see any kind of problem in it. Moreover, patristic writers did not reject all apocryphal texts but referred to and quoted from them long after the time of Irenaeus. The

---

2. See especially Andrew Gregory and Christopher Tuckett, eds., *The Oxford Handbook of Early Christian Apocrypha* (Oxford: Oxford University Press, 2015).

3. See Christopher Tuckett, "Introduction: What Is Early Christian Apocrypha?," in Gregory and Tuckett, *Oxford Handbook of Early Christian Apocrypha*, 3–12; see also Christoph Markschies, "Haupteinleitung," in *Antike christliche Apokryphen*, 1:1–183; François Bovon, "Apocrypha/Pseudepigrapha III: New Testament," *RPP* 1:308–9.

4. See Tuckett, "Introduction," 7; see also Dieter Lührmann, *Die apokryph gewordenen Evangelien: Studien zu neuen Texten und zu neuen Fragen*, NovTSup 112 (Leiden: Brill, 2004); Lührmann, *Fragmente apokryph gewordener Evangelien in griechischer und lateinischer Sprache*, MTS 59 (Marburg: Elwert, 2000).

5. See Silke Petersen, "Die Evangelienüberschriften und die Entstehung des neutestamentlichen Kanons," *ZNW* 97 (2006): 250–74.

evidence from ancient text collections that have been rediscovered in the modern era (see below) also shows that these texts were read and used during subsequent centuries. Epiphanius of Salamis (fourth century) and Athanasius of Alexandria in his Easter letter (367 CE) found it necessary to attack these texts, which indicates that a universally accepted canon was still debated among groups that defined themselves as Christians. Thus the patristic writers do not attest to the existence of a widely accepted and unquestionable fixed canon but rather to their will to form one.

2. Different Text Groups and Traditions

Collections of early Christian apocrypha, the present volume included, always involve many different kinds of texts, selected using various criteria, because apocryphal texts do not form a coherent group. In modern collections, it is common to group texts according to their genre and thus to use categories such as gospels, letters, apocalypses, and apostolic acts. This, however, is quite challenging because the titles of the texts, if they have survived at all, do not always match the modern categories. Moreover, some texts seem to belong to more than one genre, which makes their classification difficult. The texts are usually not named after their (alleged) authors; rather, the figures who lend their names to the writings, such as Thomas, Peter, Mary Magdalene, and Mary the Mother of Jesus, often appear as their main characters. Such texts include, among others, gospels associated with Thomas, Mary, and Philip and acts of apostles linked to Andrew, Paul, and Thecla. A number of texts are known only by title, while fragments of others have been preserved as quotations in patristic writings. Some are known through newly discovered fragments of ancient papyri that do not contain the slightest clue of a possible title. The heterogeneity of the material shows itself in the attempts of modern text collections to define the term *apocrypha*. Recent definitions are intentionally left quite open, such as the one by Christopher Tuckett in *The Oxford Handbook of Early Christian Apocrypha*: "'Apocrypha' are texts which either have the form of biblical texts which became canonical, or tell stories about characters in the biblical texts which became canonical, or convey words purportedly spoken by these characters."[6]

---

6. Tuckett, "Introduction," 8. See also the definition in Markschies, "Haupteinleitung," 114.

One possible way to group these texts is according to their reception histories. On the one hand, some texts were lost for centuries and were found, often by accident, and became accessible only in modern times. These include the papyrus codices found near the Upper Egyptian city of Nag Hammadi in 1945, which contain Coptic texts, most of which are presumably translations (probably from Greek). One of these codices, which has received the modern identification Codex II, has the Gospel of Thomas as its second text; the abbreviation used for the Gospel of Thomas, NHC II 2, indicates that it is the second text of the second Nag Hammadi codex. Three additional papyrus fragments of the Gospel of Thomas have been found in Greek. They belong to the large group of papyri discovered in Oxyrhynchus in Egypt at the end of the nineteenth century and prove the date of the text before the end of the second century. In addition to these, two other papyrus codices discovered in modern times deserve to be mentioned: the Codex Berolinensis Gnosticus 8502 and the Codex Tchacos. Some of the texts they contain also belong to the Nag Hammadi codices, but they also include other lost and previously unknown texts, such as the Gospel of Mary in the Berlin Codex and the Gospel of Judas in Codex Tchacos.[7]

On the other hand, other texts survived through the centuries in numerous versions and translations, often with a rich, albeit fragmentary, tradition history closely related to art, religion, and theology. Among the texts of this group, those that relate to Mary the mother of Jesus and her prehistory or that tell stories about Jesus's childhood have been particularly influential. The transmission of many parts of apocryphal acts of the apostles is characterized by a similar textual diversity, including various additions and modifications. The numerous versions of Thecla's story and the traditions related to the apostle Thomas in India serve as illuminating examples. These traditions continue in hagiographic literature, particularly those that revolve around Mary the mother of Jesus and the apostle Thecla.[8]

---

7. English translations of the Nag Hammadi texts as well as of the Gospel of Mary can be found in James M. Robinson, ed., *The Nag Hammadi Library in English*, 4th rev. ed. (Leiden: Brill, 1996); Marvin Meyer, ed., *The Nag Hammadi Scriptures: The International Edition* (New York: HarperCollins, 2007). For the translation of the Gospel of Judas, see Rodolpho Kasser, Marvin Meyer, and Gregor Wurst, eds., *The Gospel of Judas: From the Codex Tchacos* (Washington, DC: National Geographic, 2006).

8. On the transition from apocrypha to hagiographic literature and problems with definitions, see Markschies, "Haupteinleitung," 109–11.

The different transmission histories of these two text groups correspond to their different reception histories. Therefore the essays in this volume, itself part of a reception-history project named The Bible and Women, are arranged into different sections. The first two sections are titled "Newly Discovered Texts" and "Texts in Continuous Use," respectively. In addition, a third section deals with women's texts and is titled "Female Voices in Ancient Texts?" While the texts of the third section are normally not counted among apocryphal works, they have more in common with them than is obvious at first glance. We will first present possible connections by means of an example and then discuss them more theoretically.

3. Texts Written by Women, about Women, and for Women?

In one manuscript of 1 Clement, a text that did not become canonical, an appeal to women is made as part of a longer parenaetical instruction: "Let them demonstrate by their silence the moderation of their tongue" (1 Clem. 21.7).[9] This appeal, contained in the eleventh-century Codex Hierosolymitanus, is hardly surprising, given the command for women to be silent found in New Testament letters and other ancient (Christian and non-Christian) writings (see 1 Cor 14:34–35; 1 Tim 2:12; Sir 26:14; Clement of Alexandria, *Paed.* 2.7.58; Ambrose, *Virg.* 3.3.11). What is surprising, however, is a variant reading of the passage in the Codex Alexandrinus from the late fourth or early fifth century: "Let them demonstrate *by their voice* the moderation of their tongue." A difference of only three letters in Greek (τῆς φωνῆς instead of τῆς σιγῆς) leads to opposite ideas and contrary images of an ideal woman: one is silent; the other speaks with a clear voice. Codex Alexandrinus is the older of the two manuscripts, but in this case it offers a singular reading, while all other known manuscripts, including Codex Hierosolymitanus and Syrian, Coptic, and Latin translations, as well as Clement of Alexandria (*Strom.*14.17.108), prefer the reading with the silent woman.

Interestingly, according to different traditions, the scribe who produced Codex Alexandrinus was a woman named Thecla.[10] This cannot be

---

9. τὸ ἐπιεικὲς τῆς γλώσσης αὐτῶν διὰ τῆς σιγῆς φανερὸν ποιησάτωσαν. English translation by Michael W. Holmes, *The Apostolic Fathers: Greek Texts and English Translations*, 3rd ed. (Grand Rapids: Baker Academic, 2007), 75, 77.

10. See Kim Haines-Eitzen, *The Gendered Palimpsest: Women, Writing, and Representation in Early Christianity* (Oxford: Oxford University Press, 2012), 3–8.

historically accurate, if this means ascribing the manuscript to the apostle Thecla, who is linked with the time of the apostle Paul. It is possible, however, that the reference is to another woman with the same name or that the codex was produced in a monastery dedicated to Thecla. Nevertheless, it is remarkable that the reading favorable to women coincides with a reference to a female scribe.

Codex Alexandrinus is one of the so-called great codices that began to be made in the fourth century. It contained the entire text of the Greek Bible, in other words, both the Old Testament (including the so-called deuterocanonical books) and the New Testament and, following the book of Revelation, two letters ascribed to Clement (1–2 Clement) This shows that the letters of Clement were handed down and identified as biblical texts. While Codex Alexandrinus is one of the most important early biblical manuscripts in textual criticism, it contains numerous orthographic irregularities. These result particularly from confusions in spelling of individual letters and letter combinations that were pronounced identically when the texts were copied.[11] In older research, the variant voice/silence was explained as just such a mistake.[12] Alternatively, the many mistakes in the codex have been interpreted as an indication of a female scribe, for an educated scribe would not have made such orthographical mistakes.[13] Only recently have both phenomena, the women-friendly textual variant and the reference to a female scribe, been brought together.[14]

This small example shows the connection between different forms of marginalization with regard to apocryphal texts, passages that marginalize women, and texts written by women and female scribes. They all fall easily outside the mainstream tradition and history of reception, since there are few who read apocryphal writings, follow variant readings in different manuscripts, and trace marginal notes referring to the scribes of ancient codices. Nevertheless, they may allow us to hear a female voice, as

---

11. These include, for example, changes of vowels because of itacism (the identical pronunciation of ι, υ, ει, οι, etc.) or because of identical pronunciation of ο and ω.

12. See Rudolf Knopf, *Der erste Clemensbrief untersucht und herausgegeben*, TU 20.1, NS 5.1 (Leipzig: Hinrichs, 1899), 24. "Probably a great deal of negligence explains 217 φωνῆς instead of σιγῆς (γλώσσης occurs almost immediately before)."

13. See Johann Jakob Wettstein, *Prolegomena ad Novi Testamenti editionem accuratissimam* (Amsterdam: Wetstenios & Smith, 1730), 9–11.

14. See Haines-Eitzen, *Gendered Palimpsest*, 6: "Was it an attempt of some kind of 'proto-feminist' at rewriting the silencing of women?"

suggested by Athalya Brenner and Fokkelien van Dijk-Hemmes in their discussion of female authors. Male authorship is self-evidently assumed for biblical texts, usually (though not as constantly) for apocryphal texts as well, while female authorship must be proved.[15] We simply do not have enough information to prove female authorship, for ancient texts were often handed down without their authors being identified. For this reason, the concept of female voice can be helpful; it does not directly refer to a female author but to a female perspective or tone in the text through which the text is gendered.[16]

In the present volume, this means that the chapters in the third section, which assume female authorship (such as the texts by Perpetua, Proba, Eudocia, and Egeria), can also shed light on the texts of the other sections.[17] The inclusion of such women's texts in a volume on apocrypha indicates that it is possible to detect a female perspective not only in texts whose female authorship is relatively uncontroversial but also in other texts.[18] For example, some studies on the so-called apocryphal acts of the apostles have proposed that groups of women played an important role in transmitting oral stories on which the written texts are based.[19] It is

---

15. See Athalya Brenner and Fokkelien van Dijk-Hemmes, *On Gendering Texts: Female and Male Voices in the Hebrew Bible* (Leiden: Brill, 1993), 2. In the foreword to the volume, Mieke Bal asks: "The possibility that women might have contributed to the production of the Bible has not been taken seriously and yet the idea that everything is male unless otherwise proven is hardly acceptable. What can one do?" (ix).

16. See Brenner and Van Dijk-Hemmes, *On Gendering Texts*, 2, who pose the question: "Is it possible to gender a text or its author, that is, to define one or the other, or both, as a product of women's culture or men's culture?"

17. Some of the women's texts are written later than the texts that are usually defined as apocrypha. However, this is not an argument against their treatment together, as the term *ancient* in the title "Ancient Christian Apocrypha" covers the time period to the eighth century; see Markschies, "Haupteinleitung," 8.

18. On female authors in antiquity, see Ross Shepard Kraemer, "Women's Authorship of Jewish and Christian Literature in the Greco-Roman Period," in *"Women Like This": New Perspectives on Jewish Women in the Greco-Roman World*, ed. Amy-Jill Levine, EJL 1 (Atlanta: Scholars Press, 1991), 221–42; Susan Ashbrook Harvey, "Women and Words: Texts by and about Women," in *The Cambridge History of Early Christian Literature*, ed. Frances Young, Lewis Ayres, and Andrew Louth (Cambridge: Cambridge University Press, 2004), 382–90.

19. This shows how complex the production and transmission of ancient texts was and how inadequate is the concept of one identifiable male author. This applies to both the possible oral transmission processes behind the texts and the modifications during

possible to suppose that, similarly to the texts in the third section, at least some of the apocryphal texts were written and copied by women—but we do not know this exactly. The subtitle of this volume, "Marginalized Texts in Early Christianity," indicates that both sets of texts, which are usually studied in separate publications, have been similarly marginalized in their reception histories. They are found only at the margins of the normative Christian tradition; they are often regarded as less valuable, sometimes even heretical; consequently, they are read, discussed, and commented on much less frequently.

When texts usually treated separately and by different scholars are brought together, they can enrich one another. An example of this occurred during the conference that was organized in preparation of this volume, as a parallel from the texts of the Phrygian prophecy (also called Montanism) provided a solution to interpret a Nag Hammadi text.[20] From a hermeneutical perspective, it can be beneficial to shift one's perspective on familiar texts by changing their contexts and to cross the boundaries of scholarly traditions, categories, and text collections.

4. On the Contents of the Present Volume

Following this introduction, Karen L. King offers a further introduction to our topic, as she analyzes the division of early Christian texts into orthodox and heretical groups, a classification still commonly in use. Such categorization is closely linked to authority, but its persuasive power is largely based on disguising this by claiming that these categories are given, not discursively generated. The orthodoxy-heresy division also (re)produces the marginalization of women. However, if texts that have been marginalized by labeling them heretical are included within Christianity, the classification of the previously well-known texts also changes, since they are read in the context of a wider spectrum of Christian opinions.

---

copying, and offers a historical counterpart of modern theories about the "death of the author." See Roland Barthes, "The Death of the Author," in *Image—Music—Text* (New York: Hill & Wang, 1977), 142–48; Michel Foucault, "What Is an Author?," in *The Foucault Reader*, ed. Paul Rabinow (New York: Pantheon Books, 1984), 101–20.

20. Meanwhile published as Uwe-Karsten Plisch, "'Du zeigst das Übermaß des Erklärers'—Ein Verständnisproblem im Dialog des Erlösers (NHC III,5) und seine Lösung," in *Ägypten und der christliche Orient*, ed. Heike Behlmer et al. (Wiesbaden: Harrassowitz, 2018), 233–35.

The four essays that follow deal with newly discovered texts, as explained above, mostly from Nag Hammadi. Judith Hartenstein writes about "Female Disciples of Jesus in Early Cristian Gospels: The Gospel of Mary, Wisdom of Jesus Christ, and Other Gospels in Dialogue Form." Hartenstein gives an overview of women as recipients of revelation and as Jesus's dialogue partners. She asks how the texts understand female discipleship and then turns to the most important female disciples, such as Mary Magdalene, and groups of female disciples and their functions in these texts. In addition, she sheds light on the theological requirements for female discipleship.

Antti Marjanen deals with rewritten Eve traditions in the Nature of the Rulers (NHC II 4), one of the numerous Nag Hammadi texts that contain Genesis interpretations. Marjanen analyzes the motifs of the creation, rape, and fall of Eve, who is virtually split into a heavenly and an earthly Eve. In addition, the Nature of the Rulers introduces Norea, the daughter of Eve, whose role in the stories of origins is particularly important. In this text, Norea is the one who receives and mediates the salvific knowledge and thus becomes the ancestor of the Sethians; this has also been read as an indication of female authorship.

In the next contribution, Uwe-Karsten Plisch presents several female revelator figures who appear in Nag Hammadi texts: Sophia, Norea, Protennoia, and Brontē. Typically, they present themselves in the first-person and/or mediate heavenly knowledge to humans. The Sophia figure in these texts is based on the Old Testament imagery of God's Wisdom (Sophia; e.g., Prov 8). On the one hand, she is described as participating in the primeval fall, which triggers the creation of the world; on the other hand, the female figures associated with her, Norea, Protennoia, and Brontē, are central in the redemption and act as mediators of heavenly knowledge in poetic form.

Silke Petersen deals with the ideals of becoming male and eliminating gender distinctions in early Christian texts that have become apocryphal. Starting from the Gospel of Thomas, her analysis shows two ways of describing the transcendence of gender in the hierarchically structured ancient manner of speaking. Either becoming male is synonymous with becoming spiritual by overcoming corporeality, or the result of becoming spiritual is described as the overcoming or annulment of gender difference. Both modes of speech emphasize the superiority of male and spiritual over female and corporeal in the ancient conceptualizations.

In the next section, the focus is on texts that, unlike the newly discovered texts, have been in continuous use and widely transmitted through the centuries. This applies particularly to the Protevangelium of James, with the Virgin Mary as its main figure. Silvia Pellegrini deals with Mary's birth and virginity in this text, which emphasizes Mary's extraordinary purity from a narrative point of view. The text first describes her own birth and then the birth of her son, Jesus. The emphasis on Mary's virginity even after the birth of Jesus guarantees his divine origin but also exposes the text's androcentric perspective of the figure of Mary.

Ursula Ulrike Kaiser explores gender roles in the Infancy Gospel of Thomas, an early Christian collection of short stories primarily on the miracles that Jesus performed as a child. The child Jesus is not only kind and helpful but can be quick-tempered and unpredictable, which causes problems for his parents, most of all for his father. Joseph fails many times in his male role as the caretaker, while Jesus's power and self-control, a key virtue according to the ancient ideal of masculine behavior, are highlighted. The figure of Mary remains in the background.

The following four essays are devoted to apocryphal acts of the apostles. First, Carmen Bernabé Ubieta deals with the ways of life described in these texts, which propagate an ascetic ideal throughout. After an overview of previous research, she focuses on the question of the relationship between the texts and the lives of historical women, particularly whether chastity in fact had a role in increasing women's autonomy.

Next, Outi Lehtipuu examines how apostolic authority is conveyed in the Acts of Thecla and its narrative world. She argues that Paul, presented as a Christlike figure and a teacher of truth, is an authority-bearing figure in the story. His preaching of abstinence (ἐγκράτεια) is fleshed out in a series of beatitudes, which Lehtipuu analyzes in their wider context, including their connections with the Gospel of Matthew and 1 Corinthians. She concludes by asking what attraction and what consequences the preaching of abstinence might have had particularly for women.

Bernadette J. Brooten provides an intersectional analysis of gender and slavery in the Acts of Andrew. In this work the slave owner Maximilla ensures her chastity by substituting her slave Euklia in the bed of her husband, which eventually leads to the murder of Euklia. The idealization of female virginity and chastity only works against the backdrop of slavery. One woman can lead a holy life only because the other woman cannot do so.

Anna Rebecca Solevåg also carries out an intersectional analysis by relating gender and disability in the Acts of Peter. After an overview of disability studies, Solevåg analyzes how physical disability is used as a narrative device in the Acts of Peter. The text demonstrates Peter's apostolic power to paralyze—which he uses predominantly on women. Particularly instructive is the story of Peter's daughter, whom the father first heals but then unheals so she does not become a temptation for men.

The last section of this volume deals with female voices in ancient texts. The first three chapters treat texts that were most likely written by women. Part of the story of the martyrdom of Perpetua is written in a form of a diary that, according to most scholars, she wrote herself. Anna Carfora examines this prison diary, paying particular attention to Perpetua's dream visions. She analyzes how the visions adapt biblical references and set them in new combinations.

The subject of María José Cabezas Cabello is the reception of Genesis in the works of the poets Faltonia Betitia Proba and Athenais Eudokia (fourth and fifth centuries). After presenting their biography and introducing the genre of cento, she focuses on the renarrations of Genesis, which Proba undertakes in the form of a Virgilian cento and Eudocia in a Homeric cento. According to Cabello, both texts are examples of "a female discourse in a tradition dominated by men."

M. Dolores Martin Trutet treats another text written by a woman, the travel diary of Egeria, which consists of the notes she made on her pilgrimage to the holy sites in the late fourth century. Egeria's travel is inspired by the Holy Scriptures: "The biblical women find space and relevance within the textual pilgrimage, spirituality, and cartography of salvation created by Egeria." Trutet also pays attention to the connections and references to the Acts of Thecla and Egeria's encounters with historical and contemporary women.

Cristina Simonelli's essay is about another potential female (co)author of a Christian text. The name of Therasia is mentioned alongside with her husband, Paulinus of Nola, at the end of a poem (epithalamium) for the wedding of Titia and Julian, the future bishop of Eclanum. However, she is rarely mentioned in secondary literature. Simonelli presents the historical and biographical framework of the wedding poem and the biblical themes and references contained in it.

Heidrun Mader examines women of the Phrygian prophecy, a movement that was later deemed heretical and called Montanism. The works of these female prophets were systematically destroyed, and only a few logia have been preserved in writings that are hostile toward them. Mader analyzes and contextualizes the logia of two prophets, Maximilla and Quintilla. While Maximilla speaks of herself using male attributes, Quintilla describes Christ as a female figure.

The volume closes with Ute E. Eisen's treatment of grave inscriptions of early Christian women, a source that has attracted little attention thus far. Eisen first introduces the genre and assesses its value for women's and gender history, then treats two inscriptions, written for and by female deacons, in more detail. In her intertextual analysis, she shows how the inscriptions and the New Testament texts can be reciprocally interpreted. The reception of these texts opens new horizons of meaning for the inscriptions as well as for the New Testament texts and the story of the women who tell them.

No Longer Marginalized:
From Orthodoxy and Heresy Discourse
to Category Critique and Beyond

Karen L. King

In a series on women and the Bible, it is not surprising to find a volume on marginalized writings. In the established modern Western taxonomy used to classify early Christian writings and their authors, writings by and about women have traditionally been relegated to positions of obscurity if not oblivion. While much has been achieved over the last decades to retrieve these works and to place women more prominently in the history of Christianity, as this series demonstrates, many of the tools that rendered them marginal are still largely in place. One of these tools is the taxonomy itself.

In this essay I want first to briefly analyze this taxonomy, its aims, effects, and the operations by which it appears to be based on factual data that is prior to and outside discursive power relations. Second, we will turn to recent critiques of the established categories and discuss their implications. I want to examine the strategies of orthodoxy and heresy discourse and the adequacy of related categories, notably Gnosticism. Finally, I will suggest some possibilities that arise by dispensing with these categories and their surrogates.

1. Classifying Early Christian Literature

The ancient taxonomy was not neutral but took shape as an effect of strategic deployments of orthodoxy and heresy discourse.[1] Some prominent elements of this discourse include:

---

1. For a more extensive discussion, see Karen L. King, *What Is Gnosticism?* (Cambridge: Harvard University Press, 2003), esp. 20–54.

- establishing a rule of faith (later creed) to regulate what writings and teachings should be accepted and to guide interpretation;
- limiting who was allowed to preach the gospel and interpret Scripture;
- establishing a succession and hierarchy of authorized leaders;
- attacking the character of one's opponents;
- inventing names for opponents (heretics, Ophites, Barbeloites, etc.);
- contrasting the unity of the one true church with the divisiveness of heretics;
- insisting that adherence to the authority of the established leadership of the one institutional church constituted orthodoxy while doctrinal variation constituted social deviation (schism);
- alleging that heresy is produced by outside contamination of an originally pure faith (e.g., by the importation of Greek philosophy) and asserting that truth is chronologically prior to heresy;
- arguing for the theological and moral superiority of one's own views while denigrating opponents as immoral libertines or hate-filled ascetics who promulgate error.[2]

The main function of this discourse was to serve the ends of theological normativity by distinguishing truth from falsehood. It was initially based not on listing true and false writings but on determining the status of authors. Ancient author-function linked source, reliable mediation, and secure transmission through attribution to "authors."[3] Polemicists such as Irenaeus, Tertullian, and Eusebius charted two lines of transmission: truth was revealed from God through esteemed prophets and apostles to a lin-

---

2. It is notable that recently discovered literature from Nag Hammadi shows that this discourse was being deployed on all sides; see, e.g., Testimony of Truth (NHC IX 3) and Apocalypse of Peter (NHC VII 3).

3. For a discussion of author-function, see Michel Foucault, "What Is an Author?," in *The Foucault Reader*, ed. Paul Rabinow (New York: Pantheon Books, 1984), 101–20; and for application to early Christian practices, see Karen L. King, "'What Is an Author?' Ancient Author-Function in the Apocryphon of John and the Apocalypse of John," in *Scribal Practices and Social Structures among Jesus Adherents: Essays in Honour of John S. Kloppenborg*, ed. W. Arnal et al., BETL 285 (Leuven: Peeters, 2016), 15–42. Author-function in a Foucauldian sense includes the valorization of source, attestation of reliable transmission, and contextualization (e.g., situating the material object in a particular position within a history of salvation).

eage of apostolic succession, while falsehood came from Satan through fraudulent prophets and heretics to their followers. In this discourse, authors were implicitly classified on a hierarchical scale from orthodox to heretical: evangelists and apostles, apostolic and church fathers, pseudepigraphers, forgers, or heretics. Writings were assumed to be products of such authorial lineages, and they were classified accordingly, eventually distinguishing between the required (Scripture and eventually canon) and the forbidden (apocrypha), while allowing some slippage for "useful books" to be read in certain settings.[4] The resulting hierarchy applied not only to putative authors and their writings but also to categories of those who produced, interpreted, and transmitted them (teachers, preachers, exegetes). The effect of this discourse was that only individuals who could be fit into the proper categories (apostles and their authorized successors) could be the authors of orthodoxy.

It is immediately apparent that this classification is not gender neutral but is a performative iteration and (re)production of ancient patriarchal/kyriarchal and gender norms.[5] That is, insofar as authorized authors and interpreters of Scripture must fit the categories of apostle, authorized teacher, church father, or ordained clergy,[6] and insofar as women are excluded from these positions, then women cannot legitimately be authors, teachers, interpreters, or preachers of orthodox literature. As authors, only the roles of pseudepigrapher-forger-heretic are open to them. Indeed, Didymus the Blind interpreted the injunction of 1 Tim 2 against women having authority over men to exclude women from writing books in their

---

4. See François Bovon, "Beyond the Canonical and the Apocryphal Books, the Presence of a Third Category: The Books Useful for the Soul," *HTR* 105 (2012): 125–37; Bovon, "Canonical, Rejected, and Useful Books," in *New Testament and Christian Apocrypha: Collected Studies II*, ed. Glenn E. Snyder (Tübingen: Mohr Siebeck, 2008), 318–23.

5. On iteration and performance, see Judith Butler, "The Question of Social Transformation," in *Undoing Gender* (New York: Routledge, 2004), 218; on patriarchy and kyriarchy, see Elisabeth Schüssler Fiorenza, *But She Said: Feminist Practices of Biblical Interpretation* (Boston: Beacon, 1992), 7–8; on ancient gender, see Stephen D. Moore, *God's Beauty Parlor and Other Queer Spaces in and around the Bible* (Stanford, CA: Stanford University Press, 2001), 135–46.

6. By clergy, I am referring to officeholders such as priest, presbyters, and bishops. For the development of the distinction between lay and clergy, see Karen Jo Torjesen, "Clergy and Laity," in *The Oxford Handbook of Early Christian Studies*, ed. Susan Ashbrook Harvey and David G. Hunter (Oxford: Oxford University Press, 2008), 389–405.

own names (*Trin.* 3.41.3).⁷ Writing any literature with a claim to general authority would presumably be the act of a schismatic, a heretic. Of course, a few works appeared under women's names, such as Perpetua or Egeria, and some writings were ascribed to a prestigious woman or divine figure (e.g., Gospel of Mary, Wisdom of Jesus Christ); it is also possible that other women may have written pseudonymously under a male name. But the dominant taxonomy grants the highest authority and prestige only to a small group of male authors. Women are effectively marginalized by the conjunction of limited author roles with social practices that bar women from the roles of apostle, teacher, priest, or bishop.

To a great degree, the modern taxonomy of early Christian literature has reproduced the ancient classifications. Its main division is between canonical and noncanonical literature, with further subdivisions into apostolic fathers, apocrypha, and heresies (e.g., Jewish Christianity and Gnosticism), with the additional category of church fathers including the writings of those who devised and deployed the discourse of orthodoxy and heresy.

This taxonomy appears obvious and self-evident, however, only through certain operations that mask "the genealogy of power relations by which it is constituted."⁸ As Judith Butler argues,

> Insofar as power operates successfully by constituting an object domain, a field of intelligibility, as a taken-for-granted ontology, its material effects are taken as material data or primary givens. These material positivities appear *outside* discourses and power, as its incontestable referents, its transcendental signifieds. But this appearance is precisely the moment in which the power/discourse regime is most fully dissimulated and most insidiously effective.⁹

If we apply this framework here, Christianity is not to be taken as a self-evident entity. Rather, it becomes possible to see how it is constituted as an object domain, first of all by the invention of others (pagans and a usable Judaism) over against which a discrete object (Christianity) can be posited. These others make it rhetorically possible to position Christianity as an intelligible field distinct from its social-cultural context (i.e.,

---

7. My thanks to Bernadette Brooten for this reference.

8. Here I am citing the work of Judith Butler, *Bodies That Matter: On the Discursive Limits of Sex* (New York: Routledge, 1993), 35. In this paragraph, I paraphrase and apply her insights to Christianity.

9. Butler, *Bodies That Matter*, 34–35.

by figuring the world of the ancient Mediterranean as background). Once Christianity is taken for granted as an existing and intelligible domain, the products and actions of Christians appear as material data or primary givens. Canon, creed, and their embodied originators (authorized authors and interpreters) in particular appear as the indisputable material data of Christianity.[10] They appear, in Butler's terms, to be "*outside* discourses and power, as its [Christianity's] incontestable referents, its transcendental signifieds" rather than as effects of power exerted through a devised classificatory system operating within the discourse of orthodoxy and heresy. In this way, the established classification of literature—whether as orthodox or heretical, canonical or noncanonical, Christian or non-Christian—(re)produces the marginalization of women (and other abject persons) as an effect of the operation of orthodoxy and heresy discourse.

In this discourse, truth, authority, gender, and role-status have become mutually linked and aggregate such that to establish one is to reinforce the others. To establish one's beliefs and practices as orthodox, that is, true and unifying, implies that those who promulgate those beliefs and practices should have authority over others, that these persons are truly men, that their roles have preeminent status. The opposite is likewise the case. To establish that others' beliefs and practices are heretical, that is, false and divisive, implies that they should be subordinate to others or excluded entirely, that they are lesser human beings (unmen or women) who cannot occupy high-status roles.

2. Critiquing Categories

Each category of the modern taxonomy given above has been critiqued and to some extent reconceptualized.

While the division of canonical and noncanonical generally remains strong, cracks are appearing. Scholars note that in the first centuries

---

10. Note, for example, how the materiality of actual textual remains (e.g., manuscripts, books, etc.) and the presupposition that these material artifacts are the products of human activity flow naturally (invisibly) into the assumption of original authors who are real people. This authorship, however, is no simple thing, but a product of attribution practices tied, among other things, to the social construction of *types* of authors (apostles, church fathers, heretics, etc.)—types that are far from obvious givens and definitely not neutral. In this logic, actual textual remains produced by real people become material evidence for the classification system of orthodoxy and heresy, canonical and noncanonical literature, masking its circular logic along with the operations of power.

Christians had diverse collections of writings, different views about what was to be considered Scripture, and different interpretative practices. Moreover, accounts of the origin of the New Testament canon are being criticized insofar as they take a teleological perspective that begins with the current fixed canon and then looks backwards, tracing "a single line of development as though it were somehow natural and inevitable."[11] As David Brakke points out, "it is simply anachronistic to ask of writers of the second century which books were in their canon and which not—for the notion of a closed canon was simply not there. We must not continue to place Christian authors on a trajectory that leads inevitably to Athanasius's supposedly definitive list of 367." What is needed, he suggests, is to focus less on content alone and more on "how Christians used texts and how they formed groups for using them." This approach would not lead to the usual categorization of all early Christian literature in terms of whether they eventually came to reside in the canon or not, but instead to a typology of early Christian scriptural practices based on "characteristic social groups, authoritative figures, and literary activities."[12] Christians were engaged in many types of scriptural practice, only one of which points toward a closed canon.[13] The anachronistic division of canonical and noncanonical thus distorts the more complex dynamics of how Christians thought about and interpreted sacred writings in diverse social contexts and group settings, and the relation of writings to their identity.[14]

---

11. Michael W. Holmes, "The Biblical Canon," in Harvey and Hunter, *Oxford Handbook of Early Christian Studies*, 417.

12. David Brakke, "Scriptural Practices in Early Christianity: Towards a New History of the New Testament Canon," in *Invention, Rewriting, Usurpation: Discursive Fights over Religious Traditions in Antiquity*, ed. Jörg Ulrich, Anders-Christian Jacobsen, and David Brakke, ECCA 11 (Frankfurt am Main: Lang, 2012), 266, 268, 271. He offers a provisional typology: "(1) study and contemplation; (2) revelation and continued inspiration; and (3) communal worship and edification. Each of these scriptural practices had its particular social setting(s), authoritative persons, reading strategies, and spiritual goals. Each granted scriptural status to existing religious texts and so created sets or collections of scriptures, which differed in how bounded or defined they were or meant to be. Each also involved the production of new texts, oral and written, which could gain authoritative status of their own" (271).

13. Brakke, "Scriptural Practices," 263.

14. For an excellent study of practices and rhetoric of Christian identity formation, see Judith M. Lieu, *Christian Identity in the Jewish and Graeco-Roman World* (Oxford: Oxford University Press, 2004).

The category of patristic literature, too, has come under significant revision. As Elizabeth Clark notes, the field of patristics has become early Christian studies and is now considered "less often as a branch of 'church history' than as an aspect of late ancient history and literature."[15] Along similar lines, apocrypha is being redefined and expanded in scope, partly in the attempt to interrupt its narrow relation to the New Testament and partly to include a broader array of literature and hermeneutical practices.[16] Increasingly, this literature is becoming significant evidence for representing the history of ancient Christianity. All of these shifts work to decenter an anachronistic reification of the New Testament canon and to place all the phenomena in their dynamic social and intellectual contexts.

The gendered character of the dominant Christian story has been fully exposed as well. Recovering women leaders, apostles, prophets, martyrs, teachers, widows, and deacons has filled the historical narrative with active and powerful women. In a path-breaking study, *In Memory of Her*, Elisabeth Schüssler Fiorenza pioneered a rhetorical method that shows what a history of early Christianity that puts women at the center looks like.[17] These and other works have been transformative.

It is now also widely recognized that Christian constructions of Judaism and paganism are not accurate indicators of the beliefs and practices of non-Christians but were invented to aid in Christian self-definition.[18] Scholars now regularly question the parting of the ways with Jews and emphasize that Jews, Christians, and pagans (gentiles, Greeks, Romans,

---

15. See Elisabeth Clark, "From Patristics to Early Christian Studies," in Harvey and Hunter, *Oxford Handbook of Early Christian Studies*, 16.

16. On the history and controversies of the classification "apocrypha," see Stephen J. Shoemaker, "Early Christian Apocryphal Literature," in Harvey and Hunter, *Oxford Handbook of Early Christian Studies*, 521–48; Annette Yoshiko Reed, "The Afterlives of New Testament Apocrypha," *JBL* 133 (2015): 407–17; Christoph Markschies, "Haupteinleitung," in *Evangelien und Verwandtes*, vol. 1 of *Antike christliche Apokryphen in deutscher Übersetzung*, ed. Christoph Markschies and Jens Schröter (Tübingen: Mohr Siebeck, 2012), 1–24.

17. Elisabeth Schüssler Fiorenza, *In Memory of Her: A Feminist Theological Reconstruction of Christian Origins* (New York: Crossroad, 1983), 99–351.

18. It is to be emphasized that various Christians defined these "others" differently, especially in terms of how Judaism and the proper relation to Jewish Scriptures were defined. See King, *What Is Gnosticism?*, 40–47; Karen L. King, *The Secret Revelation of John* (Cambridge: Harvard University Press, 2006), 177–90, 215–24, 239–43.

and others) all shared in the fluid and complex social-political, institutional, economic, and cultural world of Mediterranean antiquity.[19]

This recognition is also starting to put some additional pressure on the subclassification of the earliest heresies. In *What Is Gnosticism?* I argue that in order to make Christian insiders appear as outsiders (heretics), polemicists attempted to identify them with Jews or pagans (i.e., gentiles or Greeks).[20] They decried their opponents for being too much like Jews ("Judaizers") or for contaminating the purity of the true gospel with Greek philosophy and pagan immorality. Modern taxonomy has reproduced this strategy of exclusion in classifying the earliest heresies as Jewish Christianity and Gnosticism, the latter famously characterized as "the acute Hellenization of Christianity."[21] Some history of religions scholars went further and traced gnostic origins to pre-Christian Oriental cults, thus defining it as essentially a non-Christian religion.[22]

Critiques of sharp divisions between Christians and Jews or pagans, however, strain the obviousness of the division of the earliest heresies into corresponding types. This point is well illustrated in the many debates that characterize the opponents of the Pauline letters, Petrine letters, the Gospel of John, or Ignatius, among others, as some kind of Judaizers or gnostics (docetists, libertines, antimarriage proponents, and so forth). The tortured and unresolvable character of these debates, however, would seem to indicate that the question may not have been properly framed. Certainly there were tensions and disputes among the early Christians, but early Christian groups were not homogeneous unities, nor were the issues under debate always well-defined.[23] Multiple voices are notable even within a single

---

19. See Adam Becker and Annette Yoshiko Reed, *The Ways That Never Parted: Jews and Christians in Late Antiquity and the Early Middle Ages* (Tübingen: Mohr Siebeck, 2003), 1–33; Andrew S. Jacobs, "Jews and Christians," in Harvey and Hunter, *Oxford Handbook of Early Christian Studies*, 169–85; Michele R. Salzman, "Pagans and Christians," in Harvey and Hunter, *Oxford Handbook of Early Christian Studies*, 186–202.

20. See King, *What Is Gnosticism?*, 22–23.

21. See Adolf von Harnack, *The History of Dogma*, trans. Neil Buchanan (New York: Dover, 1961), 1:226, 230; King, *What Is Gnosticism?*, 55–70.

22. See the discussion in King, *What Is Gnosticism?*, 71–90.

23. See esp. the critique of Stanley K. Stowers, "The Concept of 'Community' and the History of Early Christianity," *MTSR* 23 (2011): 238–56. He provides an extremely illuminating account of the genealogy of this now-common practice in New Testament studies. For our interest here in the demise of the gnostic myth, it is notable

writing, and some positions that arose within orthodox writings were later condemned while others in so-called gnostic writings were accepted.[24]

In the end, situating early Christian literature in more complex, dynamic social contexts and focusing on materials and practices in addition to content has had the effect of displacing the centrality of the New Testament canon and unsettling the tidiness of the established taxonomy of early Christian literature. A significant catalyst for much critique and reconsideration of the standard taxonomy given above, however, comes not only from new approaches but from discoveries of previously unknown Christian literature from Egypt.

In the nineteenth and twentieth centuries, Coptic manuscripts were rediscovered in Egypt that contain previously unknown Christian literature dated to the second to fourth centuries CE.[25] These were all initially categorized as Gnosticism. Work by specialists over the last decades has provided much clarity, nuance, and sophistication to the analysis of these texts, as well as to their relation to ancient philosophy and mainstream Christianity. In my opinion, it is not too much to say these works can potentially revolutionize many areas of early Christian studies.

Initially these texts were considered to be examples of ancient Gnosticism, based on descriptions of heretics preserved in the writings of well-known polemicists, such as Irenaeus, Tertullian, and Hippolytus among others. The term *Gnosticism* had been first coined by Protestant Henry More in the seventeenth century in the context of anti-Catholic polemics but was developed in the intellectual contexts of Orientalism, anti-Jewish rhetoric, Protestant church history, and in part aimed against spiritualism and theosophy.[26] Definitions, however, were derived largely

---

that one of the pillars of orthodoxy-heresy discourse, namely, the view that heresy is divisive deviance from an established, uniformly believing community, is said to stem from the Pauline (and Romantic) notion of community analyzed by Stowers. The multiplication of Christianities to include nonnormative types thus departs neither from the ancient discourse of conversion and community nor from the modern differentiation of Christian literature into the so-called varieties of early Christianity.

24. See Mark Edwards, *Catholicity and Heresy in the Early Church* (Burlington, VT: Ashgate, 2009), esp. 11.

25. Notably the Berlin Codex, the Nag Hammadi codices, and the Tchacos Codex.

26. See Bentley Layton, "Prolegomena to the Study of Ancient Gnosticism," in *The Social World of the First Christians: Essays in Honor of Wayne A. Meeks*, ed. L. Michael White and O. Larry Yarbrough (Minneapolis: Fortress, 1995), 348–49. More charged Catholicism with being "a spice of the old abhorred Gnosticism" that seduces

through homogenizing reading of early Christian polemical writings. The result of this style of reading among historians and theologians was that the construction of a gnostic redeemer myth and a set of typological characteristics reproducing many of the criticisms of the polemicists now was factual data. Gnostics were said to believe that they were saved by nature and hence they lacked any positive ethics; they promulgated an anticosmic, body-hating dualism of alienation; their teachings were esoteric and doctrinally deviant, notably rejecting the God of Hebrew Scriptures as the creator and rejecting the incarnation and suffering of Jesus (docetism).

Already before the important discovery near Nag Hammadi, much of this construction was coming under serious revision, notably in representing Gnosticism as a deviation from original Christianity and in deriving the so-called gnostic redeemer myth from later Oriental (Iranian and Mandaean) sources.[27] Once the new texts were brought into the equation, however, problems about how to define Gnosticism became acute. Michael Williams offers a convincing critique of the reigning typological definitions, which, he argues, not only do not address the mythological and social diversity displayed by the literature but actually distort interpretation. He offers alternative readings that open up new lines of interpretation while suggesting the term Gnosticism be dropped.[28]

Apart from overreliance on the distortive rhetoric of the polemicists, the enormous diversity of the literature itself also made it clear that a single term would be inadequate. Specialists rightly argue that despite the heritage of the term *gnostic* in Christian polemics, at least some texts

---

believers to idolatry. He conceptualized Gnosticism as the ancient contamination of Christianity's original purity by pagan idolatry, and charged Catholics of his own day with adherence to that legacy. Protestantism, on the other hand, he characterized as a return to the pristine origins of Christianity before its corruption by heresy. In More's usage, Gnosticism clearly functions as a rhetorical category, coined in the heat of Reformation polemics, but pointing backward to the first centuries of Christian origins for its model. On the development of the term Gnosticism in the intellectual contexts of Orientalism, anti-Jewish rhetoric, Protestant church history, see King, *What Is Gnosticism?*, 55–109. On spiritualism and theosophy, see Denise Kimber Buell, "This Changes Everything: Spiritualists, Theosophists, and Rethinking Early Christian Historiography" in *Remaking the World: Christianity and Categories*, ed. Taylor G. Petrey (Tübingen: Mohr Siebeck, 2019), 345–68.

27. See King, *What Is Gnosticism?*, 110–48.

28. See Michael Allen Williams, *Rethinking "Gnosticism": An Argument for Dismantling a Dubious Category* (Princeton: Princeton University Press, 1996).

display distinctive characteristics that make it appropriate to group sets of literature together—and we have to call those groupings something. If not gnostic, then what? One corrective strategy has been to regroup the new texts, resulting in new subcategories of Gnosticism such as Sethianism or Valentinianism, or to narrow the term gnostic to refer only to a limited set of texts.[29] In my opinion, the powerful legacy that the terms gnostic and Gnosticism carry means that their capacity to mislead remains very strong. Few who hear the terms will associate them with a carefully limited corpus of literature or a distinct social group rather than with the old typological definitions and the wider characterizations of the new Coptic literature as gnostic heresy. In that regard, the terms *Sethian* and *Valentinian* may serve better to indicate the new groupings.

However, it is important to note that the problem of nomenclature pertains not only to the new Coptic texts and related literature, but to the categorization of early Christian literature more generally. In the attempt to distance modern historiography from the blatantly interested categories of orthodoxy and heresy, terms such as *proto-orthodox, mainstream, catholic, lost gospels,* and such have been introduced, and categories such as apocrypha have been expanded, as we saw above, to include the new discoveries. In practice, however, these seemingly neutral terms tend to reproduce groupings of Christian literature nearly identical to the old ones, while yet masking their reliance on them.[30] Even emphasizing the diversity of Chris-

---

29. The 1978 conference at Yale University was organized by Bentley Layton around Sethianism and Valentinianism. See Bentley Layton, ed., *The Rediscovery of Gnosticism: Proceedings of the International Conference on Gnosticism at Yale, New Haven, Connecticut, March 28–31, 1978* (Leiden: Brill, 1981). See also Layton, "Prolegomena to the Study"; David Brakke, *The Gnostics: Myth, Ritual, and Diversity in Early Christianity* (Cambridge: Harvard University Press, 2010), esp. 29–51; Tuomas Rasimus, *Paradise Reconsidered in Gnostic Mythmaking: Rethinking Sethianism in Light of the Ophite Evidence*, NHMS 68 (Leiden: Brill, 2009). The literature Layton and Brakke identify corresponds almost identically to the literature Schenke classified by other means as Sethian. See Hans-Martin Schenke, "Das sethianische System nach Nag-Hammadi-Handschriften," in *Studia Coptica*, ed. Peter Nagel (Berlin: Akademie, 1974), 165–73; Schenke, "The Phenomenon and Significance of Gnostic Sethianism," in Layton, *Rediscovery of Gnosticism*, 2:588–616. Rasimus has argued for a category "classic gnostic" that includes Ophite and Barbeloite materials as well as the Sethian literature (*Paradise Reconsidered*, 4–5, 9–55).

30. See Karen L. King, "Which Early Christianity?," in Harvey and Hunter, *Oxford Handbook of Early Christian Studies*, 66–71.

tianities is inadequate if the categories of that diversity continue to operate within a discourse of Christian identity in which Jew, pagan, Christian, and heretic, as well as man and woman, are uncritically taken as material evidence or natural givens. To paraphrase Butler again, it is then that "the discourse/power regime [in which the reigning taxonomy operates] is most fully dissimulated and most insidiously effective." The reigning taxonomy—like all categorical schemes—not only presets how particular texts and persons will be classified, whether they will be received as authoritative or not, valuable or not, but also guides what questions should be asked, how they are framed, what counts as evidence and what is marginal.

In this regard, even the terms Valentinianism and Sethianism have their problems, suggesting isolatable social or intellectual entities. In my view, one improvement would be to speak of Valentinian Christianity or Sethian Christianity, categories that while basically reproducing the established object domain of Christianity would nonetheless challenge its boundaries. Even more significantly, these Christianities might increase awareness that discourses and power are at work in constituting religions as object domains and perhaps even make it possible to perceive more sharply that typologies are by definition positional and provisional, devised for particular but limited aims.[31]

The Sethian group, for example, does not fit comfortably within the current object domain Christianity. Several texts are currently distinguished as non-Christian Platonizing literature (Allogenes, Marsanes, Zostrianos), because they are said to lack specifically Christian terminology and myth, while having close ties with Platonizing circles, notably that of Plotinus.[32] Thus, Sethian Christianity disturbs any tidy pagan/Christian divide—a divide that in any case is far from tidy given the importance of pagan philosophical works for constructing and elaborating a wide range of Christian theology and practice.

The Valentinian group appears to fit better within the conventional bounds of Christian. Yet, it remains marginal in part because currently the lists of Valentinian literature contain only distinctive works not shared with so-called mainstream Christians, thereby reifying their differences. If the literature *used* by Valentinians for constructing and elaborating their theology were also listed, the situation would be very different. Such a list

---

31. See King, *What Is Gnosticism?*, 5–19.
32. See John D. Turner, *Sethian Gnosticism and the Platonic Tradition*, BCNH Section Études 6 (Leuven: Peeters, 2001), 499–588.

would include not only, for example, Tripartite Tractate and the Gospel of Philip, but the Gospels of Matthew and John and all the letters attributed to Paul except 1 and 2 Timothy.[33] Studies of Valentinian Christianity by specialists are currently offering a richer and more nuanced portrait of these Christians while simultaneously laying the groundwork for more accurate reconstructions of Christianity in the second and third centuries.[34]

These categories disrupt the borders of Christian and pagan, orthodox and heretical, even as other examples disturb the division of Jewish Christianity and Gnosticism.

3. From Orthodoxy and Heresy Discourse to Category Critique and Beyond

So what now? If the categories we are operating with are problematic, what is to be done? The aim is not to eliminate taxonomies as such, since intellectual analysis cannot do without categories and comparisons. Rather, the point would be to illuminate how discourses and power operate so that their operations and effects remain no longer hidden but are opened to critique as well as constructive deployment.

One immediate task would be writing a genealogy of the constitution of Christianity as an object domain through discourse and power, emphasizing how their effects (including the taxonomy of ancient religions, authors, and writings) become naturalized and taken for granted as material data and primary givens. Examining the discourse of orthodoxy and heresy and its effects is one part of this task. In this way, categories such as Valentinian Christianity or Sethian Christianity could potentially continue to do important if limited work (e.g., to expose and analyze common features of thought and practice), without automatically being subsumed into the wider framework of orthodoxy-heresy discourse. Nor would these categories need to be seen as essentialized characteristics of the literature rather than as modern analytic tools.

---

33. See the discussion of Pheme Perkins, "Gnosticism and the Christian Bible," in *The Canon Debate*, ed. Lee Martin McDonald and James A. Sanders (Peabody, MA: Hendrickson, 2002), esp. 366–69.

34. See, e.g., Christoph Markschies, *Valentinus Gnosticus? Untersuchungen zur valentinianischen Gnosis mit einem Kommentar zu den Fragmenten Valentins* (Tübingen: Mohr Siebeck, 1992); Einar Thomassen, *The Spiritual Seed: The Church of the "Valentinians,"* NHMS 60 (Leiden: Brill, 2006).

New typologies aimed at other kinds of projects are being devised as well. Brakke's proposal for types of scriptural practices is one such model, directed toward illuminating how different kinds of Christian groups used a variety of writings. His typology does not result in a neat distinction between orthodox and heretical groups, but rather each type includes examples that cross and blur those distinctions and simultaneously opens up a new way of mapping the landscape with its own insights.

Another topic ripe for new groupings would address early Christian attitudes toward marriage. Here again the categories of orthodoxy and heresy obscure more than they illumine since similar positions can sometimes be found in supposedly opposing groups.[35] The canonical Pastoral Epistles, Ephesians, and the Valentinians all argued for the legitimacy of baptized Christians' marrying, in part because baptism exorcised demons and purified believers from polluted lust.[36] So too the canonical Paul, the church father Clement of Alexandria, the Sethian Secret Revelation of John, and the Valentinian Gospel of Philip all represent Christians as capable of undefiled marriage, distinguishing them from people who rape, engage in non-Christian marital sex, and reproduce from lustful desire and demonic influence (1 Thess 4:3–5; Clement of Alexandria, *Strom.* 3.58).[37] Some, such as 1 Timothy, go so far as to condemn those who reject marriage as liars who are possessed by demons (4:1–5) and suggest that women are saved through child-bearing (2:15), a position that would need some hermeneutical sleight of hand to make it compatible with later Christian authors who considered marriage a very poor option compared with permanent virginal celibacy (e.g., Chrysostom, *Virginit.* 11.1; 13.4). And while the heretical Nag Hammadi treatise Testimony of Truth (30.28–30) offers the extreme teaching that Jesus's purpose was to end the rule of carnal procreation, in the end this work advocates

---

35. For an overview of early Christian attitudes toward marriage, see the discussion of Elizabeth Clark, "The Celibate Bridegroom and His Virginal Brides: Metaphor and the Marriage of Jesus in Early Christian Ascetic Exegesis," *CH* 77 (2008): 1–25; Karen L. King, "The Place of the Gospel of Philip in the Context of Early Christian Claims about Jesus's Marital Status," *NTS* 59 (2013): 565–87.

36. First Timothy 3:2 requires bishops to marry; see Eph 5:22–33. On the Valentinians, see Clement of Alexandria, *Strom.* 3.1.1; Irenaeus, *Haer.* 1.6.4; Testim. Truth 3.56–58.

37. Karen L. King, "Reading Sex and Gender in the Secret Revelation of John," *JECS* 19 (2011): 519–38; King, "Place of the Gospel."

a Christian life that coincides very closely with the ideals of the orthodox monastic life.[38]

Attention to the nuances and diversity of ancient Christian teaching on sexual practice and ethics thus does not line up orthodox lovers of the flesh over against heretical haters of the body. A more complex mapping might consider questions such as: How are flesh and desire conceptualized in relation to sexual practices, baptism, or demonology? What work is sexual ethics doing both rhetorically and in practice, for example in establishing the borders of various Christian groupings, proving Christian superiority, embodying devotion to God, or preparing for the resurrection?[39] How do Christians relate (various notions of) sexuality to theological images of Jesus's incarnation or the resurrected body? And so forth.

When the Coptic writings are placed within the object domain Christianity, it is transformed. Prominent images of the feminine, including representations of the divine, of female saviors, and women apostles, all expand, enrich, and complexify the traditional male and masculinized Christian story. For example, the Secret Revelation of John offers images of the divine as male, male-female, female, and polymorphic, and paints portraits of powerful female saviors. Eve appears as a savior who challenges female subordination and instructs Adam; she is a woman whom rapists cannot defile. But the story is more complex. It also sets up the ideal of a heavenly patriarchal household of God and figures the boldness of the female divine Wisdom as the cause of evil and suffering. The lower creator god is stereotypically cast as a fatherless bastard, an androgynous bestial monster. Another work, the Gospel of Mary, teaches about the soul's rise to God as a spiritual discipline for overcoming fear in the face of the dangers encountered in public preaching. And it does so in the name of a woman who is instructing fellow disciples. So, too, First Revelation of James recommends that, in order to prepare for his own violent death, James take women as his teachers and models. The Wisdom of Jesus Christ speaks of twelve male and

---

38. See Testim. Truth 44.2–19, which argues for an ascetic life of world renunciation, mystical communion with God, and quietism.

39. See, e.g., Carly Daniel-Hughes, *The Salvation of the Flesh in Tertullian of Carthage: Dressing for the Resurrection* (New York: Palgrave, 2011); Taylor G. Petrey, *Resurrecting Parts: Early Christians on Desire, Reproduction, and Sexual Difference* (New York: Routledge, 2015).

seven female disciples.[40] Placing such literature in the history of Christianity requires repositioning well-known literature as well. Texts such as 1 Timothy now can be read within wider debates—not between already sharply defined positions of orthodox and heretics but among Christians with widely varying views—debates over marriage, men and women's dress and speech, the organization of the church, the negotiation of local politics, the interpretation of Scripture, and much else.[41] The possibilities for reading this and other texts remain wide open to new lines of inquiry and imagination.

Theological anthropology offers new possibilities as well. For example, Irenaeus and Valentinians could agree that in Jesus the divine fully became flesh, lived and died a real death, but they disagreed about the reason for this union of human and divine, how it effected salvation, and indeed the ultimate status of flesh (and matter). For Irenaeus, the Gospel of Philip, or the Letter of Peter to Philip, Jesus's fleshly (incarnate) life was a model for believers to follow in attaining salvation. For Irenaeus, however, that model was needed to overcome human loss of the created likeness to God because of sin (*Haer.* 5.1.2), while for the Gospel of Philip, Jesus's embodied, historical acts were symbolic paradigms for effective salvific ritual, and for the Letter of Peter to Philip he modeled the salvific practices of teaching and healing.[42] Thus, these works would be grouped together as second-century examples of incarnational theology, but be differentiated into three subcategories regarding the purpose and efficacy of Jesus's bodily/fleshly life.

But where, we might ask, are women or other unmen?[43] By framing the question of theological anthropology in terms of Jesus's double

---

40. See Antti Marjanen, "The Seven Women Disciples in the Two Versions of the First Apocalypse of James," in *The Codex Judas Papers: Proceedings of the International Congress on the Tchacos Codex Held at Rice University, Houston, Texas, March 13–16, 2008*, ed. April D. DeConick, NHMS 71 (Leiden: Brill, 2009), 535–46.

41. For a recent discussion, see T. Christopher Hoklotubbe, *Civilized Piety: The Rhetoric of* Pietas *in the Pastoral Epistles and Roman Empire* (Waco, TX: Baylor University Press, 2017).

42. For Gospel of Philip, see King, "Place of the Gospel"; for Letter of Peter to Philip (esp. NHC VIII 2, 139.15–30), see Karen L. King, "Toward a Discussion of the Category 'Gnosis/Gnosticism': The Case of the Epistle of Peter to Philip," in *Jesus in apokryphen Evangelienüberlieferungen: Beiträge zu außerkanonischen Jesusüberlieferungen aus verschiedenen Sprach- und Kulturtraditionen*, ed. Jörg Frey and Jens Schröter, WUNT 254 (Tübingen: Mohr Siebeck, 2010), 445–65.

43. An interesting framing of this question comes in Dunning's work on Paul's Adam/Christ typology, which asks about Eve's absence. See Benjamin H. Dunning,

nature as fully divine and fully human, the assumption that full humanity is male is naturalized, a historical datum that Jesus was a man. The question of the full humanity of women is overlooked—or rather, it appears only elsewhere, in discussions of church office or reproductive roles. Portraits of Adam and Christ, such as one finds in the Secret Revelation of John, however, offer different perspectives that question the obviousness of representing God or humanity in solely male terms. Christ is represented as the divine Son of Barbelo, the Mother-Father; he is identified with the Perfect Human, the image in which the androgynous Adam is created; he is also identified with the female savior, Pronoia, in the form in which s/he descends into the body; Christ appears to his disciple John as a polymorphic old man, child, and woman.[44] Is this Christ male, female, androgynous, transgender, queer, postqueer? Here again inclusion of the full range of early Christian literature suggests the need for more complex categories and mapping of theological anthropology. The use of gender as an analytic category has opened up new avenues of interpretation that are but a few of a multitude of possibilities. We do well not to think that the people we call early Christians were less diverse, less complex, or less interesting than twenty-first-century people.

4. Some Final Musings

One effect of moving beyond orthodoxy and heresy discourse can be a perception that even though power is always at work, not everything is about conflict over authority or strategies of coercion or persuasion. The remains left to us by these people of memory whom we call Christians talk about seeking truth and salvation. At issue and at stake were belonging, meaning, and flourishing. In loosing our self-made mental shackles, all might at first appear as disorienting instabilities and ungraspable fluidities, without mooring or sense. But unmapped terrain offers fabulous opportunities to explore, to analyze, to map, to consider afresh. Opportunities that might, we hope, contribute to human flourishing in our own days.

Christ without Adam: Subjectivity and Sexual Difference in the Philosophers' Paul (New York: Columbia University Press, 2014), esp. 104–8.

44. See King, "Reading Sex and Gender."

Part 1
Newly Discovered Texts:
Nag Hammadi and Related Writing

Female Disciples of Jesus in Early Christian Gospels: Gospel of Mary, Wisdom of Jesus Christ, and Other Gospels in Dialogue Form

Judith Hartenstein

Female disciples of Jesus play a major role in many gospels that later became apocryphal. Similar to their role in the gospels that became canonical, women accompany Jesus; they are his disciples, who learn from him, and his followers, who pass on his teachings. That is particularly true for gospels in dialogue form, where women are often present and sometimes play a major role. These gospels consist of the teachings of Jesus to his male and female disciples, usually after his resurrection. An appearance of the risen Jesus then creates the setting for the dialogue with the group of disciples or with a particular person.

Mary Magdalene is the most prominent and important of all the female characters, but Salome, Martha, and the mother of Jesus (as a disciple!) are present as well.[1] The participation of women as disciples in these gospels depicts primarily the circumstances of Jesus's time (whether historically accurate or not). However, the picture is also relevant for the time in which the gospels were written, when Jesus's time is seen as normative. A discourse about the role of women at the time of their composition might be mirrored in the gospels—and on the other hand, generally accepted gospels are used as arguments in such a discourse. The position and role of women narrated in the gospels is therefore linked to circumstances of the time in which the texts were written, although they do not simply display it. Nevertheless, the gospels give indirect insights into the diversity of early Christianity.

---

1. Silke Petersen, *"Zerstört die Werke der Weiblichkeit!": Maria Magdalena, Salome und andere Jüngerinnen Jesu in christlich-gnostischen Schriften*, NHMS 48 (Leiden: Brill, 1999), 295.

Many of the gospels analyzed here belong to the Nag Hammadi library and related codices and are therefore often labeled as gnostic, although in several cases this classification is disputed. Moreover, it is not helpful in describing the diversity of early Christianity appropriately.[2] Nevertheless, it is likely that gospels of the second and third centuries were written in marginalized groups. Like the gospels that later became canonical in the first century, they aim to give new impetus for their present by means of a recourse to the founder's time. This is especially important and useful in contexts with differences from existing structures or the formation of majority opinion.[3]

Before we turn to the writings that present female disciples in a major role, a quick overview over all the extant gospels is necessary to avoid the false impression that in apocryphal texts women are generally pictured stronger than in canonical writings. In all four canonical gospels women accompany Jesus, but they are not equal to the men. The male disciples (Peter, also the Twelve) are most prominent in each gospel, and the women's full membership in the circle of disciples is in question. In the Gospel of Luke, their membership in the group of disciples is made clearest, although they have a different and subordinated role compared to the male disciples (Luke 8:1–3).[4] In the Gospel of John, the roles of male and female disciples are most similar, and the women have important positions, but even here, the men outnumber the women, and the women are not explicitly called disciples.[5]

---

2. See the contribution of Karen L. King in this volume.

3. Judith Hartenstein, "Autoritätskonstellationen in apokryphen und kanonischen Evangelien," in *Jesus in apokryphen Evangelienüberlieferungen: Beiträge zu außerkanonischen Jesusüberlieferungen aus verschiedenen Sprach- und Kulturtraditionen*, ed. Jörg Frey and Jens Schröter, WUNT 254 (Tübingen: Mohr Siebeck, 2010), 444.

4. See Judith Hartenstein, *Charakterisierung im Dialog: Maria Magdalena, Petrus, Thomas und die Mutter Jesu im Johannesevangelium im Kontext anderer frühchristlicher Darstellungen*, NTOA 64 (Göttingen: Vandenhoeck & Ruprecht, 2007), 131; Jane D. Schaberg and Sharon H. Ringe, "The Gospel of Luke," in *The Women's Bible Commentary*, ed. Carol A. Newsom, Sharon H. Ringe, and Jacqueline E. Lapsley (Louisville: Westminster John Knox, 2012), 505–7; Marinella Perroni, "Disciples, Not Apostles: Luke's Double Message," in *Gospels, Narrative and History*, ed. Mercedes Navarro Puerto and Marinella Perroni, BW 4 (Atlanta: SBL Press, 2015), 212.

5. In my opinion, women are included in the group of μαθηταί, but this is disputed. For a different assessment, see Adele Reinhartz, "Women in the Johannine Community: An Exercise in Historical Imagination," in *A Feminist Companion to*

Among the apocryphal gospels, there is one in which a woman plays the most important role of all the male and female disciples (Gospel of Mary). There are a few others in which women are clearly equal to men (Wisdom of Jesus Christ, Dialogue of the Savior, Pistis Sophia, maybe Second Book of Jeu), or where they are at least members of the group of disciples (Gospel of Thomas, Gospel of the Egyptians).[6] However, the majority of noncanonical gospels do not mention female disciples at all. Several texts describe conversations between Jesus and one or two men (Secret Book of John, Secret Book of James, Gospel of Judas, Book of Thomas) or supposedly a group of men (the Twelve or the apostles: Letter of Peter to Philip, First Book of Jeu). Other texts show men as the main recipients of revelations, although women can play a marginalized role (Epistle of the Apostles, First Revelation of James). These are the more or less completely preserved writings in dialogue form; many other gospels are too fragmentary to assess the role of male or female disciples. For the Gospel of Peter, circumstances comparable to the canonical gospels can be assumed.

1. Terminology

How is a woman who appears within a gospel identified as a disciple? In the four gospels that later became canonical, this is only indirectly indicated, because an explicit denomination with a word of the root μαθητ- is missing. Women disciples are characterized through words such as *follow* or *serve*[7] that describe discipleship (but that are nevertheless not distinct!).

John, ed. Amy-Jill Levine, 2 vols., FCNTECW 4–5 (London: Sheffield Academic, 2003), 2:26–30.

6. Of the Gospel of the Egyptians only a few quotes survive in Clement of Alexandria (*Strom.* 3.45; 63; 66; 92; *Exc.* 67), in which Salome plays a major role. It is not possible to clarify whether other (male or female) disciples were important to the story of the gospel.

7. See, e.g., Mark 15:40, where the group of women is set up as a counterpart to the group of men. This phrasing is already played down in the Synoptic parallels (Matt 27:55; Luke 8:2). Matthew does not speak of a permanent following (imperfect) in Galilee but of a following from Galilee (aorist) that can easily be understood as traveling companionship. Luke, on the other hand, specifies the serving that thereby loses the broader theological impetus it had in Mark, although the exact interpretation is disputed. See Sabine Bieberstein, *Verschwiegene Jüngerinnen—Vergessene Zeuginnen: Gebrochene Konzepte im Lukasevangelium*, NTOA 38 (Fribourg: Universitätsverlag, 1998), 53–67.

In addition, the general portrayal of women accompanying Jesus continuously suggests that they were disciples.

Some apocryphal gospels articulate this more clearly. In the Gospel of Peter (12.50) Mary Magdalene is described as a female disciple (μαθήτρια) of the Lord;[8] the Greek feminine of μαθητής is used.[9] The term μαθήτρια is also found in writings that are preserved only in Coptic translation (Pistis Sophia 136 and Second Book of Jeu 42 and 45),[10] more precisely ⲘⲘⲀⲐⲎⲦⲢⲒⲀ ⲚⲤϨⲒⲘⲈ, that is, "the female woman disciples," grammatically an unnecessary duplication.

In other texts, different phrasings are used. In the Gos. Thom. 61, Salome calls herself disciple by using the word μαθητής (the Greek singular masculine) with the feminine Coptic article.[11] First Revelation of James (NHC V 3, 38.16–18, par. CT 2, 25.19) speaks of seven women who

---

8. Gos. Pet. 12.50: "Now at dawn of the Lord's Day Mary Magdalene, a disciple [μαθήτρια] of the Lord, being afraid because of the Jews, since they were inflamed by rage, had not done at the tomb of the Lord those things which women are accustomed to do over those who have died and for those who are loved by them." Translated by Paul Foster, *The Gospel of Peter: Introduction, Critical Edition and Commentary*, TENTS 4 (Leiden: Brill, 2010), 203.

9. In the New Testament, the word μαθήτρια occurs only once, in Acts 9:36, as a description of Tabitha, and means, equivalent to μαθητής in Acts, a member of the congregation.

10. Pistis Sophia 136: "As Jesus was saying these things, however, Thomas, Andrew, James and Simon the Canaanite were in the west, with their faces turned to the east.... The rest of the disciples [ⲘⲀⲐⲎⲦⲎⲤ] and women disciples [ⲘⲀⲐⲎⲦⲢⲒⲀ ⲚⲤϨⲒⲘⲈ] however were standing behind Jesus. But Jesus was standing before the altar." Translated by Violet Macdermot, *Pistis Sophia*, NHS 9 (Leiden: Brill, 1978), 354. Second Book of Jeu 42: "Jesus said to his disciples [ⲚⲚⲈϤⲘⲀⲐⲎⲦⲎⲤ] who were gathered to him, the twelve with the women disciples [ⲘⲠⲘⲚⲦⲒⲂ ⲘⲚ ⲘⲘⲀⲐⲎⲦⲢⲒⲀ ⲚⲤϨⲒⲘⲈ]: 'Surround me, my twelve disciples and women disciples [ⲠⲀⲒⲂ ⲘⲘⲀⲐⲎⲦⲎⲤ ⲀⲨⲰ ⲘⲘⲀⲐⲎⲦⲢⲒⲀ ⲚⲤϨⲒⲘⲈ], so that I say to you the great mysteries of the Treasury of the Light, these in the invisible God which no one knows.'" Translated by Violet Macdermot, *The Books of Jeu and the Untitled Text in the Bruce Codex*, NHS 13 (Leiden: Brill, 1978), 99.

11. Gos. Thom. 61: "Jesus said, 'Two will rest on a bed: the one will die, and the other will live.' Salome said, 'Who are you, man, that you have come up on my couch and eaten from my table?' Jesus said to her, 'I am he who exists from the undivided. I was given some of the things of my father.' <…> 'I am your disciple [ⲦⲈⲔⲘⲀⲐⲎⲦⲎⲤ].' <…> 'Therefore I say, if he is destroyed he will be filled with light, but if he is divided, he will be filled with darkness.'" Translated by Helmut Köster and Thomas O. Lambdin, "The Gospel according to Thomas," in *Gospel according to Thomas, Gospel according to Philip, Hypostasis of the Archons, and Indexes*, vol. 1 of *Nag Hammadi Codex*

are disciples. To describe them, the Greek noun μαθητής and a Coptic auxiliary verb (to be, to do; NHC V 3) or the verb μαθητεύω (CT 2) is used.¹² It seems likely that the Greek original included this verb, too.¹³ The verb μαθητεύω is also used in the Wisdom of Jesus Christ (BG 3, 77.13–15) to characterize the group of seven women parallel to the twelve disciples.¹⁴ In the parallel text (NHC III 4), the verb includes not only the seven women but also the twelve disciples.

Overall, the membership of women in the group of disciples is more clearly stated in apocryphal gospels than in canonical gospels. Nevertheless, there is no fixed expression or idiom used to describe them. The term μαθήτρια as the feminine equivalent to the masculine μαθητής appears only occasionally and mostly in later writings (the exception is the Gospel of Peter). It probably was an unusual expression. Besides, using the masculine noun or the verb emphasizes the equality of the roles of men and women. Discipleship includes the same features for the women as for the men; there is no reason for a gender differentiation. It is possible, however, that the verb expresses a lower level of discipleship.¹⁵ However, in my view the frequent and slightly varying occurrences as well as the parallelism to

---

II,2–7, Together with XIII,2*, Brit.Lib.Or. 4926 (1), and P.Oxy. 1,654,655, ed. Bentley Layton, NHS 20 (Leiden: Brill, 1989), 75–77.

12. CT 2, 25.18–25: "Who are the [seven] women who have [been] your disciples [ⲣ ⲙⲁⲑⲏⲧⲉⲩⲉ ⲛⲉⲕ; NHC V 3, 38.17: ⲣ ⲙⲁⲑⲏⲧⲏⲥ ⲛⲁⲕ]? And behold, all women bless you. I also am amazed how [powerless] vessels have become strong by a perception which is in them." Translated by William R. Schoedel, "The (First) Apocalypse of James," in *Nag Hammadi Codices V,2–5 and VI with Papyrus Berolinensis 8502, 1 and 4*, ed. Douglas M. Parrott, NHS 11 (Leiden: Brill, 1979), 95.

13. That would be a likely choice in Greek, but since the noun was more frequently used, the change to the Coptic phrasing seems also plausible.

14. Wis. Jes. Chr. (BG 3) 77–78: "After he rose from the dead, when his twelve dciples and seven women who continued to be his followers [ⲡⲉϥⲙⲛⲧⲥⲛⲟⲟⲩⲥ ⲙⲙⲁⲑⲏⲧⲏⲥ ⲙⲛ ⲥⲁϣϥⲉ ⲛⲥϩⲓⲙⲉ ⲉⲧⲉ ⲛⲉⲩⲙⲁⲑⲏⲧⲉⲩⲉ ⲛⲁϥ] went to Galilee onto the mountain called 'Divination and Joy' and were accordingly perplexed about the underlying reality of the universe and the plan and the holy providence and the power of the authorities, about everything that the Savior is doing with them, the secrets of the holy plan, then the Savior appeared to them, not in his previous form but in the invisible spirit." Douglas M. Parrott, trans., "Sophia of Jesus Christ," in *Nag Hammadi Codices III,3–4 and V,1 with Papyrus Berolinensis 8502,3 and Oxyrhynchus Papyrus 1081: Eugnostos and the Sophia of Jesus Christ*, NHS 27 (Leiden: Brill, 1991), 37–39.

15. See Matt 27:57, where Joseph of Arimathea seems to be distinguished from the fixed group of disciples by using the verb instead of the noun.

the group of men show that this expression was used to enunciate the full discipleship of the women. After introductions such as these, plural forms of μαθητής are to be understood as inclusive; women are included in the group.

The Gospel of Philip is a special case; three women (all named Mary) accompany Jesus, but they are not explicitly called disciples. As in canonical gospels, their connection to Jesus can be understood as discipleship, but it can also be interpreted differently. A special status is assigned to Mary Magdalene as Jesus's companion, a position that enhances her status positively but differentiates it from the rest of the disciples.[16]

2. Individuals and Groups

The most important female disciple is Mary Magdalene. She is always present if women are mentioned by name, either as the only one or together with others.[17] She is only identified with her byname if other women named Mary are present, for example in the Gospel of Philip and Pistis Sophia. Nevertheless, through the spelling of her name and the context it is clear that it is she who is meant. She is clearly distinguished from Jesus's mother—but she might already be mixed with Mary, the sister of Martha.[18] Mary appears as the only woman or at least the only one mentioned by name in the Gospel of Mary, the Wisdom of Jesus Christ, and the Dialogue of the Savior.[19]

More interesting than individuals are groups that add an institutionalized character to the participation of women. In the Wisdom of Jesus Christ, Jesus appears to his twelve (male) disciples and seven female dis-

---

16. See Petersen, "Zerstört die Werke," 143–51. Mary's special relation to Jesus as a woman enhances her role compared to the male disciples. However, it is not transferable to other women and a gender-specific feature. It is unclear to what extend her role includes other features of discipleship such as learning from Jesus and transmission of his teachings.

17. This is the case for completely preserved gospels; the fragments of the Gospel of the Egyptians mention only Salome.

18. See Petersen, "Zerstört die Werke," 302.

19. Only half of the text of the Gospel of Mary is preserved, in which three men and Mary are mentioned by name. It is possible, however, that in the lost beginning of the text more women or a group of women were present. Mary and four men are named in the dialogue in Wisdom of Jesus Christ. In Dialogue of the Savior Jesus converses with two men and one woman who are introduced by their names.

ciples. The story of the postresurrection appearance on the mountain in Galilee clearly uses Matt 28:16–20, which emphasizes the addition of the female witnesses. The seven female disciples seem to be a fixed group equivalent to the group of the Twelve. Therefore, it could have ecclesio-political relevance even though there is nothing in the text that would depict the time of Jesus. Moreover, the text concentrates on heavenly realities. In the dialogue following the appearance of Jesus, five disciples (four men and one woman) are mentioned by name. These five characters ask questions as well as the whole group ($\mu\alpha\theta\eta\tau\eta\varsigma$ with the plural article, BG 3, 100.3 par.; 102.7 par.; 107.14 par.; 127.6 [par.]; also $\dot{\alpha}\pi\dot{o}\sigma\tau o\lambda o\varsigma$ with the plural article, BG 3, 114.12 par.). As the setting presents a male and a female group, and both men and women participate in the dialogue, these plural forms are certainly to be understood as inclusive. This is the case even for the term *apostles*—in my opinion this is the clearest example of a text that calls Mary Magdalene an apostle; she is part of the group.

A group of seven female disciples is also mentioned in First Revelation of James, but they do not take part in the reception and transmission of the revelation. The existence of the group seems to be taken for granted; James wonders who they are—but the women do not participate as equally in the event of revelation as in the Wisdom of Jesus Christ. Nevertheless, they are portrayed positively and thereby contrasted to the negatively painted group of the Twelve.[20]

In the Second Book of Jeu the group of disciples ($\mu\alpha\theta\eta\tau\eta\varsigma$ with the plural article) consists of the twelve (male disciples) and female disciples. The group of women has no fixed number, but it seems to be an established entity next to the group of the Twelve, similar to in the Wisdom of Jesus Christ.

Pistis Sophia displays another model of including women. The text speaks only of a group of disciples ($\mu\alpha\theta\eta\tau\eta\varsigma$ with the plural article), but it shows indirectly that the group consists of twelve individuals (ch. 7). Moreover, twelve characters are named, eight men and four women. Even though there is no explicit listing of names, the Twelve seem to be designed as a group of both men and women.[21]

---

20. See Silke Petersen, "'Die sieben Frauen—Sieben Geistkräfte sind sie': Frauen und Weiblichkeit in der Schrift 'Jakobus' (CT 2) und der (ersten) Apokalypse des Jakobus (NHC V,3)," in *Judasevangelium und Codex Tchacos: Studien zur religionsgeschichtlichen Verortung einer gnostischen Schriftensammlung*, ed. Enno E. Popkes, WUNT 297 (Tübingen: Mohr Siebeck, 2012), 206.

21. See Petersen, *"Zerstört die Werke,"* 122.

Perhaps a similar concept is present in Pistis Sophia (book 4), an independent text. Here too the story focuses on a general group of disciples. At the beginning, six men are introduced with their names, complemented by other male and female (μαθήτρια) disciples (ch. 136). It is possible and even likely that a group of twelve men and women is assumed here—but it could also be two groups without explicit number, as in the Second Book of Jeu.

In the Epistle of the Apostles, a group of three women—with different names in the textual tradition—witness an appearance of Jesus, drawing on the story of the women at the tomb. However, in the following dialogue with Jesus only the twelve disciples (with male names) participate.

3. The Function of Female Disciples in the Texts

The most important function of the female disciples is their participation in the dialogue with Jesus. Like his male disciples, they receive his teachings, they frequently ask questions, and they are usually responsible for the transmission of the teachings. Most of the preserved apocryphal gospels are dialogues throughout or collections of sayings including short dialogue sequences. Narratives like the story of the women visiting the tomb are rare. Therefore it is crucial for all the disciples, male or female, that they are worthy of Jesus's teachings—because of their own competence or because of a decision of Jesus—and that they receive and transmit it. In these gospels, salvation depends solely on the revelation of Jesus. In consequence, the primary witnesses acquire authority, an authority that is especially important when the transmission of the revelation is emphasized.[22] The texts show no traces of offices of the developing church, which might provide institutionalized authority. The significance of the disciples depends only on their connection to Jesus. For the readers, the disciples provide the contact to Jesus, and they are in a way representatives of them in the text. The readers, too, receive the teachings of Jesus through the gospels and can therefore connect with him.

Men and women have the same roles; there are no differences because of gender. If women receive revelations, they have the same possibilities as men. Their gender is no obstacle.[23] In some gospels, their participation is explicitly stated to be important. If the male group of the Twelve is

---

22. That applies, e.g., to Thomas in the Gospel of Thomas, and to Mary in the Gospel of Mary (see Hartenstein, "Autoritätskonstellationen in apokryphen," 436).

23. For the positive reasons to present female disciples, see below.

complemented by a group of seven women (particularly in the Wisdom of Jesus Christ) or the Twelve are understood as a group of both men and women (as in Pistis Sophia), the text is concerned with showing not only men but also women as recipients and preachers of revelations. In addition to the transmission of the teachings, it might be important that the readers are able to identify with members of the group. Women are not only able to fill this role, but they should do it. The deliberate inclusion of women is particularly distinct in the Wisdom of Jesus Christ, where the group of seven women is added to the story in Matt 28.

4. Theological Requirements for the Participation of Women

In many apocryphal gospels the participation of women is combined with (for modern ears) quite misogynist statements. In the Gospel of Thomas (logion 114), Mary has to become male in order to belong to the circle of disciples, and Dialogue of the Savior and the Gospel of the Egyptians talk about the destruction of the works of the female. This is no coincidence, as there is a connection between the two. The dissolution of femininity or, in less harsh words, the revocation of gender differences, is required if women are to participate equally.[24] All of the writings that feature female disciples represent the ideal of a spiritual state of humankind in which body and therefore sex are irrelevant. Instead, a heavenly existence is already reached or is sought. Such a true, spiritual, asexual person can be called male, in contrast to the weak, material, and female side. Nevertheless, this state can be reached by women, who will then not differ from men in their spiritual capacities.

The material conditions of life do not matter much for persons with such an orientation toward the spiritual and the heavenly because materiality is not considered as important, or it may be even rejected. That applies to body and sexuality/reproduction, but possibly also to structures and authorities within the church.

5. Why Female Disciples?

There are several possible reasons why female disciples, either alone or in a group, are found in gospels. One reason is that, historically and

---

24. See the contribution of Silke Petersen in this volume.

according to the oldest witnesses (such as the gospels that became canonical), women accompanied Jesus in his ministry and therefore are well suited as recipients of his teaching. Especially if the authors were looking for characters who could offer an alternative to Peter and the Twelve, the women could be an attractive choice. Not all but some of the apocryphal gospels show an interest in tracing their message back to persons close to Jesus other than Peter and the Twelve. Early on, Peter and the Twelve came to represent the developing church as a whole and the dominant opinion prevailing in it. However, people who wrote gospels in the second century often had divergent opinions.[25] James, the brother of Jesus, is a possible choice because he is undoubtedly close to Jesus but also a counterpart to Peter.[26] Some disciples of secondary importance from the Twelve gain prominence, for example Philip, most notably Thomas, and, to a lesser degree, Matthew and Bartholomew.[27] In some circles, Thomas is considered as Jesus's twin brother and therefore as particularly close to him. John is a special case because he is one of the leading disciples of the Twelve, but also because he plays a prominent role in the noncanonical reception history of the Gospel of John.[28] Levi is not one of the Twelve, but he is called by Jesus (see Mark 2:14).[29] Mary Magdalene and other female disciples complete this list because they too are members of the circle around Jesus and loyal even throughout the passion and on Easter morning. However, they do not belong to the established group of the Twelve. In some cases, their gender might not

---

25. Gospels were often written in marginalized groups struggling for survival and identity. That was also the case for the gospels of the first century that later became canonical (see Hartenstein, "Autoritätskonstellationen in apokryphen," 443).

26. See First and Second Revelation of James, Secret Book of James.

27. See Gospel of Philip (NHC II 3). There might have been another gospel in his name that Epiphanius quotes. Philip is mentioned as first of the disciples in the Wisdom of Jesus Christ. See the talk of a "Philip-circle" in Douglas M. Parrott, "Gnostic and Orthodox Disciples in the Second and Third Centuries," in *Nag Hammadi, Gnosticism, and Early Christianity*, ed. Charles W. Hedrick (Peabody, MA: Hendrickson, 1986), 202 and passim. Thomas gains prominence especially in the Gospel of Thomas and the Book of Thomas, but Thomas is also mentioned in the Wisdom of Jesus Christ and presumably in the Dialogue of the Savior under the name Judas.

28. E.g., in the Secret Book of John, but John also plays a special role within the Twelve in the Epistle of the Apostles.

29. Together with Mary, he is the positive antipode to Peter and Andrew in the Gospel of Mary.

be of primary importance if the main focus is on finding persons close to Jesus who could transmit specific traditions.

Some of the women are especially appropriate candidates for such a role. According to John 20, Jesus appears to Mary Magdalene and teaches her about his ascent. It is only one verse, but it contains words no one else has heard. I think this might be one, perhaps even the most important reason for her prominent role in the Gospel of Mary. There she passes on Jesus's teachings, among other things about the ascent of the soul.[30] In addition to Mary, Salome (known from the lists of women in Mark) and Martha (in Luke and John) are suited to such a role. Other female disciples with the name Mary seem to fuse early on with Mary Magdalene, thereby strengthening Martha's role. For Salome we can assume that there were traditions not preserved about her in addition to Mark.[31] Finally, there is Mary the mother of Jesus, who is clearly close to him and who is portrayed as a disciple in the Gospel of John.[32] These arguments do not differ in principle from those for James or Thomas. Even if the recourse to these alternative disciples mirrors a discourse of the time in which the gospels were written, gender issues do not have to be crucial in the decision.

Nevertheless, the fact that it is women who talk to Jesus and who are taught by him is sometimes due to the theological positions of the text. If, for example, the dissolution of femininity and the revocation of gender differences is a topic, this is particularly relevant for women, and the participation of women demonstrates this point. Not only is the state of a new, spiritual human being required for the equal participation of women, but their presence is also an illustration of these theological convictions.

However, women's presence is not always undisputed. In the Gospel of Thomas, Mary's status as a member of the group is explicitly questioned and then affirmed—therefore it is not self-evident. In First Revelation of James, women do not belong to the primary recipients of revelations. Jesus's teachings are initially meant for James and are later transmitted through other men. But female disciples are positively mentioned, whereas James wonders about the existence of the female group. Here as well their role as disciples is not self-evident.

---

30. Other than in Gospel of Mary, she plays a crucial role in the Dialogue of the Savior, the Wisdom of Jesus Christ, and Pistis Sophia.
31. See Petersen, *"Zerstört die Werke,"* 233, 300.
32. She becomes important in Pistis Sophia.

The portrayal of the participation of women in these texts possibly reflects not only theological convictions but also political opinions, a sort of feminist interest. In the second century, there were some Christian groups for whom it was important that the circle around Jesus did not consist only of men. In some writings, it is ostentatiously men *and* women who are taught by Jesus and who transmit his teachings, and in this way connect later followers to him. It can only be assumed that it was the women in these groups who had an interest in emphasizing women's participation among Jesus's followers. Still, the interest in strengthening women's roles is noticeable, in my opinion already in the Gospel of John, even more clearly in the Wisdom of Jesus Christ, Pistis Sophia, and perhaps also in the Dialogue of the Savior. In the early church, women were not always undermined, but their position was sometimes strengthened as well. Both aspects are mirrored in apocryphal gospels.

Rewritten Eve Traditions in the Nature of the Rulers (NHC II 4)

Antti Marjanen

1. Introduction

The first four chapters of Genesis belong to biblical texts that have especially stimulated later Jewish and Christian interpretative imagination. Many of the texts within the Nag Hammadi collection have, in particular, drawn their inspiration from these chapters while advancing their own views on the origin of the material world and of human beings.[1] Most studies dealing with the use of these chapters in Nag Hammadi texts focus on the figure of Adam. The purpose of the present essay is different. I will explore how the passages of the first four chapters of Genesis that deal with the figure of Eve have been employed and rewritten, and what kind of interpretive strategies these new readings serve in one Nag Hammadi text, the Nature of the Rulers (NHC II 4),[2] also called the Hypostasis of the Archons.[3] The motifs that the essay deals with are the creation, rape, and

---

1. For an instructive introduction to the Nag Hammadi collection and its content, see Marvin Meyer, ed., *The Nag Hammadi Scriptures: The International Edition* (New York: HarperCollins, 2007).

2. For the edition and an English translation of the text, see Bentley Layton, "The Hypostasis of the Archons," in *Nag Hammadi Codex II,2–7 Together with XIII,2*, Brit. Lib.Or.4926(1), and P.Oxy. 1,654,655*, ed. Bentley Layton, NHS 20 (Leiden: Brill, 1989), 234–59. For another, more readable English translation of the text, see Marvin Meyer, "The Nature of the Rulers," in Meyer, *Nag Hammadi Scriptures*, 191–98. All the English translations of the text found in this essay are nevertheless my own.

3. Other Nag Hammadi texts where Eve figures and to some of which I occasionally refer are the following: Ap. John NHC II 1 20–25 (see BG 2, 55–64); Orig. World 112.25–121.27; Gos. Phil. 60.34–61.12; 68.22–26; 70.9–22; Exeg. Soul 133.1–10; Melch. 9.28–10.11; Testim. Truth 45.23–47.14; see also Gos. Jud. (CT 3) 52. For my

-45-

fall of Eve, in addition to the motif of the children of Eve. In connection with all of these motifs, I also discuss the question of Eve's heavenly counterpart, since part of the interpretive strategy the author of the Nature of the Rulers employs is to read certain Eve texts of Genesis as references to the heavenly or spiritual Eve. All the motifs presented above, I will argue, betray the understanding of the author of the Nature of the Rulers regarding the destiny of the humans in the world and their salvation.

2. The Nature of the Rulers as a Sethian Writing

Before I enter into discussion about the specific themes of Eve in the Nature of the Rulers, I will briefly introduce this source. The text is preserved in the second codex of the Nag Hammadi texts, a Coptic collection of early Christian manuscripts. The codices are usually dated to the second half of the fourth century, but the original forms of individual texts may be earlier in. The Nature of the Rulers is usually categorized as a Sethian gnostic text.[4] What joins the Sethian texts together, which number sixteen or seventeen in all according to most scholars, is that they either narrate or presuppose a Sethian myth of origins.[5] The typical features of

---

analysis of the use of the Eve traditions of Genesis in the Secret Book of John, see Antti Marjanen, "Rewritten Eve Traditions in the Apocryphon of John," in *Bodies, Borders, Believers: Ancient Texts and Present Conversations; Essays in Honor of Turid Karlsen Seim on Her Seventieth Birthday*, ed. Anne Hege Grung, Marianne Bjelland Kartzow, and Anna Rebecca Solevåg (Eugene, OR: Pickwick, 2015), 57–67.

4. I use the term *gnostic* as a heuristic category to refer to those texts or thinkers of antiquity that maintained that the visible world was created by an evil or ignorant creator and that the human soul or spirit originates from the transcendental world, and, after having become aware of that, this divine element has the potential of returning there. For this view, see Antti Marjanen, "Gnosticism," in *The Oxford Handbook of Early Christian Studies*, ed. Susan Ashbrook Harvey and David G. Hunter (Oxford: Oxford University Press, 2008), 203–20.

5. For a brief but excellent introduction to Sethianism and Sethian writings, see Michael A. Williams, "Sethianism," in *A Companion to Second-Century Christian "Heretics,"* ed. Antti Marjanen and Petri Luomanen (Leiden: Brill, 2005), 32–63. Rather than speaking only of Sethian writings and mythology, Tuomas Rasimus has distinguished between three related mythologies—Barbeloite, Sethite, and Ophite—that together form what he calls the classic gnostic mythology, a version of what was previously called Sethian expanded by the writings that represents Ophite mythology. See Rasimus, *Paradise Reconsidered in Gnostic Mythmaking: Rethinking Sethianism in Light of the Ophite Evidence*, NHMS 68 (Leiden: Brill, 2009), 9–62. According to Rasi-

this myth are as follows: the highest God is a supreme trinity comprising the Father (Invisible Spirit), Mother (Barbelo),[6] and the Son (Autogenēs); [7]the highest God establishes a spiritual universe of various heavenly aeons and luminaries; the last of these aeons, Sophia (Wisdom),[8] undertakes a fatal project by trying to create something like herself without the consent of the Father (Invisible Spirit) and her male counterpart. The result is an evil and ignorant Creator God, Yaldabaoth, also referred to as Sakla(s) or Samael, who produces the material universe and human beings.

For Sethian texts, it is also important to stress that at least a portion of humankind bears within each of themselves a divine element derived from the realm of the highest divinity. Various versions of the Sethian myth explain this state of affairs in different ways. In the Secret Book of John, for example, Yaldabaoth has a connection to the spiritual world through his mother, Sophia. He thus has a divine element in him but is ignorant of it. While attempting to vivify the first human being, he is lured by the representatives of the spiritual universe into blowing his spirit into the face of Adam (see Gen 2:7); he thus loses his divine element, which is subsequently transferred over to Adam and his descendants (NHC II 1, 19.18–33; BG 2, 51.8–52.1). In the Nature of the Rulers, Yaldabaoth does not receive such a divine element from his mother in the first place for him to mediate to the human being he and his rulers create. It is instead the heavenly Spirit who descends to help Adam, takes up to dwell in him, and thus provides Adam with a heavenly power that vivifies him (Nat. Rulers 88.10–16).

In both versions of the Sethian myth, it is this divine element or power that gains the central role in the struggle fought between the realm of the highest God and that of the Creator God and his rulers. The struggle culminates in various attempts by Yaldabaoth's lower world to gain control

---

mus, the Nature of the Rulers should be seen as a text that combines Barbeloite and Ophite components, while underplaying the role of Seth. Therefore, the text, Rasimus argues, lacks Sethite features. I also recognize the modest role of Seth in the Nature of the Rulers, but I do not think it is due to the fact that the Nature of the Rulers should not be regarded as a Sethian text according to the traditional understanding of the term, but that it represents a form of Sethianism that emphasizes the role of Norea over Seth. For this argument, see below.

6. The name Barbelo does not occur in the Nature of the Rulers, but the figure of Incorruptibility, who appears for the first time in the text in 87.1, clearly stands for her.

7. In the Nature of the Rulers, the Son (Autogenēs) does not occur except in the final praise (97.18), which ends the text.

8. Wisdom is also called Pistis Sophia in the Nature of the Rulers (see, e.g., 87.7–8).

over the divine power. The spiritual universe of the highest God meets these attempts by sending its own Savior figures to the humans in order to bring them the salvific knowledge of the real origin of the divine element in them. With this knowledge, human beings can become capable of seeking out deliverance from the material world of Yaldabaoth. As we will see, the Eve traditions of Gen 1–4 play an important part in the way the struggle over the divine element in human beings is described and construed in Sethian myths, the Nature of the Rulers being a prime example.

Besides the common myth, there is still another feature that joins the so-called Sethian texts together: usually the addressees of the texts are seen as spiritual descendants of Seth, the third son of Adam and Eve. That is also the reason why these texts and one of the most important gnostic schools of thought are called Sethian. As we will see, the role of Seth is not particularly prominent in the Nature of the Rulers. The reason for this has to do with how the children of Eve are portrayed and what function they serve in the text.

The myth underlying the Nature of the Rulers presents a Sethian interpretation of Gen 1–6 that is embellished with typical Sethian features. However, when the story reaches a description of Noah and the building of his ark, there is a surprising change in the text. It turns into a dialogue between Elelēth, one of the heavenly luminaries, and Norea, a daughter of Adam and Eve, who plays an important part in the latter part of the narrative. It seems clear that the figure of Norea is an addition both to the narrative of Genesis and to other Sethian versions of the myth. We will get back to this later when we discuss the children of Eve, but before that we will first explore how the Nature of the Rulers deals with the traditions of the creation, rape, and fall of Eve.

3. The Creation of the Heavenly Eve

In its description of the creation of Eve, the Nature of the Rulers seemingly follows Genesis rather closely. After the creators cause Adam to fall asleep: "they opened his side <and removed his rib>[9] like a living woman. Then

---

9. The phrase between the angle brackets does not actually appear in the text, but it (e.g., ⲁⲩϥⲓ ⲉⲃⲟⲗ ⲛ̄ⲧⲉϥⲃⲏⲧⲥⲡⲓⲣ) or something similar has to be supplied in the text in order to make it understandable, as many have suggested (see, e.g., the critical apparatus in Layton, "Hypostasis of the Archons," 240). The omission of the text may easily be due to a homoioteleuton.

they built up his side with some flesh in her [= heavenly Eve] stead, and Adam became entirely psychic [ⲮⲨⲬⲒⲔⲞⲤ ⲦⲎⲢϤ]" (Nat. Rulers 89.7–11). The apparent similarity between the descriptions of Genesis and the Nature of the Rulers is nevertheless deceptive. There are two significant differences.

First, the reference to many creators is not to be understood as similar to the plural in Gen 1:27, which states: "Let us make humankind in our image." This passage in Genesis seems to imply a presence of lesser gods of the divine assembly in the creation of human beings. In the Nature of the Rulers it is not the realm of the highest God that is responsible for the creation or actually the removal of Eve from Adam, but rather Yaldabaoth. Thus, the plural "creators" refers only to his powers. Just as Adam, so too is Eve created or at least made visible as a consequence of the activity of Yaldabaoth's powers.

Second, what is removed or made visible from Adam's side is not actually the earthly Eve, as we usually read in Genesis, but the spiritual woman, a kind of spiritual element or presence, who, according to the story of the Nature of the Rulers, has earlier descended from the Adamantine Land, that is, from the spiritual universe, into Adam. Thus she, a sort of spiritual or heavenly Eve, comes to make him a living soul after he has been created by the rulers and after he has been only a psychic being lying on the ground (Nat. Rulers 88.4–5). This is indicated by the fact that when the spiritual Eve is removed from Adam and a piece of flesh has been put in his side in place of her, the text states that Adam is again only a psychic being (ⲮⲨⲬⲒⲔⲞⲤ ⲦⲎⲢϤ). But if this passage does indeed inform us of the removal of the spiritual or heavenly Eve from Adam, how and when does the earthly Eve appear on the scene in the Nature of the Rulers? We will discuss this question in the next section, which deals with the rape and fall of Eve.

4. The Rape and Fall of Eve

After the spiritual Eve has been removed from Adam, she approaches the psychic Adam, who is apparently again lying on the ground, and asks him to arise (Nat. Rulers 89.11–13). This exhortation has positive consequences. Adam is obviously awakened (from the sleep of forgetfulness?), shows his appreciation to the spiritual Eve, and says: "It is you who have given me life; you will be called 'mother of the living.'" Adam's line is reminiscent of Gen 3:20, where he names his wife Eve because "she is the mother of all living." But again, the passage of Genesis is read in the Nature of the Rulers as a reference to the heavenly or spiritual Eve instead of Adam's earthly spouse. That the spiritual Eve vivifies him does not yet have soteriological connotation, as we are about to see. It only means that the lifeless psychic creation of the archons has come alive.

The conversation between Adam and the spiritual Eve attracts the attention of the rulers, and they want to rape her. Yet the spiritual Eve flees and leaves a shadow behind, a reflection resembling herself. It is here that the earthly Eve is finally introduced into the story, but the beginning of her life is not very pleasant. The rulers attack and rape her. The text speaks about "polluting Eve" and uses the Coptic verb ϫⲱϩⲙ̄, which clearly stands for rape in this context. The function of the earthly Eve seems to be to act as a substitute for the spiritual Eve, who in docetic fashion can free herself from this unpleasant event for higher purposes. In the Nature of the Rulers, the rape does not seem to have any other purpose than to underline the violent and brutal character of the powers of the material world. In this way, the text functions as a warning of and perhaps as a protest against the cruel and shameless conduct of earthly authorities. Rape is a powerful means to subordinate and humiliate women.

Although neither the narrative of Genesis nor any other biblical Eve tradition refers to the rape of Eve, the Nature of the Rulers is not the only Nag Hammadi text that contains such an episode. The rape of Eve is also presented, for instance, in the Secret Book of John. In that text the rape leads to the birth of Yave and Elohim, two sons and servants of Yaldabaoth, who bear the names of the Jewish God but who are also called Cain and Abel (NHC II 1, 24.24-25). The purpose of this identification is to show that the two first sons of Eve belong to Yaldabaoth's realm, while Seth, the son of Eve and Adam, is of a different character and worthy of being the ancestor of the spiritual race, highlighting both the position of Seth and that of his descendants.

The rape of Eve also has another consequence in the Secret Book of John, at least according to its long recension (NHC II 1, 24.8-18). Strangely enough, the text insists that through the rape of Eve Yaldabaoth planted sexual desire in women (24.28-29). In this way, the need to procreate begins, and the divine element that has been accidentally blown into human beings by Yaldabaoth is transferred to new human bodies that keep it imprisoned. Thus, this encratic text makes sexual intercourse a condemnable act and indirectly shifts the responsibility for the desperate situation of the humans to the woman. It is interesting and significant that the short versions (NHC III 1, 31.21-32.3; BG 2, 63.1-9) maintain that the desire has been planted in Adam and do not connect this as directly with the rape of Eve, as the long version does.

Although the spiritual, heavenly Eve flees the threat of being raped, she does not entirely disappear from the scene in the Nature of the Rulers. In the form of a snake, she returns to instruct Adam and the earthly Eve about the tree of "recognizing evil and good" (Nat. Rulers 90.6–12). The negative role the snake has in Genesis and the negative act of eating from the tree of the knowledge of evil and good have thus been reversed in the Nature of the Rulers. The snake, that is, the heavenly Eve, becomes an instructor who helps Adam and the earthly Eve understand that the prohibition of Yaldabaoth against eating from the tree of the knowledge of evil and good is not given for the protection of humans but out of jealousy. Yaldabaoth knows that if the humans eat from the tree, they will become even more advanced than he and his powers are. "[Their] eyes will open and [they] will become like gods," says the snake (90.8–9). But what exactly does this mean? Is the knowledge of evil and good identical with having salvific knowledge? Is becoming like gods the same as becoming one belonging to the spiritual universe, the pleroma, as it is also called in Sethian writings?

The logic of the story seems to suggest that the right answer to both of these latter questions would have to be affirmative. In light of this, it is surprising that when the story reports that the earthly Eve and Adam eat from the tree, they receive knowledge, but not salvific knowledge. Rather, they realize "their imperfection … in their ignorance" (Nat. Rulers 90.15–16). Furthermore, they comprehend that they are spiritually naked. In other words, they do not come to know how they can be saved, but they perceive their predicament, their lack of spiritual, heavenly power. In spite of the contact Adam and the earthly Eve have with the spiritual Eve and in spite of the assistance they receive from her, it remains ambiguous in the Nature of the Rulers whether they ever attain salvation. As a matter of fact, the story of Adam and the earthly Eve seems to end on a pessimistic tone. The text states: "The rulers took Adam and threw him and his wife out of the garden. They[10] have no blessing, for they are also under the curse" (91.3–7). Even the snake appears to share the same destiny, though by the

---

10. Meyer suggests that the pronoun "they" could also refer to the archons; this is not grammatically impossible, but quite unlikely in this context ("Nature of the Rulers," 194 n. 38).

time the snake is condemned to live under the curse of the authorities (90.34–91.3), the spiritual Eve has already left the snake.[11]

In the Nature of the Rulers, it is actually in the second generation of the humans that the divine plan of salvation begins to be realized, especially in the fourth child of Eve, her daughter Norea. With this I move to the last section of the article.

5. The Children of Eve

The destiny of Cain and Abel in the Nature of the Rulers derives from two traditions. On the one hand, it draws its inspiration from the fratricide tradition of Genesis, according to which Abel was killed by his brother Cain. On the other hand, it reflects the rape-of-Eve motif found also in some other Sethian texts, such as the Secret Book of John and On the Origin of the World. As regards Cain, the Nature of the Rulers suggests that he is a result of the rape of the earthly Eve by the rulers (Nat. Rulers 89.23–28; 91.11–12).[12] Thus the text agrees with the Secret Book of John, wherein Cain also originates, together with Abel, from the rape of Eve, though there raped by Yaldabaoth himself. In the Nature of the Rulers, Abel does not seem to be a consequence of the defilement of Eve by Yaldabaoth or his rulers, but a seed of Eve's and Adam's intercourse (91.13–14). The third child of Eve, Seth, the substitute for Abel, is also mentioned in the Nature of the Rulers, but as I argued earlier, the role he is given in the text is surprisingly small when one considers that the Nature of the Rulers is a Sethian text. Seth is mentioned only once in the Nature of the Rulers, and in that passage (91.30–33) he is simply introduced as one who was given "in place of Abel." Nothing is said about his role as an ancestor of the immovable race, as in other Sethian texts.

The role that is usually assigned to Seth, the third child of Eve, in Sethian texts—for example, in the Gospel of the Egyptians (NHC) and the Revelation of Adam—is here given to Norea,[13] the fourth child of Eve in

---

11. It is interesting, at any rate, that the snake receives the promise that it will be freed from the curse when the "perfect human being" (= Jesus?) arrives (Nat. Rulers 91.2).

12. The reference to "their son" (Nat. Rulers 91.12) seems to imply that the rulers begat Cain while they raped Eve.

13. For an excellent overview of Norea in ancient writings, see Uwe-Karsten Plisch, "Norea," *RAC* 25 (2013): 1129–33; see also Birger Pearson, "The Figure of

the Nature of the Rulers.[14] The name of Norea is not mentioned in Genesis at all. Even in the Nag Hammadi texts she is a rare figure.[15] In the Nature of the Rulers, Eve introduces her birth by saying: "He [= Adam][16] has begotten [from me a virgin] to be help [for] many human generations" (Nat. Rulers 91.35–92.2). This introduction anticipates and summarizes Norea's role as a receiver and mediator of the salvific knowledge she gains through a dialogue with Elelēth, one of the four Sethian luminaries, who reveals everything about her heavenly origin. At the same time, she becomes an ancestor of the Sethians, who attain knowledge of their origin because of her and are thus saved. That Norea's offspring only appears when the true human (= Jesus) reveals the truth that was given to Norea by Elelēth does not change the fact that Norea is the mythical ancestor of these Sethians in the Nature of the Rulers (96.19–35).

There is one special feature in the description of Norea that, on the one hand, links her to her mother Eve, but, on the other hand, distinguishes her from Eve. Before Norea starts her conversation with Elelēth she, like her mother, meets with the archons of Yaldabaoth, who want to rape her (Nat. Rulers 92.18–21). Unlike her mother, Norea flees the rulers' attempt to sexually abuse her by seeking help from the God of the All, the Invisible Spirit, who sends Elelēth to her rescue. In the narrative world of the Nature of the Rulers, Norea's successful attempt to avoid the defilement consti-

---

Norea in Gnostic Literature," in *Gnosticism, Judaism, and Egyptian Christianity*, SAC (Minneapolis: Fortress, 1990), 84–93; Pearson, "Revisiting Norea," in *Images of the Feminine in Gnosticism*, ed. Karen L. King, SAC (Philadelphia: Fortress, 1988), 265–75.

14. A similar conclusion is reached by Anne McGuire, "Virginity and Subversion: Norea against the Powers in the Hypostasis of the Archons," in King, *Images of the Feminine*, 239–58, esp. 247.

15. See nevertheless the Thought of Norea (NHC IX 2) and a reference to the First Book of Noraia and the First Discourse of Oraia in Orig. World (NHC II 5) 102.10–11, 24–25.

16. Ursula Ulrike Kaiser renders the text differently and assumes that Norea was begotten by God. See Ursula Ulrike Kaiser, "Die Hypostase der Archonten (NHC II,4)," in *Nag Hammadi Deutsch: Studienausgabe; NHC I–XIII, Codex Berolinensis 1 und 4, Codex Tchacos 3 und 4*, ed. Hans-Martin Schenke, Hans-Gebhard Bethge, and Ursula Ulrike Kaiser (Berlin: de Gruyter, 2013), 170. It is not completely clear what God stands for in her interpretation, but if she thinks that God refers to the Highest God, i.e., the Father of the All, and not Yaldabaoth, the interpretation is possible. The logic of the text seems to suggest, however, that the begetter of both Seth and Norea (Nat. Rulers 91.30–92.2) is in fact Adam, although it is equally clear that Eve gives birth to these two children "through God," the Father of the All.

tutes a turning point in the story. It is after this that Norea receives Elelēth's teaching about her origin and thus gains salvific knowledge. While Eve does not succeed in resisting, Norea does, and this makes all the difference. Norea, as it were, corrects her mother's failure. Whether it is fair to make Eve responsible for her being raped can be questioned, of course, but the lesson of the story does not primarily lie in how one should react to the sexual abuse per se but how one should escape any kind of sexual activity aroused by lust.

6. Concluding Remarks

In this conclusion, I want to highlight two observations that in a very crucial way underline the interpretive strategies of the author of the Nature of the Rulers. First, the reason the author of the text is able to use and interpret the Eve traditions in Genesis in such a creative way is that he or she divides the traditions between the earthly and heavenly Eve. For example, the creation of Eve via removal from Adam's side deals with the heavenly Eve, while eating from the tree of the knowledge of good and evil deals with the earthly Eve. This bipartite interpretation probably made it possible for the author to make use of an otherwise difficult text. It is interesting that a similar interpretive strategy is employed in the Secret Book of John and On the Origin of the World, two texts very closely related to the Nature of the Rulers.

Second, while the division of the Eve traditions into two parts, those that deal with the heavenly Eve and those that deal with the earthly Eve, underlines the creativity and strategic skill of the author, one expansion of the Eve traditions may hold even greater significance when the aspirations of the author of the Nature of the Rulers are analyzed. It has been suggested that the appearance of Norea to replace Seth as the primeval ancestor of the Sethians, or at least the primeval ancestor of some of them, may have originally been an appeal to the female hearers of the Sethian myth, who would have needed a mythical hero to identify with. It has even been speculated that a woman author has produced the text.[17] Another

---

17. Birger Pearson made this proposal in the 1980s, when scholars more often looked for women among early Christian writers (see Pearson, "Revisiting Norea," 273). Now scholars tend to be more cautious. But if it is at all possible to assume that there were early Christian texts written by women, the Nature of the Rulers could be one of the better candidates.

possibility that does not necessarily rule out the earlier proposal is that the Nature of the Rulers is the product of an author participating in an intra-Sethian debate on the ultimate Sethian ancestorship whereby Norean Sethians attempt to occupy greater status for their female hero as a spiritual forerunner at the expense of Seth.[18] This would not only explain the large role Norea has in the text but would also account, in contrast, for the minimal part Seth plays in the Nature of the Rulers.

---

18. Another Sethian text that seems to imply a polemical opinion on the role of Seth as a spiritual ancestor of the Sethians is On the Origin of the World, which appears to suggest that all sons of Eve, starting from Abel and thus including also Seth, are archontic (Orig. World 117.15–18); for this, see Rasimus, *Paradise Reconsidered*, 201.

Sophia and Her Sisters: Norea, Protennoia, Brontē

Uwe-Karsten Plisch

1. Sophia

In an essay in which Sophia and her sisters are to be treated, it is an unavoidable fact that one can say only very little about the figure of Sophia herself. For this reason, I will draw attention in a certain sense to Sophia's sisters and present only the most necessary information about Sophia herself.[1]

The most important source for the gnostic Sophia figure is Old Testament wisdom (Hebrew חכמה, plural חכמות),[2] which appears in the book of Proverbs as a preexistent participant in the creation.

> *If I report to you the things that happen daily,*
>   *I will remember to enumerate the things of old.*
> The Lord created me as the beginning of his ways,
>   *for the sake of his works.*
> Before the present age he founded me, in the beginning.
> Before he made the earth *and before he made the depths*,
>   before he brought forth the springs of the waters,
> before the mountains were established
>   and before all the hills, *he begets me*....
> When he prepared the sky, I was present with him,
>   and *when he marked out his own throne on the winds.*

---

1. On the Old Testament figure of Sophia, see, among others, Gerlinde Baumann, "Die Weisheitsgestalt: Kontexte, Bedeutungen, Theologie," in *Schriften und spätere Weisheitsbücher*, ed. Christl Maier and Nuria Calduch-Benages, BF 1.3 (Stuttgart: Kohlhammer 2013), 57–74; Irmtraud Fischer, *Gotteslehrerinnen: Weise Frauen und Frau Weisheit im Alten Testament* (Stuttgart: Kohlhammer, 2006), with the literature cited in each case.

2. On the Jewish background of the gnostic Sophia mythology, see George W. McRae, "The Jewish Background of the Gnostic Sophia Myth," *NovT* 12 (1970): 86–101.

> When he made strong the clouds above
>   and when he made secure the springs
> *of what is under heaven,*
>   when he made strong the foundations of the earth,
> I was beside him, fitting together [ἁρμόζουσα];
>   it is I who was the one in whom he took delight.
> And each day *I was glad* in his presence at every moment. (Prov 8:21a–30 LXX)[3]

The act of creation is understood here naturally as quite positive, while in gnostic cosmogonies it is a fatal and, in the end, an adverse process. The Jewish background is particularly clear in the gnostic creation story in On the Origin of the World (NHC II 5): "In its main features, it follows Genesis, but its narrative begins already before heaven and earth were made."[4] Matter and envy come into being through a blunder by Sophia, and in Sophia's attempt to correct her mistake, the demiurge arises, the subordinate creator of the earthly world who falsely considers himself to be the only, the supreme god.

In the four versions of the Secret Book of John,[5] a kind of basic doctrinal text of Sethian Gnosticism, a detailed account of all creation is found—from the transcendent world of light to the deficient earthly world. From the beginning there exists an ineffable Unity, timeless, transcendent, and indescribable, "the Father of All":

> It is he who contemplates himself in his own light which surrounds him, namely, the spring of living water, the light full of purity.... And his thought [Ennoia] became actual and she came forth and attended him in the brilliance of the light. She is the power who is before the All, who came forth. She is the perfect Providence [Pronoia] of the All, the light, the likeness of the light, the image of the invisible One, the perfect power, Barbelo, the perfect aeon of glory, glorifies him, since she had come forth because of him. And she knows him. (BG 2, 26–27)[6]

---

3. Translation from NETS. The portions in italics indicate deviations from the MT.

4. Jaan Lahe, *Gnosis und Judentum*, NHMS 75 (Leiden: Brill, 2012), 199.

5. The Secret Book of John is found three times among the manuscripts of Nag Hammadi, in each case as the first text in codex II, III, and IV, as well as in the Papyrus Berolinensis Gnosticus (BG 8502) as the second text.

6. Translation by Michael Waldstein and Frederik Wisse in *The Apocryphon of John: Synopsis of Nag Hammadi Codices II,1; III,1 and IV,1 with BG 8502,2*, NHMS 33 (Leiden: Brill, 1995), 30–32.

Sophia and Her Sisters: Norea, Protennoia, Brontē

The female counterpart of the absolutely transcendent, invisible supreme god, the female Barbelo,[7] corresponds to the Sophia in Prov 8. With the approval of her counterpart, she brings forth a son, the Self-Originated One (Autogenēs). Together they form the supreme heavenly triad (BG 2, 30). The heavenly system is unfolded subsequently in more detail (the creation of the four enlighteners, Harmozel, Oroiael, Daveithe, and Eleleth, and of the four aeons, to which four ages in history correspond) but without developing any interest at all—even in the texts with the same orientation—in an absolute concurrence in the differentiations within the system.[8]

At the lower end of the system, there occurs, in the end, a fatal blunder by the (lower) Sophia, which leads to the emergence of the low god of creation, the demiurge, and to the imperfect earthly world.

> Our fellow-sister, Wisdom [Sophia], being an aeon, conceived a thought from herself, and in the conception of the Spirit and Foreknowledge. She wanted to bring forth the likeness out of herself, although the Spirit had not <agreed> with her nor had her consort approved, namely the male virginal Spirit. She, however, did not find her partner as she was about to decide without the good will of the Spirit and the knowledge of her own partner. (BG 2, 36–37: The Blunder of the [Lower] Sophia)[9]

Sophia's blunder is elaborated more mythologically, and for this reason more clearly, in Nature of the Rulers):

> Within limitless realms dwells incorruptibility. Sophia, who is called Pistis, wanted to create something, alone without her consort; and her product was a celestial thing.
>
> A veil exists between the world above and the realms that are below; and shadow came into being beneath the veil; and that shadow became matter; and that shadow was projected apart. And what she had created became a product in the matter, like an aborted fetus. And it assumed

---

7. The form of the name Barbelo, for its part, has a background in the Hebrew language: אלה בארבע = "God is in four," an allusion to the Tetragrammaton (Lahe, *Gnosis und Judentum*, 208).

8. See Hans-Martin Schenke, "Das sethianische System nach Nag Hammadi-Handschriften," in *Studia Coptica*, ed. Peter Nagel, BBA 45 (Berlin: Akademie, 1974), 165–73.

9. Translation by Waldstein and Wisse, *Apocryphon of John*, 58–60.

a plastic form molded out of shadow, and became an arrogant beast resembling a lion. (Nat. Rulers 94: Sophia's Unauthorized Work)[10]

Therewith, the creation of the lower material world is put into motion.

The tendency to differentiate between a higher, transcendent Sophia and a lower Sophia, who finally is responsible for the deficient creation of the material world, is continued in the system of Valentinian gnosis. There the lower Sophia is called Achamoth. But Achamoth is nothing other than the Greek transcription of the corresponding Hebrew expression (חכמות, plural of חכמה; see Prov 1:20; 9:1), so that the Jewish background of the gnostic Sophia figure is once again clear.

2. Norea

The figure of Norea also belongs to the sphere of mythologically oriented Sethian Gnosticism. Within the Sethian myth, she appears first of all as a sister-consort of the third son of Adam and Eve, Seth (Gen 4:25). She is there the female counterpart of Seth, the progenitor of the Sethians. She appears further in the extrabiblical tradition as a wife (?) or adversary of Noah (this must not necessarily be a contradiction) in the story of the flood (Gen 6:18) but is herself not named in the Bible. In addition, she bears traits of the heavenly Sophia in that she has an insight into, and a portion in, the world above and is finally superior to the earthly powers.

The concrete form of the name Norea varies considerably within the tradition, even within individual manuscripts: Nōrea (Nat. Rulers 92.21, 32; 93.6; Norea 27.21); Ōrea (Nat. Rulers 92.14); Norea (Norea 29.3; Irenaeus, *Haer.* 1.30.9 Latin); Nōraia, Ōraia (Orig. World [NHC II 5] 102.11, 25); Nōraia, Ōraia (Epiphanius, *Pan.* 39.5.2; 26.1.3); Nhūraitā (Mandaean, Ginza Rba 2.1.121). According to the widely accepted derivation given by Birger Pearson,[11] the Hebrew proper name Na'amah has to be seen as the background (on this Hebrew proper name, see Gen 4:22 and 1 Kgs 14:21).

---

10. Translation by Bentley Layton in *Nag Hammadi Codex II,2–7*, NHMS 20 (Leiden: Brill, 1989), 1:253.

11. Birger A. Pearson, "The Figure of Norea in Gnostic Literature," in *Gnosticism, Judaism, and Egyptian Christianity*, SAC 5 (Minneapolis: Fortress, 1990), 84–93. See also Pearson, "Revisiting Norea," in *Images of the Feminine in Gnosticism*, ed. Karen L. King, SAC (Philadelphia: Fortress, 1988), 265–75.

The meaning of the name is "delightful, pleasant"; the Greek equivalent is ὡραῖος/ὥριος. Accordingly, Na'amah would have become Nōrea/Ōrea through the act of translation.

Church father and enemy of heretics Epiphanius of Salamis (*Pan.* 26.1.3), on the other hand, reports a gnostic etymology of the name Norea, which harks back to Pyrrha via the Aramaic word *nura* (fire). With the identification of Norea with Pyrrha, there is once again a connection with the Greek flood narrative about Deukalion and Pyrrha.

As Ursula Ulrike Kaiser has demonstrated, Norea is the real chief figure in the Nag Hammadi text Nature of the Rulers.[12] In the series of the first four children of Adam and Eve, she appears in ascending order as the last of these. While Cain, as the firstborn, comes from the rape of the earthly Eve by the Rulers (Archons), Norea is a kind of divinely begotten virgin (Nat. Rulers 91.34–92.2). As a "virgin that the powers have *not* defiled" (92.2), she even surpasses her mother, Eve. She and her brother Seth are the progenitors of (true) humanity, whereby a comparatively smaller significance is laid on Seth. The Rulers attempt to seduce and to rape Norea too, as they did with their mother, but they fail because Elelēth, the fourth enlightener in the Sethian system, hurries to her aid. The entire last part of the Nature of the Rulers (93.2–97.21) is a revelatory dialogue between Elelēth and Norea in which the latter is instructed about the origin and nature of the Rulers, especially Samaēl, Sabaōth, and Jaldabōth, and about Sophia's arbitrary act through which the creation is set in motion, as well as about the origin and fate of the Children of the Light (this is the "kingless race," so a self-designation of the Sethians, 97.4). Norea is here thus a preferred recipient of the revelation and a mediatrix of the same. This narrative from Norea's birth to the revelation through Elelēth, in itself continuous, is interrupted by a short insertion (92.3–18) about the flood, in which Norea, as Noah's adversary, burns the ark with her breath. The already-mentioned Epiphanius of Salamis, on the other hand, reports about a gnostic tradition according to which Nōria, as the *wife* of Noah, burned the ark three times (*Pan.* 26.1.4–9). That she is understood as Noah's wife is not evident in Nature of the Rulers, but an extrabiblical tradition in which the protagonist is called Na'amah is likely to underlie it.

---

12. Ursula Ulrike Kaiser, *Die Hypostase der Archonten (Nag-Hammadi-Codex II,4)*, TU 156 (Berlin: de Gruyter, 2006), 271.

> Then mankind began to multiply and improve. The rulers took counsel with one another and said: "Come, let us cause a deluge with our hands and obliterate all flesh, from man to beast."
> But when the ruler of the forces [i.e., Sabaoth] came to know of their decision, he said to Noah, "Make yourself an ark from some wood that does not rot and hide in it—you and your children and the beasts and the birds of heaven from small to large—and set it upon Mount Sir." Then [N]Orea came to him wanting to board the ark. And when he would not let her, she blew upon the ark and caused it to be consumed by fire. Again he made the ark, for a second time. (Nat. Rulers 92: The Flood and the Burning of the Ark)[13]

Noah appears here as a tool of the Rulers, that is, the lower creators and lords of the world. Norea's deed is, for this reason, a good deed, since she seeks to thwart the plans of the Ruler Sabaoth. This is a typical example for the so-called gnostic protest exegesis, in which biblical traditions are, to be sure, taken up, but are assessed in a contrary manner.

Within the Nag Hammadi texts, there is a short poetic text without a title handed down in Nag Hammadi Codex IX in which Norea is the main figure (the text NHC IX 2 is sometimes named after her in research as the "Ode about Norea," "Thought of Norea," or, in French, simply "Noréa"). The text begins with a conjuration of the upper world of light through Norea; following this, the answer given to her and her elevation into the Pleroma are reported. Nothing is said about the situation in which this conjuration occurs, but this would fit in with the persecution of Norea by the Rulers as it is described in Nature of the Rulers. In contrast to the description there, all four enlighteners of the Sethian mythological system, and not just Elelēth, are designated here as her helpers. Since poetry can be only poorly recounted, and since the text is short, it may be cited here in its entirety:

> Father of the All,
> [Ennoia] of the Light,
> Nous [dwelling] in the heights
> above the (regions) below,
> Light dwelling [in the] heights,
> Voice of Truth,
> upright Nous,

---

13. Translation by Layton in *Nag Hammadi Codex II,2–7*, 247–49.

untouchable Logos,
and [ineffable] Voice,
[incomprehensible] Father!

It is Norea who [cries out] to them.
They [heard,] (and) they received her into her place
forever. They gave her the Father of Nous, Adamas,
as well as the voice of the Holy Ones,
in order that she might rest
in the ineffable Epinoia,
in order that <she> might inherit
the first mind which <she> had received,
and that <she> might rest in the divine Autogenes,
and that she (too) might generate herself,
just as [she] also has inherited the [living] Logos,
and that she might be joined to all of the Imperishable Ones,
and [speak] with the mind of the Father.
And [she began] to speak with the words of Life,
and <she> remained in the [presence] of the Exalted One,
[possessing that] which she had received before
the world came into being.

[She has] the [great mind] of the Invisible One,
and [she gives] glory to <her> Father,
[and she] dwells within those who […] within the Pleroma,
[and] she beholds the Pleroma.
There will be days when she will [behold] the Pleroma,
and she will not be in deficiency,
for she has the four holy helpers
who intercede on her
behalf with the Father of the All, Adamas,
the one who is within all of the Adams,
that possess the thought of Norea,
who speaks concerning the two names
which create a single name. (NHC IX 2, 27–29)[14]

---

14. Translation by Søren Giversen and Birger Pearson, "The Thought of Norea," in *Nag Hammadi Codices IX and X*, ed. Birger Pearson, NHMS 15 (Leiden: Brill, 1981), 95–99, with my poetic division.

3. Protennoia

The female mediatrix of the creation, Sophia, appears in the prologue of the New Testament Gospel of John transformed into the grammatically masculine Logos, which then is identified with Jesus Christ, the preexistent mediator of creation:[15]

> In the beginning was the Logos,
>> and the Logos was with God
>> and the Logos was God....
> All things were made by him;
>> and without him was not made any thing made that was made....
> He came unto his own, and his own did not receive him.
> But to those who received him,
> he gave power to become children of God....
>> And the Logos became flesh and pitched his tent among us,
> and we have seen his glory—
>> the glory as of the only begotten of the Father,
>> full of grace and truth. (John 1:1–14)

The Nag Hammadi text Three Forms of First Thought (also known as Trimorphic Protennoia; NHC XIII 1), which likewise is to be attributed to Sethian Gnosticism, is the divine revelatory oration of a female revealer. In this work, the three-part speech of revelation, according to which the Protennoia (first thought) reveals herself as father, as mother, and also as son, conforms to the principle of continuous revelation. In a short passage in the third revelation, the Protennoia, as a redemptive figure, herself reflects once again on her threefold revelation. The elements of the pro-

---

15. Wisdom traditions, including the interpretation of Jesus as a personification of Wisdom, are found also elsewhere in the New Testament. See, e.g., Matt 11:25–30, especially the so-called Savior's call, 11:28–30. See on this Ulrich Luz, *Das Evangelium nach Matthäus (Mt 8–17)*, EKKNT 1.2 (Neukirchen-Vluyn: Neukirchener Verlag, 1990), 217. See also the parallels in Gos. Thom. 90. On the entire phenomenon, see Hermann von Lips, "Christus als Sophia? Weisheitliche Traditionen in der urchristlichen Christologie," in *Anfänge der Christologie: Festschrift Ferdinand Hahn*, ed. Cilliers Breytenbach and Henning Paulsen with Christine Gerber (Göttingen: Vandenhoeck & Ruprecht, 1991), 75–95; von Lips, *Weisheitliche Traditionen im Neuen Testament*, WMANT 64 (Neukirchen-Vluyn: Neukirchener Verlag, 1990).

logue placed before the Gospel of John give the impression of being somewhat contrived and appear here in a certain sense (again) in their natural place—precisely in a revelatory oration, which also, by the way, contains numerous self-predications in the style of the Johannine "I am" sayings.[16] Remarkable about this text is, beyond this, the fact that the few Christian elements in it are clearly secondary additions; Three Forms of First Thought is at its core essentially a non-Christian—feminine—revelatory address.

> (The first time I came …)]
> I [told all of them about my mysteries]
> that exist in [the incomprehensible], inexpressible Aeons.
> I taught [them the mysteries] through the [Voice
> that exists] within a perfect Intellect,
> [and I] became a foundation for the All, and [I empowered] them.
> The Second time I came in the [Speech] of my Voice.
> I gave shape to those who [took] shape,
> until their consummation.
> The Third time I revealed myself to them
> [in] their tents as Word (Logos),
> and I revealed myself in the likeness of their shape.
> And I wore everyone's garment,
> and I hid myself within them,
> and [they] did not know the one who empowers me.
> For I dwell within all the Sovereignties and Powers,
> and within the angels,
> and in every movement [that] exists in all matter.
> And I hid myself within them
> until I revealed myself to my [brethren].
> And none of them (i.e., the Powers) knew me,
> [although] it is I who work in them.
> Rather [they thought] that the All was created [by them]
> since they are ignorant, not knowing [their] root,
> the place in which they grew.
> [I] am the Light that illumines the All.
> I am the Light that rejoices [in my] brethren,
> for I came down to the world [of] mortals

---

16. On the Johannine "I am" sayings and their relationships with, and parallels to, wisdom literature, Isis aretalogies, and texts from Nag Hammadi, see Silke Petersen, *Brot Licht und Weinstock: Intertextuelle Analysen johanneischer Ich-bin-Worte*, NovTSup 127 (Leiden: Brill, 2008), esp. 143–99, 235–85.

on account of the Spirit that remains [in] that which [descended] (and) came forth [from] the [innocent] Sophia. (NHC XIII 1, 47)[17]

4. Brontē

The second text in Nag Hammadi Codex VI, Brontē, Perfect Mind, is the revelatory oration of a female divine figure. However, one cannot establish with certainty whether Brontē (Greek: thunder) is her name (or one of her names) or whether the thunder describes only one—not really very unusual—attendant state of the heavenly revelation (or the way she is perceived by outside observers; see Sir 46:17; Ps 29:3; Jer 25:30; John 12:28; Rev 14:2; 19:6). The text not only takes gnostic myths (such as the fall and rescue of Sophia) and mythic (female) figures for granted, but also reflects on them on a high level and connects them with one another. The Egyptian Isis, too, has left her traces here; the "I am" predications, for example, remind one in form and content of the Isis aretalogy of Cumae.[18] The revelatory oration is characterized, on the one hand, by paradoxically and antithetically formulated self-predications on the part of the feminine revealer, which are best understood as conundrums, and, on the other hand, by likewise repeatedly and frequently antithetically formulated requests made of the male and female hearers. Within the Nag Hammadi texts, Codex VI 2 has its closest formal equivalent in Codex XIII 1, Three Forms of First Thought, which, as in Brontē, is the revelatory oration of a female figure. Along with these formal parallels, references to the content of Sethian texts and traditions can be demonstrated. Thus, the female revealer discloses her identity as Epinoia, for example, who also appears in the Three Forms of First Thought. In the Secret Book of John, Epinoia, who hides herself in Adam, serves the first Ruler as a model for the creation of Eve. Some of the conundrums in Brontē, on the other hand,

---

17. Translation by John D. Turner, "The Trimorphic Protennoia," in *Nag Hammadi Codices XI, XII, XIII*, ed. Charles W. Hedrick, NHMS 28 (Leiden: Brill, 1990), 427.

18. On the text of this Isis inscription and further Isis aretalogies, see the collection of texts in Maria Totti, *Ausgewählte Texte der Isis- und Sarapis-Religion*, SubEp 12 (Hildesheim: Olms, 1985). On the influence of the Isis texts on Jewish wisdom literature, see, among others, John S. Kloppenborg, "Isis and Sophia in the Book of Wisdom," *HTR* 75 (1982): 57–84; Burton L. Mack, *Logos und Sophia: Untersuchungen zur Weisheitstheologie im hellenistischen Judentum*, SUNT 10 (Göttingen: Vandenhoeck & Ruprecht, 1973); Silvia Schroer, *Die Weisheit hat ihr Haus gebaut: Studien zur Gestalt der Sophia in den biblischen Schriften* (Mainz: Grünewald, 1996).

refer to the carnal Eve, taken out of Adam, as well as to the heavenly Eve. The female speaker then calls herself the "Sophia of the Greeks" and the "Gnosis of the Barbarians" (NHC VI 2, 16.3–4).

The text Brontē has been handed down in very good Coptic and enfolds a poetic power that constitutes a part of its appeal, as well as also a part of the challenge that it offers to the understanding of the men and women who read it today.[19] In order to illustrate this, several exemplary citations are placed here at the conclusion of this essay:

> I was sent forth from the power,
> and I have come to those who reflect upon me,
> and I have been found among those who seek after me.
> Look upon me, you who reflect upon me,
> and you hearers, hear me....
> For I am the first and the last.
> I am the honored one and the scorned one.
> I am the whore and the holy one.
> I am the wife and the virgin.
> I am <the mother> and the daughter.
> I am the members of my mother.
> I am the barren one
> and many are her sons.
> I am she whose wedding is great,
> and I have not taken a husband.
> I am the midwife and she who does not bear.
> I am the solace of my labor pains.
> I am the bride and the bridegroom,
> and it is my husband who begot me.
> I am the mother of my father
> and the sister of my husband
> and he is my offspring.
> I am the slave of him who prepared me.

---

19. The fascination that emanates from NHC VI 2 has found expression—unusual for a Nag Hammadi text—also in pop culture: for example, in the album *Thunder Perfect Mind* by the neo-folk band Current 93 (1992) with two like-named numbers that are based on NHC VI 2; or the album by the same name from the same year by the industrial band Nurse with Wound. In a commercial video for a Prada perfume made by British director and cultural icon Ridley Scott and his daughter Jordan, a young woman wanders through Berlin while, in part from off screen and in part by the woman herself, texts from Brontē are recited from a book (see https://www.prada.com/ww/en/pradasphere/films/2005/thunder-perfect-mind.html).

I am the ruler of my offspring....
I am the silence that is incomprehensible
and the idea whose remembrance is frequent.
I am the voice whose sound is manifold
and the word whose appearance is multiple.
I am the utterance of my name.
Why, you who hate me, do you love me,
and hate those who love me?
You who deny me, confess me,
and you who confess me, deny me....
For I am knowledge and ignorance.
I am shame and boldness.
I am shameless; I am ashamed.
I am strength and I am fear.
I am war and peace. (NHC VI 2, 13–14)[20]

---

20. Translation by George W. MacRae, "The Thunder, Perfect Mind," in *Nag Hammadi Codices V,2–5 and VI with Papyrus Berolinensis 8502,1 and 4*, ed. Douglas M. Parrott, NHMS 11 (Leiden: Brill, 1979), 235–39.

Becoming Male and the Annulment of Gender Difference: Return to Paradise?

Silke Petersen

Speech about gender difference differs in different cultures and at different times. This is true already concerning the shifts in gender discourse within the West-oriented world of the past fifty years, but a comparison between the ancient world and modern times shows considerable changes still more clearly. The modern discourse about gender difference is marked by the recourse to natural and social sciences; the ancient world, on the other hand, often argued mythologically, that is, on the basis of certain fundamental narratives. A special role is played here by the first chapters of Genesis, which, as a fundamental text of the Jewish-Christian tradition, often stands in the background, even if this is not obvious.

In the following, I will first start with several statements from Nag Hammadi texts that deal explicitly with the theme of gender difference. Other texts can then be easily classed with these texts, that is, their statements can be integrated into the general ancient view of gender difference, as they are not categorically different from one another.

1. Gender Concepts in the Gospel of Thomas

I would like to begin with a well-known example of speech about gender difference from the Gospel of Thomas (NHC II 2) from the second century. The following exchange is found at the very end of the text:

> Simon Peter said to them, Let Mary leave us, for women are not worthy of life. Jesus said, I myself shall lead her in order to make her male [ϩⲟⲟⲩⲧ], so that she too may become a living spirit [ⲡⲛⲉⲩⲙⲁ] resembling

you males. For every woman who will make herself male will enter the kingdom of heaven.¹ (Gos. Thom. 114 [51.18–26])

This text has triggered some irritation that has led to critical comments or even to the thesis that the passage might be a secondary addition to the text.² One reason for such ideas is that the text appears to stand in contradiction to another passage of the same gospel (Gos. Thom. 22), in which gender difference is spoken about in a divergent manner:

> Jesus saw infants being suckled. He said to his disciples, These infants being suckled are like those who enter the kingdom. They said to him: Shall we then, as children, enter the kingdom? Jesus said to them, When you make the two one, and when you make the inside like the outside and the outside like the inside, and the above like the below, and when you make the male and the female one and the same, so that the male not be male nor the female female; and you fashion eyes in place of an eye, and a hand in place of a hand, and a foot in place of a foot, and a likeness [ϩⲓⲕⲱⲛ] in place of a likeness; then will you enter the kingdom. (Gos. Thom. 22 [37.20–35])³

Here the formulation is symmetric, and the gender difference is eliminated finally in "a single one." In Gos. Thom. 114, on the other hand, women are asked to become male. At first sight there appears to be a contradiction, since that which is the condition intended in Gos. Thom. 114, that is, becoming male, is, according to Gos. Thom. 22, eliminated. However, the end of both texts is formulated in parallel: the goal is in both cases to "enter the

---

1. Coptic text and English translation are taken from Helmut Köster and Thomas O. Lambdin, "The Gospel according to Thomas," in *Nag Hammadi Codex II,2–7, Together with XIII,2*, Brit.Lib.Or. 4926(1), and P.Oxy. 1,654,655*, vol. 1, *Gospel according to Thomas, Gospel according to Philip, Hypostasis of the Archons, and Indexes*, ed. Bentley Layton, NHS 20 (Leiden: Brill, 1989), 92–93. The references given in square brakets are to NHC II 2.

2. See, e.g., Johannes Leipoldt, *Das Evangelium nach Thomas: Koptisch und Deutsch*, TU 101 (Berlin: Akademie, 1967), 77; Marvin W. Meyer, "Making Mary Male: The Categories 'Male' and 'Female' in the Gospel of Thomas," *NTS* 31 (1985): 561; Stevan L. Davies, *The Gospel of Thomas and Christian Wisdom* (New York: Seabury, 1983), 21; and the discussion in Ivan Miroshnikov, "'For Women Are Not Worthy of Life': Protology and Misogyny in Gospel of Thomas Saying 114," in *Women and Knowledge in Early Christianity*, ed. Ulla Tervahauta et al., VCSup 144 (Leiden: Brill, 2017), 175–86.

3. Köster and Lambdin, "Gospel according to Thomas," 62–63.

kingdom."[4] In addition, both kinds of speech about gender difference also appear in other texts from the same period—this too is an indication that we do not have to do with categorically different concepts, but rather with different forms of expression against the background of a common concept.

Fundamentally, this concept is hierarchically structured. The spiritual is placed above the corporeal just as the masculine is placed over feminine. Gender difference is not conceived as symmetric or complementary but rather poses a problem that must be overcome. What is finally striven for is an ideal original state before the corporeal differentiation of the genders was instituted—an original state that can be found also in Gen 1:27 (LXX), in the middle of the verse:

καὶ ἐποίησεν ὁ θεὸς τὸν ἄνθρωπον
κατ' εἰκόνα θεοῦ ἐποίησεν αὐτόν
ἄρσεν καὶ θῆλυ ἐποίησεν αὐτούς.

And God made man,
in the image of God he made him,
male and female he made them.

The ideal ἄνθρωπος is created in the image of God; he stands in the singular (αὐτόν). Only in the next part of the sentence follows the statement that this man apparently consists of two human beings (αὐτούς, plural) and is sexually differentiated: "male and female he created them." In order to resolve this contradiction, one can assume a two-stage creation, in which the ideal human being in the image of God is differentiated sexually only in a secondary stage. Such a notion is likely also to be at the basis of Gos. Thom. 22, where the last step in creation is rescinded. The Coptic text makes this clear through the fact that the keyword εἰκών (as a loanword from Greek) is taken up from Gen 1:27, the "image" or "likeness," according to which the creation of human beings occurs.[5] What in Gos. Thom. 22 replaces the secondary condition in the history of creation is thus an image

---

4. This formulation appears otherwise only in Gos. Thom. 99 (49.21–26; Köster and Lambdin, "Gospel according to Thomas," 88–89), where the issue likewise is overcoming fundamental social orders when Jesus disassociates himself from his family of birth.

5. See on this in more detail Silke Petersen, "Nicht mehr 'männlich und weiblich' (Gen 1,27): Die Rede von der Aufhebung der Geschlechterdifferenz im frühen Christentum," in *Geschlechterverhältnisse und Macht: Lebensformen in der Zeit des frühen*

closer to the original image ("a likeness in place of a likeness") that is not yet subjugated through worldly differentiations to space (see the contrary pairs of concepts of inner and outer and above and below) and gender. What appears to be here is an original human being with a very special body, in which the body parts are renewed and which neither has spatial extent nor is subject to sexual differentiation. Thereby, gender difference is not simply negated but rather annulled through unification ("when you make the male and the female one and the same"), whereby the condition of the original God-likeness is attained once again.

The text from Gos. Thom. 22 has several parallels in early Christian literature. The best known is found in Gal 3:26–28, where, through the formulation "no male and female," reference likewise is made to Gen 1:27: "For you are all sons/children [υἱοί] of God through faith in Christ Jesus, for those of you who have been baptized in Christ have put on Christ. There is neither Jew nor Greek; there is neither slave nor free; there is no male and female [ἄρσεν καὶ θῆλυ]: For you all are one [εἷς] in Christ Jesus." There is a whole series of further texts in which the motif of the annulment of opposites is shaped in different ways, such as 1 Cor 12:13, Col 3:9–11, 2 Clem. 12.2, and the fragments of the Gospel of the Egyptians (see below). Male and female is not always listed among the opposites; the logion is apparently variable according to the context. Connected with this is the fact that it is hardly possible to reconstruct an original form, even though one can assume an origin of the logion in the Antiochene theology before Paul.[6]

It is interesting that the new human being emerging in Gal 3:28 is not quite so sexless as might appear at first. That is, the human being is Christlike and not "one" in neuter form but "one" in masculine form. This is not visible in many languages, such as English, but is obvious in German and Greek, since these languages use different numeral words for mascu-

---

Christentums, ed. Irmtraud Fischer and Christoph Heil, EUZ 21 (Vienna: LIT, 2010), 78–109.

6. So Jürgen Becker, "Der Brief an die Galater," in *Die Briefe an die Galater, Epheser und Kolosser*, by Jürgen Becker and Ulrich Luz, NTD 8.1 (Göttingen: Vandenhoeck & Ruprecht, 1998), 59. On the extensive discussion of Gal 3:26–28 in the research literature, see the surveys by Angela Standhartinger, "Geschlechterkonstruktionen bei Paulus: Feministische Zugänge zu Gal 3,27f und Röm 7,1–6," *US* 58 (2003): 339–49; François D. Tolmie, "Tendencies in the Interpretation of Gal 3:28 since 1990," *AcT* 34 suppl. 19 (2014): 105–29.

line, feminine, and neuter cases. Thus it becomes obvious that the result of the annulment of the difference in Greek is masculine: εἷς (masculine) and not ἕν (neuter). With this, we move once again into the proximity of Gos. Thom. 114. Apparently, the result of the annulment of the difference is a spiritual-masculine human being,[7] precisely that which is formulated explicitly in Gos. Thom. 114.

This means that in the hierarchically structured ancient manner of speaking, there are two possibilities for describing the transcendence of gender: either becoming male as a synonym for becoming spiritual, for the overcoming of corporeality (type A), or overcoming or annulment of the difference with the result of becoming spiritual (type B)—which in the end also means becoming male, since the male is closer to the spiritual than the feminine. Philo of Alexandria formulates this in the following way:

> For progress is indeed nothing else than the giving up of the female gender by changing into the male, since the female gender is material, passive, corporeal and sense perceptible, while the male is active, rational, incorporeal, and more akin to mind and thought. (QE 1.18)[8]

The female gender is described as being closer to matter, body, and sensory impressions; the masculine is incorporeal, rational, and closer to spirit and thought. Active and passive also are clearly divided between masculine and feminine. Hereby it is clear that what is better is always to be found on the masculine side. Aristotle already formulates this in a passage of unsurpassed clarity:

> In addition, the relation of the male to the female is by nature [τὸ ἄρρεν πρὸς τὸ θῆλυ φύσει] that of better to worse and ruler to ruled. (Pol. 1.5.1254b13–14)[9]

---

7. In addition, Gen 2:7 can also stand in the background (see Miroshnikov, "Protology and Misogyny," 180–82).

8. Since the original text exists only in the Armenian language, quoted here is the translation from Richard A. Baer, *Philo's Use of the Categories Male and Female*, ALGHJ 3 (Leiden: Brill, 1970), 46. On the interpretation of the passage in the context of Philonic statements, see 45–49.

9. Translated by Peter L. Phillips Simpson in *The Politics of Aristotle* (Chapel Hill: University of North Carolina Press, 1997).

In this (and in many other statements), the recourse to nature disguises the fact that in the end it does not describe nature; rather, the argument serves to establish cultural postulates that are supposedly antecedent and natural.[10] Recent theories on gender difference describe this phenomenon as *doing gender*. The gender difference is not described objectively but is produced by means of the ostensible description. That the gender difference is a constructed one becomes evident in the fact that the attributions vary over time, which is also true in case of the supposedly clear recourse to nature, biology, or genes—all these are time conditioned and determined by antecedent notions of what is masculine and feminine.[11]

Comparison of these time-conditioned attributions shows, however, that the model of the complementarity of genders, disseminated in the modern age, is not valid in the same way for antiquity. According to Thomas Laqueur, the modern two-sex model is preceded by a one-sex model, in which women are conceived of and are described, not only socially but also biologically, as imperfect men.[12] Accordingly, becoming male always describes a development that leads "from a lower to a higher stage of moral and spiritual perfection."[13]

This higher, spiritual perfection is also the goal that Mary (Mariham in Gos. Thom. 114) is mean to reach—and is able to reach.[14] On closer examination, Gos. Thom. 114 proves to be not only negative. Peter, to be sure, wants to exclude Mary, and with her all women, from the group, "for women are not worthy of life," but Jesus formulates *the condition for membership* and thus counters Peter's request clearly (we have here one of the clearest early Christian pieces of evidence for female disciples of

---

10. On this rhetorical strategy, see the chapter by Karen L. King in this volume.

11. Present-day biology distinguishes between four variables in the differentiation of gender: chromosomal, gonadal, hormonal, and morphological gender. The characteristics named do not always indicate the same sex in regard to a person. On the fundamental critique of supposedly neutral biology, see Judith Butler, *Gender Trouble: Feminism and the Subversion of Identity* (New York: Routledge, 1991), esp. 106–11.

12. See Thomas Laqueur, *Making Sex: Body and Gender from the Greeks to Freud* (Cambridge: Harvard University Press, 1990); on the differentiation of this model, see Caroline Vander Stichele and Todd Penner, *Contextualizing Gender in Early Christian Discourse: Thinking beyond Thecla* (London: Continuum, 2009), esp. 44–62.

13. So Kari Vogt, "'Männlichwerden': Aspekte einer urchristlichen Anthropologie," *Concilium* 21 (1985): 434.

14. On the role of Mary Magdalene in other Nag Hammadi texts and in the Gospel of Mary (BG 1), see the chapter by Judith Hartenstein in this volume.

Jesus). Not only does Mary belong to the group, but this is true of all other women, as the doubling of the becoming-male motif at the end of the text shows. What is put into effect in regard to the example of Mary is valid for all women, even in the absence of direct leadership by Jesus. Mary is the paradigmatic woman for the assessment of femininity. The striking asymmetric formulation in Gos. Thom. 114, in contrast to Gos. Thom. 22, is likely to be indebted precisely to this line of argument; namely, the formulation of the procedure involved in change comes from the perspective of the woman, and the difference is no longer spoken of in general terms.

Under these preconditions, becoming male means a real progress for Mary Magdalene—as for all women. This becomes clear when one looks at the alternative concept for dealing with femininity as the roughly contemporary Pastoral Letters formulate it. Because of Eve's transgressions, the only salvation for women consists in keeping silence and subordination, as well as in bearing children (see 1 Tim 2:11–15). In the Gospel of Thomas, on the other hand, Mary Magdalene (and with her the other women) must, to be sure, become masculine—but they are able to do it too and thus are not committed to a single feminine model of life, prescribed by the Pastoral Letters as the only saving model.

2. Further Examples: Origen and the Gospel of the Egyptians

The two ways of seeing gender difference I have presented are found in many further early Christian texts, among them texts found in Nag Hammadi as well as others. Origen is successful in integrating both ways of seeing gender difference in a single context:

> For divine Scripture does not know how to make a separation of men and women according to sex. For indeed sex is no distinction, but a person is designated either a man or woman according to the diversity of spirit. How many out of the sex of women are counted among the strong men before God, and how many of the men are reckoned among slack and sluggish women? (*Hom. Josh.* 9.9)[15]

---

15. Latin text: Annie Jaubert, *Origène, Homélies sur Josué*, SC 71 (Paris: Cerf, 1960), 266: "Etenim sexus apud Deum nulla discretio est, sed pro animi diversitate vel vir vel mulier designatur. Quantae ex mulierum sexu apud Deum in viris fortibus numerantur, et quanti ex viris inter remissas et languidas mulieres reputantur?" English translation by Barbara J. Bruce in Origen, *Homilies in Joshua*, FC (Washington, DC: Catholic University of America Press, 1984), 106.

The difference denied in the first sentence returns immediately in the second and, to be sure, includes the hierarchic formulations observed already above that codify the superiority of the masculine. Even if the difference is seen as irrelevant before God, it permeates the earthly way of speaking.

Both ways of speaking described in regard to gender difference are found also in the so-called Gospel of the Egyptians, which became apocryphal. The Gospel of the Egyptians comes from the second century; only some fragments of it have survived in the writings of Clement of Alexandria. From the context in Clement's text, it is clear that the Gospel of the Egyptians was used by encratite (ascetically living) groups. Clement himself does not reject it but interprets it differently from those groups. Thus, he quotes a statement by Jesus directed to the female disciple Salome (see Mark 15:40; 16:1), in which the motif of becoming male (type A) is encountered more or less in reverse:

> Those who are opposed to God's creation, disparaging it under the fair name of continence, also quote the words to Salome which we mentioned earlier. They are found, I believe, in the Gospel according to the Egyptians. They say that the Savior himself said "I came to destroy the works of the female" [τὰ ἔργα τῆς θηλείας]. meaning by "female" desire, and by "works" birth and corruption. (*Strom.* 3.63.1)[16]

The last sentence does not appear to have originated in the Gospel of the Egyptians; it is probably a secondary interpretation of the Jesus logion. Clement himself is of the opinion that the *Kyrios* has made an end to the works of desire, namely, greed, dogmatism, hunger for fame, addiction to women, love of young boys, gluttony, and so on.

In a further text from the Gospel of the Egyptians, Clement also argues in a similar allegorical way. This time, though, we have a text with type B, annulment of difference:

---

16. Greek text in Otto Stählin and Ludwig Früchtel, *Stromata Buch I–VI*, GCS 52 (Berlin: Akademie, 1960), 225. English translation in Henry Chadwick and John E. L. Oulton, eds., *Alexandrian Christianity: Selected Translations of Clement and Origen*, LCC 2 (repr., Philadelphia: Westminster, 2006), 69. See also the parallels in the Dialogue of the Savior (NHC III 5) with the claim: "Destroy the works of womanhood!" (144.19). On this, see Silke Petersen, "*Zerstört die Werke der Weiblichkeit!*": *Maria Magdalena, Salome und andere Jüngerinnen Jesu in christlich-gnostischen Schriften*, NHMS 48 (Leiden: Brill, 1999), esp. 115–18.

On this account he says: "When Salome asked when she would know the answer to her questions, the Lord said, When you trample on the robe of shame, and when the two shall be one, and the male with the female, and there is neither male nor female" [οὔτε ἄρρεν οὔτε θῆλυ]. In the first place we have not got the saying in the four Gospels that have been handed down to us, but in the Gospel according to the Egyptians. Secondly Cassian seems to me not to know that it refers to wrath in speaking of the male and to desire in speaking of the female. When these operate, there follow repentance and shame. (*Strom.* 3.92.2–93.1)[17]

Clement conducts the discussion through citing a text to which his opponent (Cassian) refers. He argues on two levels. First, he takes something of the dignity from the text he quotes stating that this text is not to be found in the "four Gospels that have been handed down to us."[18] Second, Clement opposes the interpretation, which he finds false because of its exaggerated encratism by interpreting masculine and feminine allegorically as human desires. Beyond this dispute concerning interpretation, it becomes clear that the Gospel of the Egyptians contains both manners of speaking in one text, similar to Gospel of Thomas and Origen. A hierarchical way of speaking that wants to overcome the feminine stands next to a variant formulated in an egalitarian sense, in which masculine and feminine are to be annulled in a "one." Interesting in this context is a further fragment from the Gospel of the Egyptians, in which the issue is, somewhat surprisingly, eating:

> But why do they [Clement's opponents] not go on to quote the words after those spoken to Salome,—these people who do anything rather than walk according to the true evangelical rule? For when she says, "I would have done better had I never given birth to a child," suggesting that she might not have been right in giving birth to a child, the Lord replies to her saying: "Eat of every plant, but eat not of that which has bitterness in it." (*Strom.* 3.66.1–2)[19]

---

17. Stählin and Früchtel, *Stromata Buch I–VI*, 238; trans. Chadwick and Oulton, *Alexandrian Christianity*, 83–84.

18. The text reflects a stage of the canonization process when the priority of the four gospels is confirmed while further gospels are not rejected out of hand.

19. Stählin and Früchtel, *Stromata Buch I–VI*, 226; trans. Chadwick and Oulton, *Alexandrian Christianity*, 70.

Salome's observation that she "would have done well not to have borne a child" implies the question of whether this is in fact the case. Jesus's remark about the bitter plant, however, is at first glance puzzling. To understand this statement one can draw on parallels within the Nag Hammadi texts, in which bitterness (πικρία or the Coptic equivalent ϭⲓϣⲉ) is connected with sexuality.[20] In this way, Jesus's exhortation to Salome can be understood as a warning about the bitter consequences of producing children, somehow similar to the encratite opponents of Clement mentioned above.

Nevertheless, this does not yet completely explain why sexuality and bearing children are spoken about with a metaphor from the world of food. Again a parallel from a Nag Hammadi text can illuminate this. The Secret Book of John (NHC II 1; II 1; IV 1; BG 2), originating from the second century, speaks about food (τροφή) and bitterness (ϭⲓϣⲉ) in connection with the tree in paradise and with the fruit that was poison.[21] From this perspective, the exhortation in Gospel of the Egyptians not to eat the bitter plant seems to be an allusion to the story of the fall in Genesis. The world in which Jesus has destroyed the works of the female corresponds to the world before the fall, before the separation of the human being into feminine and masculine. This interpretation of the Gospel of the Egyptians is confirmed by the other fragment, which speaks of the annulment of the difference between ἄρρεν and θῆλυ in their union using terminology from Genesis. Beyond this, the speech about the robe of shame that is taken off and trampled underfoot is to be understood against the background of Gen 2:25, where Adam and Eve, although unclothed, are not ashamed. This condition changes only after eating the fruit from the tree of knowledge.

In the Gospel of the Egyptians, as far as we are able to determine on the basis of the existing fragments, it is Salome, not—as frequently otherwise—Mary Magdalene, who appears as the paradigmatic disciple of Jesus and as a partner in conversation with him. Common to both texts is that the gender difference is discussed with an important woman from the circle of female and male disciples—not, however, together with an

---

20. The concepts of bitterness or bitter are almost always found in contexts that speak of ἐπιθυμία (Ap. John [NHC II 1] 18.28; Bk. Thom. 139.33; 140.32; 141.34; 143.28; 145.9; Paraph. Shem 37.34), πορνεία (Teach. Silv. 104.28), or ἡδονή (Orig. World [NHC II 5] 106.34).

21. Ap. John [NHC III 1] 27.5–14 parr.

important male disciple. The problem discussed is either femininity or the difference as such, but not masculinity.

This possibly has to do with the fact that only femininity is distinguished, that is, that the feminine is, in the end, the only sex. Monique Wittig formulates correspondingly: "There are not two genders. There is only one: the feminine; the 'masculine' not being a gender. For the masculine is not the masculine but the general."[22] It is likely that this idea was more applicable to antiquity (according to everything that we know) than to the modern period—even if the structures of our languages still continue to function according to such a model. In many languages, the masculine form stands for the general, the feminine for the particular, for feminine alone is distinguished as gender and perceived as different.

3. Gender, Difference, and Baptism

Formulations of the two types described above appear repeatedly in contexts in which baptism plays a role, as in Gal 3:26–28, cited above. The trampling on the clothes in Gospel of the Egyptians could also be an allusion to baptismal practice, in which clothing was taken off completely.[23] There is also a series of examples where gender difference is connected with baptism among the Nag Hammadi texts. Thus, the Valentinian Tripartite Tractate (NHC I 5) from the third century discusses the significance of baptism (possibly alluding to Gal 3:26–28):

> For when we confessed the kingdom which is in Christ, <we> escaped from the whole multiplicity of forms and from inequality and change. For the end will receive a unitary existence just as the beginning is unitary, where there is no male nor female [ⲘⲚ̄ ϨⲞⲞⲨⲦ ⲘⲚ̄ ⲤϨⲒⲘⲈ], nor slave

---

22. Monique Wittig, "The Point of View: Universal or Particular," in *The Straight Mind and Other Essays* (Boston: Beacon, 1992), 60; see also Butler, who refers to Wittig comprehensively (*Gender Trouble*, 112–21).

23. See Jonathan Z. Smith, "The Garments of Shame," in *Map Is Not Territory: Studies in the History of Religion*, SJLA 23 (Leiden: Brill, 1978), 1–23; Silke Petersen, "'Wenn ihr Christus anzieht …' (Gal 3,27): Kleidung, Taufe und Geschlechterdifferenz im frühen Christentum," in *Das neue Kleid: Feministisch-theologische Perspektiven auf geistliche und weltliche Gewänder*, ed. Elisabeth Hartlieb, Jutta Koslowski, and Ulrike Wagner-Rau (Sulzbach: Helmer, 2010), 157–79.

> and free, no circumcision and uncircumcision, neither angel nor man, but Christ is all in all. (Tri. Trac. 132.16–28)[24]

In this case, we have again a formulation of type B, annulment of the gender difference. At the same time, it becomes clear that the ideal future human condition resembles the original primal state. If Christ is for the baptized "all in all," this leads back to a paradisiacal state without differences, inequality, or change.

In the next text, the issue is again baptism, this time combined with a hierarchical conception of masculinity and femininity. In the text Zostrianus (NHC VIII 1; second–third century), an especially clear formulation of type A, the hierarchical view of gender difference, is found:

> Do not baptize yourselves with death nor entrust yourselves to those who are inferior to you as if to those who are better. Flee from the madness and the bondage of femaleness [ⲙⲛ̄ⲧⲥϩⲓⲙⲉ], and chose for yourselves the salvation of maleness [ⲙⲛ̄ⲧϩⲟⲟⲩⲧ]. (Zost. 131.2–8)[25]

Masculinity in these texts is not a given natural biological state but rather something that must be acquired. Moisés Mayordomo, following Laquer and others, summarizes the Greco-Roman notion in the following manner: "In view of the always inherent 'danger' of feminization, masculinity is not a given, but rather something that must be learned, earned and preserved."[26] Especially in texts that are not closely connected with Roman power politics, but rather reflect philosophy and/or deal with the theme within Jewish and early Christian tradition, a close connection between

---

24. Coptic text and translation in Harold W. Attridge and Elaine H. Pagels, "NHC I,5: The Tripartite Tractate," in *Nag Hammadi Codex I (The Jung Codex)*, ed. Harold W. Attridge, NHS 22 (Leiden: Brill, 1985), 1:328–29. An expression of type A also appears in this text; see 78.11–13 and 94.16–20.

25. Coptic text and translation in John H. Sieber and Bentley Layton, "NHC VIII,1: Zostrianus," in *Nag Hammadi Codex VIII*, ed. John H. Sieber, NHS 31 (Leiden: Brill, 1991), 222–23, corrected according to the facsimile edition. A further text derogative of femininity is found in 1.10–13. On both passages, see Frederik Wisse, "Flee Femininity: Antifemininity in Gnostic Texts and the Question of Social Milieu," in *Images of the Feminine in Gnosticism*, ed. Karen L. King, SAC 4 (Harrisburg, PA: Trinity Press International, 2000), 299–301.

26. Moisés Mayordomo, "Jesu Männlichkeit im Markusevangelium: Eine Spurensuche," in *Doing Gender—Doing Religion*, ed. Ute E. Eisen, Christine Gerber, and Angela Standhartinger, WUNT 302 (Tübingen: Mohr Siebeck, 2013), 364.

masculinity and spirituality is dominant. The Teachings of Silvanus (NHC VII 4), a wisdom text that was probably written in Alexandria, summarizes this in the following way:

> Reason [ⲗⲟⲅⲟⲥ] and Mind [ⲛⲟⲩⲥ] are male names. (Teach. Silv. 102.15)[27]

From this, one can also derive concrete requests:

> Live in accord with the mind [ⲛⲟⲩⲥ]. Do not think about things belonging to the flesh: Acquire strength, for the mind is strong. If you fall from this other, you have become male-female [ϩⲟⲟⲩⲧⲥϩⲓⲙⲉ]. And if you cast out of yourself the substance of the mind, which is taught, you have cut off the male part and turned yourself to the female part alone. (Teach. Silv. 93.3–13)[28]

Here it is not only the feminine but also the male-female state that is inferior to the masculine. The close connection between spirituality and masculinity leads to a negative assessment of all that no longer corresponds to what is pure masculinity. Thereby, the positive assessment of the idea of a union of gender opposites expressed in other texts falls in this case into the maelstrom of the negative assessment of femininity.

4. Masculine Women

The rather theoretically formulated concepts of the texts presented thus far raise the question about their implementation for concrete women in concrete situations. Witnesses for this are not easy to find since, especially in the Nag Hammadi texts, there is hardly any information on daily life or data that can be assessed sociologically. Nevertheless, something can be said by expanding the horizon of the cited texts.

The Apophthegmata Patrum collects stories and sayings from early Egyptian eremitism. In spite of the title, it includes not only sayings from the desert fathers but also several from desert mothers, among them the following apophthegm of Amma Sarah:

---

27. Coptic text and translation in Malcolm Peel and Jan Zandee, "The Teachings of Silvanus," in *Nag Hammadi Codex VII*, ed. Birger A. Pearson, NHMS 30 (Leiden: Brill, 1996), 324–25.

28. Peel and Zandee, "Teachings of Silvanus," 300–303.

> Another time two old men, great anchorites, came to the district of Pelusia to visit her. When they arrived one said to the other: "Let us humiliate this old woman." So they said to her, "Be careful not to become conceited thinking to yourself, 'Look how anchorites are coming to see me, a mere woman.'" But Amma Sarah said to them, "According to nature I am a woman, but not according to my thoughts [τῇ μὲν φύσει γυνή εἰμι ἀλλ' οὐκ τῷ λογισμῷ]."[29]

In her discussion of this text, Anne Jensen speaks of Sarah's "self-consciousness" of being equal to the men: "It is possible even for a woman to overcome her feminine nature and through the spirit become equal to men—she would then be the exception to the rule. The sense of Sarah's statement, however, is much more likely that through the every human being is a sexual being, yet the spirit is independent of gender—here women and men are not different."[30] I believe, though, that the text has still another point of emphasis; namely, the last sentence does not say that women and men do not differ spiritually, but rather that Sarah, in regard to her mind, is not a woman but a man. The opposition behind this, feminine nature versus masculine understanding, reminds one of the statement from the Teachings of Silvanus cited above: Sarah's dictum shows how women could use this scheme to their own advantage against malevolent men. But it also shows that a separation of intellect and femininity was likely great in women's minds, too.

Another implementation of the becoming-male motif, but this time a more practical one, is encountered in the Apocryphal Acts of the Apostles. There one reads repeatedly about women who undertake wanderings in order to preach, to missionize, and occasionally even to baptize. The best-known example is found in the Acts of Thecla, from the second century, in which Thecla leaves her fiancé and, during her wanderings, changes her hairstyle and her clothing to resemble a man (see Acts Thecla 25, 40).[31] In the later Acts of Xanthippe and Polyxena, the motif appears

---

29. Apophthegmata Patrum (PG 65:420).
30. Anne Jensen, *God's Self-Confident Daughters: Early Christianity and the Liberation of Women* (Louisville: John Knox, 1992), 44.
31. Greek text in Richard Adelbert Lipsius and Maximilianus Bonnet, *Acta Petri, Acta Pauli, Acta Petri et Pauli, Acta Pauli et Theclae, Acta Thaddei* (repr., Darmstadt: Wissenschaftliche Buchgesellschaft, 1959), 1:253, 266. On women's ways of life in the Apocryphal Acts of the Apostles, see also the chapter by Carmen Bernabé Ubieta in this volume.

again, accompanied by an explicit reference to the Acts of Thecla (Acts Xanth. 33, 36).[32] What is most interesting in our context is a manuscript of the Acts of Philip, likewise a rather late composition (probably from the fourth century), which has recently become accessible again. The text describes how a certain Mariamne (Mary) is exhorted to accompany the apostle Philip, who is introduced as her brother. He is very much in need of her companionship, which Jesus justifies in the following way in words directed to Mariamne:

> I know that you are good and manly in soul [ἀνδρεία τῇ ψυχῇ] and blessed among women; and the woman's way of thinking has entered into Philip, but the masculine [ἀρρενικόν] and manly [ἀνδρεῖον] thinking is in you. (Acts Phil. 8.3)[33]

Accordingly, Mariamne is supposed to remove her feminine clothing and character, in order to wander with Philip in masculine clothing (Acts Phil. 8.4).[34] They enter a city that is dominated by serpents and by a serpent cult, and this serves as justification for the change of clothing, which, accordingly, is not motivated only by practical reasons:

> Now when you enter into that city, the serpents of that city must see you dissociated from Eve's appearance, with nothing of a feminine appearance. Since Eve's appearance is woman, she is the form itself; Adam's form is man. And you know that from the beginning hostility arose between Adam and Eve. Such was the beginning of the serpent's standing against that man, and its affection for the woman; and Adam was deceived by his wife Eve. And what the serpent puts off, that is, its poison, he, Adam, put on through Eve; and by this process the ancient enemy found a place in

---

32. Greek text in Montague R. James, "Actae Xanthippae et Polyxenae," in *Apocrypha Anecdota*, TS 5.1 (Cambridge: Cambridge University Press, 1893), 81, 83. See also Hans-Josef Klauck, *The Apocryphal Acts of the Apostles: An Introduction*, trans. Brian McNeil (Waco, TX: Baylor University Press, 2008), 250–51.

33. Greek text in François Bovon, Bertrand Bouvier, and Frédéric Amsler, *Acta Philippi 1: Textus*, CCSA 11 (Turnhout: Brepols, 1999), 243. ET in François Bovon and Christopher R. Matthews, *The Acts of Philip: A New Translation* (Waco, TX: Baylor University Press, 2012), 74. Interesting here, too is the transferal of the motif in Luke 1:42 ("blessed among women") from Jesus's mother to Mariamne in the Acts of Philip.

34. Bovon, *Acta Philippi*, 244; see Acts Phil. 95 (2), in Maximilianus Bonnet, *Acta Philippi et acta Thomae: Accedunt acta Barnabae*, AcApAp 2.2 (repr., Darmstadt: Wissenschaftliche Buchgesellschaft, 1959), 37.

Cain, Eve's son, so that he killed Abel, his brother. So you, Mariamne, flee the poverty of Eve and be rich in yourself. (Acts Phil. 8.4)[35]

The text plays throughout with terminology related to putting on and removing clothing. The formulations indicating change are so extensive that they give the impression that Mariamne not simply changes her clothing, but in fact discards her feminine shape, in order to resemble Eve as little as possible—and to return to a state before the fatal alliance between woman and serpent. Mariamne's ability to transform herself bodily is confirmed in a later part of the Acts of Philip, where the apostles Philip, Bartholomew, and Mariamne, all three traveling, missionizing, and baptizing together, are made to unclothe themselves in the early stages of martyrdom. In the case of Mariamne, the explicit goal is to determine that she is in fact a woman, which, however, is not easy:

> And when they stripped Mariamne, immediately the likeness of her body was changed [ὁμοιότης τοῦ σώματος αὐτῆς] and became a glass shrine filled with light [ἐγένετο κιβωτὸς ὑελίνη γέμουσα φωτός], and they were unable to approach her. (Acts Phil. Mart. 20 [A])[36]

Mariamne's feminine body is protected through transformation—through a transition into another state, which, however, is not a masculine body. The idea of a woman becoming masculine was conceivable in early Christianity, as shown in the Passio Perpetuae et Felicitatis. The young Christian woman Perpetua discusses several dream visions that she saw while waiting in prison on her execution. In one of the visions, she is led into the

---

35. Bovon, *Acta Philippi*, 245–47; trans. Bovon and Matthews, *Acts of Philip*, 75. See David Konstan, "Suche und Verwandlung: Transformation von Erzählmustern in den hellenistischen Romanen und den apokryphen Apostelakten," in *Askese und Identität in Spätantike, Mittelalter und früher Neuzeit*, ed. Werner Röcke and Julia Weitbrecht, TA 14 (Berlin: de Gruyter, 2010), 251–68; François Bovon, "Facing the Scriptures: Mimesis and Intertexuality in the *Acts of Philip*," in *Christian Apocrypha: Receptions of the New Testament in Ancient Christian Apocrypha*, ed. Jean-Michel Roessli and Tobias Nicklas, NTP 26 (Göttingen: Vandenhoeck & Ruprecht, 2014), 267–80.

36. Bovon, *Acta Philippi*, 373–75; trans. modified from Bovon and Matthews, *Acts of Philip*. Later, Mariamne changes herself back to her original state; see Acts Phil. Mart. 25 (A) (Bovon, *Acta Philippi*, 383); 32 (A) (Bovon, *Acta Philippi*, 399). Interesting is the use of the word κιβωτὸς, here translated as "shrine," which is used in biblical contexts also for the ark of Noah and the ark of the covenant.

arena in order to fight with a fearsome Egyptian. She is unclothed and becomes masculine (Pass. Perpet. Felicit. 10.7).[37] The Passion of Perpetua, in contrast to the apocryphal apostle acts, does not originate from an ascetic environment; Perpetua is not a wandering misfit but is attached to a family and has a child. However, the majority of the numerous texts in which women are praised as masculine or give up their traditional women's roles belong in an ascetic context.[38] Even if the stories about women in the apocryphal acts are not historically verifiable stories, their dissemination and their extensive later reception show that the change they depict in women's lifestyle was conceivable and certainly also put into practice.[39] A conquest of their femininity was obviously possible for women particularly in ascetic contexts.

5. Back to Paradise?

After the masculine women who dominated the last section, I would like to deal with the other possibility in the reception of the Genesis story, in which the motif of the union of genders is central. In the Gospel of Philip (NHC II 3; second–third century), it says:

> When Eve was still in Adam, death did not exist. When she was separated from him, death came into being. If he enters again and he takes him up into himself, death will be no more. (Gos. Phil. 71 [NHC II 3, 68.22–26])[40]

---

37. "Et expoliata sum et facta sum masculus." See Peter Habermehl, *Perpetua und der Ägypter oder Bilder des Bösen im afrikanischen Christentum: Ein Versuch zur Passio Sanctarum Perpetuae et Felicitatis*, TU 140 (Berlin: Akademie, 1992), 20. On the motif of becoming male, see 122–33. See also the chapter by Anna Carfora in this volume.

38. See the examples in Elizabeth Castelli, "Virginity and Its Meanings for Women's Sexuality in Early Christianity," *JFSR* 2 (1986): 61–88; Susanna Elm, *Virgins of God: The Making of Asceticism in Late Antiquity* (Oxford: Clarendon, 1996), 91, 101, 120, 134, and passim; John Anson, "The Female Transvestite in Early Monasticism: The Origin and Development of a Motiv," *Viator* 5 (1974): 1–32.

39. See Ruth Albrecht, *Das Leben der heiligen Makrina auf dem Hintergrund der Thekla-Traditionen: Studien zu dem Ursprüngen des weiblichen Mönchtums im 4. Jahrhundert in Kleinasien*, FKDG 38 (Göttingen: Vandenhoeck & Ruprecht, 1986), 283.

40. Coptic text in Wesley B. Isenberg and Bentley Layton, "The Gospel according to Philip, Nag Hammadi Codex II,3," in Layton, *Nag Hammadi Codex II,2–7*, 1:178. My translation differs from Isenberg's (on p. 179).

Death here is not the result of eating the forbidden fruit but rather originates earlier, namely, in the separation of Eve from Adam. This likely refers back to Gen 2:21–23, where Eve comes into being from out of Adam's side (πλευρά).[41] Odd, however, is the continuation, in which it is not easy to grasp to what the several masculine personal pronouns refer: Who goes into whom, and who takes up whom? I see two possibilities for understanding this passage. First, one could assume that Adam enters once again into Eve. Surprising in this reading is that it was Eve who previously separated herself. Thus, it should be she who must enter again into him. The reversal could indicate a positive assessment of sexuality[42] if one understands "If he, the man, goes into the woman once again." The next statement ("when he takes him up into himself") would then be interpreted to mean that the original two-sex primordial human being is repaired through the act of taking up Adam again, which would imply an interesting reversal of Genesis.

A second possibility for reading the text sees paradise as the location of entering into once again; the last part of the sentence would then mean "If Adam once again would enter *into paradise* and would take up *Christ* in himself, there will be no more death."[43] These interpretations do not necessarily exclude each other; in the complex, multileveled world of lan-

---

41. See Karen L. King, "The Place of the Gospel of Philip in the Context of Early Christian Claims about Jesus' Marital Status," NTS 59 (2013): 574.

42. Scholars disagree about the position held by the Gospel of Philip toward marriage and sexuality. According to Clement of Alexandria, Valentinian groups did not reject marriage but rather practiced "spiritual unions" (πνευματικὰς κοινωνίας; see Strom. 3.1.1; 3.4.29; Stählin and Früchtel, *Stromata Buch I–VI*, 209). April D. DeConick is of the opinion that this could mean sexual intercourse without lust, which Clement himself sees as the ideal. See DeConick, "The Great Mystery of Marriage: Sex and Conception in Ancient Valentinian Tradition," VC 57 (2003): 315. On the basis of the highly symbolic and metaphorical language of the Gospel of Philip, this solution appears to me to be too simple, the more so since a criterion for a successful union (κοινωνία) in Gospel of Philip is "resembling one another" (whatever that may mean). So Cain became a murderer because Eve committed adultery with the serpent, who became Cain's father (Gos. Phil. 42 [NHC II 3, 61.5–12]; see Gos. Phil. 112–113 [NHC II 3, 78.12–79.13]).

43. This reading gains in plausibility in the light of the text appearing directly before it (Gos. Phil. 70 [NHC II 3, 68.17–22]; Isenberg and Layton, "Gospel according to Philip," 178–79), which reads: "Before Christ some came from a place where they no longer able to enter [i.e., paradise], and they went where they were no longer able to come out [i.e., in the body/the world]. Then Christ came. Those who went in he

guage and understanding in Gospel of Philip, both are possible. Clear in any case is the fact that the statements about Adam are meant also to be general statements about the human being, as is also shown by another passage in Gospel of Philip formulated in parallel with that just cited:

> If the woman had not separated from the man, she would not die with the man. His separation became the beginning of death. Because of this Christ came to repair the separation which was from the beginning and again unite the two, and to give life to those who died as a result of the separation and unite them. (Gos. Phil. 78 [NHC II 3, 70.9–17])[44]

What was just said about Eve's separation from Adam is here generalized as "the woman" and "the man," whereby the subject of speech is Eve and Adam as well as also the human gendered constitution in general. The continuation is different from that in the previous text since Christ here appears explicitly as the one taking action in order to annul the original separation and to unite woman and man once again. Where death ruled before, now Christ gives life through this union. This associates with both creation stories. The separation of the woman from the man refers to Gen 2:21–23, which is rescinded through their reunion. But likewise, one can also imagine a connection with Gen 1:27 if one reads this text, like Gos. Thom. 22, as a restitution of the two-sex primordial human being. Both ways make clear that the annulment of gender difference will lead us back into paradise.

---

brought out, and those who went out he brought in [i.e., into paradise]." My suggestions for interpreting the riddles are found in the brackets.

44. Isenberg and Layton, "Gospel according to Philip," 182–83.

Part 2
Texts in Continuous Use:
Infancy Gospels and Apocryphal Acts of Apostle

Birth and Virginity in the Protevangelium of James

Silvia Pellegrini

1. Research Question

"For man is not from woman, but woman from man.... Nevertheless, neither is man independent of woman, nor woman independent of man, in the Lord" (1 Cor 11:8, 11–12).[1] This is how Paul, a representative of the first-century CE Jewish culture, discusses the ancient *querelle* regarding the precedence of the genders: Who comes first, man before the woman or vice versa?

It is clear to all that life starts in the woman who gives birth, but it is precisely this fact that is turned upside down in the androcentric narrative (of the Yahwist tradition) of Gen 2:22–23, where males are given the precedence over females: "She shall be called woman, because she was taken out of man" (Gen 2:23b). In this text, birth is treated as secondary and not as a brilliant and vital event—as is the case in Gen 1:28a, which reads: "Be fruitful and multiply; fill the earth and subdue it." Instead, childbirth is marked with the shadow of negativity and sin ("I will greatly multiply your sorrow and your conception; In pain you shall bring forth children"; Gen 3:16a). The woman's real origin is the rib of Adam, and he is the first of all men. The text suggests that even if man has to come through the woman, man cannot derive from a woman! In this archaic vision, birth contains an aura of negativity combined with the impurity assigned to it.[2]

Paul was a Jew by culture and a Christian through his faith, and he is able to surpass the supremacy problem when he writes: "Neither is man inde-

---

1. Biblical quotations follow the NKJV, unless otherwise noted.
2. See Lev 12 and in particular Luke 2:22: "When the days of their [αὐτῶν] purification ... were completed." Here the plural form would also include the child. (My translation here differs from the NKJV.)

pendent of woman, nor woman independent of man, in the Lord" (1 Cor 11:11). However, this was not the cultural perception of his time. Instead, a dream of being born without the help of a woman, a dream of male purity and male dominance, had been cultivated and refined throughout antiquity.[3] Mary, the mother of Jesus, the prototype of the new human being (see 1 Cor 15:45; Rom 5:12–21), was predestined to fulfill this impossible dream of purity and a type of autogenesis: male from male, a virgin birth.

The character of Mary embraces paradigmatic features for the image of women and transcends the limits of the biblical canon. While the canonical texts only give little and limited information about the mother of Jesus, apocryphal texts, in particular the Protevangelium of James, which elaborates the topics of birth and virginity in the Jewish purity context, give her a remarkable role. Therefore, it is necessary to approach and analyze this theme in its cultural context, also taking general anthropological problems, including gender conflict, into consideration.

2. Setting and Aim of the Protevangelium of James

The title "Protevangelium," given to the text by Guillaume Postel,[4] presents its themes and intents clearly: it claims to narrate the events that precede the story of Jesus in the form we know it on the basis of the canonical gospels. The need to investigate preceding events is already evident in the Synoptic Gospels that go further back from the baptism narrated by Mark and tell about the birth of Christ (Matt 1–2; Luke 1–2) and that of John the Baptist (Luke 1).

The Protevangelium is a composite work in which we can identify three intertwined traditions:

1. the first part focusing on Mary (chs. 1–17, or about 60 percent of the text); this is the so-called Secret Book of James;

---

3. The archaic idea of the birth from the father and not from the maternal womb is traditionally associated with power. For example, in the patriarchal version of the myth of Athena, the virgin goddess of war is not born from the mother but from the head of her father, Zeus (see Pindar, *Ol.* 7.35; Euripides, *Ion* 454).

4. See Silvia Pellegrini, "Protevangelium des Jakobus: Einleitung und Übersetzung," in *Evangelien und Verwandtes*, vol. 1.2 of *Antike christliche Apokryphen in deutscher Übersetzung*, ed. Christoph Markschies and Jens Schröter with Andreas Heiser (Tübingen: Mohr Siebeck, 2012), 909 n. 32.

2. the second part on the birth of Christ (chs. 18–21, or about 30 percent of the text); this is the so-called Secret Book of Joseph; and
3. the third part, which is an appendix on Herod and on the assassination of Zechariah in the temple (chs. 22–24, or about 10 percent of the text); this is the so-called Secret Book of Zechariah. However, it was not known to Origen (185–254) and is therefore dated toward the end of the third century.

Consequently, the final editing of the three parts is presumed to have taken place toward the end of the third and the beginning of the fourth century by a Jewish-Christian editor[5] who knew and valued Jewish literature. According to the current understanding,[6] the first two parts were composed around the middle of the second and the last part toward the end of the third century.

Differently from the canonical gospels, this text is written in a popular style. It takes pleasure in describing the marvelous phenomena and at times minute details of Mary as a child, for example, how she, placed for the first time on the third step of the altar, danced graciously with all Israel looking at her admiringly (Prot. Jas. 7.3). At other times she is described with vividly realistic terms, as in the scene of the manual testing of her postpartum virginity by the midwife Salome (Prot. Jas. 19.3–20.4). In particular, similarities have been sought with contemporary Hellenistic novels,[7] a genre that originated around the beginning of the Christian era and flourished from the second century CE onward. However, the similarities are limited to some stylistic features and joint narrative details that are also found in the novels *Daphnis and Chloe, Leucippe and Clitophon,*

---

5. See also Pellegrini, "Protevangelium des Jakobus," 908–9. For a contrasting view, see Ronald F. Hock, *The Infancy Gospels of James and Thomas: With Introduction, Notes, and Original Text Featuring the New Scholars Version Translation* (Santa Rosa, CA: Polebridge), 1995, 10. Hock maintains that the numerous inaccuracies in the text and the modest knowledge of Jewish customs show that the author is not Jewish-Christian. However, the constant reference to the Jewish environment and the attachment to Jewish values, such as purity, seem to suggest that the author's religious education, while perhaps secondhand or received in the diaspora, was based on a thorough study of the Old Testament and the LXX, to which he frequently refers.

6. On the gradual revision of the dating, see Pellegrini, "Protevangelium des Jakobus," 907–8.

7. These similarities are noted by Hock, *Infancy Gospels*, 26.

and (*The Ephesian Tale of*) *Anthia and Habrocomes*.⁸ In my opinion, this does not allow us to make any far-reaching conclusions about the origins of the text or the interpretation of its contents. In particular, the praise of virginity, which the Protevangelium of James defends and elevates as emphatically as the Hellenistic novels,⁹ appears, at a closer look, rather different as far as the cultural origins, sensibilities, problems, and arguments are concerned.

In the novels, the question is of endangered virginity that needs to be defended to acquire wealth for the family or, for a nobler purpose, to achieve a greater spiritual and carnal pleasure through mutual fidelity.¹⁰ Nothing could be further from the concern for Mary's purity that is never in danger in the Protevangelium. Her purity isolates her from everyone and gives her, the eternal virgin, the aura of static solemnity and surreal eternity. However, the Protevangelium shares its narrative style with the Hellenistic novel and popular literature in general, as well as its folktale, anecdotal, poetic, and sometimes even lyrical features—as in the verses that describe the sudden standstill of the whole world, which holds its breath and barely moves in amazed silence at the moment of the virgin birth of the Savior (Prot. Jas. 18.2–3).

In order not to collide with the canonical gospels, the text shares the essential elements of the nativity narrative: the annunciation made by an angel (Prot. Jas. 11.2), the virginal conception of Jesus (Prot. Jas. 11.2; 14.2), the husband figure of Joseph (Prot. Jas. 8.2; 15.4; 17.1), the birth in Bethlehem (Prot. Jas. 18.1), and the magi and the massacre of the innocents (Prot. Jas. 22). Using this limited background, the narrative freely paints its scenography, with some additional touches here and there. As already noted, there are many historical inconsistencies, which reveal a modest knowledge of Jewish customs of the narrated period; for example,

---

8. Both the lament of Anna (Prot. Jas. 2.4) and that of Daphnis (*Daphn.* 4.28.2) take place in a garden. On the symbolic value of παράδεισος in Prot. Jas. 2.4, see Alexander Toepel, *Das Protevangelium des Jakobus: Ein Beitrag zur Diskussion um Herkunft, Auslegung und theologische Einordnung* (Münster: Aschendorff, 2014), 66–68. See the test of virginity in Prot. Jas. 16.2 and in *Leuc. Clit.* 8.6.12–14. See Xenophon of Ephesus, *Eph.* 5.14, regarding the purity of the two.

9. See, for example, *Leuc. Clit.* 5.20.2: "I have imitated your virginity, if there be any virginity in men." Translated by Stephen Gaselee in Achilles Tatius, *Leucippe and Clitophon*, LCL (Cambridge: Harvard University Press, 1969), 283.

10. See *Daphn.* 3.25.2; Michel Foucault, *The Care of the Self*, vol. 3 of *The History of Sexuality* (London: Lane, 1988), 228–32.

educating a girl in a temple like a Vestal and inventing a "custody of the virgin" by the husband-to-be bring to mind a *virgo subintroducta* of the first Christian centuries, among other examples.[11]

However, such malleable details fulfilled the needs of a large audience who yearned for color, form, faces, names, and concreteness in the nativity scene and made this text a huge success, especially in the Eastern churches. The *Wirkungsgeschichte* of the Protevangelium is so extensive that it cannot be treated in detail here. For a long time, the Protevangelium of James was considered an apologetic text in defense of Mary against accusations of adultery (see Celsus, *True Doctr.* 1.28), but the text rather seems to be an encomiastic story (ἐγκώμιον)[12] about the mother of Christ. While the text was never a candidate to be included among canonical texts, it was widely read, and it is possible to trace its influence in art history and the history of ideas all the way to the point when the dogma of the immaculate conception was proclaimed on December 8, 1854.

The central theme of the text is the purity of the mother of the Lord.[13] It is noteworthy that, during the period in which the Protevangelium was written, the virginity of Mary was a topic extensively discussed by theologians (all male; there is no sign of female theologians pondering the topic). This debate was more intense than we might be willing to believe now and did not lack harsh or sarcastic remarks. The theological tension underpinning these heated disputes can be understood as a reaction to the emergence of early heresies. The first significant challenge was posed by docetists. Virgin birth fitted well to the denial of the corporeal and to their conviction that the suffering and humanity of Jesus Christ were only apparent, not real: a body that was not real certainly did not need a real birth.

Ignatius of Antioch (ca. 35–107 CE) was one of the first who raised his voice against docetic beliefs. Defending the real humanity and corporeality of the Savior, he underlined the reality and materiality of the birth on the basis of Gal 4:4 ("born of a woman"): "Be deaf, therefore, whenever anyone speaks to you apart from Jesus Christ, who was of the family of David, who was the son of Mary; who *really was born*, who both ate and drank, who really was persecuted under Pontius Pilate, who really was

---

11. For further details, see Pellegrini, "Protevangelium des Jakobus," 908 n. 23.
12. See Hock, *Infancy Gospels*, 15, 18–20.
13. As argued, with good reason, by Lily C. Vuong, *Gender and Purity in the Protevangelium of James* (Tübingen: Mohr Siebeck, 2013), 4.

crucified and died ..., who, moreover, really was raised from the dead" (Ignatius, *Trall.* 9.1–2).[14] In the *Letter to the Ephesians* (about 107 CE), Ignatius also suggests that the birth of Christ "from the virgin" was one of the "three mysteries to be loudly proclaimed" that materialized "in the silence of God" (*Eph.* 19.1).[15]

Tertullian (ca. 150–220 CE) was harsher in his treatise against Marcion (ca. 85–160 CE), who had rejected the birth of the Savior as something impure and repulsive, and even suggested that Jesus appeared suddenly and unexpectedly as an adult, spiritual being from heaven. Tertullian attacks Marcion with his own uncultivated vocabulary and vehemently refuses the idea of virgin birth in the defense of Christ's humanity:

> Come on then, use all your eloquence against those sacred and reverend works of nature, launch an attack upon everything that you are: revile that in which both flesh and soul begin to be: characterize as a sewer the womb, that workshop for bringing forth the noble animal which is man: continue your attack on the unclean and shameful torments of child-bearing, and after that on the dirty, troublesome, and ridiculous management of the new-born child. And yet, when you have pulled all those things to pieces, so as to assure yourself that they are beneath God's dignity, nativity cannot be more undignified than death, or infancy than a cross, or <human> nature than scourging, or <human> flesh than condemnation. (Tertullian, *Marc.* 3.11)[16]

Origen (ca. 185–254 CE), perhaps influenced by Tertullian, appears first critical but later begins to defend Mary's virginity at the time of giving birth. In his *Homily 14 on Luke*, written around 233 CE, he suggests that

---

14. PG 5:681; trans. Michael Holmes in *The Apostolic Fathers: Greek Texts and English Translations*, 3rd ed., ed. and trans. Michael W. Holmes (Grand Rapids: Baker Academic, 2007), 221, emphasis added. See also Ignatius, *Smyrn.* 1.1. Others follow Ignatius, e.g., Justin Martyr (ca. 100–165) and Irenaeus of Lyons (ca. 130–202); see Irenaeus, *Haer.* 4.33.11 (PG 7:1080 B): "Quonam Verbum caro erit et Filius Dei filius hominis, purus pure puram aperiens vulvam, eam quae regenerat hominem in Deum, quam ipse puram fecit" ("the pure One opening purely that pure womb which regenerates men unto God, and which He Himself made pure"). Latin text taken from Irénée de Lyon, *Contre les hérésies*, ed. Adelin Rousseau et al., SC 100 (Paris: Cerf, 1965), 4:830; trans. *ANF*.

15. PG 5:659–60, trans. Holmes, *Apostolic Fathers*.

16. Translated by Ernest Evans in Tertullian, *Adversus Marcionem* (Oxford: Oxford University Press, 1972), 203.

"in the Mother of Christ (unlike all other mothers), the womb opened for the first time precisely when she gave birth to the Son."[17] Thus, Origen denies virginity at birth.

However, in the comment to Ps 22:10 ("From birth I was cast on you; from my mother's womb you have been my God"), he writes that Jesus has been "the only" to have been taken from the mother's womb by the Father himself, and for this reason, the "obstetrician" of Jesus was—according to Origen—his very Father (*Fr. Ps.* 21).[18] He does not explicitly affirm Mary's virginity but clearly understands the birth of Jesus as an extraordinary, miraculous event, different from any other childbirth.

Over a century later, a similar turn is found in Jerome (ca. 347–420 CE), who in 384 wrote, "Add, if you like, Helvidius, the other humiliations of nature, the womb for nine months growing larger, the sickness, the delivery, the blood, the swaddling-clothes. Picture to yourself the infant in the enveloping membranes.... We do not blush, we are not put to silence" (*Helv.* 20).[19] However, in his treatise against the Pelagians in 415 he has changed his mind (*Pelag.* 2.4). What strikes most in this long-lasting debate is the rough tones of both parties, their emotions, and the shared conviction that childbirth is something shameful, impure, and embarrassing.

The idea of virginal childbirth is thus easily accepted. This is not a peculiarity only of the Protevangelium but rather a common notion widely shared in the early Christian circles that were influenced by Jewish thinking, as evidenced by other apocryphal writings that testify to a spontaneous popular belief in the virginal childbirth.[20] As an example, I quote from the Ascension of Isaiah (11.7–10), dated to the second century CE,[21] which narrates the birth of Jesus as follows:

---

17. "Omne, inquit, masculinum quod apérit vulvam. Sacratum quidpiam sonat. Quaecunque enim de utero effusum marem dixeris, non sic apérit vulvam matris suae, ut Dominus Jesus, quia omnium mulierum non partus infantis sed viri coitus vulvam reserat. Matris vero Domini eo tempore vulva reserata est quo et partus editus, quia sanctum uterum et omni dignatione venerationis venerandum ante nativitatem Christi masculus omnino non tetigit" (Origen, *Hom. Luc.* 14; PG 13:1836).

18. PG 12:1254D–1255A.

19. Translated in *NPNF*[2] 6:344.

20. Three such texts are known: Odes Sol. 19.7–9; Ascen. Isa. 11.7–10; Gos. Phil. 83 (NHC II 3, 71.16–21).

21. The work is a composite of Jewish and later Christianized parts that are dated between the first century BCE to the second or fourth century CE. Chapters 6–11 (where the cited text belongs) are usually dated to the second century CE.

> And after two months of days, while Joseph was in his house, and Mary his wife, but both alone, it came about, when they were alone, that Mary then looked with her eyes and saw a small infant, and she was astounded. And after her astonishment had worn off, her womb was found as [it was] at first, before she had conceived. And when her husband, Joseph, said to her, "What has made you astounded?" his eyes were opened, and he saw the infant and praised the Lord, because the Lord had come in his lot. And a voice came to them, "Do not tell this vision to anyone." But the story about the infant was spread abroad in Bethlehem. Some said, "The virgin Mary has given birth before she has been married two months." But many said, "She did not give birth; the midwife did not go up [to her], and we did not hear [any] cries of pain." And they were all blinded concerning him; they all knew about him, but they did not know from where he was. (Ascen. Isa. 11.7–10)[22]

Another but even more emblematic testimony of Mary's virginal childbirth is in the Odes of Solomon (first to third century CE). In Ode 19, dedicated to incarnation, we read:

> The womb of the Virgin took it,
> and she received conception and gave birth.
> So the Virgin became a mother with great mercies.
> And she labored and bore the Son
> but without pain, because it did not occur without purpose.
> And she did not require a midwife,
> because He caused her to give life.
> She brought forth like a strong man with desire,
> and she bore according to the manifestation,
> and she acquired according to the Great Power. (Odes Sol. 19.6–10)[23]

This popular literature shows us clearly how one part of postapostolic Christianity conceived the virginity of Mary at her childbirth. The debates and discussions did not cease easily but continued in the long story of Marian dogmas that are not dealt with here, as they fall outside our topic. A short note suffices to show where this troublesome road led.

Among the four Marian Dogmas (the divine motherhood, or Maria Θεοτόκος = *Deipara*; the perpetual virginity = ἀειπαρθενεία; the immaculate conception; and the assumption), only the first two have christological

---

22. Translated by Michael Knibb in *OTP*.
23. Translated by James Charlesworth in *OTP*.

relevance. They were also the first to be defined, in the Council of Ephesus in 431 and the Second Council of Constantinople in 553.

The first council (431) defined Mary as the "mother of God" (θεοτόκος), against Nestorius, who only acknowledged her the attribute of χριστοτόκος (the mother of Christ). This means that the humanity of the mother is defined as the guarantee of the authenticity of the Son, while the divinity of Jesus guarantees the divine motherhood of Mary. The second council (553) affirmed that the Word "became flesh from the glorious Theotokos and perennially virgin Mary" (σαρκωθέντος ἐκ τῆς ἁγίας ἐνδόξου θεοτόκου καὶ ἀειπαρθένου Μαρίας, DH 422), thereby sanctioning the perpetual virginity of Mary.

Faced with this heated and confusing situation, the author of the Protevangelium of James (or their sources) had to consider several demands. On the one hand, they had to defend the corporeal reality of Jesus against docetic ideas, but on the other, to stick to the idea of Mary's absolute virginity, which is the sign of her purity. According to the text's logic, Mary's virginity is not in contrast with or detracting from the corporeality of the Savior; the author readily notes, for example, the first suckling of the baby Jesus, commenting that he fed like any baby. There is nothing in the Protevangelium that would show docetist contempt for the material world; on the contrary, it is both appreciated and vividly described as a part of the divine story (see, e.g., Prot. Jas. 18.2–3). On the other hand, the essential information of the canonical gospels could not be ignored, for example, concerning Joseph as the husband of Mary,[24] even though this narrative element was in open contrast with the concern for chastity. Having such narrow space to maneuver, the main purpose of the narrative is to defend Mary's absolute purity, both in cultic and in moral sense—purity that, in contemporary discourses, is linked to her virginity.[25] The virginal purity is therefore what the narrative is all about, and we are now going to analyze its essential features.

3. Mary's Birth in the Protevangelium of James

There are two narrative centers that revolve round Mary: her own birth and that of her son Jesus, both associated with the theme of purity. In the

---

24. On Joseph, see section 4 below.
25. The growing value of virginity as the premise for the closeness to God is variably shown in contemporary literature. See, e.g., Philo, *Congr.* 7; *Cher.* 42–50 (regarding Sarah and the other matriarchs).

first narrative, the particular interest lies with the parental figures, Anna and Joachim, while the second highlights Mary's husband, Joseph. Let us first look at the first birth.

In the wake of the other great matriarchs of Israel (Sarah, Rebecca, Rachel),[26] Mary is also born as a gift from the Lord to a childless couple with the stigma of not being able to procreate looming over them. However, the narrative does not begin with the usual focus on a woman in crisis, because she has not become a mother but is forgotten by the Lord (see Gen 30:1, 6, 22; 1 Sam 1:6). Instead, it is the father, righteous both in spirit and in deeds, who encounters accusations of childlessness and who, for this reason, is dismissed from the honors of the altar (Prot. Jas. 1.2). He is in crisis, as he finds out that "all the righteous had raised offspring in Israel … and Joachim was very sad" (Prot. Jas. 1.4).[27] Because of this, he separates from his wife to go to the desert and fast for forty days in order to seek God and his forgiveness. Anna also seeks forgiveness, and her prayers are heard—all biblical clichés are in use—and the much-awaited descendant finally arrives.

The birth of a child takes on the aspect of a social and religious redemption: being infertile is seen as sign of sin and is strongly punished in the religious community. Against this background, the Protevangelium sees the birth as an expression of divine justice. Both Joachim and Anna have a descendent, not for their own merits but through their faith and humility. It is a free gift that brings life (fecundity) and the joy of birth. From the religious and social perspective, Mary's birth is an indispensable divine gift, the fruit of justification. Joachim expresses this clearly by concluding: "'Now I know that the Lord God is gracious to me and has forgiven all my sins.' And he came down from the temple of the Lord justified, and went to his house" (Prot. Jas. 5.1).

In this sense, the birth of Mary is pure, in other words, not contaminated by sin, and a result of justification, but it is not a miracle.[28] In fact,

---

26. Sarah (Gen 16:1; 17:17; 18:11–15; passim), Rebecca (Gen 25:21), and Rachel (Gen 29:31; 31:1) were (believed to be) infertile. The same is suggested for Elizabeth in Luke 1:7.

27. English translation of the Protevangelium of James consistently follows J. K. Elliot, *The Apocryphal New Testament: A Collection of Apocryphal Christian Literature in an English Translation* (Oxford: Clarendon, 1993).

28. Contra Vuong, who speaks of "the miraculously-born Mary" (*Gender and Purity*, 95). According to Vuong, *Gender and Purity*, 94 and passim, the priests in the

it is fair to assume that in this text, Anna and Joachim have had normal sexual intercourse before separating to pray, as the baby girl is born six months after their separation (Prot. Jas. 5.2).[29] The text does not yet mention *immaculata conceptio*, which later became the dogma, proclaimed by Pope Pius IX on December 8, 1854.[30]

The annunciation of the birth of the mother of the Savior takes place, not by chance, on the "great day of the Lord" (Prot. Jas. 2.2), which alludes to Yom Kippur. The coincidence with the Day of Atonement preludes the saving mission of this mother and her son. According to Lily Vuong,[31] the narrative framework of Yom Kippur expresses the idea that Mary, the mother of the Savior, was conceived on the Day of Atonement or close to it. According to the manuscript tradition, that dates the birth of the child at about six months after Yom Kippur; however, this coincidence does not hold. Yet, the link to Yom Kippur and the idea of atonement is undeniable, since the angel promises the birth of a child to Anna while she prays on the Day of Atonement (Prot. Jas. 4.1). Following this line of thought, Vuong sees Mary as a sacrifice ("child-sacrifice") according to the model of Isaac, which preludes the theme of self-sacrifice ("a self-sacrificing son") and the redemptive death in which Mary would play a role.[32] More moderately, Alexander Toepel confirms a link between Yom Kippur and the offering of Mary at the temple as a Nazirite, but he distances himself from a sacrificial-redemptive interpretation in line with Isaac or Iphigenia. He

---

temple had mistakenly judged Anna and Joachim as sinners; even if they were and remained righteous, and they corrected their mistake when Mary was born. I believe that the point of the text is not in the act of rectification the priest, but in emphasizing that life is a gift from God. Being righteous is not a result of one's own action but of the mercy of God: Mary is "the fruit of His righteousness" (Prot. Jas. 6.3)—here "His" (αὐτοῦ) refers to God's justice and not to that of Joachim.

29. In certain manuscripts, the time is nine months, while in others it is six. Vuong opts for the nine-months version while I, among others, prefer the variant "about six months." The expression "Anna will conceive" (Prot. Jas. 4.1, 4) in the future tense is explained as belonging to the annunciation by the angel. This corresponds to the uncertainty during the first few months of pregnancy concerning the exact time of conception. There were no technical means to ascertain such a date.

30. According to the bull *Ineffabilis Deus*, Virgin Mary remained immune to the original sin from the first moment of her conception. However, the concept of original sin was not sufficiently developed in the second century CE.

31. See Vuong, *Gender and Purity*, 79.

32. See Vuong, *Gender and Purity*, 100–103.

concludes that the Protevangelium redefines the Jewish and pagan concept of sacrifice.[33] The closest model to the consecration of Mary thus appears to be Samuel (1 Sam 1), who was dedicated to the Lord and belonged to him but was not sacrificed to him. Mary is thus assigned a sacerdotal function ("a priestly function").[34]

Following the model of Samuel, son of Anna and Elkanah (1 Sam 1), Mary is also a gift from God, and she is received and consecrated to the temple already before her birth. Perhaps, as Jürgen Becker has suggested, the name of the mother, Anna, is also a reference to the Samuel story.[35] As a firstborn male, Samuel belonged to the Lord in compliance with the law of the redemption of the firstborn (Exod 13:15), which commanded that every firstborn, if male, had to serve at the temple of the Lord, and if he was not given to the temple, he had to be redeemed. The presentation (and redemption) of Jesus in the temple (Luke 2:22–24) fulfilled this law, but it certainly would not have applied to Mary. In fact, there are no documents that would indicate the presence of virgins, either of service or of residence, in the temple.[36] Yet, in the Protevangelium, Mary is indeed consecrated as if she were male. The variant is intentionally constructed and appropriately announced in advance in the text when Anna says: "As the Lord my God lives, if I bear a child, whether male *or female*, I will bring it as a gift to the Lord my God, and it shall serve him all the days of its life" (Prot. Jas. 4.1).

---

33. See Toepel, *Das Protevangelium des Jakobus*, 76.

34. Toepel, *Das Protevangelium des Jakobus*, 76 (my translation).

35. See Jürgen Becker, *Maria: Mutter Jesu und erwählte Jungfrau* (Leipzig: Evangelische Verlagsanstalt, 2001), 258. As a reference text for the name of the father (Joachim), Becker suggests 2 Kgs 24, but this in my opinion is not convincing.

36. It is unwarranted to refer here to the "the women who assembled at the door of the tabernacle of meeting" (1 Sam 2:22) or the prophet Anna (Luke 2:36–38). As for the first case, it is not from the same period, it is not about the temple, and (whatever the service they provided) these women were certainly not virgins since the children of Eli joined them. In the second case, Anna was not a virgin, and no reference is made to a group of virgins to which she would belong. Moreover, Protevangelium of James does not say that Mary would be in service but, quite cleverly and in line with its aim, says only that she resided in the temple (Prot. Jas. 8.1: "Mary *stayed* at the temple of the Lord," emphasis added), irrespective of what the mother had in mind (Prot. Jas. 4.1). In the time when Protevangelium of James was written, the temple of Jerusalem no longer existed. Perhaps this opening of the exclusively male Jewish liturgical service to females was an adaptation of the Roman Vestal virgin tradition?

This shows that from the beginning the text does not treat Mary as a woman. The progressive redefinition of her sexuality begins with the destiny of a nonfemale and proceeds, as we will see, with the successive stripping of all sexual characteristics of a mother.

This anomalous fate is strengthened after birth. For Mary, birth does not mark the beginning of life in the world, as for all other children, but of a separation from the world. "[As] the Lord my God lives, you shall walk no more upon this earth until I bring you into the temple of the Lord" (Prot. Jas. 6.1), says the mother to her little daughter of only six months of age when she takes her first seven steps.[37] In this ascetic vision, the whole world is impure and, if possible, should not even be touched. In Mary's bedroom, Anna builds a "sanctuary," where she watches that nothing "common or unclean" reaches the child's hands (Prot. Jas. 6.1). The aura of purity around Mary is an exact counterbalance of an implicitly negative vision of the impure and sinful world. With purity as the basic concept of the Protevangelium,[38] everything that is considered impure or profane must be rejected.

In this respect, it should be emphasized that the meaning of pure/impure in the Protevangelium does not correspond to the concept in the Jewish Bible, which clearly distinguishes between cultic purity and moral purity. The former regulates access to the temple and participation in the sacrificial cult; the latter involves the decision making and the will of the person.[39] The Protevangelium does not make such a distinction but links them together, as already happens in Philo, in Qumran, and in the subsequent rabbinic literature.[40] In the case of the Protevangelium, this link is seen in the mutual development of the two sides of purity. Cultic purity is highlighted as the premise of the pure offering of Mary to the Lord as a gift (δῶρον, Prot. Jas. 7.1) on which the moral purity is invoked by removing Mary from sin.

---

37. In child development, the first steps are normally not taken before the child is ten to twelve months. The incredible age of six months can be interpreted as a sign of extraordinary precocity. However, it could also suggest that the author was a man, not very well informed about the development of an infant during the first year. It is difficult for me to think that any woman would not know that a normal baby does not walk at six months of age.
38. See Vuong, *Gender and Purity*, 4.
39. See Vuong, *Gender and Purity*, 60–64.
40. See Vuong, *Gender and Purity*, 64–88.

Throughout the narrative, Mary remains pure ("pure before God"; Prot. Jas. 10.1), in other words, not contaminated. She is ritually pure, that is, uncontaminated by the impure, since her infancy, and morally pure, that is, uncontaminated by sin, as a woman. In this regard, Ignace de la Potterie notes: "The concern that there was no 'stain' in the mother of Jesus has remained alive in the patristic period but the non-contamination was apparently interpreted more and more in religious and Christian sense as the synonym for *virginity*."[41]

4. Virginity in Birth of Jesus according to Protevangelium of James

The fundamental concern for the preservation of Mary's virginity is evident in the annunciation scene, when the young woman asks the angel: "Shall I conceive by the Lord, the living God, and bear *as every woman bears*?" (Prot. Jas. 11.2, emphasis added.) Perhaps also the curious detail that Mary soon forgets about this announcement and is surprised with Elizabeth that all women call her blessed and mother (Prot. Jas. 12.2) can be explained as a trait of purity, in a simple, naive, and humble form. Not even the idea of an event so impure as the childbirth comes to her mind!

With these premises, virginity, now as a symbol of moral purity, fully dominates the second central event of the narrative, that is, the birth of Christ.[42] The text contains a strong link between purity and absence of sin. In the Protevangelium, *pure* refers to noncontamination both by impure things and by sin (Prot. Jas. 6.1; 8.1; 10.1; 13.3; and passim). The narrative evolves toward the climax of the purity theme, passing from a ritual quality (Mary as a girl) to a moral quality (Mary as a woman).

Both these forms of purity are seen not only as successive to each other (first ritual purity, followed by moral purity) but also in relation to each other (ritual purity is the basis for moral purity; in other words: moral purity comes from ritual purity), as in the vision of conservative Judaism (e.g., Qumran).[43] In fact, when the text discusses moral purity, it

---

41. Ignace de la Potterie, "Il parto verginale del Verbo incarnato: 'Non ex sanguinibus …, sed ex Deo natus est' (Gv 1,13)," *Marianum* 45 (1983): 127.

42. This is strongly emphasized by Mary F. Foskett, "Virginity as Purity in the Protoevangelium of James," in *A Feminist Companion to Mariology*, ed. Amy-Jill Levine and Maria Mayo Robbins, FCNTECW (London: T&T Clark, 2005), 75.

43. Vuong compares the ideal of extreme purity in Protevangelium of James with the writings of Qumran. Both show a combination of ritual purity and moral purity

makes a causal link to ritual purity. This is the structure of the accusation made by the priest against Mary: "You who were brought up in the Holy of Holies and received food from the hand of an angel, and heard hymns, and danced before Him, why have you done this?" (Prot. Jas. 15.3; see also 13.2).

The concept of purity is so emphasized as to exclude the common (reference to the holy of holies) and the material (reference to the food from the hand of an angel),[44] to the degree of dematerializing and desexualizing the feminine features. How does the reference to Mary's puberty find place and sense in this context? As Vuong correctly notes,[45] Mary is not free from the menstrual cycle, a feature of impure sexuality. This is mentioned for narrative purposes but only in passing and is then relegated to the background. It serves as a justification of Mary's exclusion from the temple (Prot. Jas. 8.2), allows the introduction of the figure of Joseph, and initiates the theme of moral purity, linked to active sexuality and therefore identified as chastity.

As we see, Mary is partly desexualized;[46] in other words, the reproductive sexual characteristics of her femininity are reduced as much as possible. Female characteristics (meekness, joy, service, diligence, menstrual cycle) are preserved in her figure, while those of a mother are denied or distorted (no sexual activity, no childbirth).

Before discussing the virginal childbirth, we have to see how the author presents the virginal conception of Jesus vis-à-vis the canonical gospels. Here Joseph is the key figure. Joseph's function and figure are quite different from the canonical gospels. In contrast to Matthew (1:20; 2) and Luke (2:3; 3:31), the Protevangelium presents Mary, not Joseph, as a descendant of David (Prot. Jas. 10.1.) This change can be explained by the concentrated interest in the figure of Mary and the weakening of the role of Joseph. In the beginning of the narrative, he does not want her, does not

---

that is stricter than in the Jewish Bible, and interpret it much more rigidly (*Gender and Purity*, 66).

44. For the purposes of my discussion, it is not useful to split hairs about the food consumed by Mary, whether it is angelic food or just normal food received from the hand of an angel. In any case, it is obvious that, mirroring the nature of the Redeemer Son, the author transfers Mary out of the real human, i.e., the daily, concrete, and material world, and sets her between the human and the divine.

45. Vuong, *Gender and Purity*, 147.

46. However, she is not fully desexualized; she is removed from the temple because of her puberty.

guard her but leaves her (Prot. Jas. 9.1–3); he does not really marry her but accompanies her like a servant. In the Protevangelium, Joseph is a weak figure who echoes Mary's actions. He is afraid (Prot. Jas. 9.3; 14.1) and cries like her (Prot. Jas. 13.3; cf. Prot. Jas. 16.1), he is pure like her (Prot. Jas. 15.4), he is consulted only after her (Prot. Jas. 15.4), and he asks Mary for explanations and advice as to what to do (Prot. Jas. 17.2; 18).

According to the biblical and Jewish way of thinking, the loss of virginity is not a sin as such, but being sexually active outside marriage is (Anna is not a virgin but not a sinner). However, Mary was duly married to Joseph—both in the canonical gospels and in the Protevangelium. While the perspective of the Synoptic Gospels is limited to the (divine!) origins of Jesus, and they concentrate on the prenatal virginity of the conception, in the second century the request for absolute purity raised questions about the subsequent family life of Mary, whose sons and daughters are named in the Synoptic Gospels without any problem (Mark 6:3). As a response, the Protevangelium insists that Mary is a wife, with a husband, and that must not make her a mother! It is evident that the text is willing to shake any historical and religious canon to protect Mary's purity at any cost.

According to Matthew and Luke (Matt 1:18; Luke 1:27), Joseph is the bridegroom who marries Mary and presumably also has children with her (Mark 6:3). Therefore, he is seen as a young man. In the Protevangelium, however, Joseph is transformed into an old widower who already has offspring (Prot. Jas. 9.2). As such, he seems to give guarantee for the protection of Mary's virginity. Following this path, the tradition makes the brothers and sisters of Jesus into Joseph's children from his first marriage or into Jesus's cousins. It is obvious that the narrative must here fulfill two needs. On the one hand, it has to agree with the gospel stories that describe Joseph as the husband (not least to safeguard Christ's lineage from David! see Matt 1:20); on the other hand, its aim is to preserve the purity of the virgin Mary. Therefore, Mary is given as a bride to a man with whom she was not supposed to consummate the marriage—evidently against Jewish norms, which provide that the man has the right to children or the marriage could be dissolved.

Having laid these foundations, the narrative proceeds with increasingly bold turns. First, Joseph accuses Mary of fornication (Prot. Jas. 13.2), as he knows that he is not responsible for her pregnancy. Then the high priest accuses Joseph of having "defiled" Mary and of having "consummated his marriage in secret": "You have consummated your marriage in secret, … and have not bowed your head under the mighty hand in order that your seed might be blessed" (Prot. Jas. 15.2). In other words, Joseph would have consummated the marriage without the ritual blessing.[47] But why should he not have consummated the marriage—after all, he was her husband? The accusation is quite artificial, and the whole narrative construction is weak from the logical and historical perspective, but it holds up well in preserving Mary's purity. Purity—in what sense? The sexuality that makes her a mother also makes her impure in a phobic vision of female sexuality, quite common in the epoch. Bernhard of Clairvaux (d. 1153) writes that Mary's privilege of the perpetual virginity makes it possible to combine the joy of maternity with the honor of virginity ("gaudia matris habens cum virginitatis honore") and makes it obvious in what extreme manner maternity was perceived as damage and virginity as honor within this ascetic culture.[48]

Reassessing the *christological* sense of the virginal birth against modern cultural standards, I would turn to the demonstration of the divinity of Christ and his sublime meekness. Just like the Jesus in the gospels was meek and nonviolent, this same Jesus came to life without causing any violence to his mother. In this sense, he is divine.

5. Birth and Virginity: Theological-Cultural Intersection

Among the many interests that underlie the Protevangelium of James (religious piety, popular curiosity, questions of truth concerning Jesus and Mary, etc.), we can distinguish, in my opinion, two fundamental levels. First is the theological aspect that is interested in the reality of Jesus and, based on this, speculates on Mary. Second is the cultural aspect, which, in keeping with the (androcentric) culture of the time, sees female sexuality, childbirth, and other related sexual aspects as fundamentally impure, negative, and contaminated. For certain writers quoted above, they are even repugnant and disgraceful. These contemporary cultural convictions

---

47. See Ermenegildo Pistelli, *Il Protevangelo di Jacopo: Prima traduzione italiana con introduzione e note di E. Pistelli. Segue un appendice dallo Pseudo-Matteo* (Lansiano: Carabba, 1919), 84. He gives as an example of such ritual blessing the text of Ruth 4:11, which is quite remote from the context of Protevangelium of James. Toepel refers to Gen 22:18 and Isa 65:23, and interprets the reference as an emphasis of Mary's fertility (*Protevangelium des Jakobus*, 190). However, this seems quite farfetched.

48. Bernard of Clairvaux, *In assumptione B.V.Mariae sermo* 4.5, PL 183:428.

concerning childbirth and virginity significantly influence theological discussions. It is our task to recognize and analyze them.

Above all, the focus on virginity and its verification postpartum is not an end in itself but derives from theological reflection about the nature of Jesus and the trouble to guarantee his divine origin. For this reason, I want to emphasize that my reflections do not diminish the merit of the theological speculations on the human and divine nature of Christ, fixed in the christological and in the two first Marian dogmas. However, from the New Testament perspective, such an effort seems unnecessary, given that the virginal conception and the incarnation fully guarantee Jesus's divine origin. A christological interest alone is, therefore, not enough to support the idea of virginity *in partu*—a notion that is not found in the canonical gospels.

However, as the theologians of the time considered giving birth as an unclean and impure event that would threaten (by mere contact!) the divinity of the Savior, Mary's virginity in childbirth was a cultural necessity. Naturally, this kind of argumentation is extremely weak, but the logic of the discourse here follows cultural, not theological standards.

On the other hand, the reflection on motherhood, focused on childbirth, is theological. Childbirth does not exist in paradise (except for the happy greeting in Gen 1:28, "Be fruitful and multiply!") but is read—in the wake of the original Yahwist story—as a sign of sin. For this reason, it is taken away from Mary, whose purity is not just ritual but above all moral in the eyes of the author of the Protevangelium.

So, on the one hand, the virginity of Mary tells about a birth that is not a childbirth. It is a coming into being, like a light, *without* passing through a woman. On the other hand, the Virgin Mother becomes a symbol of the structural absence of sin. Mary is not like Eve and the daughters of Eve, but she relates to the time *before* Eve's sin; in other words, she is the heroine of a birth without labor. In the Protevangelium, this child Jesus, who is surrounded by light and mystery, brings to mind the birth of Eve from Adam rather than a real infant in his mother's arms—this is why the Ode of Solomon says: "She brought forth like a strong man" (Odes Sol. 19.11).[49]

The combination of childbirth and the preservation of virginity is a bold and ingenious religious synthesis that became enormously successful in Christian history. It simultaneously fulfills two ancient dreams: a female

---

49. See above, section 2.

dream of having children without suffering pain and damage, and a male dream of receiving life that is not contaminated by female impurity and is not dependent on woman.

Alongside the sincere and sound theological question, this text is dominated by a distorted view of female sexuality that interprets maternity solely through childbirth and considers it to be a sign of sin. The author is not able to conceive a harmonious vision of female sexuality that would naturally develop into maternity. He adapts Mary to his ideal image of woman, extrapolating an abstractly pure femininity and reducing the reality of pregnancy at the climax of childbirth, as if he did not have much experience or interest in the pregnancy itself. In the Protevangelium of James, Mary is "like a dove" (Prot. Jas. 8.1), an ideal of a docile woman who is meek, joyful, pure, faithful, silent, skillful, healthy, hardworking, courageous, respected, and obedient. Is this not an "androcentric portrayal of the virgin,"[50] the female ideal and dream decidedly constructed by a man of that epoch and culture?

---

50. Foskett, "Virginity as Purity," 76.

Gender Roles in the Infancy Gospel of Thomas

Ursula Ulrike Kaiser

1. Introduction to the Text and Related Questions

The earliest core of the narrative about the childhood deeds of Jesus (Greek Paidika), better known under the undoubtedly secondary title of the Infancy Gospel of Thomas,[1] can be presumably traced back to the late second or early third century. It was rapidly and widely distributed, as shown by the many differing textual editions and versions in a wide variety of languages.[2] It is evident that this partly astonishingly violent but abundantly miraculous Childhood Deeds of Jesus between the ages of five and twelve enjoyed great popularity.

To the present, only Reidar Aasgaard has dealt extensively with the question of the gender roles in the Paidika.[3] He quite correctly certifies a "male focus" in the text.[4] A cursory glance already shows that the fig-

---

1. A long form of the original title could have been Τὰ παιδικὰ τοῦ κυρίου ἡμῶν Ἰησοῦ Χριστοῦ. On the question of the title, see, among others, Ursula Ulrike Kaiser, "Die sogenannte 'Kindheitserzählung des Thomas': Überlegungen zur Darstellung Jesu als Kind, deren Intention und Rezeption," in *Infancy Gospels: Stories and Identities*, ed. Claire Clivaz et al., WUNT 281 (Tübingen: Mohr Siebeck, 2011), 460.

2. On the dating, see, among others, Tony Burke, *De infantia Iesu evangelivm Thomae*, CCSA 17 (Turnhout: Brepols, 2010), 202; Reidar Aasgaard, *The Childhood of Jesus: Decoding the Apocryphal Infancy Gospel of Thomas* (Eugene, OR: Cascade, 2009), 182. On the transmission, text families, and the usual sigla in research, see the overview by Ursula Ulrike Kaiser with Josef Tropper, "Die Kindheitserzählung des Thomas: Einleitung und Übersetzung," in *Antike christliche Apokryphen in deutscher Übersetzung*, ed. Christoph Markschies and Jens Schröter (Tübingen: Mohr Siebeck, 2012), 1:931–35; and in more detail, Burke, *Infantia Iesu evangelivm Thomae* 14.127–71.

3. See Aasgaard, *Childhood of Jesus*, especially ch. 7.

4. Aasgaard, *Childhood of Jesus*, 111.

ures discussed in the Paidika in more detail are, in the striking majority, male. They are encountered as fathers, husbands, scribes, and teachers, but also as woodchoppers and construction workers (the last, though, only in later expansions of the text). The children playing with Jesus, insofar as they emerge from out of the anonymity of the group, are also always boys. Mary, on the other hand, is encountered only seldom. In the compilation of episodes in the Paidika as documented by the oldest preserved Greek text form and the Syrian version,[5] there are only two episodes in which she speaks and acts actively, and a further episode in which she is a passive figure. In respect of the gender roles that influence the text,[6] and that the text itself contains and promotes, the figures of Joseph and Jesus are thus the most interesting; among the women, this figure is Mary. The following analysis will be limited to these three.

How does one detect gender roles in a text that never explicitly emphasizes certain manners of conduct and characteristics as masculine or feminine? In his study of the masculinity of Jesus in Mark, Moisés Mayordomo points out that in a narrative text, masculinity can "be brought into play most easily as a useful analytical category when [it] is considered as an aspect of the characterization of the figures."[7] In a comparable way, Thomas Späth, in his study of masculinity and femininity in the work of Tacitus, begins his analysis with the actions of the persons portrayed and

---

5. The siglum for the oldest preserved Greek textual witnesses from the eleventh century is Gs. Aasgaard refers essentially to this text, which, for him, goes back to an archetype from the fifth century (*Childhood of Jesus*, 15; see also the appendix with edition and translation). The present essay also refers to Gs as far as the content, the text form, and the numbering of the episodes are concerned, but I do this according to Burke's critical edition. However, when passages are cited, the translation is in each case my own. The Syrian textual witness, which originates already from the sixth century, will also be cited along with further versions when there are deviations that are significant for gender roles. The Syrian version will be quoted from the translation by Josef Tropper in Kaiser, "Kindheitserzählung des Thomas."

6. Apart from later added passages, the core narrative of the Paidika undoubtedly belongs in the cultural framework of late antiquity. So also Aasgaard: "It shares the social and cultural values current in late antiquity, such as honor codes and perceptions of gender" (*Childhood of Jesus*, 215).

7. Moisés Mayordomo, "Jesu Männlichkeit im Markusevangelium: Eine Spurensuche," in *Doing Gender—Doing Religion: Fallstudien zur Intersektionalität im frühen Judentum, Christentum und Islam*, ed. Ute E. Eisen, Christine Gerber, and Angela Standhartinger, WUNT 302 (Tübingen: Mohr Siebeck, 2013), 362.

with the relationships emerging in them.⁸ Aasgaard has a similar approach in his analysis of the gender roles in the Paidika: "the issue of gender ... looms large in the writing: in the ideas and values reflected in it, *in the figures involved, and not least in Jesus, its main character.*"⁹

Here I will follow this approach in the analysis of the main characters. In contrast to Aasgaard, I will not only concentrate on Jesus but also and even more on Joseph. I will also direct my attention to reception processes and consider in which ways characters and roles that have become familiar from the later canonized gospels are taken up and changed in the Paidika.¹⁰

As female figures play only a marginal role in the Paidika in its earlier form, as already indicated, the question of masculinity is central in the analysis of gender roles in this text. What constitutes a man in the framework of late antiquity? How is masculinity construed? The "dominant aspects of antique masculinity,"¹¹ worked out by Mayordomo, prove to be useful for my analysis. These aspects can be summarized as follows:

- Masculinity must be acquired and learned, as a rule primarily from the father.¹²
- Masculinity is performed in the mode of public self-representation and takes place in competition with others, toward whom strength must be shown.¹³ Preferred possibilities for doing so are

---

8. Thomas Späth, *Männlichkeit und Weiblichkeit bei Tacitus: Zur Konstruktion der Geschlechter in der römischen Kaiserzeit*, GG 9 (Frankfurt: Campus, 1994), 30.

9. Aasgaard, *Childhood of Jesus*, 103, emphasis added.

10. The emphasis here lies quite decisively on figures and roles, not on direct textual dependence. The question of which of the canonical gospels the Paidika may have drawn is disputed in research. See Ursula Ulrike Kaiser, "Jesus als Kind: Neuere Forschungen zur Jesusüberlieferung in den apokryphen 'Kindheitsevangelien,'" in *Jesus in apokryphen Evangelienüberlieferungen: Beiträge zu außerkanonischen Jesusüberlieferungen aus verschiedenen Sprach- und Kulturtraditionen*, ed. Jörg Frey and Jens Schröter, WUNT 254 (Tübingen: Mohr Siebeck, 2010), 260–64.

11. See Mayordomo, "Jesu Männlichkeit im Markusevangelium," 362–67; see also Colleen M. Conway, *Behold the Man: Jesus and Greco-Roman Masculinity* (New York: Oxford University Press, 2008), 15–34.

12. See Mayordomo, "Jesu Männlichkeit im Markusevangelium," 364; on the role of the man as *pater/paterfamilias* see also Späth, *Männlichkeit und Weiblichkeit bei Tacitus*, 306–11.

13. See Mayordomo, "Jesu Männlichkeit im Markusevangelium," 365, 371.

offered by the realms of war and the military, sporting competitions, rhetoric, and political office.
- Masculinity means the exercise of control and supremacy in the political as well as the private sphere.[14]
    - Self-control, moderation, and strength of will are to be demonstrated as the inner side of this control and supremacy.[15]
    - Masculine supremacy is to be exercised also in the area of sexuality, whereby what is specifically masculine is expressed in personal freedom and sovereignty.[16]

This brief description in unavoidably general terms of the aspects that formed the measure of masculinity in antiquity is used in the following as a tool in assessing the development of the characters of Joseph and Jesus in the Paidika.[17]

2. Joseph: The Tested Father

Joseph plays a central role in the Paidika. He appears in almost all the episodes and is the most important reference point for Jesus. His chief role is that of the father. This role is quite clearly a *social* role. That Joseph is not the *biological* father of Jesus shines through in several passages for the informed reader and is, in my opinion, assumed by the text,[18] even

---

14. See Mayordomo, "Jesu Männlichkeit im Markusevangelium," 366.
15. See Mayordomo, "Jesu Männlichkeit im Markusevangelium," 367.
16. See Mayordomo, "Jesu Männlichkeit im Markusevangelium," 366.
17. In the part devoted to gender, Aasgaard focuses on comparable parameters: "I take my point of departure from dominance and self-restraint as basic notions.... I break the former down into more specific categories, namely strength, violence, persuasive speech, honor, and female exclusion" (*Childhood of Jesus*, 104). Aasgaard orients himself, above all, on categories that Clines transferred from his studies on David and other OT figures to the analysis of Paul. See David J. A. Clines, "Paul, the Invisible Man," in *New Testament Masculinities*, ed. Stephen D. Moore, SemeiaSt 45 (Atlanta: Society of Biblical Literature, 2003), 181. However, for the Paidika, the construction of masculinity in the late antique world, on which Mayordomo and Späth, among others, focus, is of greater significance than the OT characterization, even though there is some overlap. Aasgaard also briefly touches on the broad research landscape on "ancient masculinity" (see *Childhood of Jesus*, 103.
18. The boy Jesus himself makes reference to his special origin in 6.2b with clear echoes of John 8:58. See also the integration of Luke 2:49 in ch. 17[19].3. (The number

though it is not dealt with directly in any of its passages. In view of the miracles that the little boy Jesus performs and of the words with which he demonstrates a wisdom far transcending his age, the observing crowd at times expresses suspicion that all this has to have something to do with a special origin of the child Jesus. Nevertheless, Joseph's social role as father, with related duties, is in no way infringed upon by it.[19] This takes a quite different form in the Gospel of John, where the knowledge about Jesus's earthly family, in the two passages in which Joseph is at all mentioned in John, interferes with the true understanding about Jesus (John 1:45) or even makes it impossible (John 6:42).[20]

Somewhat more about the figure of Joseph can be acquired from Luke and Matthew. The connection of the Paidika with Luke is quite clear: the story of the twelve-year-old Jesus in the temple (Luke 2:41–52) serves as the closing story of the collection of Jesus's childhood deeds and functions as a hinge to the narratives around the adult Jesus.[21] With this pericope, the Paidika also takes up the role that Joseph plays in the canonical text (whereupon Mary is, at the same time, given more significance; see below). However, while Joseph in Luke *always* appears in the shadow of Mary (and not only in this episode, but also in the remaining text of Luke 2), in the Paidika, this is the case *only* in chapter 17 [19].

Thus, the figure of Joseph in the apocryphal childhood stories about Jesus is more comparable with the somewhat more independent description of Joseph in Matt 1–2, even if, in content, none of the incidents narrated by Matthew are taken up as such in the Paidika. In contrast to the Lukan birth and childhood stories, in the Matthean version Joseph is the

---

in square brackets indicates the numbering of the episodes in the Greek long version, Ga, which in many editions of the Apocrypha still forms the basis of translation.)

19. The child Jesus also criticizes Joseph's physical attempts at education in 5.3. He does not do this, though, by denying Joseph's responsibility as a father. Rather, he questions Joseph's discernment into the situation and, accordingly, the appropriateness of the punishment (see more on this passage below).

20. The issue in John 1:45 is not so much whether Joseph is Jesus's earthly father but whether Nazareth can be the place of origin of the Messiah, which is questioned by Nathanael. The situation in John 6:42 is similar to Mark 6:2–3, although there is no mention of Jesus's father at all.

21. On the relationship to Luke, see esp. Tony Chartrand-Burke, "Completing the Gospel: The Infancy Gospel of Thomas as a Supplement to the Gospel of Luke," in *The Reception and Interpretation of the Bible in Late Antiquity*, ed. Lorenzo DiTommaso and Lucian Turescu (Leiden: Brill, 2008), 101–19.

more active person. He doubts and intends to leave Mary (Matt 1:19). He changes his mind after divinely sent dreams and assumes responsibility for the family (Matt 1:20–24). Threatened by Herod in Bethlehem, he leads his family out of the danger to Egypt, and later from there to Nazareth (Matt 2:13, 19–23). In this sense, he fulfills his role as *paterfamilias* and cares for the external security of the family.

He appears in this role as *paterfamilias* in the Paidika, too. In respect to content, however, this role develops in a completely different direction. Not only must Joseph do without the helping guidance of dreams, but also he is asked only once to care for the preservation of the external security of the family (see below). Rather, his responsibility for the *upbringing* of Jesus is central.[22] While the canonical gospels, with the exception of Luke 2:41–52, completely ignore Jesus's adolescent life, that is, the hard school of masculinity, and while Joseph, too, drops out unnoticed from the repertoire of active figures after the infancy of Jesus, it is precisely this part of life that the Paidika describes.[23] Other people repeatedly remind Joseph of his responsibility for the upbringing of Jesus, and he himself takes the appropriate initiatives in this regard.[24] A paraphrase of various parts of the text makes this clear.

As the five year-old Jesus, in chapter 2, plays in the mud on the banks of the stream on a Sabbath, forms waterholes, and miraculously cleans the water, then forms sparrows out of the clay, he is observed by a Jew. The observer goes to Joseph and informs him that Jesus is doing something not allowed on the Sabbath. Thereby, Joseph is made responsible for Jesus's action. Joseph reacts appropriately by going to Jesus and scolding him with the words: "Why do you do these things on the Sabbath?"

The continuation of this episode already begins to indicate that Joseph's role as Jesus's legal guardian will not be easy, for Jesus reacts to

---

22. So too Aasgaard, *Childhood of Jesus*, 66: "In keeping with ancient practice, Josef as *paterfamilias* emerges as having primary responsibility for Jesus' upbringing."

23. See Mayordomo, "Jesu Männlichkeit im Markusevangelium," 364. See also Späth, *Männlichkeit und Weiblichkeit bei Tacitus*, 317–19.

24. On the responsibility of the father for the upbringing of children, see Cornelia B. Horn and John Wesley Martens, *"Let the Little Children Come to Me": Childhood and Children in Early Christianity* (Washington, DC: Catholic University of America Press, 2009), 132. Their view of the upbringing of the child Jesus in the Paidika, however, remains limited to formal education and thus concentrates too much on the three episodes with Jesus's teachers (129–32).

Joseph's scolding plainly and simply by clapping his hands, bringing the birds to life, and letting them fly away. What Joseph thereupon does is not reported.

The miracles performed by Jesus are not all of this rather harmless kind. In the next episode, in chapter 3, he lets the son of the scribe Hannas wither because the child had destroyed Jesus's waterholes willfully.[25] When Jesus later (in ch. 4) walks through the village with Joseph, another boy runs by him and bumps into his shoulder.[26] This makes Jesus furious, and he curses the boy with the words: "You shall not continue on your way!"[27] The boy immediately dies.

While the crowd, still filled with astonishment and dismay, discusses the power that lies in Jesus's words, the parents of the dead boy come and make Joseph responsible for what has happened: "Wherever you have this child from—you cannot live with us in this village! If you want to stay here, then teach him to bless and not to curse!" Here Joseph is questioned not only in regard to Jesus's upbringing. Rather, Jesus's conduct threatens the existence of the entire family within village society.

Joseph at first does not react any differently than he did in the case of the sparrows. He takes the boy Jesus to task and reproaches him because of his deed (5.1). Jesus once again interprets Joseph's disciplinary efforts at first as an understandable and excusable reaction to the threats of the other villagers (5.1) and spares Joseph. All the others who had criticized his conduct, though, he strikes with blindness. Thereupon, Joseph gives up his previously only verbal rebukes and firmly pulls Jesus's ear (5.2). Now the boy Jesus again becomes furious, this time with Joseph, and rebukes him (5.3): "That's enough! You have acted unwisely! Just do not grieve me!"[28]

---

25. In the later, in part expanded, Greek textual versions Ga, Gb, and Gd, Joseph is again made responsible by others for this act of Jesus (see ch. 2).

26. The versions differ concerning whether this occurred inadvertently or with evil intention. See Kaiser, "Überlegungen," 464–68, and the synopsis of ten versions of chapter 4 of the Paidika in Ursula Ulrike Kaiser, "Jesus als enfant terrible in verschiedenen Versionen der apokryphen 'Kindheitserzählung des Thomas'—Ein synoptischer Vergleich von KThom 4," uukaiser (blog), March 18, 2011, https://tinyurl.com/SBL6010a.

27. This is the wording of the Ga variant, which agrees with with Syriac. Gs offers a more difficult text here: the "hegemon" of the boy is cursed. Here Gs appears not to have preserved the older text but more likely has revised it (see also the previous note).

28. The textual transmission of this passage shows clear signs of textual corrup-

This remains the only instance in the Paidika where Joseph exercises physical force against Jesus in his pedagogical efforts. It is also the only time that Jesus so clearly criticizes Joseph. This indicates that the possibilities and limits of the upbringing of the child are explored here. Joseph obviously realizes that he makes no progress with his verbal rebukes of Jesus. For this reason, he resorts next to the means of corporal punishment. Those were in no way exceptional in the upbringing of children in antiquity. In this case, however, the punishment turns out to be relatively moderate. Thereupon, the roles reverse themselves completely. What Jesus says does not belong in the mouth of a five-year-old who answers his father, but rather would be expected the other way around. In regard to the gender roles, Joseph's masculinity suffers a defeat here all along the line. Neither does he adequately fulfill the role of father in relationship to his son, nor is he a match rhetorically for the child. The corporal punishment he applies does not lead to success, either, and thus cannot be interpreted as an indication of strength. Finally, all of this takes place in public.

It is not quite clear how the public audience is exactly to be envisioned, but at least the following chapter (ch. 6) describes an appropriate reaction to this astonishing verbal exchange that presupposes that a certain teacher has witnessed the confrontation.[29] On the basis of what he has heard, the teacher concludes that the child has an extraordinary intelligence (6.1). However, he also perceives the lack of respect that Jesus has for other people and for this reason desires to take him as his student and to teach him not only reading and writing but, not least of all, reverence for human beings and, above all, for his elders (6.2). Again, it is Joseph, in his typical role of the father who is responsible for the upbringing of his son, to whom this inquiry is addressed and who must decide about it. Since Jesus is still somewhat too young for a school career that in antiquity

---

tion. The Greek versions appear to revise in different ways an unclear passage; see the Syriac (5.3) with Jesus's words to Joseph: "Is it not enough for you that you seek me and find me? You have acted unreasonably." In the Greek transmission, these words are negated and used as a reproach against Joseph, who precisely does *not* find Jesus. Subsequently, they are further interpreted, but they aim at the emphasized *affiliation* of Jesus to Joseph: "I am yours."

29. As has become evident from the paraphrase, the individual episodes of the Paidika clearly refer to each other, and Jesus's deeds and the confrontations growing out of them escalate. Thus, this first third of the text does not lack cohesion, as was often the charge leveled at the text, especially in earlier research.

normally began around the age of seven,[30] it is not astonishing that Joseph himself already has not taken the corresponding initiative. He does this later in the Paidika precisely at the point at which Jesus is seven years old and after his first attempt at schooling in chapters 6–8 has been a thorough failure (see below, section 3). But this second attempt (ch. 13 [14]) is not successful, either. Neither teacher is a match for this special student, and they both are humiliated and punished by him. Thereupon (ch. 13[14].3), Joseph orders Mary not to let Jesus go outside the house anymore, so that no more people might be harmed by him.

Here another aspect of Joseph's role as *paterfamilias* becomes visible. He is not only the father of Jesus but also the husband of Mary and, as such, gives her orders to be obeyed. Mary herself remains the pure object of those orders and is not given a voice or opinion of her own. Since the inside of the house is normally the area for which the wife is responsible, it is quite a matter of course that she receives the task of caring for compliance with the order for Jesus's detention.

Already in the next episode (ch. 14 [15]), though, Jesus is again liberated, for a third teacher asks Joseph to be allowed to instruct the child. By adding one school story directly to the next, there is, on the one hand, the possibility to directly compare the different teachers (the third of whom is finally successful by—literally—doing nothing and letting Jesus do as he wants). On the other hand, though, it becomes clear that the house, as the area for women and girls, is no longer the proper place for the education of a seven-year-old boy.

Another aspect of Jesus's education is highlighted in chapter 12 [13]. Here Joseph actively takes part in the training of his son by introducing him to his own craft. The canonical gospels show only traces of this. Taking Mark 6:3 and Matt 13:55 together suggests that Jesus as well as Joseph is known to the people in Nazareth as a carpenter (τέκτων). In the framework of late antiquity, this implies that Jesus learned his trade from his father,[31] just as the Paidika tells. However, here, too, there is a reversal

---

30. See further Kaiser, "Sogenannte 'Kindheitserzählung des Thomas,'" 475–77, esp. n. 75.

31. Horn and Martens, among others, describe how in the Jewish context, the future trades of the sons "were learned at the feet of one's father" (*Let the Little Children*, 175). See also Boris Dreyer, "Ausbildung und Beruf," in *Handbuch der Erziehung und Bildung in der Antike*, ed. Johannes Christes, Richard Klein, and Christoph Lüth (Darmstadt: Wissenschaftliche Buchgesellschaft, 2006), 175.

of roles: Joseph is to make a bed, but one sidepiece is not the same length as the other. Thereupon, Jesus orders him to lay the two boards one on top of the other and to hold them fast. Then Jesus pulls the shorter board to the proper length and asks Joseph to carry out what he had planned to do. Here it is not Joseph who assumes the role of the foreman but rather Jesus. In contrast to the teacher in the first school episode, though, Joseph does not break out in lamentation over his lost honor[32] but rather praises God for having given him this child.

A second episode (ch. 11 [12]), which Aasgaard reckons as a further part of the training that Jesus receives from Joseph,[33] describes how Jesus sows grain and achieves a miraculously large harvest. Differently from the Greek tradition, the Syrian tradition does not describe this as a joint action, in which Joseph takes the seven- or eight-year-old Jesus along.[34] According to the Syriac text, Jesus, while playing alone and without Joseph nearby, sows one grain (or, depending on the manuscript, a "sea," a Syrian unit of measure equal to approximately seven liters) and from this harvests a hundredfold.[35] An indication of the originality of the Syriac is that the episode in the Greek transmission has gone through a further interpretation that indicates a revision: Joseph gives the rich harvest of grain to the poor of the village, while at the same time he retains some of Jesus's special seeds.

In sum, one can say that, in his central role as Jesus's father and teacher, Joseph cannot conform to the late antique ideal of a *paterfamilias*: the roles are reversed twice so that Joseph becomes the one instructed (the same takes place in the school episodes, where the teachers have a similar experience with Jesus). The goal of the Paidika is certainly not to portray *Joseph* as an unmanly man but rather to emphasize the special nature and greatness of *Jesus*. Joseph *must* fail within the typical role models because he has accepted, and attempts to exercise, the role of father, but Jesus does not fit into the role of a typical son. Jesus, rather, is

---

32. On the honor-shame dynamics, as they become effective in the teacher episode (ch. 7; but not in Syriac), see also Aasgaard, *Childhood of Jesus*, 106.

33. Aasgaard, *Childhood of Jesus*, 109.

34. The reference to Jesus's age stands between this episode of sowing and harvesting and the following episode about the bed, and can be applied either to the previous episode or to the following one (in my opinion, the latter is more probable).

35. The Latin text family Lm, the Old Irish tradition, and the Ethiopian transmission also let Jesus sow and harvest alone.

described as one endowed with divine power and divine knowledge. This puts Joseph in a role conflict, which he cannot solve and, indeed, which he does not even recognize as such. Like the other figures in the text who encounter Jesus, he is torn between indignation at Jesus's conduct (see, e.g., ch. 5) and, at the same time, being impressed by miraculous positive changes (ch. 12 [13]). This, however, does not lead him to a deeper knowledge about Jesus.

3. Jesus: The Masculine Child

With the exception of the pilgrimage story in Luke 2:41–52 (see below, section 4), there is little material from the later canonized gospels that the Paidika could have adopted for the portrayal of Jesus as a child. Still, the baby Jesus in Luke and Matthew already receives veneration and adoration from those who encounter him (see Luke 2:17–20, 28, 38; Matt 2:11). The Paidika takes up this aspect in several stories as an element reminiscent of a so-called Chorschluss (see 2.5; 6.2c; 9.3) and adds stories that justify the veneration through miraculous deeds done by Jesus. This adoration, however, is partly mixed with dismay (see 4.1), for, especially in the first few chapters of the Paidika, more people come to harm through Jesus's powerful, miracle-working words than have good done to them. Measured against the portrayals of the Jesus figure in the canonical gospels (which also undoubtedly unite different features in themselves), it is hardly possible to overlook in the Paidika the one-sided emphasis of a quick-witted, miracle-working Jesus who emerges as the victor in all his encounters—including miracles that produce death or injury. In contrast, the stories of the Paidika do not take up features of a Jesus who calls for forgiveness and the renunciation of status, or describe a suffering Jesus.

If one reflects on these observations under the aspect of masculinity in late antiquity, this leads to the paradoxical-sounding thesis that the boy Jesus of the Paidika is more masculine than the adult Jesus of the gospels. Several concrete textual observations confirm this.[36]

In chapter 2, Jesus forms sparrows out of clay on a Sabbath. When he is criticized for this, he lets the sparrows fly away. Instead of complying, that is, admitting to a transgression of a commandment, and even perhaps

---

36. The examples take up much of what already has been mentioned above (in section 2).

destroying the birds, he creates life. In the framework of the discourses about masculinity in antiquity, this incident shows that Jesus has put up a successful defense against public reproach. At the same time, this story expresses much more in theological terms. Jesus's action shows that he is in no way inferior to God the Creator, who first established the Sabbath as a day of rest. The child, criticized by experts of the Jewish law, stands above the Sabbath.

In chapter 3, the son of Hannas, for no recognizable reason, destroys the waterholes Jesus has built. Thereupon, Jesus publicly berates his childish adversary and punishes him with the same fate that the child himself had applied to the waterholes: he lets the child wither. Once again, Jesus successfully defends himself and proves to be the stronger one. Chapter 4 reports something similar. Another boy, running through the village, bumps into Jesus's shoulder. Jesus takes this as an attack on his person and immediately curses the boy. He is not to continue on his way! At these words of Jesus, the boy falls to the ground and dies.[37]

In chapter 5, Joseph reprimands Jesus because of the public protests against his behavior but becomes the recipient of passionate rebuttal from Jesus. The roles of father and son reverse themselves (see this in detail in section 2 above). In chapters 6–8, Jesus puts up a defense against the teacher who bores him with his teaching of things Jesus already knows, and knows better than the teacher, who also hits him. Through his clever speech, Jesus corners the teacher and makes him appear ridiculous as a teacher. The teacher finally acknowledges Jesus's superiority and complains about his public humiliation at the hands of a child (the keyword for lost honor [αἰσχύνη] is explicitly used in 7.3). The events repeat themselves with the second teacher in chapter 13 [14], although the narrative is shorter. At the end, the teacher is left behind unconscious, or dead (so in the Syrian version), in the schoolroom.

In chapter 9, Jesus is unjustly accused of having thrown his playmate Zenon from the roof. Jesus defends himself successfully against this charge by awakening Zenon to life and letting him testify to Jesus's advantage.

---

37. Stephen J. Davis reads ch. 4 of the Paidika "as an agonistic scene," where the boy Jesus conducts and defends himself in a completely understandable way. See Davis, *Christ Child: Cultural Memories of a Young Jesus* (New Haven: Yale University Press, 2014), 72–87. Davis refers exclusively to the textual version Gs, although the text is known in strikingly different transmissions (see above).

In all of these examples, Jesus successfully defends himself against attacks from others who question his reputation or his actions or judge them as unlawful and inappropriate. In all of these episodes, he gives proof of his strength over against others (men) in the public realm. This occurs above all through words, which then also become deeds, as the crowd repeatedly emphasizes with astonishment.

In his gender-oriented analysis of the Jesus figure, Aasgaard makes similar observations[38] and interprets the portrayal of the child Jesus, which, as I have shown, fits into the matrix of antique constructions of masculinity, as a gradually progressive *training* in masculinity: "Step by step, from age five to twelve, the boy Jesus makes it: he becomes a man."[39] This assessment, in my opinion, is not the whole story. It is correct that the stories about the child Jesus do not follow on each other arbitrarily but describe phases of a child's life, including the informal and formal steps in training belonging to those phases. This has already become clear in the analysis of the Joseph figure above.[40] The analysis also made clear that Jesus repeatedly reverses the roles and stands as the one who instructs and knows. Thus the stories of the Paidika describe a life path and course of training typical for boys in late antiquity. At the same time, however, it is precisely this boy whose path is described here who repeatedly reverses the typical conditions. Time and again, Jesus makes clear that he does not need advice and instruction. Jesus is portrayed not only as a child but also as divine; he is equipped with the power to create and to destroy through his words and, moreover, has insight into things far beyond the life experience of the other characters in the narrative. In these role reversals, he shows repeatedly that he knows much more than what his father and his teachers can ever show him.

There is only one aspect in which Jesus does not come up to the standard of the antique ideal of masculinity and which shows more distinctly

---

38. See Aasgaard, *Childhood of Jesus*, 104–9; on his methodological presuppositions, see above.

39. Aasgaard, *Childhood of Jesus*, 112.

40. Through Joseph, Jesus experiences the introduction into the public world that is appropriate for a boy. Joseph walks with him through the village (ch. 4); brings him to the place where he himself cannot carry out the necessary formal training, to teachers (chs. 6, 13 [14], 14 [15]); introduces him to his own trade; and finally takes him with him on the pilgrimage to Jerusalem (ch. 17 [19]). This last episode, which is taken over from Luke 2:41–52, is the only passage in the text that explicitly mentions a *religious* aspect of Jesus's education.

Aasgaard's educational idea and the necessity for a development "from boy to man" in the Jesus figure; this is Jesus's lack of self-control.[41] Especially in the first chapters of the Paidika, Jesus appears as impulsive and quick-tempered. This becomes clear, for example, in his reactions to the destruction of his waterholes (ch. 3) or to the boy who bumps into his shoulder on his way through the village (ch. 4). Aasgaard interprets this trait in the Jesus figure as one that is not compatible with "ancient masculinity standards." At the same time he determines that "such behavior was acceptable for one particular group of males, namely young males, i.e. boys."[42] They have to learn in the course of their adolescence to control not only others but also themselves. But does Jesus *learn* this according to the Paidika? Certainly, his fits of anger and his uncontrolled reactions diminish in the course of the narrative, but the text does not suggest that this might be the result of a development and increasing internal maturation. Jesus, for example, never shows a critical consciousness for his previous deeds. A conclusive judgment in this case is, for this reason, difficult.

A last point to be briefly considered concerns the boy Jesus who *plays*. He does this at the water ford after the rainstorm with clay, sticks, and water; on the flat roof of a house; with other children; and by himself. This domain of childlike play could definitely be understood according to gender-specific aspects within late antique notions and thus could also serve the (informal) preparation for the boy's later role as *paterfamilias*[43] (e.g., with short cart races, or with other competitive games). But the stories of the Paidika do *not* exploit this possibility. Jesus's play is not gender-specific, and later additions to the text do not change this, although he plays only with boys.

---

41. Aasgaard, *Childhood of Jesus*, 103.

42. Aasgaard, *Childhood of Jesus*, 106–7.

43. "Schon in der Spielphase findet in der Philosophie, die sich ausschließlich mit Knaben beschäftigt, aber auch in der Realität, wie die archäologischen Zeugnisse zeigen, eine Trennung der Geschlechter statt." ("A separation of genders appears already in the playing phase in philosophy, which concerns itself exclusively with boys, and also in reality, as archaeological witnesses show.") What Marieluise Deissmann-Merten describes here for ancient Greece continues similarly also in Roman late antiquity. See Deissmann-Merten, "Zur Sozialgeschichte des Kindes im antiken Griechenland," in *Zur Sozialgeschichte der Kindheit*, ed. Jochen Martin with Klaus Arnold (Freiburg: Alber, 1986), 299; see also Horn and Martens, *Let the Little Children*, 193.

4. Mary: The Mother on the Margin

Apart from later expansions and connections of the text with the Protoevangelium of James, Mary is given a rather marginal role in the Paidika. This is remarkable, especially in contrast to the strong emphasis given to Joseph, since the canonical gospels, especially Luke, show a clearly different position toward the importance of the characters in the narrative.

A limited presence in the narrative does not necessarily mean a lower esteem for the figure of Mary in the Paidika. In comparison with Joseph, her relationship to Jesus is clearly much less marked by conflict. In chapter 10, she sends Jesus with a jug to fetch water, and when the jug is broken because of the jostling crowd, this does not lead to a confrontation. Rather, Jesus brings the needed water home in his spread-out robe, and Mary is astonished at what has happened.

Some versions (Gs, Gd, Lt) attach here Mary's prayer to God for the preservation of the child. In addition, one textual witness (Gs) transmits Mary's fear that someone could "bewitch" (βασκαίνειν) Jesus. Aasgaard compares Mary's fear from a gender-specific point of view with Joseph's concern, who in chapter 14[15].2 prefers to have Jesus shut up in the house so that Jesus can no longer cause any more harm in public (see section 2 above). According to Aasgaard,[44] the concern of the mother for the well-being of her child is completely limited to the private sphere, which is in contrast to the concern of the father, related to the public sphere. This interpretation, however, works only with the text of Gs, which might not represent the original, and is not supported by the Syriac (or by the other Greek witnesses).

The concluding story of the twelve-year-old Jesus in the temple differs from the Lukan model as it sheds a more positive light on Mary. By not taking over Luke 2:50, the Paidika removes the stigma of nonunderstanding from the parents—and above all from Mary as the spokesperson of the family. Instead, a short dialogue between the scribes and Pharisees and Mary is inserted, in which her status as mother is emphasized and, above all, the wisdom of her child is praised.

If Mary is such a positive figure who appears to understand and accept Jesus and his significance much better than Joseph, why does the Paidika in its earliest form tell so little about her? The reason, in my opinion, is

---

44. See Aasgaard, *Childhood of Jesus*, 110.

that in a story of a boy who grows to manhood and who, in many respects, gives impressive proof of his masculinity already as a five- to seven-year-old, the mother has no decisive role. Thus, the Paidika tells a story that is to a great extent free of women but in which there are enough masculine figures against whom Jesus can compete. Especially the father, Joseph, strives honestly on behalf of the gender-specific masculine upbringing of his son but fails repeatedly because Jesus is more than just a male child. He is endowed with divine powers and wisdom and thus remains unresponsive to most of Joseph's all-too-human educational attempts.

Ways of Life in the Apocryphal Acts of the Apostles: Chastity as Autonomy?

Carmen Bernabé Ubieta

1. Introduction

Many studies on the role and place of women in early Christianity revolve around the question of a possible relationship between the rejection of marriage or the interruption of conjugal sexual relations on the one hand, and achieving more autonomy on the other. Rejection of marriage, or continence in it, is a central theme in many of the apocryphal acts, including the five oldest ones: the Acts of Paul, the Acts of Peter, the Acts of John, the Acts of Andrew, and the Acts of Thomas.[1] They were written between the middle of the second and the middle of the third century CE. Continence also appears as a theme in the later acts, such as the Acts of Philip and the Acts of Xanthippe and Polyxena.[2]

These stories belong to the literary genre of the Hellenistic novel,[3] even though their message is the opposite, as the objective of the heroines

---

1. The Acts of Paul and Thecla have circulated both as part of the Acts of Paul and independently.

2. Hans-Joseph Klauck, *The Apocryphal Acts of the Apostles: An Introduction*, trans. Brian McNeil (Waco, TX: Baylor University Press, 2008), 231–53. For a different chronology of the five great apocryphal acts, see Dennis R. MacDonald, "The Acts of Paul and the Acts of John: Which Came First?," in *Society of Biblical Literature 1992 Seminar Papers* (Atlanta: Scholars Press, 1992), 506–10; MacDonald, "The Acts of Peter and the Acts of John: Which Came First?," in *Society of Biblical Literature 1993 Seminar Papers* (Atlanta: Scholars Press, 1993), 623–26.

3. The question of genre has been and remains to be disputed. A great majority accepts the inclusion of the apocryphal acts among ancient novels, but there are also other opinions (see Klauck, *Apocryphal Acts of the Apostles*, 7–14). In her earlier work, Virginia Burrus maintained that the acts did not belong to this genre but has

in the apocryphal acts is the reverse of marriage. In these texts, women choose a life of continence after they hear the preaching of an apostle or are healed by him. This choice often means that they face opposition and suffer, sometimes even risk their lives. Nevertheless, there are important differences between these texts: neither the image of women, nor their roles, nor the function of continence in their lives is the same.

In the studies carried out during the last three decades on the lifestyles of women in the apocryphal acts, there are differing opinions regarding whether choosing continence offered women more possibilities of autonomy. These studies have also generated an interesting debate on how to use the apocryphal acts to better understand the lives of historical women, their voices, and their desires—a debate on the usefulness of these texts in reconstructing a picture of early Christian women.

Changes in epistemological perspectives and exegetical methods have also changed the assessment of the importance of the apocryphal acts. In the following, I will first briefly summarize the different phases of their research history. Then I will give some hermeneutical indications that should be taken into account when we read and analyze these texts in order to decide whether they present chastity as a means for women of gaining more autonomy. Finally, I will discuss the links between these texts and the lives of historical women.

2. From Optimism to More Nuanced Visions

In the early 1980s, a number of studies prompted a fruitful line of inquiry in discussing the presence of women in the apocryphal acts. The conclusion that emerged was that these texts present women in an extremely positive light and show that, for some groups of historical women, staying celibate offered them a degree of autonomy not open to married women.

---

later accepted their inclusion, albeit with a different purpose. See Burrus, *Chastity as Autonomy: Women in the Stories of the Apocryphal Acts*, SWR 23 (Lewiston, NY: Mellen, 1987). While the novels served to strengthen marriage and marital fidelity, the acts reject marriage and the social order it promotes. See also Virginia Burrus, "Mimicking Virgins: Colonial Ambivalence and the Ancient Romance," *Arethusa* 38 (2005): 49–88. For a different opinion, see Antonio Piñero and Gonzalo del Cerro, eds., *Hechos Apócrifos de los Apóstoles*, BAC 646 (Madrid: Biblioteca de Autores Cristianos, 2004), 1:36–44.

The first of these three pioneering studies, written by Stevan Davies and titled *The Revolt of the Widows*,[4] was based on the premise that the apocryphal acts not only bear witness to the diversity of Christian beliefs in the second century but also show that some Christian women adopted a continent lifestyle. In these stories, Davies finds an empowering intent and a form of "popular piety." His aim is to discover the social circumstances of the writers of these stories as well as those of their recipients, whom Davies calls "simple people." Through the analysis of the female characters who convert to an ascetic way of life (men appear rarely in this role), Davies offers the probable hypothesis that both the audience and authors of these texts were groups of widows and celibate women. Davies interprets the rejection of marital sex as a conscious rebellion against the wishes of husbands in the traditionally patriarchal family model, which required the wife to submit to wishes that were not her own. The significance of these choices had repercussions for the political order of the city, which is the reason the author uses the term *revolt* to designate the actions of these groups of women. In doing so, he underlines the political ramifications of an action that might seem purely domestic.

Dennis R. MacDonald, in *The Legend of the Apostle*,[5] focuses on the Acts of Paul and Thecla, relating it to what the Pastoral Epistles say regarding appropriate behavior for women in Christian society. Using theories developed in the study of folklore, MacDonald maintains that behind the Acts of Paul and Thecla lie oral legends created and told by women. This was customary in the ancient world, as demonstrated by multiple literary testimonies of the time. Women transmitted and used these oral accounts to legitimize their own position with the authority of Paul. According to MacDonald, the author of the Pastoral Epistles knew these tales and wrote the letters in the name of Paul to contradict their message and their impact by interpreting the apostolic memory and tradition in a significantly more traditional way regarding the social and community role of women.

---

4. Stevan L. Davies, *The Revolt of the Widows: The Social World of the Apocryphal Acts* (Carbondale: Southern Illinois University Press, 1980). To be exact, the topic was discussed briefly a little earlier by Ross S. Kraemer, "The Conversion of Women to Ascetic Forms of Christianity," *Signs* 6 (1980): 298–307; Elisabeth Schüssler Fiorenza, *In Memory of Her: A Feminist Reconstruction of Christian Origins* (New York: Crossroad, 1983), 173–75.

5. Dennis R. MacDonald, *The Legend and the Apostle: The Battle for Paul in Story and Canon* (Philadelphia: Westminster, 1983).

Virginia Burrus, in her work *Chastity as Autonomy*, identifies in the apocryphal acts what she calls "chastity stories," whose origin she finds, following MacDonald, in the oral traditions passed down from woman to woman. Unlike Davies, Burrus does not claim female authorship of these tales (though she does concede that this could have been the case in the oral phase), but she does confirm that they represent a female point of view. Even though she acknowledges the difficulties pertaining to their historical evaluation, Burrus believes that these stories offer glimpses to the ancient world from a feminine perspective.[6] In order to understand what these stories may tell us, Virginia Burrus uses social scientific models to analyze the social and psychological factors that these stories reflect. She believes that in so doing she can better understand the context of the lives and struggles of the women, correcting certain androcentric portraits of female chastity in the early church. Following Ross Kraemer,[7] Burrus believes that the continent lifestyle offered women greater freedom and autonomy. She has developed and nuanced this idea in her later works, in which she is much more cautious about the possibility of accessing the lives of these historical women via text.[8] This caution has a great deal to do with the criticism these studies received in the middle of the 1990s due to a change in epistemological perspective.

However, the first criticisms that these works received in the early 1990s were not due to this change in epistemological perspective but rather from diverse ideological positions. Some scholars, without having fully considered their own positions, criticized the results and proposals of these studies for imposing a modern feminist ideology on the texts rather than keeping with an objective analysis.[9] However, the most

---

6. Burrus, *Chastity as Autonomy*, 3. This work is developed from her master's thesis. A little earlier she had presented her position in Virginia Burrus, "Women in Apocryphal Acts," *Semeia* 38 (1986): 101–17.

7. See Kraemer, "Conversion of Women."

8. Virginia Burrus, "Word and Flesh: The Bodies and Sexuality of Ascetic Women in Christian Antiquity," *JFSR* 10 (1994): 27–51; Burrus, "Mimicking Virgins." In the latter she analyzes the Acts of Paul and Thecla from the perspectives offered by postcolonial criticism and hybridity to show how this text, similarly to Hellenistic novels, uses irony and reverses readers' expectations to criticize established standards and to propose alternative ones.

9. Peter W. Dunn, "Women's Liberation, the Acts of Paul, and Other Apocryphal Acts of the Apostles: A Review of Some Recent Interpreters," *Apocrypha* 4 (1994): 245–61. See also Lynne C. Boughton, "From Pious Legend to Feminist Fantasy: Dis-

important criticism of studies on the apocryphal acts were not written until the mid-1990s.[10]

Some scholars strongly questioned the optimism of these three earlier works: (1) they doubted whether the feminine image the texts transmitted was actually as positive as maintained by them; (2) they questioned whether chastity actually meant autonomy and thus whether the texts had a liberating function for women; (3) they criticized that the studies conducted had been blind to the varying situations of women (slaves, married women, foreign women); and (4) they questioned the possibility of accessing the lives of historical women through texts.[11]

The origin of this criticism and its skepticism was in the so-called linguistic turn,[12] a philosophical change that affected all historical studies because it questioned whether a text could directly access reality and underlined the ability of language to construct and give shape to reality.[13]

---

tinguishing Hagiographical License from Apostolic Practice in the Acts of Paul/Acts of Thecla," *JR* 71 (1991): 362–83. There some of the topics the author discusses would need greater precision. See Esther Yue L. Ng, "Acts of Paul and Thecla: Women's Stories and Precedent?," *JTS* NS 55 (2004): 1–29. Shelly Matthews criticizes accurately these and other scholars who claim that a feminist perspective invalidates historical studies, whereas they consider themselves as representing an "objective" position. See Matthews, "Thinking of Thecla: Issues in Feminist Historiography," *JFSR* 17 (2001): 39–55, esp. 43–46.

10. Anna Rebecca Solevåg, *Birthing Salvation: Gender and Class in Early Christian Childbearing Discourse*, BibInt 121 (Leiden: Brill, 2013), 11–41; Stephen J. Davis, "From Women's Piety to Male Devotion: Gender Studies, the *Acts of Paul and Thecla*, and the Evidence of an Arabic Manuscript," *HTR* 108 (2015): 579–93.

11. Part of the criticism has concentrated on the failure to take into account the intersection of such analytical variables as gender and class, particularly in the accounts where autonomy is achieved at the cost of other women (e.g., Acts Andr. 17–22.)

12. In early Christian studies, this epistemological change meant questioning the possibility to get access to the social reality behind texts through studying the texts. The historical-critical sensitivity and methodology lost its central position and gave way to literary criticism, discourse theory, and gender studies. In the case of feminist historical studies, this change cast doubt on the possibility of learning about the historical reality of the women who appear in the texts.

13. Kate Cooper, *The Virgin and the Bride: Idealized Womanhood in Late Antiquity* (Cambridge: Harvard University Press, 1999); Elisabeth A. Clark, "The Lady Vanishes: Dilemmas of a Feminist Historian after the 'Linguistic Turn,'" *CH* 67 (1998): 1–32; Elizabeth Castelli, "Heteroglossia, Hermeneutics, and History: A Review Essay of Recent Feminist Studies of Early Christianity," *JFSR* 10 (1994): 73–98.

Not all scholars gave up the claim to know and say something about historical women behind the texts, even if it had to be done indirectly, using comparative references to other sources and contexts. This less skeptical position was more common among scholars with biblical training than among those with predominantly historical training. This is not surprising, given that historical criticism of biblical texts had been conducted for over a century and biblical studies had left behind the frustrating period that had focused on the immanence of texts. On the other hand, a new feminist sensibility criticized the reading of these texts for being excessively dualistic and one-sided in addressing only women and their experiences, without taking into account other differences, such as race, religion, class, or sexual orientation.[14]

Today the less skeptical line of study regarding the relationship between narrative and history is again affirmed. Without denying the possibility of reconstructing the lives of historical women (though not necessarily as real people), the recent contributions from the perspectives of discourse theory and gender studies, including the criticisms of so-called third-wave feminism and its awareness of difference, have undoubtedly enriched and facilitated a better understanding of these texts.

3. Hermeneutical Principles

3.1. Physical Body, Social Body, Ideological Body

The human body has the capacity both to express and to reflect sociocultural aspects and to be modeled by them (that is, by ideals, norms, or prohibitions). It also has the ability to express countercultural objections and the ideas of individuals and groups. "The external world, including the

---

14. Some authors have accepted the expression "third-wave feminism" (Rebecca Walker) as an umbrella term for this critique. See Solevåg, *Birthing Salvation*, 11–41; Outi Lehtipuu, "The Example of Thecla and the Example(s) of Paul: Disputing Women's Role in Early Christianity," in *Women and Gender in Ancient Religions: Interdisciplinary Approaches,* ed. Stephen P. Ahearne-Kroll, Paul A. Holloway, and James A. Kelhoffer, WUNT 263 (Tübingen: Mohr Siebeck, 2010), 349–78; Margaret Y. MacDonald, "Women as Agents of Expansion," in *A Woman's Place: House Churches in Earliest Christianity,* ed. Carolyn Osiek and Margaret Y. MacDonald with Janet H. Tulloch (Minneapolis: Fortress, 2006), 220–43.

human body, is not a given, but an historical reality constantly mediated by human labour and interpreted through human culture."[15]

Anthropologist Mary Douglas speaks of the physical body as a natural symbol, as a microcosm of the social body, the place where ideals, fears, and social norms that define physical bodies are reflected.[16] Bodies can also be thought of as texts where the script of the group's worldview is inscribed or written, or as a territory that is constructed and ordered according to norms, prohibitions, and symbolic limits.[17]

The action of the social body on the physical body calls for a third body—the ideological body, which is made up of the philosophical or theological ideas that create and sustain the worldview of that group. Cultural rules on the body manifest the values of this culture or group,[18] its idea of the world, and the place that each person occupies within it. This ideological body is usually that of the hegemonic discourse, but alternative discourses may justify different social practices and different treatments of the body.[19] The apocryphal acts reflect the variety of different, sometimes conflicting positions concerning the physical body.

Women's bodies are central to the discourses through which the stories of the apocryphal acts affected the social dynamics of early Christianity.[20] The spatial metaphor allows us to see the extent to which women's bodies

---

15. Bryan S. Turner, *The Body and Society: Explorations in Social Theory* (London: Sage, 1996), 34.

16. Despite the criticism it has received, this theory is by and large acceptable. Mary Douglas, *Natural Symbols: Explorations in Cosmology* (London: Cresset, 1970); Douglas, *Purity and Danger: An Analysis of Concepts of Pollution and Taboo* (London: Routledge, 1966); Douglas, *Implicit Meanings: Selected Essays in Anthropology* (London: Routledge, 1975).

17. This image is taken from the study of territoriality, which examines how a person or a group can control, configure, or influence people, phenomena, or relationships by delimiting a certain geographical area and by giving it a concrete shape. See Robert D. Sack, *Human Territoriality: Its Theory and History*, CSHG 7 (Cambridge: Cambridge University Press, 1986), 19. It is also possible to speak of a political body because societies tend to reproduce and socialize the type of body they need. See Jennifer A. Glancy, *Corporal Knowledge: Early Christian Bodies* (New York: Oxford University Press, 2010). She cites Michel Foucault and Pierre Bourdieu as fundamental authors on this subject.

18. Jon L. Berquist, *Controlling Corporeality: The Body and the Household in Ancient Israel* (New Brunswick, NJ: Rutgers University Press, 2002), 5.

19. Berquist, *Controlling Corporeality*, 10.

20. Glancy, *Corporal Knowledge*.

are presented as a symbolic territory, organized according to the norms and criteria born of the group's philosophical or religious worldview. We can also see that women's bodies are a disputed territory, in which various ideas, ideologies, and power struggles are visible. Throughout history, the physical body, especially that of women, has been defined and controlled by male-influenced philosophical, religious, and medical discourses. Therefore, it is interesting to examine whether there are groups with alternative visions on the body of women, with different ways of defining it and treating it, and whether they open new possibilities for women—without forgetting to consider whether women themselves respond in some way or construct some kind of discourse.

3.2. Feminine Virtues, Gendered Virtues

In the apocryphal acts, a series of virtues appear that need to be properly contextualized within the society where relationships operated in two areas, within the family and in the polis, and where each gender had one of the two as its natural place. Along with this, certain virtues were associated—in view of the common good, which was equated with and maintained by this male order. Whether a person met these expectations or not determined whether they were respected and honored by those around them.[21] The virtues that were expected and demanded from respectable women had to do with the functions by which their identity was defined, namely, the role of wife and mother. Therefore, sexual loyalty and proper behavior (modesty, humility) were what was expected of them, but not much more. In the apocryphal acts, various terms refer to female sexual behavior:[22]

1. Ἁγνεία, translated as chastity and sometimes purity (Acts Andr. 39 (7); 14.2; 48.8; Acts John 9; 2; 27), is a virtue that reinforces the

---

21. Aristotle goes so far as to say that the greatest virtues are those that are most useful to others. Therefore, justice and courage come first (see *Rhet.* 1366b). Text and English translation in Aristotle, *The "Art" of Rhetoric*, trans. John H. Freese, LCL (Cambridge: Harvard University Press, 1926), 1.9.5–13.

22. See Joy L. Lapp, "Chaste Women: Characterization in the Apocryphal Acts of the Apostles and Greek Romance Novels" (PhD diss., University of Denver/Iliff School of Theology, 2002), 4–6.

institution of marriage and the family and, with it, the order of the polis.

2. Σωφροσύνη designates the moderation of desires and behavior as well as restraint and decency expected from a woman (Acts Andr. 14.2; 23.2). In the apocryphal acts, the term sometimes stands for sexual abstinence.[23] Occasionally, men used it to praise certain women, since the term indicated a capacity for moderation and self-control, and these were attributes normally denied as characteristics of female nature. According to Aristotle, "Virtues and actions are nobler, when they proceed from those who are naturally worthier, for instance, from a man rather than from a woman" (*Rhet.* 1.1366b [Freese]).[24]

3. Ἐγκράτεια and παρθενία. The women in the apocryphal acts do not actually choose chastity (which would imply moderate and regular sexual activity within marriage), but rather the total abstinence from sex both within and without marriage, which is better described as ἐγκράτεια (self-control) and παρθενία (virginity).

Virginia Burrus sees a certain irony in this presentation of feminine virtues. Given that the patriarchal marriage system requires chastity only from women, undertaking ἐγκράτεια, a male virtue, results in a subversion of the system and offers women greater autonomy (αὐτάρκεια). For this reason, Burrus chose to use the term *chastity*, despite recognizing that it is not quite exact.[25] We will next move to examine whether the practice

---

23. In Acts Andr. 14, Maximilla prays to God to help her stay σώφρονα, referring to sexual abstinence. Just a little earlier in the text, her husband praises that her restraint (σωφροσύνη), meaning her chastity and sexual loyalty, give him peace of mind.

24. Weakness of body and weakness of character were associated with the woman. Her own place was inside the house, and she needed the guidance of the man and his reason. When Aristotle lists the components of virtue, namely, justice (δικαιοσύνη), courage (ἀνδρεία), self-control (σωφροσύνη), magnificence (μεγαλοπρέπεια), magnanimity (μεγαλοψυχία), liberality (ἐλευθεριότης), gentleness (πραότης), practical wisdom (φρόνησις), and speculative wisdom (σοφία), he speaks of male virtues, seen from the perspective of his activity in the polis. If some of these features were recognized in a woman, the rarity would not go without notice, and she would be compared to men.

25. Virginia Burrus prefers the term *chastity*, since it best reflects the irony she detects in the text. "In this work, the term chastity will generally be used to denote

of ἐγκράτεια or παρθενία allows these women to exercise a greater degree of autonomy (αὐτάρκεια) or whether a careful analysis of the texts forces to qualify this belief.

3.3. Rhetorical Framework of the Apocryphal Acts

When analyzing the apocryphal acts to find answers to these questions, it is necessary to take into account several aspects of the "rhetorical structure of the argument that the stories develop." Elisa Estévez summarizes them as follows: (1) gender and social position are interrelated; (2) the main objective of these texts is to exalt the apostle, who appears as a mediator of the divine power manifested in wonders, healings, and resurrections; (3) the claim to create an alternative social order to empire is reflected in the treatment of the body, sexuality, and the construction of gender; (4) despite the proximity to the literary genre of ancient novel, the objective of the apocryphal acts is not so much to entertain as to convert and spread the gospel.[26]

4. Women in the Apocryphal Acts of the Apostles

A narrative analysis offers several clues that can be used to examine how the characters in these stories are constructed. The manner in which they are presented and the manner in which they relate to others are two fundamental aspects in this analysis. The former takes into account how the characters are described, how they speak, think, and act. The latter addresses

---

women's abstinence from sexual relations, *not* their abstinence from extra-marital sexual relations alone. Despite the confusion which may result from this slightly unconventional use of the word 'chastity' ('continence' or 'celibacy', for example, might have been less ambiguous), I have chosen it for its power to evoke stereotypes of 'womanly virtue.' Chastity … enables the women in the stories of apocryphal Acts to break out of their marriages. From the point of view of patriarchal marriage, 'chastity' is thus subverted. It becomes a means not to women's restriction or subjugation but to women's autonomy" (Burrus, *Chastity as Autonomy*, 4 n. 4).

26. Elisa Estévez López, "Breaking or Submitting? Male Control of Female Body in the Apocryphal Acts," in *Geschlechterverhältnisse und Macht: Lebensformen in der Zeit des frühen Christentums*, ed. Irmtraud Fischer and Christoph Heil, EUZ 21 (Berlin: LIT, 2010), 137–41.

the ways in which their relations to others are described, how they are compared to other people, and whether there are conflicting expectations.[27]

Among these aspects, Joy Louise Lapp chose three for the part of her study that has to do with the presentation of women in the apocryphal acts and especially the question of whether choosing celibacy offered them a greater personal autonomy and freedom of action.[28] The three aspects are character description, the actions they undertake, and their comparison with other people, particularly men (among whom the apostle occupies a prominent place).

The analysis of the stories and the most striking features of their portrayals of women that follows here will start with the oldest and most original one: the Acts of Paul and Thecla. Other apocryphal acts will be presented in a chronological order that is not the most commonly held but defended by some scholars:[29] Acts of Paul and Thecla, Acts of Peter, Acts of John, Acts of Andrew, and Acts of Thomas. One reason for this choice is the intertextual links that are evident in some of these works. In all likelihood, their aim is to interpret the female figure and her role in the Acts of Paul and Thecla in a more restrictive and domesticated fashion.

4.1. Thecla and Her Transformation to Religious Authority and Autonomy

Thecla is introduced at the beginning of the story as a young woman, promised to Thamyris, an important citizen of the city of Iconium. When Thecla hears Paul's preaching, she begins her transformation. Contrary to what was expected from a young fiancée, she obeys neither her mother nor her future husband, refuses to marry, and is determined to follow Paul despite his doubts about her perseverance and endurance. Thecla remains self-confident and adheres to a way of life that causes her to leave her home and city and to ignore social conventions and expectations that her family and the whole city place on her as a woman.

---

27. Robert Alter, *The Art of Biblical Narrative* (New York: Basic Books, 1981), 114–30; Shimon Bar-Efrat, *Narrative Art in the Bible*, JSOTSup 70 (Sheffield: Almond, 1989); Adele Berlin, *Poetics and Interpretation of Biblical Narrative*, BLS 9 (Sheffield: Almond, 1983).

28. Lapp, *Chaste Women*.

29. MacDonald, "Acts of Paul"; MacDonald, "Acts of Peter." For a more nuanced view, see Judith B. Perkins, "The Acts of Peter as Intertext: Response to Dennis MacDonald," in *Society of Biblical Literature 1993 Seminar Papers*, 627–33.

The resistance of her mother, who would rather see her dead than following Paul, leads Thecla to leave her home, although she finds a new family (that of the widow Trypheaena), with whom she shares her new faith and life. The decision to travel leads her to cut her hair and dress as a man,[30] to face dangers, to be convicted, even to face death in animal battles in the arena, and to confess her faith. The narrative portrays her as determined, steadfast, courageous, energetic, verbose and increasingly independent of Paul. When she meets him again, she has already earned religious authority and has baptized herself. She has preached and taught, and knows what she is about to do. Before Paul tells her to "go and teach" (ch. 48), she has already announced her decision to go to Iconium (ch. 41), and it goes without saying that she will preach, teach, and enlighten many (ch. 43), as she has already done in Tryphaena's house.

Paul's role diminishes as Thecla's increases until she becomes the main character in this part of the Acts of Paul, which seem to have been distributed separately. She has gone from a conventional virgin to a celibate servant of God, a Christian teacher with authority.[31] For Thecla, renouncing marriage and celibacy brings her greater autonomy.

4.2. The Daughter of Peter: A Virgin's Body, Sick and Mute for the Salvation of Men

The Acts of Peter begins with a tale of Peter's virgin daughter, whose name is never mentioned. She does not act herself but remains an object of other people's actions. She does not choose her virginity nor celibacy; it is her father who imposes it on her. He prefers to have her forever ill and paralyzed in order not to provide temptation for men with a free and healthy body. This was the case with a certain Ptolemy who tried to rape her. As Estévez says, this woman "is seen only as a body and a virgin, capable of

---

30. The meaning and purpose of these gestures are debated. In my opinion, the reason for the haircut and dressing up as a male was to make the journey easier and safer. The same was done by female travelers in the nineteenth century. For this topic, see Julia L. Welch, "Cross-Dressing and Cross-Purposes: Gender Possibilities in the Acts of Thecla," in *Gender Reversals and Gender Cultures: Anthropological and Historical Perspectives*, ed. Sabrina P. Ramet (London: Routledge, 1996), 66–78; Stephen J. Davis, "Crossed Texts, Crossed Sex: Intertextuality and Gender in Early Christian Legends of Holy Women Disguised as Men," *JECS* 10 (2002): 1–36.

31. See the detailed analysis in Lapp, *Chaste Women*, 32–42.

tempting and damaging men. Her body suffers the punishment of having been wanted by another."[32] While her attacker regains the "health of his soul" on witnessing a miracle, she is left damaged forever. Her purity remains intact, at the cost of her health; her inability to move and her inability to speak for herself at the cost of her autonomy. She neither acts nor decides—it is all done for her.

A similar story about the virgin daughter of a gardener follows. At the request of her father, Peter prays to God to grant her what is useful for her soul—whereupon God grants her death (Acts Pet. 2). When the father complains about this, Peter resurrects her, and she runs off with a guest of the house. Again, the body of a young healthy woman is portrayed as dangerous and an opportunity for seduction and sin for men. This story shows the negative consequences of the autonomy that Peter's daughter was denied and thus confirms its message.

The story of Peter's daughter offers a model of silence, passivity, obedience, and quiet suffering for Christian women.[33] The (possibly encratite) group to whom the text was produced radicalized certain cultural ideas surrounding the weak, irrational, seductive, and seducible nature of women. These ideas were present in the collective imagination, which legitimized treating women as subordinate and in need of male guidance. While the message of the story is on the one hand that only God knows what is best for humanity,[34] on the other hand it underlines that it is men, the patriarchs, who are designed to interpret God's word and ensure that it is done.

At the end of the Acts of Peter, known as Martyrdom, the sense of the story changes but, contrary to what one might expect, not the perception of the role of women. It again takes up the concept of ἁγνεία ("chastity" or "purity")[35] when, thanks to Peter's preaching on chastity, four concubines of Agrippa (Agrippina, Nicaria, Euphemia, and Doris) decide to follow the teachings of the apostle and abandon the royal bed (ch. 33). The same is done by Xanthippe, the wife of Albinus, a friend of Agrippa, and by many other women and their husbands (ch. 34). These actions cause a

---

32. Elisa Estévez López, "Identidades y (de)construcciones socio-religiosas en los relatos de curación de los Hechos Apócrifos de Pedro, Juan, Pablo y Tecla," *EstBib* 62 (2004): 211.
33. Estévez, "Identidades y (de)construcciones socio-religiosas," 213.
34. Piñero and del Cerro, *Hechos Apócrifos*, 1:490.
35. Piñero and del Cerro, *Hechos Apócrifos*, 1:651–52.

great upheaval in Rome and lead to Peter's denunciation before Agrippa, who condemns him to the cross. These women are portrayed as if they are freely choosing a continent life, rejecting sexual relations with the king or with a husband. However, in spite of their independent actions, they do not speak, nor set out their reasoning, nor do they influence the further course of the story, which soon forgets them. They are quite different from Thecla, who grows in stature as the story unfolds.[36] For these women, abstinence does not bring autonomy.

4.3. Drusiana: Silent Chastity and Self-Punitive Self-Denial

The Acts of John introduces two married women: Cleopatra and Drusiana. The first is the wife of Lycomedes, who is able to bring her husband back to life after John has healed her. However, this action is not a sign of autonomy, authority, or power, because it is John who takes her by the hand and leads her when she raises her husband. In reality, the miracle simply highlights the importance of the apostle John, who is presented as a holy man, mediator of the healing power of God. The promise to all disciples in Mark 16:17–18 is in the Acts of John manifest in John, who is portrayed as a necessary agent of God's salvation.[37] The story does not say that Cleopatra and Lycomedes opt for a chaste marriage,[38] as is the case with the marriage of Drusiana and her husband, Andronicus. In this marriage, it is the woman who overcomes the resistance of the husband, who has gone so far as to enclose her in a tomb.[39]

Drusiana appears as a determined, courageous, and independent woman when it comes to choosing an abstinent lifestyle, renouncing sexual relations with her husband and opposing him. However, she does not display the same determination and bravery toward her harasser, Callimachus, but directs his violence and guilt toward herself and inflicts a kind of self-imposed martyrdom that ends with his

---

36. Lapp, *Chaste Women*, 65.

37. See Estévez López, "Breaking or Submitting?," 145.

38. Perhaps John's words can be interpreted in this sense, although this is not certain: "The colours which I bid you use … the whole range of colours, which … mutilates your abdomen" (Acts John 29.2). English translation in John K. Elliott, *The Apocryphal New Testament: A Collection of Apocryphal Christian Literature in an English Translation* (Oxford: Clarendon, 1993), 314.

39. The text is fragmentary. Its construction is based on later allusions.

conversion (chs. 76–78).⁴⁰ Just as in the case of Peter's daughter, the community receives an example of a woman's self-denial and destruction, which leads to the conversion and salvation of evildoers. The same does not happen in stories about men. Drusiana is portrayed as an object of male action, while her personal performance is much more limited than theirs.

Jan Bremmer finds the portrayals of women in the Acts of John more positive but admits that there is a big difference between elite women and the rest (e.g., widows).⁴¹ In my opinion, however, the presentation of these women is not really positive. It is true that Cleopatra is presented and defined according to typically masculine characteristics, such as moderation and self-control (the opposite is said of her husband), but this has no consequences in terms of autonomy, freedom of choice, or decision making. The only decision Drusiana makes is to choose continence against her husband's will. No further mention is made of any other autonomous actions. I agree with Bremmer that the protagonists are presented in a way that allows readers, possibly elite women, to identify with them. The text offers a model of women who, like Thecla in the Acts of Paul and Thecla, can opt for abstinence, but without the same consequences for their personal autonomy, authority, teaching, or preaching.

4.4. Maximilla: Chastity in the Apostolic Surveillance

The broad strokes of this story are very similar: an upper-class woman, healed by Andrew, converts to faith and a chaste life, abandoning sexual relations with her husband. She goes so far as to pray to God, "Rescue me at last from Aegeates' filthy intercourse and keep me pure and chaste [καθαρὰν καὶ σώφρονα]" (Acts Andr. 14.2).⁴² The text presents Aegeates as a loving and caring spouse who praises his wife's behavior (σωφροσύνη), which he calls a relief for him. Maximilla, for her part, is portrayed as

---

40. Lapp, *Chaste Women*, 236.
41. Jan N. Bremmer, "Drusiana, Cleopatra and Some Other Women in the Acts of John," in *A Feminist Companion to the New Testament Apocrypha*, ed. Amy-Jill Levine with Maria Mayo Robbins, FCNTECW 11 (London: T&T Clark, 2006), 77–87; Bremmer, "Women in the Apocryphal Acts of John," in *The Apocryphal Acts of John*, ed. Jan N. Bremmer (Kampen: Kok Pharos, 1995), 37–56.
42. Jean-Marc Prieur, *Acta Andreae*, CCSA 5 (Turnhout: Brepols, 1989), 461; trans. Elliott, *Apocryphal New Testament*, 249.

a woman of great initiative, with power to act and control her sexuality. Because she is strong enough to resist desires, she is described as having reversed the fall of Eve. Andrew calls her for help and addresses her as ἀνήρ and ἄνθρωπος. The use of these terms seems to support the idea of seeing Maximilla as a male woman or the "perfect man."[43] She has overcome her femininity, considered inferior and sinful, and, unlike her husband, she is able to control her passions and desires, associated with a manly man. This resembles the model of Thecla, but it is reinterpreted in a way that gradually loses the independence and autonomy so characteristic of Thecla.

Nonetheless, the message that this woman conveys is ambiguous because her autonomy is reduced by her constant dependence on the apostle, whom she asks for help and advice. She passes from the guardianship of a husband to the guardianship of the apostle.[44]

The Acts of Andrew presents only upper-class women as those who choose an abstinent lifestyle. The bodies of slave women pose no problem in this context. They can be used as instruments in obtaining the purity of the highborn woman, as happens in the case of Euclia.

4.5. Mygdonia: From the Obedient Wife of Charisius to the Obedient Wife of Jesus

The Acts of Thomas portrays Mygdonia as a beautiful wife of an important man. She converts to the message of the apostle Judas Thomas and renounces sexual relations with her husband, who is repeatedly said to be close with the king (chs. 82, 87, 93, 102) and whose position and wealth are underlined. The text presents Mygdonia as highly determined and strong. She has courage to challenge the expectations of her surroundings and the desires of her powerful husband, who imprisons the apostle. She defies her husband and bribes the jailer to visit Thomas in prison. This gesture is a reminiscence of Thecla, as is also the cutting of her hair. However, her autonomy is far from that of Thecla's, since Mygdonia remains submissive to the apostle, obeying his wishes and throwing herself at his feet. Mygdonia too moves from the authority of her husband to the authority of the apostle. Her gender role seems very traditional, even though her rejecting power and wealth holds some sociocritical potential.

---

43. See Kerstin Aspegren, *The Male Woman: A Feminine Ideal in the Early Church* (Stockholm: Almqvist & Wiksell International, 1990), 125–29.

44. Estévez, "Breaking or Submissing?"; see also Lapp, *Chaste Women*, 95.

In conclusion, the only independent act committed by the women in the apocryphal acts is choosing continent life and rejecting the sexual desire of their husbands. This, however, does not grant them autonomy.[45] Thecla is an exception. She achieves an independent life free from men, including the apostle Paul, and travels, teaches, and exercises authority.

5. The Apocryphal Acts and Historical Women

I have already alluded to the question of the relation between historical women and the women in the apocryphal acts, as well as to the loss of interest in research in this question and the conviction that it is not possible to access the lives of early Christian women. However, unlike Kate Cooper, I see good reasons to assume that the women who appear in these and similar texts were not mere conceptual tools used to discuss male issues.[46] Behind these stories hide conflicts related to attitudes, desires, and behavior of real and historical women that an elite group of men considered improper or dangerous—according to the standards that they themselves had established and maintained. This is reflected in the Greco-Roman literature of the time and in the early Christian writings that allude to groups of women who behaved in ways considered inappropriate. Many scholars think that it is an exaggeration to say that the apocryphal acts do not allude to the lives of women of this time. With Margaret MacDonald, I believe that, judging by the diverse testimonies from Christian and non-Christian sources, the behavior of women was an important aspect of the social order, and it became problematic.[47] Apparently, the elites of the empire, at least at certain times and in certain places, viewed the Christian position in this regard as a challenge to the ruling order, as the criticism

---

45. Lapp, *Chaste Women*, 235, 243.

46. Shelly Matthews criticizes Cooper correctly, showing that both her work and that of Peter Brown, on which she builds, depend on Claude Levi-Strauss, who was first to use the expression "use women to think with" (see Matthews, "Thinking of Thecla," 46–51). However, both of them forget part of Levi-Strauss's argument. He maintains that women are also producers of signs and cannot be reduced to "symbols of tokens." Similarly, Ross S. Kraemer, *Unreliable Witnesses: Religion, Gender, and History in the Greco-Roman Mediterranean* (Oxford: Oxford University Press, 2011), 117–52.

47. Margaret Y. MacDonald, *Early Christian Women and Pagan Opinion: The Power of the Hysterical Woman* (Cambridge: Cambridge University Press, 1996).

of non-Christian writers such as Celsus or Apuleius and the polemics of Christian authors such as Tertullian show (see Tertullian, *Bapt.* 17.4–5).

Texts give insight into the reality their authors want to influence but also into the reality in which these authors lived and wrote. This reality becomes present through the explicit and implicit allusions to the values and cultural schemes in which the authors have been socialized and from which they interpret and express reality, and the often-implicit or incidental allusions to the situations and problems they encounter. Therefore, it is possible to reconstruct the reality behind texts to a certain degree.[48]

When these stories are read critically in their context and in relation to each other and to other texts of the same period, it is possible to get a glimpse of the situation of some women—their interests, complaints, and transgressions. We can also see the reactions they provoked in men, the measures they took, and the arguments they used to justify these measures. As we have seen, the intertextual links in some of these texts seems to exist in order to modify earlier traditions, undoubtedly due to the repercussions they had, manifested, among others, in the abovementioned testimony of Tertullian (late second century). It allows us to conclude that certain groups of women used texts and traditions, such as that of Thecla, with which they identified and which legitimized their claim for a greater role for women in the church.

The same tradition continued to be used by advocates as well as opponents of female autonomy and participation. In the centuries that followed, Thecla's example was softened (1) by additions and reinterpretations of her life, as in Life and Miracles of Saint Thecla,[49] an expanded version of the Acts of Thecla; and (2) by writing other apocryphal acts that implicitly refer to her example but interpret it in a more conventional way, as in the Acts of Xanthippe and Polyxena (fourth century). According to Jill C. Gorman, this text revises Thecla's story to propose a model of submission

---

[48]. Adriana Destro and Mauro Pesce, "Dentro e fuori le case: Mutamenti del ruolo delle donne dal movimento di Gesù alle prime chiese," in *I Vangeli, narrazioni e storia*, ed. Mercedes Navarro Puerto and Marinella Perroni (Trapani: Il Pozzo di Giacobbe, 2011), 290–309.

[49]. Stephen J. Davis, *The Cult of Saint Thecla: A Tradition of Women's Piety in Late Antiquity* (Oxford: Oxford University Press, 2001). For a more nuanced discussion of Thecla's domestication, see Susan E. Hylen, "The 'Domestication' of Saint Thecla: Characterization of Thecla in the *Life and Miracles of Saint Thecla*," *JFSR* 30 (2014): 5–21.

for women, to create a new ideal of Christian marriage for their audience, and to propagate a new model of female asceticism.[50] Fasting, which had become a "source of female empowerment," was condemned, and women were only allowed to teach other women (in line with Did. Apost. 25 and precisely when, in the fourth century, Pricillianist women maintained the practice of feminine teaching). Female travelers were seen as a temptation, and men and women were advised to travel separately. It should not be forgotten that there was a sanctuary dedicated to Thecla (Hagia Thecla) in Seleucia, where ascetics of both genders kept her memory alive. Egeria tells in her diary at the end of the fourth century that she visited this place as part of her pilgrimage to the holy places.

It is not possible to confirm on the basis of the apocryphal acts that chastity or continence gave women greater autonomy, participation, and authority within the ecclesial community, since there were several factors in play. Nevertheless, when we read these texts in context, they offer us a window into the struggles of women to obtain autonomy and the barriers the social and ideological body tried to put in their way.

---

50. Jill C. Gorman, "Reading and Theorizing Women's Sexuality: The Representation of Women in the Acts of Xanthippe and Polixena" (PhD diss., Temple University, 2003).

Apostolic Authority in the Acts of Thecla

Outi Lehtipuu

The Acts of Thecla is one of the few ancient texts that features a female figure as its protagonist.[1] According to the manuscript evidence, the narrative circulated both independently and as part of the larger Acts of Paul. The surviving manuscripts attest to the wide popularity of the narrative: in addition to the nearly fifty Greek manuscripts, there are early translations into Coptic, Latin, Syriac, Armenian, Slavonic, Arabic, and Geʻez.[2] Moreover, several ancient writers allude to Thecla, mostly in praise and admiration, and her cult was widespread.[3]

While the Acts of Thecla has been studied intensively, particularly in the past forty years, scholarship remains divided on what the text reveals about the role of women in early Christianity, with conclusions that variously see "chastity as autonomy" as a running theme or dismiss the work as "feminist fantasy."[4] This range in scholarly interpretation derives partly

---

1. While the text is often referred to as the Acts of Paul and Thecla, the narrative circulated under various titles, most of which only speak of Thecla (e.g., the Martyrdom of Saint Thecla). See Anne Jensen, *God's Self-Confident Daughters: Early Christianity and the Liberation of Women* (Louisville: John Knox, 1992), 82; Glenn E. Snyder, *Acts of Paul: The Formation of a Pauline Corpus*, WUNT 2/352 (Tübingen: Mohr Siebeck, 2013), 103. Here I refer to the text as the Acts of Thecla, both to appreciate her leading role in the narrative and for the sake of brevity.

2. See Maurice Geerard, *Clavis apocryphorum Novi Testamenti*, CCSA (Turnhout: Brepols, 1992), 117–26.

3. See Susan E. Hylen, *A Modest Apostle: Thecla and the History of Women in the Early Church* (Oxford: Oxford University Press, 2015), 91–113; Snyder, *Acts of Paul*, 101–5; Stephen J. Davis, *The Cult of Saint Thecla: A Tradition of Women's Piety in Late Antiquity* (Oxford: Oxford University Press, 2001); Monika Pesthy, "Thecla among the Fathers of the Church," in *The Apocryphal Acts of Paul and Thecla*, ed. Jan N. Bremmer (Kampen: Kok Pharos, 1996), 164–78.

4. For a brief summary of the research history on the Acts of Thecla, see Carmen

from the ambiguity surrounding the figure of Thecla, allowing for different readings in both ancient and modern contexts.[5] That the protagonist of the narrative is a woman has prompted speculations about female authorship of the text, but there are hardly any features in the text that would securely identify the gender of its author.[6] For the same reason, we cannot establish male authorship, however likely, beyond a reasonable doubt. According to Tertullian, the Acts of Thecla is a forgery, composed by a presbyter in Asia Minor, but his description of the work is highly polemical and should not be taken at face value.[7] While most composers of texts and scribes in antiquity were in all likelihood male, there is also evidence of literate women,[8] and it is intriguing that a marginalia note in Codex Alexandrinus

---

Bernabé's contribution to this volume. See also Shelly Matthews, "Thinking of Thecla: Issues in Feminist Historiography," *JFSR* 17 (2001): 39–55; Stephen J. Davis, "From Women's Piety to Male Devotion: Gender Studies, the *Acts of Paul and Thecla*, and the Evidence of an Arabic Manuscript," *HTR* 108 (2015): 579–93.

5. Outi Lehtipuu, "The Example of Thecla and the Example(s) of Paul: Disputing Women's Role in Early Christianity," in *Women and Gender in Ancient Religions: Interdisciplinary Approaches*, ed. Stephen P. Ahearne-Kroll, Paul A. Holloway, and James A. Kelhofer, WUNT 263 (Tübingen: Mohr Siebeck), 361; Hylen, *Modest Apostle*, 91–113.

6. According to the influential thesis of Dennis MacDonald, the text displays a sensitivity to the concerns of women and was based on stories circulated orally and preserved by communities of women. See Dennis R. MacDonald, *The Legend and the Apostle: The Battle for Paul in Story and Canon* (Philadelphia: Westminster, 1983), 34–56. Stevan Davies has argued for a female authorship of the Acts of Thecla. See Davies, *The Revolt of the Widows: The Social World of the Apocryphal Acts* (Carbondale: Southern Illinois University Press, 1980), 95–109. Both scholars point out that the text casts women and female characters—including female animals—in a positive light, and men and male characters in a negative light. This is, however, a broad generalization, overlooking the role of Thecla's mother as one of the chief actors against Thecla and that of the she-bear that attacks Thecla. See Elisabeth Esch-Wermeling, *Thekla –Paulusschülerin wider Willen? Strategien und Leserlenkung in den Theklaakten*, NTAbh 53 (Münster: Aschendorff, 2008), 153 n. 331. Furthermore, how women are presented in the narrative might have nothing at all to do with the gender of its author.

7. Several scholars who speculate about women's active role in composing stories of Thecla still follow Tertullian's claim unquestioningly, viewing the role of the presbyter as that of a collector of women's stories. See, e.g., MacDonald, *Legend and the Apostle*, 26–33; Jeremy W. Barrier, *The Acts of Paul and Thecla: A Critical Introduction and Commentary*, WUNT 2/270 (Tübingen: Mohr Siebeck, 2009), 21–22.

8. Kim Haines-Eitzen, *The Gendered Palimpsest: Women, Writing, and Representation in Early Christianity* (Oxford: Oxford University Press, 2012), 5–6, 23–38; Erja

(fifth century CE) states that the scribe of the codex was a certain "Thecla the martyr."[9]

While it is impossible to know who wrote the Acts of Thecla or for what purpose the text was written, even if we were somehow to know the answers to these questions, we might still raise doubts as to whether these answers would help us understand and interpret the text. Furthermore, scholarship widely acknowledges "authorial intent" as a problematic hermeneutic[10]—texts are read, reread, and reinterpreted in numerous ways, varying according to context. Later interpreters may also have subscribed to certain opinions about the author's intentions—for example, Tertullian thinks that the presbyter forged the Acts of Thecla "out of love for Paul" (*amore Pauli*) yet, by his judgment, produced an imperfect work. The notion that, in the Acts of Thecla, the apostle would have authorized women to teach and baptize must be false, Tertullian claims, for Paul did not even allow women an independent right to learn: "let them keep silence, he says, and ask their husbands at home" (*Bapt.* 17.4–5; see 1 Cor 14:35).

Tertullian's words offer an illuminating example of the competing images of Paul that circulated among early Christians. The Pauline legacy was complex and diverse and developed in different directions.[11] The question, however, was not only of how Paul's letters were to be interpreted; it was first and foremost the figure of the apostle and the stories about him as a preacher, miracle worker, and martyr that were invested with apostolic authority.[12] The Acts of Thecla clearly attests to this fact. Paul is the author-

---

Salmenkivi, "Some Remarks on Literate Women in Roman Egypt," in *Women and Knowledge in Early Christianity*, ed. Ulla Tervahauta et al., VCSup 144 (Leiden: Brill, 2017), 62–72.

9. W. Andrew Smith, *A Study of the Gospels in Codex Alexandrinus: Codicology, Palaeography, and Scribal Hands* (Leiden: Brill, 2014), 15–18, 32–34.

10. Annette Merz, *Die fiktive Selbstauslegung des Paulus: Intertextuelle Studien zur Intention und Rezeption der Pastoralbriefe*, NTOA 52 (Göttingen: Vandenhoeck & Ruprecht, 2004), 31–35.

11. For a discussion, see Outi Lehtipuu, "Apostolic Authority and Women in Second-Century Christianity," in *Receptions of Paul in Early Christianity: The Person of Paul and His Writings through the Eyes of His Early Interpreters*, ed. Jens Schröter, Simon Butticaz, and Andreas Dettwiler, BZNW 234 (Berlin: de Gruyter, 2018), 609–24.

12. Several recent contributions to the study of the reception of Paul emphasize that reception is not simply textual reinterpretation; the image of the apostle often

ity-bearing hero of the story, and no mention is made of his letter-writing, except for one direct quotation from Paul's letters. In this respect, the Acts of Thecla resembles the canonical Acts of the Apostles, where Paul is likewise preacher and healer—no mention made of his epistolary life.

In this essay I study how Paul is portrayed in the Acts of Thecla, how his authority is constituted and wielded, and how that authority relates to women. My focus is on the narrative world of the Acts of Thecla. I thus do not concern myself with whether this portrait of Paul corresponds to the "historical Paul" or whether the author of the Acts of Thecla "got Paul right."[13] Paul was an ambiguous figure, and both he and his letters were interpreted in different ways and used as evidence in support of different ideas.[14]

In what follows, I show that Paul is a figure of authority in the Acts of Thecla, an authority constituted by presenting Paul as a Christlike figure and a teacher of truth, emphasizing his ascetic message to women and men alike, albeit according to gendered ancient ideals.

1. Paul as Christ

One of the striking features in how Paul is portrayed is his sudden disappearance and abandonment of Thecla every time peril befalls her. This is discernible already in the first part of the story, when Thecla is condemned to death by burning and Paul is driven out of the city. In the latter part of the story, Paul denies knowing Thecla, exposing her to the advances of a certain Alexander. Between these two episodes, Paul also expresses doubts over her determination, spurning her request to be baptized. On these grounds, several scholars claim that the Acts of Thecla

---

predates and even surpasses the influence of Paul's letters. See James W. Aageson, *Paul, the Pastoral Epistles, and the Early Church* (Peabody, MA: Hendrickson, 2008), 1–2; Benjamin L. White, *Remembering Paul: Ancient and Modern Contests over the Image of the Apostle* (Oxford: Oxford University Press, 2014), 55, 79–90.

13. See Outi Lehtipuu, "Who Has the Right to Be Called a Christian? Deviance and Christian Identity in Tertullian's *On the Prescription of Heretics*," in *Methods, Theories, Imagination: Social Scientific Approaches in Biblical Studies*, ed. David Chalcraft, Frauke Uhlenbruch, and Rebecca Sally Watson (Sheffield: Sheffield Phoenix, 2014), 80–98; White, *Remembering Paul*, 10–13.

14. Outi Lehtipuu, "'Flesh and Blood Cannot Inherit the Kingdom of God': The Transformation of the Flesh in Early Christian Debates," in *Metamorphoses: Resurrection, Body and Transformative Practices in Early Christianity*, ed. Turid Karlsen Seim and Jorunn Økland (Berlin: de Gruyter, 2009), 150.

is highly critical of Paul, portraying him as "a bad shepherd who leaves his lamb in danger and flees away"[15] and who "often lacks solidarity and indeed humiliates her."[16]

In the overall context of the narrative, this kind of reasoning, in my opinion, is not convincing. On the contrary, Paul is depicted as a hero in the Acts of Thecla, one whose authority goes unquestioned.[17] How, then, can Paul's absence in the crucial parts of the story be explained? One solution is to refer to the textual history of the narrative. According to one popular theory, the latter part of the narrative, the Antioch incident, forms the core of the story, to which the first part, the Iconium episode, was later added.[18] The incorporation of different materials would explain why the narrative does not always run smoothly and also accounts for Paul's occasional absence. This may well be true, but it is also worth noting that Paul's absence is necessary to the narrative logic of the Acts of Thecla. In the story world, Paul's actions seem to lead Thecla into trouble but in fact end up confirming her autonomy.[19] Thecla must be left alone to challenge Alexander and consequently to undergo her trials. Similarly, Thecla would not have been able to baptize herself had Paul baptized her.

At the narrative level, Paul's actions are never called into question. On the contrary, the narrator seems even to admire Paul—as does Thecla. Upon hearing his teaching, she devotes herself to him as if bewitched, inciting accusations that Paul was a sorcerer who, not without double

---

15. Eung Chun Park, "ΑΓΝΕΙΑ as a Sublime ΕΡΩΣ in the Acts of Paul and Thecla," in *Distant Voices Drawing Near: Essays in Honor of Antoinette Clark Wire*, ed. Holly E. Hearon (Collegeville, MN: Liturgical Press, 2004), 221.

16. Beate Wehn, "'Blessed Are the Bodies of Those Who Are Virgins': Reflections on the Image of Paul in the Acts of Thecla," *JSNT* 79 (2000): 164.

17. This is even clearer in the overall context of the Acts of Paul. It seems that the compiler of this larger work did not discern any criticism at all of Paul in the Acts of Thecla.

18. Anne Jensen, *Thekla—Die Apostolin: Ein apokrypher Text neu entdeckt*, FKG 3 (Gütersloh: Kaiser, 1999), 83–84; Esch-Wermeling, *Thekla—Paulusschülerin wider Willen?*, 71–148; Richard I. Pervo, *The Acts of Paul: A New Translation with Introduction and Commentary* (Eugene, OR: Cascade Books, 2014), 87–88.

19. Johannes N. Vorster, "Construction of Culture through the Construction of Person: The Construction of Thecla in the Acts of Thecla," in *A Feminist Companion to the New Testament Apocrypha*, ed. Amy-Jill Levine with Maria Mayo Robbins, FCNTECW 11 (London: T&T Clark, 2006), 115.

entendre, "has misled all our wives" (Acts Thecla 15).[20] The narrative further plays with erotic language in its description of Thecla's relationship to Paul.[21] When Thecla is separated from Paul, she goes after him, seeking after him until she finds him. She is clearly his faithful disciple, and he exercises authority over her. He is the one who commissions her to "go and teach the word of God" (Acts Thecla 41). Thecla and her deeds are thus authenticated through the figure of Paul—and vice versa, the figure of Thecla adds to the fame and attests to the amiability of Paul.[22]

Paul's authority is further enhanced by styling him as a Christ figure.[23] His preaching is represented through beatitudes, which makes him "sound like Jesus."[24] He also looks like Jesus—or Christ looks like Paul—when he appears to Thecla in the likeness of the apostle as she is undergoing her first trial, to be burned at the stake. Thecla, who keeps searching for Paul "as a lamb in the wilderness looks around for the shepherd" (Acts Thecla 21), takes this figure to be Paul. While the readers soon learn that this is in fact Christ, in the narrative world, this is never explained to Thecla. This conflation of the apostle and Christ suggests the question as to who Thecla's shepherd is. The story has often been seen as a love triangle between Thecla, her fiancé, and, indeed, who? Is Thecla's partner and the object of her emotions Paul, Christ, or God? While Thecla calls herself "a servant of the living God" who has come to believe "in the Son of God" (Acts Thecla 37), it is still Paul for whom she longs (Acts Thecla 40). Clearly, Paul is on the side of God and Christ, with divine authority vested in his words and deeds.

---

20. All translations of the Acts of Thecla are taken from J. Keith Elliott, *The Apocryphal New Testament: A Collection of Apocryphal Christian Literature in an English Translation* (Oxford: Clarendon, 1993), 364–72, if not otherwise noted.

21. Jensen, *Thekla—Die Apostolin*, 108–9; Jan N. Bremmer, "Magic, Martyrdom and Women's Liberation in the Acts of Paul and Thecla," in Bremmer, *Apocryphal Acts of Paul and Thecla*, 41–42.

22. Barrier, *Acts of Paul and Thecla*, 18. In the words of Richard Pervo, "If you like Thecla, you'll love Paul, as she in fact did" (Pervo, *Acts of Paul*, 88).

23. Snyder, *Acts of Paul*, 103; Richard I. Pervo, "Shepherd of the Lamb: Paul as a Christ-Figure in the Acts of Paul," in *Portraits of Jesus*, ed. Susan E. Myers, WUNT 2/321 (Tübingen: Mohr Siebeck, 2012), 355–69.

24. Pervo, *Acts of Paul*, 102.

2. Paul as a Teacher of the True Faith

Not just the actions of Paul but also his teachings in the Acts of Thecla have been regarded as dubious, as striking an unfamiliar chord.[25] This claim is related to the ascetic tone of Paul's teaching. But how strange is it after all? A closer look at his beatitudes shows, as we shall see, that they echo the teachings of Paul in his letters, most prominently in 1 Corinthians. However, an even closer comparison can be drawn between Paul's teachings in the Acts of Thecla and his teachings in the canonical Acts of the Apostles. The narrator of the Acts of Thecla gives Paul's message in a nutshell as λόγος θεοῦ περὶ ἐγκρατείας καὶ ἀναστάσεως (Acts Thecla 5), which in most English translations is rendered as "the word of God about abstinence and the resurrection." In the canonical Acts, Paul's teaching is described using a strikingly similar phrase, but in most translations ἐγκράτεια is here taken in the more general sense of "self-mastery" or "self-control" as Paul discusses περὶ δικαιοσύνης καὶ ἐγκρατείας καὶ τοῦ κρίματος τοῦ μέλλοντος (justice, self-control, and the coming judgment) with the governor Felix (Acts 24:25).

Paul's message would be unfamiliar only if compared to the teaching of the pastoral Paul, the author(s) who penned the epistles to Timothy and Titus in the name of Paul. The way the Pastoral Epistles, particularly 1 Timothy, depict Paul's stance toward women and asceticism is strikingly different from that in the Acts of Thecla.[26] According to the Paul of 1 Timothy, women will be saved through childbearing (1 Tim 2:15), while the Paul of the Acts of Thecla teaches that "there is for you no resurrection unless you remain chaste and do not pollute the flesh" (Acts Thecla 12).[27]

---

25. Sheila E. McGinn, "The Acts of Thecla," in *Searching the Scriptures: A Feminist Commentary*, ed. Elizabeth Schüssler Fiorenza (New York: Crossroad, 1994), 2:807–8; see also Wehn, "Blessed Are the Bodies," 161.

26. For an analysis of the differences among the Pastoral Letters, including their attitudes toward women, see Matthijs den Dulk, "I Permit No Woman to Teach Except for Thecla: The Curious Case of the Pastoral Epistles and the *Acts of Paul* Reconsidered," *NovT* 54 (2012): 176–203.

27. Several scholars claim that Demas and Hermogenes are untrustworthy witnesses and thus they misrepresent Paul (see McGinn, "Acts of Thecla," 812; Barrier, *Acts of Paul and Thecla*, 93–94; Hylen, *Modest Apostle*, 87–88). However, their statement coheres with Paul's overall teaching in the Acts of Thecla, and there is no reason not to take their words seriously.

These two texts exemplify the different lives Paul's legacy led in the early days of Christianity.

In addition to their stark differences, however, the texts also bear similarities. Both sets of texts depict Paul as an authoritative teacher and a heresy fighter. While this observation is a scholarly commonplace concerning the Pastoral Letters,[28] it is less often acknowledged in relation to the Acts of Thecla. Indeed, Paul's defense of the "true faith" is not as straightforward in the latter text, mostly, I would argue, due to the different genres of the texts. However, it is important to note that the pastoral letters are rather vague about what the true faith entails, other than belief in the goodness of the created world (1 Tim 4:1–5) and in the coming resurrection (2 Tim 2:16–19). On this point, the Acts of Thecla is more explicit. When Paul arrives in Iconium at the beginning of the narrative, his message is described as "the words of the Lord" (τὰ λόγια κυρίου) concerning "the birth and resurrection of the beloved" (καὶ τῆς γεννήσεως καὶ τῆς ἀναστάσεως τοῦ ἠγαπημένου; Acts Thecla 1).[29] In addition to incarnation and resurrection, Paul also teaches belief in only one God (ἕνα καὶ μόνον θεὸν; Acts Thecla 9)—all three of these aspects were hotly debated among early Christians, and, in all three, the Paul of the Acts of Thecla seems to expound the views that would later come to be regarded as orthodox.

While the narrative genre is less polemical in nature compared to the Pastorals, the opponents of the true faith are nevertheless prominent. They take the form of Paul's deceitful companions, Demas and Hermogenes, who are portrayed as hypocrites, subscribed to ideas of which the narrator disapproves.[30] Their depiction as false associates of Paul is polemically motivated: Christians who teach in such a manner are not true Christians. The false teachings of Demas and Hermogenes are best exemplified in their views on resurrection: "It has already taken place in the children whom we have and that we rise again, after having come to the knowledge

---

28. See Aageson, *Paul, the Pastoral Epistles*, 91–93.

29. See McGinn, "Acts of Thecla," 807. Paul's teaching is variously described in the narrative as the "word of God" (λόγος θεοῦ; Acts Thecla 5, 40), the "word of Christ" (τὸν τοῦ Χριστοῦ λόγον; Acts Thecla 7), or the "words of God" (τὰ λόγια τοῦ θεοῦ; Acts Thecla 42).

30. Outi Lehtipuu, "The Distorters of Resurrection in Apocryphal Acts and Other Early Christian Texts: The Threat of Deviance," in *Voces Clamantium in Deserto: Essays in Honor of Kari Syreeni*, SEJ (Åbo: Teologiska fakulteten, 2012), 186–91.

of the true God" (Acts Thecla 14). This narrative polemic is comparable to what the author of 2 Timothy says about the false teachers Hymenaeus and Philetus: their "profane chatter," according to which the resurrection has already happened, indicates that they have deviated from the truth (2 Tim 2:16–18). Thus, insofar as resurrection is concerned, the authors of 2 Timothy and the Acts of Thecla are in line with each other—opposed additionally to those who, in the name of Paul, promote the understanding of resurrection as knowledge of the true God (see Col 3:1–4; Eph 1:17–21; 2:5–7.) Thus, in both sets of texts, Paul is similarly depicted as a teacher of the true faith—but what that true faith entails partly differs between these texts.

3. Paul's Encratite Message

The key word in Paul's teaching is ἐγκράτεια, the classic Greek virtue of self-control.[31] The term itself is often rendered as "abstinence" or "continence" but, in a wider sense, denotes mastery over any emotions, impulses, or desires and was first and foremost a manly virtue, a characteristic of the rational man (see, e.g., Aristotle, *Eth. nic.* 7.1145a–1154b; [Pseudo-]Aristotle, *De virtutibus et vitiis*).[32] In his discussion of ἐγκράτεια, Aristotle treats τὰ ἀφροδισία (sexual matters) as only one of the bodily pleasures to be controlled—his main focus lies elsewhere.[33] Accordingly, some scholars prefer the translation "self-control" in the Acts of Thecla.[34] I, however, have chosen the more traditional translation of "abstinence," as this word preserves both the ambiguity of the Greek and its connotation of sexual continence. Furthermore, the overall narrative context of the Acts of Thecla makes it abundantly clear that this is the meaning ἐγκράτεια carries in this text, most visibly in Theocleia's summary of Paul's teaching as "one must fear only one God and live in chastity" (ἕνα καὶ μόνον θεὸν φοβεῖσθαι καὶ ζῆν ἁγνῶς; Acts Thecla 9), which can be taken as a paraphrase to the

---

31. Pervo, *Acts of Paul*, 101.

32. These discussions are addressed to a male audience, and they do not mention female ἐγκράτεια. This inherently gendered quality of ἐγκράτεια is also reflected by many early Christian texts; see, e.g., Herm. Vis. 3.8.4.

33. For further examples, see Henry Chadwick, "Enkrateia," *RAC* 5 (1962): 343–65.

34. Wehn, "Blessed Are the Bodies," 152; Barrier, *Acts of Paul and Thecla*, 78; Pervo, *Acts of Paul*, 99.

earlier "resurrection and ἐγκράτεια." Thus, both ἐγκράτεια and ἁγνεία refer to a life of sexual abstinence.³⁵

In other early Christian texts, ἐγκράτεια and related words (ἐγκρατεύομαι, ἐγκρατής) sometimes occur in the general sense of self-mastery, as in Paul's simile of Christ-believers as athletes who exercise self-control (1 Cor 9:25) or in his list of the fruit of the Spirit (Gal 5:23).³⁶ While these short references do not need to be interpreted as speaking only about sexual continence, they by no means exclude this connotation—an ascetically inclined reader might even find in them a justification for sexual abstinence. In some other early Christian texts, examples of ἐγκράτεια explicitly include controlling one's sexuality, even though the term is not confined to this meaning.³⁷

Paul uses the verb ἐγκρατεύομαι once in a similar sense with clear sexual overtones. In his discussion in 1 Cor 7, which Elizabeth Clark characterizes as "probably the most ascetically charged chapter of the New Testament," Paul concedes that those who cannot exercise ἐγκράτεια should be allowed to marry, "for it is better to marry than to burn" (1 Cor 7:9 NKJV).³⁸ Paul's teaching in the Acts of Thecla is quite the opposite: the followers of Christ ought to extinguish all sexual passions without exception—even within marriage.

These references in Paul's letters demonstrate that ἐγκράτεια indeed belongs to Paul's teaching, even if it might be uncertain whether, on their basis, we could summarize his teaching as "the word of God about abstinence and the resurrection." Furthermore, ἐγκράτεια belongs to the reception of Paul and his teaching in the Acts of the Apostles, as we have

---

35. The early Latin versions of the text usually render ἐγκράτεια as *abstinentia*, sometimes as *continentia*.

36. Similar lists of Christian virtues occur in Titus 1:8; 2 Pet 1:6; 1 Clem. 35.2; 62.2; 64; Barn. 2.2; Pol. *Phil.* 5.2.

37. In the Shepherd of Hermas, ἐγκράτεια is a particularly central virtue. The first commandment in the Mandates has three parts: to believe in God, to fear him, and to exercise ἐγκράτεια (ἐγκράτευσαι; Herm. Mand. 26.2). The eighth commandment is devoted to ἐγκράτεια, guiding Hermas to exercise self-control over all evil. A list of vices follows, starting with adultery and fornication but also including drunkenness, luxury, certain foods, extravagant wealth, arrogance, lying, slander, hypocrisy, and blasphemy (Herm. Mand. 38.3; see also Herm. Vis. 2.4; 1 Clem. 38.2; 2 Clem. 4.3).

38. Elizabeth A. Clark, *Reading Renunciation: Asceticism and Scripture in Early Christianity* (Princeton: Princeton University Press, 1999), 13; 1 Cor 7:9: εἰ δὲ οὐκ ἐγκρατεύονται, γαμησάτωσαν, κρεῖττον γάρ ἐστιν γαμῆσαι ἢ πυροῦσθαι.

seen, even though the overall impression of Paul in the canonical acts is very different from that of the antiestablishment preacher in the Acts of Thecla.[39] We may thus safely say that the author of the Acts of Thecla did not invent the notion of Paul as a preacher of ἐγκράτεια but rather gave his or her own interpretation of what Paul might have meant in his use of the word.

Other texts betray a quite different understanding of ἐγκράτεια in relation to controlling one's sexuality. Whereas the Acts of Thecla seems to use ἐγκράτεια and ἁγνεία interchangeably to denote celibacy on the part of the unmarried and the married alike, other texts show that they can be, as Glenn Snyder puts it, "reimagined in a variety of ways."[40] For example, in his letter to the Philippians, Polycarp uses both ἐγκράτεια and ἁγνεία to discuss the virtues of a faithful wife.[41] From his perspective, chastity does not amount to a total renunciation of sexual relations but denotes rather faithfulness to one's spouse and proper modesty. Similarly, according to 1 Clement, wives are to exhibit purity (ἁγνεία), which in its literary context seems to denote proper behavior, including silence and faithfulness in marriage (1 Clem. 21.6-7).

The letters of Polycarp and Clement share many similar features with the Pastoral Epistles, where, likewise, adjectives such as ἐγκρατής (continent), ἁγνός (chaste), καθαρός (pure), and σώφρων (temperate) appear side by side, denoting proper εὐσέβεια (piety).[42] Thus, the Pastoral Letters and the Acts of Thecla share the same ideal of purity, expounding this view in Paul's name, albeit understanding this ideal differently.

4. Blessed Abstinence

Paul's preaching is fleshed out in a series of beatitudes, wherein he declares blessed different groups of people, promising them great rewards, not all of

---

39. Richard I. Pervo, *The Making of Paul: Constructions of the Apostle in Early Christianity* (Minneapolis: Fortress, 2010), 164.

40. Snyder, *Acts of Paul*, 138.

41. "Instruct your wives to continue in the faith delivered to them and in love and purity [ἁγνείᾳ], cherishing their own husbands in all fidelity and loving all others equally in all chastity [ἐγκρατείᾳ]" (Pol. *Phil.* 4.2). Translated by Michael W. Holmes, *The Apostolic Fathers: Greek Texts and English Translations*, 3rd ed. (Grand Rapids: Baker Academic, 2007).

42. See Aageson, *Paul, the Pastoral Epistles*, 199; Park, "ΑΓΝΕΙΑ as a Sublime ΕΡΩΣ," 225.

which concern abstinence and the resurrection. In fact, the word *resurrection* does not appear at all.[43] On the other hand, the rewards are expressed in future tense, reflect an intimate relationship with God, and thus seem to be intimately related to resurrection. While not all of the beatitudes point to sexual abstinence, the structure of the section, which begins with purity and ends with lauding the bodies of virgins, gives a strong ascetic ring to the whole:[44]

> Blessed are the pure in heart, for they shall see God.
> Blessed are those who have kept the flesh chaste, for they shall become a temple of God.
> Blessed are the continent, for God shall speak with them.
> Blessed are those who have kept aloof from this world, for they shall be pleasing to God.
> Blessed are those who have wives as not having them, for they shall inherit God.
> Blessed are those who have fear of God, for they shall become angels of God.
> Blessed are those who respect the word of God, for they shall be comforted.
> Blessed are those who have received the wisdom of Jesus Christ, for they shall be called the sons of the Most High.
> Blessed are those who have kept the baptism, for they shall be refreshed by the Father and the Son.
> Blessed are those who have come to a knowledge of Jesus Christ, for they shall be in the light.
> Blessed are those who through love of God renounce the form of the world, for they shall judge angels, and shall be blessed at the right hand of the Father.
> Blessed are the merciful, for they shall obtain mercy and shall not see the bitter day of judgment.
> Blessed are the bodies of the virgins, for they shall be well pleasing to God and shall not lose the reward of their chastity. For the word of the Father shall become to them a work of salvation in the day of his Son, and they shall have rest for ever and ever. (Acts Thecla 5–6)

---

43. Nine out of the thirteen beatitudes are directly connected to the teaching on self-control, while none relate explicitly to Paul's teachings about resurrection (Barrier, *Acts of Paul and Thecla*, 82).

44. The translation is slightly modified from that of Elliott to retain the original wording.

The number of the beatitudes varies in different manuscripts, which has led to speculation that they originally numbered eleven, following Jesus's beatitudes in the Gospel of Matthew.[45] However many there may have been, the beatitudes in the Acts of Thecla certainly borrow both form and formulation from the Gospel of Matthew,[46] echoing several of the Matthean beatitudes: blessing the pure-hearted (Matt 5:4) and the merciful (Matt 5:7) and promising comfort (Matt 5:4), inheritance (Matt 5:5), and beholding of God (Matt 5:8), and dubbing the blessed as sons of the Most High (Matt 5:9).[47] These parallels invoke the authority of Jesus himself—that is, the Paul of the Acts of Thecla teaches and sounds like Jesus.

The beatitudes are also partly built on expressions reminiscent of Pauline literature, especially 1 Corinthians.[48] Particularly close is the second beatitude, which promises those who have kept the flesh pure (οἱ ἁγνὴν τὴν σάρκα τηρήσαντες) that they will become "a temple of God" (ναὸς θεοῦ). Similarly, Paul teaches in 1 Corinthians that the body is a temple of God that must be kept holy by not defiling it (1 Cor 3:16–17; cf. 2 Cor 6:16; 1 Cor 6:16–19). An even closer link to 1 Corinthians is the fifth beatitude in the list in Acts of Thecla, which resembles verbatim Paul's words in 1 Cor 7:29. Having wives as if not having them can only mean, both in the context of 1 Corinthians and in the Acts of Thecla, that even married men should abstain from sexual relations with their wives—which, naturally, means that married women must also abstain from sex. This radical idea is

---

45. The first six are missing from Coptic because of the fragmentary condition of the manuscript, while variation exists throughout in some Greek and Latin manuscripts. The second-to-last beatitude ("blessed are the merciful"), for instance, is absent from the Coptic and some Greek manuscripts. See Carl Schmidt, *Acta Pauli aus der Heidelberger koptischen Papyrushandschrift Nr. 1: Tafelband* (Leipzig: Hinrichs, 1904); see also Barrier, *Acts of Paul and Thecla*, 83–85. The study of the Acts of Thecla suffers greatly from the fact that the only available edition of the Greek text is that of Lipsius, originally published in 1891, based on only eleven manuscripts (compare to the approximately fifty manuscripts known today). See Richard Adelbert Lipsius and Maximilianus Bonnet, *Acta Petri, Acta Pauli, Acta Petri et Pauli, Acta Pauli et Theclae, Acta Thaddei* (Darmstadt: Wissenschaftliche Buchgesellschaft, 1959).

46. See the table in Barrier, *Acts of Paul and Thecla*, 54; see also Martin Ebner, "Paulinische Seligpreisungen à la Thekla: Narrative Relecture der Makarismenlehre in ActThecl 5f," in *Aus Liebe zu Paulus? Die Akte Thekla neu aufgerollt*, ed. Martin Ebner (Stuttgart: Katholisches Bibelwerk, 2005), 67–70.

47. Thecla uses the same expression ("son of the Most High") to denote Christ in her prayer (Acts Thecla 29).

48. Merz, *Fiktive Selbstauslegung des Paulus*, 326–30.

missing from at least one manuscript, where the word γυναῖκας is omitted, and the resulting text reads as follows: "blessed are those who have as if not having" (οἱ ἔχοντες ὡς μὴ ἔχοντες).[49] While it cannot be ruled out that this omission resulted from an unintentional mistake, it is also possible that the copyist had wished to broaden the beatitude to a renunciation of all possessions, harmonizing it with the preceding beatitude.

Despite the similarity in both formulation and meaning, the literary context of the sentence is different. Only a partial endorsement of the ascetic ideal exists in 1 Cor 7. While his overall discussion is aimed at the purity of the body, Paul seems to think in 1 Corinthians, contrary to the Acts of Thecla, that acquiring and maintaining bodily holiness is possible without abandoning sexual relations altogether.[50] Even though his chief recommendation is to remain unmarried, Paul's teaching was ambiguous enough to allow for the development of different interpretations. To argue for sexual renunciation on the basis of 1 Cor 7, ascetically inclined Christians were forced to read and use the passage eclectically.[51] There were others who used the same text for quite opposite purposes, emphasizing Paul's advice to married couples not to abandon their sexual relations (7:2–5), his instruction not to divorce (7:10–16), or his permission to let virgins marry (7:36–38). This is quite the opposite of the example of Thecla, who rejects her fiancé and shows in her actions that it is literally better to burn than to marry, as she is prepared to be burned alive instead of marrying.

According to the Acts of Thecla, a total renunciation of sexual relations, also within marriage,[52] is the only possibility for salvation: "there is for you no resurrection unless you remain chaste and do not pollute the flesh" (Acts Thecla 12). There is no compromise. This same rigidity is reflected in the last beatitude, which lauds "the bodies of the virgins" (τὰ

---

49. Barrier, *Acts of Paul and Thecla*, 80.

50. Luise Schottroff, "Purity and Holiness of Women and Men in 1 Corinthians and the Consequences for Feminist Hermeneutics," in Hearon, *Distant Voices Drawing Near*, 83–93.

51. Clark, *Reading Renunciation*, 259–329. Other Pauline texts raise similar kinds of difficulties—e.g., the exhortation to have young widows marry in 1 Tim 5:14. See Outi Lehtipuu, "To Remarry or Not to Remarry: 1 Timothy 5:14 in Early Christian Ascetic Discourse," *ST* (2017): 29–50.

52. Onesiphoros and his wife seem to be an example of a couple who stay married but abstain from conjugal relations (McGinn, "Acts of Thecla," 808). In so doing, they have already "become angels of God" (see beatitude six), participating in an angelic life, unimpaired by sexuality (see Luke 20:36).

σώματα τῶν παρθένων) and serves as a sort of synopsis of the whole story, which centers on Thecla, her body, and the threats against the preservation of its purity.[53]

This focus on bodies in turn reveals a high esteem for the body. The body is where the true spiritual relationship is tried and tested. Whoever can keep the flesh pure will become a temple of God.[54] I understand the ninth beatitude, recognizing the blessedness of those who keep their baptism (οἱ τὸ βάπτισμα τηρήσαντες), in the same way. If "keeping baptism" is an equivalent of "keeping the flesh pure," this would partly explain why Paul refuses to baptize Thecla. It is perhaps not so much about doubting Thecla's perseverance but an expression of his fear that someone might violate her sexually, meaning that Thecla would not be able to keep her baptism. From the perspective of polluting the female body, the ancient ideal did not differentiate between a willing initiator of sexual activity and an innocent victim of rape.[55]

What also distinguishes the ascetic teaching of the Acts of Thecla from 1 Corinthians is their different temporal frames. Paul's exhortation originally appears in an eschatological context: "The time is short, so that from now on even those who have wives should be as though they had none … for the form of this world is passing away" (1 Cor 7:29–31 NKJV). It is because the end is drawing near that the normal circumstances of life are no longer valid. In the beatitudes in the Acts of Thecla, however, this sense of eschatological urgency has disappeared; the exhortation to live as if not having a wife has become a timeless ideal.[56]

How is this ideal put into practice—or is it, in fact, meant to be put into practice? As I have argued elsewhere, the ascetic ideals reflected in the text were only achievable by very few elite women.[57] A slave woman, for exam-

---

53. See McGinn, "Acts of Thecla," 809.

54. In some Latin manuscripts, the emphasis on the body is downplayed, altering the text to "their souls will be temples"; see Pervo, *Acts of Paul*, 105.

55. Perhaps the best-known example of this is Lucretia, who committed suicide after she was raped.

56. This is all the more striking, since the notion of casting off "the form of this world" (τὸ σχῆμα τοῦ κόσμου τούτου) appears in another beatitude. Many ancient commentators of Paul similarly overlooked the eschatological dimension of 1 Corinthians. They often interpreted the comment on the shortness of time as an allusion to the brevity of an individual's life, claiming that chastity, on the other hand, was eternal (see Clark, *Reading Renunciation*, 308–12).

57. Outi Lehtipuu, "Example of Thecla," 362–64.

ple, was in no position to, in the author's words, "remain pure," to reject the advances of her male partner or that of her owner. A particularly reprehensible example of such a situation occurs in the Acts of Andrew, where the heroine, Maximilla, the elite wife of the proconsul, manages to preserve her own purity by using her slave girl as her surrogate body, sending her to sleep with her husband (Acts Andr. 17–22).[58] If virginity and abstinence from sex are required for salvation, however, Maximilla has denied her slave girl any possibility for salvation. The author of the Acts of Andrew takes no notice of this fact; for him, the slave girl is simply an instrument by means of which Maximilla can pursue a pure and virtuous life.

5. Paul's Apostolic Authority and Early Christian Women

To whom, then, are the beatitudes and the whole of the Acts of Thecla addressed? Because the protagonist is female, the text has often been referred to as women's literature. However, Paul does not speak to women only; the groups he declares blessed are addressed in masculine plural.[59] While most of these gendered forms can be taken inclusively to refer to both men and women, the reference to those who have wives as if not having them clearly focuses on men.[60] According to Annette Merz, this shows that the beatitudes form an earlier text unit that was later incorporated into the Acts of Thecla.[61] This does not, however, need to be the case, for Paul's audience in the narrative comprises both men and women. "All the women and the young men go to him," Theocleia complains (Acts Thecla 9).[62] While Paul's followers are mainly described as virgins (παρθένοι),[63] (married) women (γυναῖκες), and young men (νέοι), the other named follower of his is a married adult man, Onesiphorus. Thecla's companions

---

58. See Bernadette Brooten's chapter in this volume.

59. They are constantly referred to as μακάριοι and αὐτοί, and all nouns and adjectives used are in masculine plural—see especially υἱοὶ ὑψίστου.

60. Ebner, "Paulinische Seligspreisungen," 65.

61. Merz, *Fiktive Selbstauslegung des Paulus*, 320–33.

62. See Acts Thecla 12: "He deprives the young men of wives and young women of husbands" (στερεῖ δὲ νέους γυναικῶν καὶ παρθένους ἀνδρῶν).

63. The word παρθένος can also refer to male virgins; see Rev 14:4. However, in the Acts of Thecla the use of the word seems to be restricted to young women alone, as the young men are called οἱ νέοι throughout the text. Thus, the last beatitude of "the bodies of the virgins" seems to refer to women. This does not exclude the possibility that a later male reader might take it to include himself.

also include both males and females (νεανίσκους καὶ παιδίσκας), probably slaves from Trypheaena's household (Acts Thecla 40). Later manuscript tradition shows that the text was copied and read by men who regarded Thecla as their model.[64]

Thus, even though Paul's message is intended for both men and women, in practice, male self-control and female self-control took on different meanings according to the wider cultural gender expectations. In the case of women, their modesty, which included controlling their sexuality, was paramount. Even though the same ideals were also important for men, it was the purity of women that was taken to indicate social morality and piety.[65] At the narrative level, this double standard manifests in the different sentences handed to Paul and Thecla when they are taken to the governor: Paul, albeit the instigator of the unrest, is driven out of the city, while Thecla is condemned to be burned alive (Acts Thecla 21).[66]

The prevailing scholarly opinion emphasizes that Thecla's trade of marriage for a life of celibacy validated her autonomy and authority. Recently, Susan Hylen has suggested the opposite: since a good marriage offered the means of freedom and authority especially for elite women, the ancient readers of Thecla's story might have understood her choice as voluntarily abandoning her own autonomy.[67] Hylen rightly notes that the popularity of Thecla's story indicates that ancient readers did not see her as a countercultural figure but as someone who fulfilled the cultural expectations of a modest woman.[68] Most patristic commentators praise Thecla and other ascetic women without reserve. Particularly in the fourth century, several treatises were written to promote virginity and widowhood. Intriguingly, one common approach by male authors was to remind women that celibacy will free them from pangs and sufferings of birth, thus gaining control over their own body and sexuality (see Cyprian, *Hab. virg.* 22; John Chrysostom, *Iter. conj.* 5; Jerome, *Ep.* 54.15). None of these authors, however, are concerned that a life of celibacy might offer women

---

64. See Davis, "From Women's Piety," 586–87.
65. Ross Shepard Kraemer, *Unreliable Witnesses: Religion, Gender, and History in the Greco-Roman Mediterranean* (Oxford: Oxford University Press, 2011), 147. See Pol. *Phil.* 5.3, where sexual purity (ἁγνεία) is listed among the principles to which young men should adhere.
66. Wehn, "Blessed Are the Bodies," 154.
67. Hylen, *Modest Apostle*, 85.
68. Hylen, *Modest Apostle*, 91–113.

such autonomy as would elevate them beyond male dominion. Some of the most influential early Christian women, such as Macrina or Olympias, were celibate and highly praised by men.

While celibacy was an ideal for both genders, then, exhortations to preserve one's virginity were predominantly aimed at women—those that discouraged remarriage almost exclusively so. One reason for this gender disparity might be that moneyed widows might have considered remarriage beneficial and had thus to be reminded of the benefits of staying celibate. As far as I know, there are no ancient texts praising widowerhood. This might imply that controlling male sexuality was considered more of a matter of exercising self-control more generally. Men did not need advice in the same manner as did women, children, and slaves. Moreover, if the claim that ecclesiastical officeholders should be men who have married only once was taken seriously (see 1 Tim 3:2), men had more to lose in remarriage than women.

Another question that might be asked is whether women themselves might have interpreted a life of celibacy as a road to freedom and authority. Tertullian's attack of women who follow the example of Thecla has often been taken as evidence that there were female teachers who followed Thecla's example and practiced baptism (Tertullian, *Bapt.* 17.4–5). It is not certain, however, whether Tertullian was actually familiar with such baptizing women or whether he was simply conjuring to mind a worst-case scenario, too dreadful to be true.[69] Be that as it may, Tertullian's words show the potential of the figure of Thecla to inspire and empower women who read and heard her story.

---

69. Lehtipuu, "Apostolic Authority and Women," 617–19.

Gender and Slavery in the Acts of Andrew

Bernadette J. Brooten

1. Introduction

In the Passion of Andrew, part of the Acts of Andrew, which was first composed in the second or third century and enjoyed great popularity among Christians throughout the ancient Mediterranean from the third through the ninth centuries, pious Maximilla, determined to keep her body pure for Christ, enlists her slave woman Euklia into having sex with her snake of a pagan husband, Aigeates, so that she herself can avoid the "polluting defilement" of sex.[1] Euklia's name ironically and euphemistically means

---

I thank the following for their support of this research: the Ford Foundation, the National Endowment for the Humanities, the Harvard Women's Studies in Religion Program, Brandeis University, and the Israel Institute for Advanced Studies, as well as those who read and provided comments: Ann Braude, Rachel Adler, Michelle Wolf, Julia Watts-Belser, Hauwa Ibrahim, Michael VanZandt Collins, and Elizabeth Stoker. A special thanks to Arianna Rotondo for organizing a memorable conference in Catania, Sicily, and to the editors of this volume.

1. The Acts of Andrew dates to around the late second century. See Dennis R. MacDonald, *The Acts of Andrew* (Santa Rosa, CA: Polebridge, 2005), 7-9; Jean-Marc Prieur, ed., *Acta Andreae*, CCSA 5 (Turnhout: Brepols, 1989), 413-14, followed by Rebecca Solevåg, *Birthing Salvation: Gender and Class in Early Christian Childbearing Discourse*, BibInt 121 (Leiden: Brill, 2013), 140; and Andrew S. Jacobs, "A Family Affair: Marriage, Class, and Ethics in the Apocryphal Acts of the Apostles," *JECS* 7 (1999): 105-38. Hans-Josef Klauck and John K. Elliott date it to the early third century. See Klauck, *The Apocrphyal Acts of the Apostles: An Introduction*, trans. Brian McNeil (Waco, TX: Baylor University Press, 2008), 116; Elliott, *The Apocryphal New Testament: A Collection of Apocryphal Christian Literature in an English Translation* (Oxford: Clarendon, 1993), 236. For the tradition, see, e.g., Eusebius, *Hist. eccl.* 3.25.6, and the *Epitome* by Gregory of Tours (sixth century) in Prieur, *Acta Andreae*, 119, 551-651.

"of good reputation," and I translate it as "Miss Respectable." Maximilla teaches Euklia to impersonate her in bed, thereby successfully tricking Aigeates for a time. Maximilla ultimately prevails in her goals, whereas Euklia fails.

In what follows, I will argue that the intersection between gender and legal status as enslaved or free is necessary to comprehending the Passion of Andrew. The narrator depicts the four freeborn protagonists (the apostle Andrew; Maximilla; her husband, Aigeates; and her brother-in-law Stratokles) as complex, full-fledged characters, frequently presents their words as direct speech, provides character development for the protagonists other than Andrew (who is presented as already a complete person from the outset), and reports on their inner feelings and motivations. In contrast, with two exceptions, the enslaved figures in the narrative, who are either intermediate or background figures, do not speak in their own words, and the narrator does not describe their inner feelings or thoughts and depicts no character development. These flat figures fit ancient stereotypes of enslaved household servants as either domestic enemies or faithful servants.[2] The narrator portrays all believers as enslaved to the Lord, but slaveholders Maximilla and Stratokles enjoy a freedom to pursue Christian philosophy to a higher degree than legally enslaved believers. The narrator presents Stratokles's journey as largely a philosophical one of attaining better and better understanding through questioning Andrew. In contrast, the narrator depicts Maximilla's main challenge as leading a holy life by refusing sex with her husband, although she also comes to a better philosophical understanding through learning from Andrew. The freeborn Maximilla needs her slave woman Euklia to serve as her sexual surrogate with her husband, and she needs her slave woman Iphidama to serve as a public companion who confirms that she is not herself enslaved and as a physical surrogate who can go out on dangerous missions to find Andrew.

Slavery and freedom are both deeply embedded within the Passion of Andrew and yet invisible—hidden in plain sight, to which contemporary readers have paid insufficient attention. Narrative strategies within the Passion of Andrew itself, however, serve both to reveal and to obscure slavery and freedom. The Passion of Andrew exemplifies a particular strand

---

2. On the Roman and Christian anxiety of enslaved persons as the domestic enemy, see J. Albert Harrill, *Slaves in the New Testament: Literary, Social, and Moral Dimensions* (Minneapolis: Fortress, 2006), 145–63.

of the early Christian idealization of female virginity and celibacy that, combined with an individualistic notion of salvation, depends on slavery.

Maximilla needs both her own freedom and Euklia's enslavement to be pure and holy. Euklia's pagan body, itself unholy, unites with the pagan body of Aigeates, Maximilla's husband, thereby freeing Maximilla to devote herself to prayer and study with the apostle Andrew. The holiness of the one woman depends on the unholiness of the other. Euklia's legally enslaved body enables Maximilla's enslavement to the Lord, which includes both prayer and keeping her own body pure for the Lord. Maximilla's enslavement to the Lord implies sisterhood with other believers, including to her loyal slave woman. In the Roman world, a legally enslaved person has no legal relatives, but the metaphorical enslavement to the Lord in the Passion of Andrew signifies both being bound to Christ and bound to other believers in a kinship relationship. Legally free believers and legally enslaved believers form one community of sisters and brothers enslaved to Christ, although the social aspects of the legal roles persist. The metaphorical terms for a woman enslaved to the Lord (δούλη) and a man enslaved to the Lord (δοῦλος) do not simply designate servitude but rather legal enslavement. Thus, slavery, whether legal in the physical sense or metaphorical in the spiritual sense, imbues this text.

2. The Narration

2.1. The Narrator and the Places of Action

The third-person narrator knows everything about the events and internal thoughts and feelings of the characters (i.e., is omniscient), is able to narrate from and about every location (i.e., is omnipresent), and knows the past, present, and future (i.e., is omnitemporal).[3] These are the privileges of a narrator external to the narrative itself. The large picture (i.e., without focalization or narrowing to a specific perspective) that this narrator is able to portray serves to create confidence in the narrator.[4] At the very end,

---

3. For the narratological analysis in all that follows, I am deeply indebted to Ute Eisen, *Die Poetik der Apostelgeschichte: Eine narratologische Studie* (Göttingen: Vandenhoeck & Ruprecht, 2006).

4. In narratological terms, the narrator is extradiegetic and heterodiegetic, that is, external to the narrative (*diēgēsis*) itself and not directly involved in the workings of the narrative.

the narrator switches, first, to the first-person plural and then to the first-person singular, which I take to be devices for challenging the narratee to become part of this specific believing community. The first-person narrator at the end is directly involved in the events and the message and speaks directly to the narratee.[5] The Passion of Andrew does not define the narrator as male or female.[6] The narrator's philosophical knowledge could mark the narrator as male for ancient readers, although some ancient women were philosophically educated.[7]

The protagonists of the story are the apostle Andrew, Maximilla, Stratokles, and Aigeates. The narrator depicts them as complex by means of direct speech in the form of both long monologues and dialogues, reports on their inner feelings, and provides external descriptions and descriptions of their actions. Andrew's speeches are by far the longest. Whereas Maximilla and Stratokles show character development as they progress toward greater perfection, Andrew does not, presumably because he has already attained the highest level, and Aigeates does not, because he never engages Andrew's message.

Intermediate characters include Euklia and Iphidama, both enslaved to Maximilla; Alkmanes, enslaved to Stratokles; an unnamed enslaved servant belonging to Aigeates; a comely boy who greets Iphidama at the prison; and the executioner soldiers who crucify Andrew.[8] With two exceptions, the

---

5. On the switch to the first person in Pass. Andr. 64–65, see Laura S. Nasrallah, "'She Became What the Words Signified': The Greek Acts of Andrew's Construction of the Reader-Disciple," in *The Apocryphal Acts of the Apostles*, ed. François Bovon, Ann Graham Brock, and Christopher R. Matthews (Cambridge: Harvard University Press, 1999), 231–58; Dennis R. MacDonald, *Christianizing Homer: The Odyssey, Plato, and the Acts of Andrew* (New York: Oxford University Press, 1994), 287–89; Prieur, *Acta Andreae*, 38. I am following Nasrallah's interpretation.

6. In contrast, see, e.g., Luke 1:3, which defines the narrator as male through the masculine participle, on which see Eisen, *Poetik der Apostelgeschichte*, 89.

7. Stevan L. Davies has posited female authorship for the apocryphal Acts, which might also imply a female narrator. See Davies, *The Revolt of the Widows: The Social World of the Apocryphal Acts* (Carbondale: Southern Illinois University Press, 1980); see also Dennis R. MacDonald, *The Legend and the Apostle: The Battle for Paul in Story and Canon* (Philadelphia: Westminster, 1983).

8. One might also consider the demon cast out of Alkmanes by Andrew to be an intermediate character, Pass. Andr. 5 [334]. In what follows, I cite according to Prieur's edition, here "5," followed by the page number in the Detorakis edition, here "[334]." See Theocharis Detorakis, "ΤΟ ΑΝΕΚΔΟΤΟ ΜΑΡΤΥΡΙΟ ΤΟΥ ΑΠΟΣΤΟΛΟΥ ΑΝΔΡΕΑ," in *Acts of the Second International Congress of Peloponnesian Studies 1*,

enslaved figures do not speak directly.[9] Instead, the narrator describes them and their actions while refraining from describing their inner feelings.

Background characters include unnamed groups of enslaved and freed staff persons, of believers (not defined as free or enslaved), of Stratokles's and of Aigeates's friends, the executioners/soldiers, and the largely pagan crowd that witnesses Andrew's crucifixion. With the exception of the crowd that speaks directly to Aigeates, background characters do not engage in direct speech.

The narrative unfolds in relation to the places in which events occur and in response to two adversarial figures: the proconsul Aigeates, with the power of Rome, and the apostle Andrew, with the power of persuasion. The governor's palace (*praetorium*) in Patras, which the Passion of Andrew inaccurately depicts as the capital of the province of Achaia in southern Greece, and especially its bedrooms, is the site of boundaries breached by the figures in the narrative.[10] Inside the palace, the believers pray, heal, learn, and encourage one another, but polluting sex and the proconsul's decision making also happen there. In the outside world, in an unnamed location, Andrew and the believers sleep, learn, and pray together. There also is the street where Euklia is left to be eaten by dogs, the market, the prison where Andrew is kept, and the place of public execution, where the network among believers is strengthened and expanded to the broader public. The outside is the place of death.

2.2. The Context (Pass. Andr. 1–16 [333–39])

In what follows, I will focus on one sequence within the narrative that best illustrates the intertwining of slavery and gender. The narrative itself begins *in medias res*, presupposing that both Maximilla and her loyal slave woman, Iphidama, already believe in Christ and that they know that Andrew is a healer.[11] Andrew heals Alkmanes, the beloved slave boy of

---

Patras 25.–31. Mai 1980, JSPSSup 8 (Athens: Hetaireia Peloponnēsiakōn Spudōn, 1981–1982), 325–52. Translations are mine.

9. Aigeates's unnamed enslaved servant informs Aigeates at length about Andrew's effect on Aigeates's family (Pass. Andr. 24–25 [341–42]), and Iphidama speaks a prayer (Pass. Andr. 28 [343]).

10. Corinth was the capital of the province of Achaia.

11. The beginning is missing in the ancient manuscripts. On the complex situation of the manuscripts and other witnesses to the text, see Prieur, *Acta Andreae*, 1–65.

Aigeates's brother Stratokles, which results in their both coming to faith in Christ. The believing community is gathered in a palace bedroom when Proconsul Aigeates returns home, and Andrew protects them from being seen by making them invisible to him while he sits on his chamber pot for hours. Maximilla refuses sex with Aigeates, who is thereupon quite downcast. Andrew urges Maximilla to refrain from sex with her husband, reciting a long prayer over her.

2.3. Miss Respectable Helps the Blessed Lady to Remain Holy (Pass. Andr. 17–18 [339])

One might have expected that the narrator would follow Andrew's prayer, recited in the very bedroom in which Aigeates might tempt Maximilla to engage in "foul corruption," with an account of her next valiant act of resistance to his direct entreaties, but that is not what happens. Instead, Maximilla devises a plan of her own. The placement of Maximilla's plan immediately after Andrew's prayer leads the narratee to view the plan as her own action taken with Andrew's blessing and in accordance with the Lord's wish for her, as her way of helping the Lord to protect her.

Apparently still in the bedroom, Maximilla summons her slave woman, named Euklia, which means "of good reputation" and which I translate as "Miss Respectable." The narrator's description of her as "totally gorgeous and exceedingly wanton by nature" renders the name Euklia ironic.[12] The name and description serve to contrast Euklia with Iphidama, Maximilla's faithful enslaved servant and fellow believer, whose appearance the narrator at no point describes. Maximilla tells Euklia what she herself takes pleasure in and desires, promising to give Euklia whatever she wants: "If you will enter into a pact with me and keep safe what I am confiding in you."

Maximilla speaks here in the first person. Through direct speech, Maximilla is able to define herself as a benefactress and as willing to grant to Euklia all that she wishes, if Euklia will remain silent. That agreement, however, contains dangerous seeds, because of Euklia's potential to speak. At any moment, Euklia has the potential to become a domestic enemy, which is now heightened because of her proximity to the most politically powerful person in the story, Aigeates. The distancing narrative report of

---

12. Pass. Andr. 17 [339]: Πάνυ εὔμορφος καὶ φύσει ἄτακτος ὑπερβολῇ.

Euklia's speaking renders her a flat, noncomplex character, as one who spells trouble, rather than as one who might evoke sympathy.

Maximilla's words show that she, although determined to avoid Aigeates for spiritual reasons, actually has desires. Maximilla communicates the pleasures that she enjoyed with her husband, so that Euklia can act her part as persuasively as possible. Euklia does not speak directly; instead the narrator describes her response to Maximilla's initiative: "when she had been ... reassured by her." The ancient freeborn reader would expect to hear the direct words of other freeborn persons, including of the antagonist Aigeates, but might not expect to hear enslaved persons speaking directly to them. In line with that, the narrator reports on the speech of the enslaved, which creates greater distance between the narratee and their speech than either direct or indirect speech. With direct speech, the narratee may evaluate the words.

Euklia's reassurance comforts Maximilla and supports her in her wish to "lead a holy life." The narrator depicts an intimate moment of female space in which Maximilla adorns Euklia "and let[s] her sleep with Aigeates in her place."

The ancient narratees understand the surrogacy entailed by enslavement and know that slaveholders can reduce the risk to their own persons through employing persons enslaved to them as extensions of themselves. They would not be surprised that Maximilla sends Iphidama out into the streets to find Andrew. The sexual surrogacy described here is unusual, but still in keeping with an owner's expectation that her enslaved servant act as a buffer between herself and the unpleasantness of the world. The narrator creates sympathy with Maximilla's proposal by having it follow directly on the prayer that delineates the high stakes of the enmity between "foul corruption" at the hands of the "serpent," by portraying Euklia as well suited for this task by virtue of her wantonness and by depicting her as a flat character. The narrator controls the narratee's view of Euklia through the name and adjectives and by the evaluative reports on her speech. Beyond this, the omniscient narrator does not describe Euklia's inner thoughts or feelings. This narrative leaves no space for Euklia herself to have chosen a path of sexual purity; indeed, the phrase "exceedingly wanton by nature" implies that she had already rejected that path before Maximilla asked her to agree to the pact. Ancient readers who lived with slavery all around them both knew of the severe constraints on enslaved persons and of the many intelligent enslaved servants who employed all kinds of strategies to stay alive and to improve their life circumstances. This narrator, however, does not portray

Euklia as constrained by her state of bondage, but rather as fully capable of entering into a contractual agreement with Maximilla. The only indication given by the narrator as to why she might agree is her wantonness.

Aigeates uses Euklia as if she were his own wife and then lets her return to her own room, just as he has been accustomed to do with Maximilla. The Roman practice of having sex in dark bedrooms might help to explain why Aigeates does not know that he is sleeping with Euklia rather than his own wife (Ovid, *Ars* 2.619–20; *Am.* 1.5.7–8; Martial, *Epigr.* 11.2.4; 11.104.5; 12.43.10; Tacitus, *Ann.* 15.37).[13] Or perhaps, just as the Lord made the Christians invisible and allowed them to pass by Aigeates after having gathered in the bedroom, so too the Lord is protecting Maximilla by concealing Euklia's identity from Aigeates. Alternatively, Aigeates's own carnality and self-preoccupation, as exhibited in his sitting on the chamber pot for hours, could suggest to the narratee why Aigeates does not notice with whom he is actually sleeping.

Maximilla utilizes the reprieve well; "restored and rejoicing in the Lord" (Pass. Andr. 17 [339]), she spends the time with Andrew and escapes notice. Nevertheless, a boundary violation has occurred in that Euklia freely enters and leaves Aigeates's bedroom. An enslaved woman being in the master's bedroom would not count as a boundary violation in the narratee's world, but an enslaved woman impersonating the master's wife in his bedroom would. The narrator signals that this cannot go on forever: Maximilla "escaped detection for a long time." The deception of a powerful man in his own space will not end well.

The Passion of Andrew suggests that the Lord approves of Maximilla's clandestine use of Euklia as a sexual surrogate. While Euklia sleeps with her "hostile snake" of a husband, Maximilla is "rejoicing in the Lord" (Pass. Andr. 17 [339]).

2.4. Euklia's Breach of Contract (Pass. Andr. 18 [339–40])

Euklia's action defines her as bold but it sets in motion the beginning of the end. Although within the terms of the contract with Maximilla, freedom is the most precious, the most expensive gift that Euklia can ask for.

---

13. See Jan. N. Bremmer, "Man, Magic, and Martyrdom in the Acts of Andrew," in *The Apocryphal Acts of Andrew*, ed. Jan N. Bremmer, SECA 5 (Leuven: Peeters, 2000), 21. For a rabbinic assumption that a husband recognizes his wife at night by her voice, see b. Git. 23a.

Freedom only partially removes Euklia from Maximilla's authority, for as a freedwoman she still has duties to her patroness. Maximilla is said to free her the same day. The ancient reader would know, however, that a slaveholder could not normally manumit an enslaved person in a day. The Passion of Andrew represents Maximilla as a Roman matron, the wife of the Roman proconsul, who would certainly be subject to Roman law. Full manumission was a formal process, requiring the approval of a Roman magistrate. Maximilla could obviously not ask her husband to approve the manumission, nor any official who answered to him, because that could unmask the deception. Roman law did recognize "manumission among friends" (*manumissio inter amicos*), which consisted of an oral declaration of manumission in the presence of witnesses.[14] This would also be totally contrary to the secret arrangement depicted in the Passion of Andrew. Thus, the freedom obtained by Euklia has little to do with legal manumission, but is rather simply a narrative device that demonstrates Maximilla's largesse.

As the first thing for which Euklia asks, freedom epitomizes Euklia's earthly nature, the fact that she is tied to the things of this world. If the eight months suggest pregnancy, freedom for Euklia would mean that her child would be born free and not subject to natal alienation. According to the theology of the Passion of Andrew, both childbearing and concern about the status of one's child as free or enslaved denote imprisonment in the material world, as opposed to the recognition that the transcendent realm is all that matters. In contrast, Iphidama does not and would not ask for her freedom. As Maximilla's sister in Christ, Iphidama is her fellow slave woman of the Lord, which renders her earthly legal status irrelevant.

Just a few days after Euklia has ostensibly received her freedom, she asks for a considerable amount of money, which Maximilla immediately gives her. Then Euklia asks for fine clothing and jewelry, none of which Maximilla refuses her. Thus, Euklia repeatedly asks and Maximilla repeatedly gives without delay. The repetition paints Euklia as greedy, sensual, and focused on the things of this world—freedom, money, beautiful clothing, headbands, and jewelry—and Maximilla as generous, charitable, selfless, and spiritual.

---

14. Under the *lex Iunia Norbana* (perhaps 17 BCE), a person so manumitted was free, but not a citizen, during their lifetime, and their patron inherited their property upon death. For Justinian's alteration, see Corpus Iuris Civilis, Institutiones 1.5.3.

Euklia's escalating demands over eight months—suggestive of pregnancy—after she begins sleeping with Aigeates may allude to the enslaved Hagar in Genesis.[15] The matriarch Sarah hands her slave woman Hagar over to Abraham in order to bear her child for her, albeit without subterfuge (Gen 16:2–3). Later, both Rachel and Leah hand over their slave women Bilhah and Zilpah to Jacob (Gen 30:3–4, 9).[16] Like Maximilla, biblical figures can also deceive. Judah's daughter-in-law Tamar and Ruth employ ruses to obtain their ends—with God's approval (Gen 38; Ruth).[17] Early Christians could plausibly read the Bible as giving a woman the right to hand over a slave woman to her husband. The early Christian reading, of course, contains a very new twist. Sarah, Leah, and Rachel hand over their slave women for the purpose of having children by their enslaved servants, whereas Maximilla hands over Euklia to Aigeates in order to keep her body pure and to remain holy. In Genesis, children are God's purpose; in the Passion of Andrew, celibacy is God's will. In these stories in Genesis and the Passion of Andrew, all of the enslaved women fulfill their duty. Hagar, Zilpah, and Bilhah all bear sons for their mistresses. In contrast to Genesis, the Passion of Andrew does not say that Euklia bears a child. Whereas in Genesis, the status of Hagar's child is a matter of struggle and dispute, in the Roman world, everyone knows that the child of a slave woman is enslaved. Any child that she might have borne to Aigeates would have increased the size of his estate but would not be his heir. Therefore, and because the Passion

---

15. On ancient thinking about the eighth month as a particularly dangerous time in a pregnancy, see especially Solevåg, *Birthing Salvation*, 190–91; Ann Ellis Hanson, "The Eight Months' Child and the Etiquette of Birth: *Obsit Omen!*," *BHM* 61 (1987): 589–602. On an eighth-month pregnancy and on pregnancy as the feared outcome of adultery that renders it public, see Saundra Schwartz, "From Bedroom to Courtroom: The Adultery Type-Scene and the Acts of Andrew," in *Mapping Gender in Ancient Religious Discourses*, ed. Todd C. Penner and Caroline Vander Sitchele (Leiden: Brill, 2007), 303–4.

16. See Jennifer A. Glancy, *Corporal Knowledge: Early Christian Bodies* (New York: Oxford University Press, 2010), 67–68. She notes the echoes of the Hagar narrative in the Acts of Andrew. Ancient readers of Greek novels may also have seen a parallel to the Euklia sequence in Heliodoros, where a stepmother named Demainete hands over her slave woman Thisbe to have sex with her stepson Knemon for the purpose of tricking him (*Aeth.* 1.11.15–17).

17. See Rachel Adelman, "Seduction and Recognition in the Story of Judah and Tamar and the Book of Ruth," *Nashim* 23 (2012): 87–109.

of Andrew promotes celibacy and not progeny, there is no narrative reason for Euklia to give birth.

When Hagar finds that she is pregnant, "she looked with contempt on her mistress" (Gen 16:4 NRSV). Reminiscent of Hagar, Euklia tells her fellow enslaved laborers about the affair, "boasting and bragging" (Pass. Andr. 18 [339]). Euklia's insubordination lies in her speech. First she speaks to her mistress, demanding worldly things. Although her verbal demands are within the limits of the agreement, they signify her escalating insubordination: first freedom, then money, clothing, and adornments. Euklia cannot hold her tongue. By describing Euklia's speech with such laden terms as "boasting and bragging," rather than attributing direct speech to her, the narrator maintains greater control over the representation of Euklia. In the absence of Euklia's own words, the narratee sees only that Euklia asks and asks and asks, but that the gifts do not satisfy her, whereupon she boasts and brags. Maximilla assumes that her gifts, each given in accordance with the contract, have made Euklia "loyal and not gossipy."[18] The narrator thereby portrays Maximilla as fully abiding by and trusting in a contract that was freely entered into by both parties, although a critical reader of today might see her as living in a parallel universe of upper-class obliviousness.

Gossip is what Euklia seems to desire most of all. She wants the world—or at least her world—to know that she is sleeping with the master, the most powerful man in the province. Marianne Bjelland Kartzow ascertains that ancient Mediterranean writers depicted gossip as potentially destabilizing the gendered spaces of the public and the private realms by leaking information, through powerful alternative networks, between the two.[19] Enslaved women sometimes figure prominently in such leaking.[20] Thus, the belittling depiction of women's speech as gossip may indicate anxiety about its powerful subversive potential. Euklia is intent on speaking, on letting everyone around her know the news. A master's sexual liaison with a slave woman is hardly unusual. That alone would not make for good gossip. The juicy gossip instead lies in the fact that Euklia has

---

18. Pass. Andr. 19 [339]: ἀφλύαρος καὶ πιστής (transposed in English for the sake of felicity).

19. Marianne Bjelland Kartzow, *Gossip and Gender: Othering of Speech in the Pastoral Epistles*, BZNW 164 (Berlin: de Gruyter, 2009).

20. See Bjelland Kartzow, *Gossip and Gender*, 211. Her examples include Lysias, *Erat.* 15–17; Plutarch, *Garr.* 507b–f; Plutarch, *Curios.* 519f.

successfully impersonated Maximilla for eight months, that Aigeates considers her to be his wife, a fact about which Euklia is determined to boast.

In the section on Euklia, the omniscient narrator does not apply verbs that denote thinking or perceiving to Euklia, nor does the narrator describe any of Euklia's internal thoughts, feelings, or motivations. Instead, the descriptions of her boasting, bragging, gossiping, and laughing direct the narratee to view her in a very particular light.

Euklia's boasting, like Hagar's contempt for her mistress, foreshadows violence in her future. In Genesis, Sarah deals so harshly with Hagar that she flees (Gen 16:6). At first, Euklia's fellow enslaved laborers, vexed with her boasting, simply speak ill of her among themselves. (The term σύνδουλοι [Pass. Andr. 18 (339)], "fellow enslaved laborers," shows that Euklia is actually not free, in spite of the ostensible manumission.) Their vexation at Euklia demonstrates their loyalty to the master and mistress. As if to justify the far greater violence that will befall Euklia, Euklia does not rest content with verbal boasting. She wants to prove to the others that she sleeps with the master as if she were the mistress. She waits until the master is dead drunk, which does not seem to take very long, and sets two of her fellow enslaved servants at the head of his bed. When Euklia awakens Aigeates from a deep sleep, he addresses Euklia as "Maximilla, my lady" (Pass. Andr. 18 [339]), words that reveal his affection for Maximilla. In his drunken state, Aigeates does not notice the other two at all. The narratee now grasps a major cause of the ruse's success: Aigeates is a drunken viper who cannot even recognize with whom he has been sleeping for the last eight months.

2.5. Maximilla Unveiled and Betrayed by Her Enslaved Servants (Pass. Andr. 19–21 [339–40])

While Euklia is boasting and betraying her mistress by revealing the secret arrangement, Maximilla is spending nights with Andrew and other believers, relying on the contract to keep her husband at bay. Far from persuading Euklia to do her this favor on moral grounds, she has instead selected Euklia based in part on Euklia's bad moral character. Thus, Euklia's compliance depends solely on the gifts. And trouble is brewing. Andrew has a portentous dream about a contrivance in the house of Aigeates that is "full of disturbance and wrath" (Pass. Andr. 19 [340]).

Andrew's words confirm Andrew's spiritual powers; he can see what has happened in another place and what will happen in the near future.

Andrew is the third of the three freeborn persons to speak directly in the section on Euklia. Their direct speech serves to evoke empathy with them, even with Aigeates, who, though deceived, loves his wife. In contrast, none of the enslaved characters in the sequence speak directly, which enables the narrator more effectively to portray their boundary-breaching speech as the central problem.

Maximilla begs to know what the dream means, but Andrew tells her that she will know soon enough. Maximilla regularly disguises herself to leave the house to be with Andrew. In comparison, Aigeates's brother Stratokles apparently does not have to disguise himself in order to join the other believers. Maximilla seems to need a double camouflage: Euklia acting in the role of Maximilla and a veil concealing her own person. The double ruse enables her to avoid sex with her own husband and to spend nights of holy celibacy with Andrew and the other believers.

When Maximilla returns to the house this time, however, the enslaved household staff members have decided to switch loyalties. The narrator does not comment on their reasons, but their actions constitute the crisis that Andrew saw in his dream. Ancient freeborn readers familiar with slavery might have assumed fear of the master or mistress or hope of reward from one of them. Enslaved or freed readers familiar with the moral ambiguities and pressures of slavery might recognize these staff members as clever, defiant persons carefully maneuvering the Scylla and Charybdis of slavery, although their own experience would have led them to such a reading far more than what the narrator tells them. The enslaved staff members now know of Euklia's affair with Aigeates and of Maximilla's daily trips to see Andrew, which they presumably assume are adulterous. Right at the entrance, they grab Maximilla as if she were a stranger and rip off her veil. In front of them is their mistress, caught in the act of deceiving their master by leaving home under cover of a disguise. Whereas the biblical Tamar had veiled herself to conceal her identity from her father-in-law Judah as a means of obtaining her rightful offspring by him (Gen 38:14), Maximilla veils herself to escape the marriage bed. Pandemonium breaks out. The ancient reader would understand the imminent danger to the enslaved staff members. If they do not tell Aigeates, he could punish them brutally. Some cast their lot with Aigeates, victim of deceit, but others stand by Maximilla, "moved by a simulated affection toward their mistress" (Pass. Andr. 20 [340]). Their lives at stake, they beat one another. Maximilla uses the minor riot as a chance to escape to her bedroom, where she prays to the Lord "to avert all evil from her" (Pass. Andr. 20 [340]).

Seizing on Maximilla's vulnerability, her enslaved supporters rush into her bedroom and flatter her in the hope of a bribe. The "blessed woman"[21] instructs her faithful and Christian slave woman Iphidama to open the coffers. Giving them the generous sum of one thousand denarii, she "commanded them not to make the affair known" (Pass. Andr. 21 [340]); in response, they swear that they will remain silent.

The ancient Christian narratee would suspect that enslaved persons demanding such a bribe are of the devil, and so they are. Once again, Maximilla's gifts are to no avail. "Their father the devil" guides them to betray Maximilla to Aigeates (Pass. Andr. 21 [340]). Aigeates learns about it all: how Maximilla has arranged for Euklia to sleep with him in her place so as to avoid sex with him and how Euklia has boasted about it. Confirming that Euklia is hardly free, Aigeates interrogates her under torture.[22] When Euklia confesses that she has received gifts from Maximilla to keep her quiet, Aigeates's rage knows no bounds.

Maximilla's, Aigeates's, and Andrew's hopes, fears, and desires all converge on Euklia's enslaved body, which now bears the brunt of it all. As Maximilla's surrogate, Euklia's body extends Maximilla's own. Paradoxically, Euklia is both merged with Maximilla as her sexual extension and yet totally separate from her as a barrier between wife and husband.

---

21. Pass. Andr. 21 [340]: ἡ μακαρῖτις. Maximilla remains "the blessed" throughout the narrative.

22. Ancient readers would have understood that Aigeates was hardly conforming to Roman law, but they would also have known that enslaved persons were generally able to be tortured, while free persons were usually not. Emperor Hadrian (117–138) wrote that free persons already condemned to capital punishment could be tortured, i.e., the state enslaved persons convicted of capital crimes (*servi poenae*), and they were therefore subject to torture; otherwise free persons could not legally be tortured (Dig. 48.19.29 [Gaius]; see also 48.18.12 [Macer]). By the end of the second century, however, and under the Christian Roman emperors, lower-ranking free persons could also be legally interrogated under torture (*quaestio per tormenta*). See Dig. 48.18 on criminal investigations, especially 48.18.1.1 (Ulpian, citing Emperor Hadrian, who both assumes that torture is for enslaved persons and limits it) and 48.18.1.9 (Ulpian, who reports that freed persons may not be tortured when their patrons have been accused of capital crimes). For differentiated overviews of the historical development of investigations under torture, see Janne Pölönen, "Plebeians and Repression of Crime in the Roman Empire: From Torture of Convicts to Torture of Suspects," *RIDA* 51 (2004): 217–57; Joachim Ermann, "Folterung Freier im römischen Strafprozeß der Kaiserzeit bis Antoninus Pius," *ZSS* 117 (2000): 424–31, who notes that enslaved persons were not witnesses but rather evidence.

Euklia can therefore simultaneously protect Maximilla's chastity and fulfill Aigeates's carnal desires. As long as Euklia serves as the buffer between Maximilla and Aigeates, she serves Andrew's mission of helping Maximilla to maintain her purity, a purity that elevates Maximilla spiritually. But when Euklia's body no longer serves these multiple purposes, Aigeates rushes to torture, while Maximilla and Andrew remain passive. Within Maximilla's and Andrew's moral universe, there would be no reason for them to try to prevent the torture of Euklia. Euklia lives in and for the flesh and has betrayed her mistress.

2.6. Death to Slavish Slander (Pass. Andr. 22 [340–41])

In his rage at Euklia for boasting to her fellow enslaved laborers and for "slandering the mistress"[23] (note again, not "the patroness," which would be the proper term if Euklia were legally free), Aigeates cuts out Euklia's tongue, cuts off her hands and feet, and has her put out into the street, where dogs will eat her after she herself has gone without food for some days.[24] Cutting out Euklia's tongue suits her crimes of boasting and slander.[25] Cutting off her extremities may signify definitively removing her agency. He crucifies the three enslaved staff members who reported the matter to him. As the narrator has it, out of love for Maximilla, Aigeates "wanted the matter to be kept silent" (Pass. Andr. 22 [341]).

Rather than causing a crisis in the narrative, either for Aigeates or for Maximilla or her fellow believers, these killings restore a balance that Euklia's and her fellow servants' speech had disrupted. Both Maximilla and Aigeates wanted silence, Maximilla so that she could avoid Aigeates, and Aigeates because he loved Maximilla. Enslaved speech has foiled them both. The enslaved persons' death restores the silence desired by both

---

23. Pass. Andr. 22 [341]: ὑποδιαβάλλουσα τὴν δέσποιναν.

24. On contemporaneous views of dogs as exposing their sex lives to public view and as voracious, both of which might be said of Euklia and Aigeates, see Solevåg, *Birthing Salvation*, 191–93. See also Mark Nanos, "Paul's Reversal of Jews Calling Gentiles 'Dogs' (Philippians 3:2): 1600 Years of an Ideological Tail Wagging an Exegetical Dog?," *BibInt* 17 (2009): 458–59.

25. See ancient Christian "tours of hell," in which the narrator reports seeing punishments in hell that suit specific sins, including hanging by the tongue for having slandered (Acts Thom. 56), having lips cut off or the tongue bit through and the mouth filled with fire for having lied (Apoc. Pet. 9 [Ethiopic]; 29 [Akhmim]), and chewing the tongue for having reviled God (Vis. Paul 39).

Maximilla and Aigeates. The killings do, however, rupture the triangular structure of the narrative (Aigeates's and Andrew's struggle over Maximilla), but the rupture is temporary and will heal quickly.

In this sharply dualistic narrative, Euklia stands for the earthly things that Maximilla, Andrew, and other believers transcend: physical beauty, legal status as free, money, clothing, jewelry, and peer acknowledgement that she is sleeping with the most powerful man in the province. Far from leading the narratee to mourn Euklia's death or to mark it in any special way within the narrative, the narrator instead turns back to the freeborn figures whose lives have been purged of Euklia's demands and boasting. Aigeates, although a "snake" and the "enemy," shows genuine affection for Maximilla and is now unable to eat, not because he has killed four human beings but rather owing to his anguish over Maximilla. In contrast even to Aigeates, Euklia is only carnal and bound to the things of this earth. She is slavish in every way that slaveholders imagine: inordinate, eager for a bribe and quick to betray its giver, and arrogant beyond her position in life. In the logic of this narrative, Euklia's death is her own fault. She is a tool in Maximilla's long struggle to keep her body pure, a tool that has failed at its task.

2.7. Silence Restored: Aigeates's Plea to Maximilla (Pass. Andr. 23 [341])

Silence now falls over the slavish gossiping, revealing the underlying conflict between Aigeates and Maximilla. Without the buffer that Euklia's body provided, Maximilla is at greater risk of defiling her body with Aigeates. The eight months of Euklia's surrogacy provided a reprieve. Now that silence has been restored, the grief-stricken Aigeates tearfully pleads on bended knee with Maximilla to take him back. He even says that he will forgive any adultery that she may have committed and keep it secret. Offering to forgive one's wife of adultery is not only culturally astounding; it is illegal. A statute promulgated by the Emperor Augustus required husbands to divorce their adulterous wives, who were to forfeit their property and be banished to a remote island.[26] The state was to criminally prosecute as a pimp (*leno*) a husband who did not divorce his adulterous wife (Sen-

---

26. The *lex Julia de adulteriis coercendis* (after 18 BCE). See Thomas A. J. McGinn, *Prostitution, Sexuality, and the Law in Ancient Rome* (New York: Oxford University Press, 1998), 140–247.

tences of Paul 2.26.8; Dig. 48.5.2.2).[27] Not all women, as ancient readers knew, fell under this law.[28] For example, enslaved women could not be prosecuted for adultery, because they could not legally marry (e.g., Dig. 48.5.6 [Papinian]; 23.2.24 [Modestinus]). Prostitutes, even if they were married, could not be prosecuted (Tacitus, *Ann.* 2.85.1–3).[29] In fact, a woman's liability to the law of adultery was actually a mark of status, for it signified that she was honorable. In the Passion of Andrew, Maximilla epitomizes both Christian purity and Roman honor. If she were guilty of adultery, as an abettor of that crime, Aigeates would himself be a criminal, and his status would immediately sink. The risk that Aigeates takes with his offer to forgive even adultery on Maximilla's part and his affectionate praise of her prudence and moderate character serve to portray his character as complex. At this moment, Aigeates is more tragic than evil. Far from criticizing Aigeates for having silenced the gossipy Euklia and the three servants who reported the story to him, the narrator portrays him as a man in anguish about the loss of the love of his life, as unable to comprehend what has befallen him.

Maximilla patiently explains to Aigeates that she does not love another man but rather something that is not of this world.

2.8. Aigeates Crucifies Andrew and Kills Himself (Pass. Andr. 25–65 [341–52]

Aigeates now focuses his attention on discovering what has caused the change in Maximilla, which another servant tells him. Knowing that Aigeates crucified the other enslaved attendants who spoke ill of their mistress, this servant nevertheless decides to take his chances and secretly tell all to his master. In a rare instance of direct speech by an enslaved person, the servant tells Aigeates that not only has Maximilla followed her slave woman Iphidama's lead, but that the slave-holding Stratokles—without any shame—goes out into public to buy his own vegetables and bread, and that he actually carries them through the streets himself (Pass. Andr. 25 [341–42]).

---

27. See McGinn, *Prostitution, Sexuality*, 171–94.

28. See McGinn, *Prostitution, Sexuality*, 194–202; Theodor Mommsen, *Römisches Strafrecht* (Leipzig: Duncker & Humblot, 1899), 691–92.

29. A woman named Vistilia registered as a prostitute in an attempt to avoid prosecution as an adulteress.

The male slaveholder Stratokles behaves differently from Maximilla. Stratokles's Christian faith causes him to do the work that enslaved persons should be doing for him, whereas the story does not anywhere depict Maximilla as doing the work of enslaved attendants. On the contrary, she continues to rely heavily on enslaved women. The cultural requirement for Maximilla, but not for Stratokles, to sleep with a spouse may partly explain the discrepancy. Maximilla's elite female body is under legal obligation to Aigeates and at risk of being dishonored if she appears on the open streets alone. For these reasons, Maximilla needs both Euklia and Iphidama in a way that Stratokles does not need enslaved attendants. Happily, Alkmanes decides to follow Andrew, leading to a harmonious relationship between the master and his slave boy, which may continue to be homo-affectional. Alkmanes's legal status remains ambiguous. On the one hand, Stratokles has given up all of his possessions, which presumably includes his human property, but, on the other hand, after Stratokles has relinquished his property, Aigeates's enslaved attendant says, "he who has many slaves shows himself a servant" (Pass. Andr. 25 [342]).

Ultimately, Aigeates casts Andrew into prison and crucifies him. Andrew remains alive for four days on the cross, from which he preaches, bringing many to belief. Aigeates quietly kills himself, and Maximilla lives a peaceful life with the believing community.

3. Andrew, Maximilla, and Aigeates: An Inverted Love Triangle?

On the surface, the Passion of Andrew seems to be structured around an inverted love triangle, but only without taking account of slavery: Maximilla is at the center, fought over by her pagan husband, Aigeates, and the apostle Andrew.[30] Aigeates loves Maximilla and longs to resume their

---

30. On a love triangle in the Passion of Andrew, see Schwartz, "From Bedroom to Courtroom," 267–311. See also Kate Cooper, *The Virgin and the Bride: Idealized Womanhood in Late Antiquity* (Cambridge: Harvard University Press, 1996), 51. Cooper mentions Euklia only briefly and fails to mention that Aigeates later brutally kills her. Similarly, in *Women in Early Christianity*, the editor, Patricia Cox Miller, does not include the section on Euklia, summarizing it only briefly in square brackets and not mentioning her killing. See Cox Miller, *Women in Early Christianity: Translations from Greek Texts* (Washington, DC: Catholic University of America Press, 2005), 182. János Bolyki suggests that triangular structures in the Bible may have served as models. See Bolyki, "Triangles and What Is beyond Them: Literary, Historical, and Theological Systems of Coordinates in the Acts of Andrew," in *The Apocryphal Acts*

sexual relationship, while Andrew, out of love for Christ, urges Maximilla to keep her body pure and unsullied for Christ. Numerous features in the text certainly point to an inverted love triangle: Andrew's meeting with Maximilla in her bedroom, nightly visits by Maximilla to sleep with Andrew and other followers, and the overt struggle between Andrew and Aigeates, ending in the deaths of both. Of course, Maximilla does not have sex with Andrew, but spending nights at his side has erotic overtones. Aigeates certainly sees the triangle, saying that he will torment Maximilla through Andrew, whom she loves more than her husband.

Andrew's seeing in Maximilla a new Eve, and in himself a new Adam, certainly makes them a couple, albeit a celibate one (Pass. Andr. 37, 39 [345]). Andrew is not an autonomous saintly man but rather dependent on Maximilla's virtue. Maximilla has freed herself from Eve's passions, and Andrew perfects Adam's imperfection by fleeing to God. "What she took no heed of, you listened to, and what he consented to, I escape" (Pass. Andr. 37.26–27 [lacking in Detorakis]). Just as Adam died in Eve by agreeing to Eve's proposal, "so I now live in you who follow the Lord's commandment" (Pass. Andr. 39.2–4 [345]). This new Eve rejects the advances of Aigeates, whose father is the devil (Pass. Andr. 40 [346]). By recognizing her essence, her true spiritual nature, Maximilla inverts the Eve narrative. Whereas Eve had led her husband astray through ignorance, Maximilla does not lead her husband on a false path. While her refusal of Aigeates's sexual advances may seem to constitute disobedience, the Passion of Andrew depicts Maximilla as obeying a higher power. Rather than luring her husband into sin, she lives out Andrew's vision of holiness and chastity. In that sense, she becomes Andrew's mate in the immaterial, spiritual realm. She has reached the highest level of awareness, namely, knowledge of God.[31]

---

of Andrew, ed. Jan N. Bremmer (Leuven: Peeters, 2000), 70–80. For sober recognition of the role of slavery in the Passion of Andrew, see Solevåg, *Birthing Salvation*, 137–97; Outi Lehtipuu, "The Example of Thecla and the Example(s) of Paul: Disputing Women's Role in Early Christianity," in *Women and Gender in Ancient Religions: Interdisciplinary Approaches*, ed. Stephen P. Ahearne-Kroll, Paul A. Holloway, and James A. Kelhofer, WUNT 263 (Tübingen: Mohr Siebeck, 2010), 362–64.

31. Lautaro Roig Lanzilotta argues that the earliest form of the Acts of Andrew presents three stages of cognitive-spiritual development: (1) receiving Andrew's knowledge (the believing brothers and sister), (2) possessing that knowledge but not yet applying it (Stratokles), and (3) applying it to achieve knowledge of God (Maximilla). See Lanzilotta, *Acta Andreae Apocrypha: A New Perspective on the Nature,*

At a deeper level, however, the structure is not that of pure triangle, because enslaved women enable Maximilla to become and remain enslaved to Christ. Metaphorical enslavement to Christ differs radically, of course, from legal slavery. We have seen how Euklia's sexual surrogacy frees Maximilla to pray and spend nights with the apostle Andrew and the other believers as she learns how to recognize her true essence and focus on deeper spiritual matters, as well as Iphidama's vital role in enabling her mistress's religious development. Like the other enslaved persons in the narrative, Euklia and Iphidama are peripheral to Maximilla's story, which, according to Maximilla's culture, is as it should be. Faithful enslaved persons buffer the lives of their mistresses or masters, protecting them from and within a public arena that is subject to the violence endemic to highly stratified societies built on forced and exploitative labor. When these enslaved persons do their work properly, they register only on the periphery. We could read Euklia's and Iphidama's peripheral appearances within the narrative as confirming its triangular structure. Maximilla uses Euklia as a sexual surrogate for her husband, Aigeates, and Iphidama as a messenger surrogate to Andrew. In this reading, the enslaved women enable the actions of the female protagonist but are inessential to the narrative's primary struggle between Aigeates and Andrew over Maximilla.

But in fact, without these enslaved women, the story falls apart. Maximilla uses her legal freedom, as well as the women whom she holds in bondage, to resist her husband, follow Andrew, and become a slave woman of Christ. Without Iphidama's accompaniment in public, Maximilla would be unable to maintain her elite status and visit Andrew, and she would be cut off from information concerning him. Iphidama may also serve in the narrative as a kind of chaperone whose presence makes clear that Maximilla's nightly visits with Andrew are not adulterous. (On the other hand, an enslaved attendant would not necessarily be seen as a reliable witness in these matters.)[32] Iphidama forges a path between Maximilla and Andrew, physically moving from one to the other and communicating between them. Thus, Iphidama does not disrupt the

---

Intention and Significance of the Primitive Text (Geneva: Cramer, 2007), 206 n. 215; 218–19.

32. For the early rabbinic view that a divorced woman may not be trusted alone with her former husband in the presence of an enslaved woman belonging to her, because she is too familiar with her own servant (although other enslaved men and women may be trusted as witnesses), see m. Git. 7:4.

triangular structure. She disrupts nothing, because she is an obedient slave woman. Euklia, who asserts her full personhood, on the other hand, disrupts everything. As an enslaved worker, she counts as both a person and a thing.[33] With respect to criminal liability, enslaved persons in the Roman world are always persons.[34] Aigeates treats Euklia as criminally liable, torturing and killing her and exposing her body to the wild dogs. To be sure, Aigeates does not hear her case in court, but then he is himself the highest magistrate in the province and is himself the law. As an insubordinate who speaks, Euklia bursts from the periphery to the center of the narrative. Had Euklia stayed compliant, she would have remained as a buffer between Maximilla and Aigeates. Instead, she disrupts the triangular structure by boasting about her sexual surrogacy and the gifts. But why is Euklia necessary in the first place?

As a Roman matron, Maximilla does not actually need a buffer, because she has the legal power to divorce Aigeates (Dig. 24.2). In fact, at the end of the story, she unilaterally separates from him and lives the celibate life that she wishes to live with her fellow believers (Pass. Andr. 64.6 [352]). Perhaps Maximilla needs Euklia as a sexual surrogate early in her spiritual journey, because she is not yet ready to make the definitive break with Aigeates. Maximilla's ongoing need for the sexual body that is Euklia may signify that Maximilla has not yet severed her own ties with the carnal realm. She needs to become more aware of her own essence before she can finally separate from Aigeates. Aigeates's ongoing presence in her life presents Maximilla with temptations that she needs to resist and that she does resist. Maximilla, of course, does not resist temptation alone; Andrew supports her, and Euklia takes her place in the marriage bed. In this reading, the triangle is not a pure triangle because Maximilla needs time, prayer, study, and the support of both enslaved and free persons before she has become sufficiently aware of her essence to leave Aigeates behind. Euklia fulfills one of the classic roles of an enslaved person: freeing her mistress to develop herself through thought and study.

The Acts of Andrew, which enjoyed widespread circulation over a broad geographical region for centuries, surely inspired women to follow

---

33. See Gaius, *Inst.* 1.9; 2.12–13.

34. See William W. Buckland, *The Roman Law of Slavery: The Condition of the Slave in Private Law from Augustus to Justinian* (1908, repr., Holmes Beach, FL: Gaunt, 1994), 91–97.

their vision of the ascetic holy life. That vision may have even included using enslaved women as sexual surrogates.

Gender and Disability in the Acts of Peter: Apostolic Power to Paralyze

Anna Rebecca Solevåg

1. Introduction

In the Acts of Peter, there are several stories of apostolically inflicted paralysis. In this essay, I analyze how gender and disability intersect in these stories. The most well-known is probably the story of how Peter first heals, then unheals his own daughter.[1] I argue that in this story and the others I will present, Greco-Roman understandings of disability, sexuality, and gender intersect. The complexity of the characters' interaction is, in my view, best understood by means of an intersectional hermeneutic. Intersectionality is an interdisciplinary approach at the crossroads of feminist, gender, antiracist, postcolonial, and class-sensitive modes of analysis.[2] An intersectional approach tries to identify how different vectors of domination and oppression function together, taking seriously that categories sometimes overlap and that identities are complex.[3] With a view to intersectional analysis of early Christian texts, Elisabeth Schüssler Fiorenza has coined the term *kyriarchy* and puts it forward as a useful model for interpretation. She defines the term like this: "derived from the Greek term lord, this coinage underscores that domination is not simply a matter of patriarchal, gender-based dualism but of more comprehen-

---

1. The story is only found in the Coptic papyrus document Codex Berolinensis 8502 (BG 4).

2. Paulina de los Reyes and Diana Mulinari, *Intersektionalitet: Kritiska reflektioner över (o)jämlikhetens landskap* (Stockholm: Liber, 2005).

3. Marianne Bjelland Kartzow, *Destabilizing the Margins: An Intersectional Approach to Early Christian Memory* (Eugene, OR: Pickwick, 2012), 10.

sive, interlocking, hierarchically ordered structures of discrimination."[4] By employing this term, Schüssler Fiorenza shows how important the role of the *kyrios/paterfamilias* is for understanding the intersecting power structures of antiquity.

In this essay, I employ an intersectional hermeneutic drawing particularly on insights from feminist and disability theory. Whereas feminist interpretation has a long history in biblical and early Christian studies, disability perspectives are fairly new in these fields and therefore need more of an introduction in a volume such as this.[5] Disability studies' intellectual roots are found in the social sciences, humanities, and rehabil-

---

4. Elisabeth Schüssler Fiorenza, *Rhetoric and Ethic: The Politics of Biblical Studies* (Minneapolis: Augsburg Fortress, 1999), ix.

5. The literature on feminist hermeneutics has grown enormously since the 1980s, and here I only pay tribute to the publications that have been the most formative for me. They include Elizabeth Schüssler Fiorenza, *In Memory of Her: A Feminist Theological Reconstruction of Christian Origins* (New York: Crossroad, 1983); Schüssler Fiorenza, *Searching the Scriptures: A Feminist Commentary* (New York: Crossroad, 1994); Turid Karlsen Seim, *The Double Message: Patterns of Gender in Luke-Acts*, trans. Brian McNeil (Edinburgh: T&T Clark, 1994); Jorunn Økland, *Women in Their Place: Paul and the Corinthian Discourse of Gender and Sanctuary Space*, JSNTSup 269 (London: T&T Clark, 2004); Carolyn Osiek and Margaret Y. MacDonald, *A Woman's Place: House Churches in Earliest Christianity* (Minneapolis: Fortress, 2006).

For biblical studies anthologies and monographs informed by disability studies, see Hector Avalos, Sarah J. Melcher, and Jeremy Schipper, eds., *This Abled Body: Rethinking Disabilities in Biblical Studies*, SemeiaSt 55 (Philadelphia: Fortress, 2007); Candida R. Moss and Jeremy Schipper, *Disability Studies and Biblical Literature* (Basingstoke: Palgrave Macmillan, 2011); Rebecca Raphael, *Biblical Corpora: Representations of Disability in Hebrew Biblical Literature*, LHBOTS (London: Continuum, 2009); Saul M. Olyan, *Disability in the Hebrew Bible: Interpreting Mental and Physical Differences* (New York: Cambridge University Press, 2008); Jeremy Schipper, *Disability and Isaiah's Suffering Servant*, BibRef (Oxford: Oxford University Press, 2011); Schipper, *Disability Studies and the Hebrew Bible: Figuring Mephibosheth in the David Story* (New York: T&T Clark, 2006); Louise Joy Lawrence, *Sense and Stigma in the Gospels: Depictions of Sensory-Disabled Characters* (Oxford: Oxford University Press, 2013). For works on the ancient Mediterranean world, see Henri-Jacques Stiker, *A History of Disability* (Ann Arbor: University of Michigan Press, 1999); Robert Garland, *The Eye of the Beholder: Deformity and Disability in the Graeco-Roman World* (Ithaca, NY: Cornell University Press, 1995); Martha L. Rose, *The Staff of Oedipus: Transforming Disability in Ancient Greece* (Ann Arbor: University of Michigan Press, 2003); Christian Laes, Chris F. Goodey, and Martha L. Rose, eds., *Disabilities in Roman Antiquity: Disparate Bodies a Capite ad Calcem* (Leiden: Brill, 2013).

itation sciences.⁶ Similar to feminist approaches and critical race studies, it stands at the intersection of political activism and academia. At the core of disability studies is a critique of the medical model of disability or other "property definitions" that see disability as the property of the person with an impairment.⁷ Instead, "the social model of disability" focuses attention on social oppression, cultural discourse, and environmental barriers rather than biological deficit.⁸

As a hermeneutical tool to understand ancient texts, disability offers some of the same insights as gender; it helps to understand how power is negotiated. Drawing on Joan Scott's famous article on the usefulness of gender as an analytical category in historical studies, Catherine J. Kudlick argues that disability provides "a new analytical tool for exploring power" and that it is crucial for understanding "how Western cultures determine hierarchies and maintain social order."⁹

2. Apostolic Disablement in the Acts of Peter

The Acts of Peter is one of the so-called apocryphal acts.¹⁰ It is not preserved as one coherent whole, and in my analysis I rely on several different text corpora in three different languages that together make up the (incomplete) Acts of Peter: the Act of Peter from the Coptic Berlin Codex, the Latin Actus Vercellenses, and the Greek Martyrdom of Peter.¹¹ The Acts of

---

6. Gary L. Albrecht, Katherine D. Seelman, and Michael Bury, "Introduction: The Formation of Disability Studies," in *The Handbook of Disability Studies*, ed. Gary L. Albrecht, Katherine D. Seelman, and Michael Bury (Thousand Oaks, CA: Sage, 2001), 2.

7. Gareth Williams, "Theorizing Disability," in Albrecht, Seelman, and Bury, *Handbook of Disability Studies*, 124–25.

8. Tom Shakespeare, "The Social Model of Disability," in *The Disability Studies Reader*, ed. Lennard J. Davis (New York: Routledge, 2006), 197.

9. Catherine J. Kudlick, "Disability History: Why We Need Another 'Other,'" *AHR* 108 (2003): 763–93. See Joan W. Scott, "Gender: A Useful Category of Historical Analysis," *AHR* 91 (1986): 1053–75.

10. There are five apocryphal acts that can be dated to the second and third centuries. See Hans-Josef Klauck, *The Apocryphal Acts of the Apostles: An Introduction*, trans. Brian McNeil (Waco, TX: Baylor University Press, 2008), 3.

11. Actus Vercellenses and the Martyrdom of Peter are published in Richard Adelbert Lipsius and Max Bonnet, *Acta Petri, Acta Pauli, Acta Petri et Pauli, Acta Pauli et Theclae, Acta Thaddei* (Darmstadt: Wissenschaftliche Buchgesellschaft, 1959). The Coptic Berlin Codex is published in Douglas M. Parrott, ed., *Nag Hammadi Codices*

Peter is commonly dated to the end of the second or the beginning of the third century.[12]

The Coptic Act of Peter tells the story of how Peter heals and unheals his paralyzed virgin daughter. The story is considered to be part of the otherwise lost first part of the Acts of Peter.[13] The Actus Vercellenses gives us the longest portion of text. After a brief prelude on how Paul leaves Rome for Spain, this Latin text focuses on Peter's contestations with the Jewish sorcerer Simon Magus in Rome and ends with Peter's martyrdom. The martyrdom is also preserved, in fairly similar phrasing to Actus Vercellenses, in the Greek Martyrdom of Peter. It is assumed that the original Acts of Peter was written in Greek and that it had more material in the beginning than we have preserved from the Actus Vercellenses.[14] In Actus Vercellenses, Peter recalls previous conflicts with Simon Magus in Jerusalem, and the lost beginning presumably covered Peter's ministry in Jerusalem before he travels to Rome.[15] In the Actus Vercellenses much of the narrative revolves around the conflict between Peter and Simon Magus, who claims to be some sort of Christ figure. Seduced by his magic tricks and deceitful speech, Roman Christians turn away from their former beliefs and follow Simon instead, worshiping him like a god. Peter

---

V,2–5 and VI with Papyrus Berolinensis 8502, 1 and 4, NHMS 1 (Leiden: Brill, 1979). The Epistle of Titus is published in RBén 37 (1925). For English translations of the texts, see "The Acts of Peter," in *The Apocryphal New Testament*, ed. John K. Elliott (Oxford: Clarendon, 1993), 397–427; Wilhelm Schneemelcher, "The Acts of Peter," in *Writings Relating to the Apostles, Apocalypses and Related Subjects*, vol. 2 of *New Testament Apocrypha*, ed. Wilhelm Schneemelcher and R. McLeod Wilson (Louisville: Westminster John Knox, 2003), 285–316. It is likely that all these texts belonged to the original Acts of Peter. However, the arguments I make in this essay are not dependent on the original unity of these texts.

12. Bremmer dates the Acts of Peter to the last two decades of the second century. See Jan N. Bremmer, "Aspects of the Acts of Peter: Women, Magic, Place and Date," in *The Apocryphal Acts of Peter: Magic, Miracles, and Gnosticism*, ed. Jan N. Bremmer (Leuven: Peeters, 1998), 18. Klauck dates it to ca. 200 CE (*Apocryphal Acts of the Apostles*, 84). Some also argue that the story "The Gardener's Daughter," from the Epistle of Titus (Pseudo-Titus), belonged to the original Acts of Peter (see Klauck, *Apocryphal Acts of the Apostles*, 106–7).

13. See, e.g., Klauck, *Apocryphal Acts of the Apostles*, 105–7.

14. Klauck, *Apocryphal Acts of the Apostles*, 82–83.

15. See, e.g., Schneemelcher, "Acts of Peter: Introduction," 279; Christine M. Thomas, *The Acts of Peter, Gospel Literature, and the Ancient Novel: Rewriting the Past* (Oxford: Oxford University Press, 2003), 68.

travels to Rome to win them back, and the narrative depicts these two men as archenemies representing good and evil, God and the devil. Peter and Simon compete for the favor of the Christian community in Rome, and their contestations for power are acted out through miracles, including healing and raising the dead, casting out demons, and even flying. Finally, Peter exposes Simon as a fraud, and Simon is driven from the city.

In the Acts of Peter miracles of unhealing are as common as healing miracles. There are some summary statements about Peter's healing miracles (BG 4, 128.4–6; Act. Verc. 29; Mart. Pet. 2) and a (possibly purely metaphorical) healing of some blind widows (Act. Verc. 21–22), but it is the stories of apostolic disablement that stand out. I want to look closer at four such episodes: the healing and unhealing of Peter's daughter, the condemnation and paralyzation of Rufina, a vision of the slaying of an Ethiopian demon, and the final undoing of Simon Magus, in which he falls, breaks his leg, and finally dies.

The story about Peter's daughter is fascinating and troubling. At a gathering on the Lord's Day, Peter, who is known for curing many sick people, is asked why he has not healed his own daughter, who is paralyzed and present at the gathering (BG 4, 128.10–19). "It is apparent to God alone why her body is not healthy" is Peter's answer, but, he adds, "God was not weak or unable to give this gift to my daughter" (BG 4, 129.10–12).[16] To prove this point, Peter proceeds to heal his daughter. He asks her to rise and walk toward him, and to the amazement of the crowd, she does so. Peter again addresses his daughter and says: "Go to your place, sit down, and become an invalid again. For this is beneficial for you and me" (BG 4, 129.14–19). So she goes back to her place and becomes paralyzed again. The crowd laments this turn of events, but Peter again assures them that "this is beneficial for her and me" (BG 4, 131.13–14). The reason she is lame, explains Peter, is that when she was ten she became so beautiful that she was a stumbling block to many men. One man in particular, Ptolemy, who had seen her when she was bathing, wanted to take her as his wife. But the girl's mother did not consent to Ptolemy's repeated marriage proposals. At this point in the story, two pages of the papyrus document are missing, so it is unclear what happens next. The story resumes as Peter and his wife find their daughter paralyzed on the doorstep, left there by

---

16. English quotations are from James Brashler and Douglas M. Parrott's translation in "The Act of Peter," in Parrott, *Nag Hammadi Codices V,2–5 and VI*.

Ptolemy (or his slaves). "We picked her up, praising the Lord who had saved his servant from defilement, pollution and destruction," Peter recalls (BG 4, 135.10–13).

The second story is from the beginning of Actus Vercellenses. Paul is about to leave Rome, to go to Spain "to be a Physician to the Spaniards."[17] The Roman Christians gather to receive the Eucharist from Paul before he leaves, and as one woman, Rufina, comes forward, Paul is filled by God's spirit and accuses her of improper behavior. She is an adulterer, he claims, and Satan will destroy her: "But if you repent of your deed, he is faithful to forgive your sins" (Act. Verc. 2). Upon hearing Paul's words, Rufina collapses, "being paralyzed on the left side from head to foot [*a capite usque ad ungues pedum*]. Nor could she speak anymore, for her tongue was tied" (Act. Verc. 2). Rufina's collapse seems to be a punishment for her misbehavior. It also affects the other believers, who start to worry whether God will forgive them their sins. Paul takes advantage of the situation to preach forgiveness to those who repent. Rufina's loss of speech is juxtaposed to Paul's eloquence. Her tied tongue and paralyzed body perhaps also serve as a foreshadowing of her eternal fate if she does not repent. Paul warns her that "Satan will trample down your heart and expose you before the eyes of all who believe in the Lord," so when she falls down it is a warning to "repent while you are still in the body" (Act. Verc. 2).

The third story is not a (un)healing miracle story but a vision. It seems perhaps ill fitting, but it will hopefully become clear why I have chosen to include it in this discussion. After a series of contestations between Peter and Simon Magus, Peter has slowly won back most of the Christians in Rome from Simon's grasp. Jesus appears to Simon in a vision, warning that on the coming Sabbath the two will meet for a final contest in the Roman forum. The night before the contest, the senator Marcellus, Peter's patron and a leading figure in the Christian community, also has a vision. It is this vision that seems to me to have affinities with the unhealing/paralysis theme. In Marcellus's vision, he sees a demon in the likeness of an Ethiopian woman; she is "very black, clad in filthy rags" (Act. Verc. 22). A figure who seems to be both Christ and Peter appears with a sword and cuts off the woman's limbs and decapitates her. The woman represents "the whole power of Simon and of his god [i.e., Satan]" (Act. Verc. 22),

---

17. Unless otherwise noted, all English quotations from Actus Vercellenses and the Martyrdom of Peter are from Elliott's translation in *Apocryphal New Testament*.

and the vision encourages Peter and Marcellus that "the Lord always takes care of his own" (Act. Verc. 22) and hence that they will defeat Simon in the forum.

The fourth and last story about paralysis and disablement is the story of Simon's fall from the sky, which is the final demise of Simon's power over the Christians in Rome. With the contest in the forum, in which Peter has raised three dead men but Simon none (he has, however, killed one), it has become clear to the crowd that Peter represents the more powerful god. In a desperate move to win back the favor of the Romans, Simon promises that he will fly over the *via sacra*. Clearly this is in imitation of Jesus's ascension. Simon claims to be divine, to be Christ, when he says: "I ascend to my father and shall say to him: 'Me, your son who stands, they desired to bring low; however, I had no deal with them, but returned to myself'" (Mart. Pet. 2). If Simon flies, he proves that he is Christ. So Peter prays that Simon may fall: "let him fall down and become crippled but not die; let him be disabled and break his leg in three places" (Mart. Pet. 3). Simon falls down, and his attempt at *imitatio Christi* becomes a parody. His power is obviously broken, as he lies on the ground with a broken leg. One of his earlier followers drive home the point: "Simon, if God's power is broken, shall not that God, whose power you are, be darkened?" (Mart. Pet. 3).

In many respects, the stories about Rufina's and Simon's unhealing are quite different from Peter's daughter's. Their disability is clearly a punishment for misdeed. In these two stories there is, I would argue, symbolic overtones to their falling down—it is both physical and spiritual. The vision of the Ethiopian demon highlights this metaphorical level. In the vision, the physical disablement of the female demon *is* the eradication of the evil power. There is the same juxtaposition of a powerful, male, able-bodied apostle and a powerless, disabled woman (or emasculated man) in all these stories.

Another interesting likeness between these episodes is that they are all played out in front of an audience of Christian believers. Even in the vision it is pointed out that the slaying takes place in front of "a great multitude" (Act. Verc. 22). It has been noted that in the healing and unhealing miracles of the Acts of Peter it is the community rather than the individual that seems to be the main beneficiary. Magda Misset-Van de Weg has argued that both the healing and the unhealing miracles are performed for the benefit of the community. Phrases such as "God watches over those who are his and he prepares what is good for each one" (BG 4, 139.19–140.4) and "the Lord always takes care of his own" (Act. Verc. 22) underscore this point.[18] In the story about Peter's daughter, Peter's act of healing and unhealing is clearly for the sake of the audience: to teach them what he believes to be beneficial to himself and his daughter. Moreover, Peter's story about his daughter's paralysis includes the tale of how the seducer, Ptolemy, regretted his actions against the daughter and after his death left her his fortune. Peter, as executor of the will, sold the property and distributed the money among the poor. Thus the community has benefited both spiritually and materially from the episode. Similarly, Rufina's *Strafwunder* becomes an opportunity for the community to repent their sins, and the demon vision strengthens the believers' faith that Peter will prevail. Last, Simon's fall leads to the conversion to Christianity of Simon's most dedicated followers.

There is, however, a gender dimension to this community concern that needs to be further scrutinized. In the following, I will discuss more closely the interconnections between disability, gender, and sexuality in the stories I have presented.

3. Paralysis, Gender, and Sexuality

Both stories of female unhealing are tied to the woman's sexuality. Rufina is punished for her adultery, while Peter's daughter is saved from sexual defilement. She has been paralyzed, as an act of God, to preserve her from being raped by Ptolemy. That this is a good thing is clearly stated. The daughter's disability is explained and given positive value by understanding it according to a hierarchy of valued goods. Two different afflictions are juxtaposed, and the daughter's disability is held up as the preferred alternative. Which is better, to be lame or to have a violated body? To have a broken leg or a broken hymen? As if it were a game of divine "Would you rather," Peter juxtaposes these two scenarios and argues that his daughter is better off as she is, and so is he.

Peter's argument reflects Greco-Roman gender values. A young girl was a future bride, and as such young, free women's most important asset was their virginity. Peter's argument also reveals his position as a householder, a male *kyrios*, whose responsibility it was to rule over his household and keep wife, children, and slaves under control. It was shameful for the

---

18. Magda Misset-van de Weg, "'For the Lord Always Takes Care of His Own': The Purpose of the Wondrous Works and Deeds in the Acts of Peter," in Bremmer, *Apocryphal Acts of Peter*, 101.

whole family if a daughter was sexually violated, especially for the head of the household, whose responsibility it was to protect his women's sexual honor. The story of Verginia, told by Livy, has clear likenesses with that of Peter's daughter.[19] In a desperate attempt to prevent his daughter from being abducted and raped, the statesman Verginius kills his own daughter (Livy, *Ab urb. cond.* 3.44–48). Abduction marriages were well known in antiquity. *Raptus* involved the abduction of an unmarried girl by a man who had not made a formal betrothal agreement with her. The assumption that the union had been consummated during the abduction period would then force the consent of the girl's parents.[20] Hence, the hoped-for end result was that the abductor would marry his victim. Ptolemy's scheme bears the resemblance of a typical *raptus*. After his marriage offer is (repeatedly) turned down, Ptolemy becomes impatient and abducts the girl, but something happens, so he returns her to her father's home, paralyzed. Exactly how paralysis rescued the daughter from violation is unclear due to the lacuna. Although Peter creates a clear either-or scenario, becoming paralyzed does not necessarily exclude being raped. On the contrary, from what we know about the experiences of disabled women today, it seems likely that paralysis would make the daughter more vulnerable to a sexual assault.[21]

A disability of this kind would probably render a virgin unmarriageable. Her impairment is described in vivid terms as "completely paralyzed" on one side of her body (BG 4, 129.4), and she "lies crippled" in the corner of the room (BG 4, 129.4–5). Even if she would be able to carry out the roles expected of a *matrona*, of caring for the household and bearing children, marriage in a kyriarchal economy was a trade, and a disabled bride had less value. It is clear from the narrative that marriage is not an option after the kidnapping, for the daughter remains a virgin because of this episode. Ptolemy does not complete the *raptus* scheme of offering to marry the girl. The inherent logic of the *raptus* scenario is that the girl does not

---

19. Noted also by Klauck, *Apocryphal Acts of the Apostles*, 107.

20. Judith Evans-Grubbs, "Abduction Marriage in Antiquity: A Law of Constantine (Cth. Ix. 24. I) and Its Social Context," *JRS* 79 (1989): 61.

21. According to the United Nations, women and girls with disabilities are particularly vulnerable to physical abuse such as rape and domestic violence worldwide. See Office of the United Nations High Commissioner for Human Rights, "Thematic Study on the Issue of Violence against Women and Girls and Disability," 30 March 2012, https://tinyurl.com/SBL6010b.

necessarily have to be raped; her reputation is ruined simply by the possibility that she is no longer a virgin.[22] The narrator glosses over this fact, that her reputation is in fact ruined by the abduction, by insisting on her virginity and by focusing on her disability, which likewise renders her unmarriageable.

Another seeming flaw in the logic of the plot is the girl's current situation. Because she is still described as beautiful, we can assume that she is still a potential stumbling block for men, but she is, according to Peter's argument, less of a risk to herself and the men in Peter's congregation if she remains lame. A possible explanation can be found if we consider the spaces in which Peter's daughter has been vulnerable. She is first seen and lusted after when she is "bathing with her mother" (BG 4, 132.14–15), that is, when she is at the public baths. She is again absent from her father's house when she is abducted. It has been noted that in ancient myths, virgins are vulnerable to rape when they are outside the house and thus removed from their father's protection.[23] According to the *raptus* law of Constantine, the victims are themselves to blame, even if they were abducted against their will, because "they could have kept themselves at home till their marriage day and, if the doors were broken ..., they could have sought help from the neighbours by their cries."[24] A virgin, then, is best protected by staying in her father's house and in his presence. This seems to be the case also for Peter's daughter. Her paralysis becomes a protection because it anchors her to her father's house (church). Cornelia Horn has pointed out that the combination of householder and apostle that we find in the narrative construction of Peter in this story renders him extremely powerful.[25] As a child, a female, and a disabled person, Peter's daughter has no say when her father declares her situation "beneficial." Peter has absolute power over his daughter's body, and the benefit seems

---

22. Evans-Grubbs, "Abduction Marriage in Antiquity," 62.

23. Susan Deacy, "The Vulnerability of Athena: *Parthenoi* and Rape in Greek Myth," in *Rape in Antiquity: Sexual Violence in the Greek and Roman World*, ed. Susan Deacy and Karen F. Pierce (London: Duckworth, 1997), 44–45.

24. Cod. theod. 9.24.1, quoted in Evans-Grubbs, "Abduction Marriage in Antiquity," 59–60.

25. Cornelia B. Horn, "Suffering Children, Parental Authority and the Quest for Liberation? A Tale of Three Girls in the Acts of Paul (and Thecla), the Act(s) of Peter, the Acts of Nerseus and Achilleus and the Epistle of Pseudo-Titus," in *A Feminist Companion to the New Testament Apocrypha*, ed. Amy-Jill Levine with Maria Mayo Robbins, FCNTECW 11 (London: T&T Clark, 2006), 135.

to be rather for the crowd, whose faith is increased, and for Peter, whose honor is preserved.[26]

Rufina is severely punished for her immoral behavior. We do not learn more of what becomes of her, so we do not know whether she is healed again or remains mute and lame. If an adulterer is punished so harshly, it may seem strange that Peter elsewhere in the narrative has no qualms taking money from a rich woman, Chryse, who serves as a patron of the Christian community, despite rumors that she is promiscuous and even sleeps with her slaves (Mart. Pet. 1). Perhaps Rufina is punished because she brings shame not only over herself, but also over the congregation by her promiscuous behavior? In addition, she serves, as noted, as an example, to teach the believers a lesson about repentance. I suggest that the Rufina episode also serves as a "preview" of what will become of Simon. The two things that happen to her—she is paralyzed and struck dumb—also befall Simon. He becomes mute after the first contest with Peter and breaks his leg after the last. Simon's sin is illicit worship (idolatry) whereas Rufina's is illicit sex (adultery). In the Hebrew Bible idolatry and adultery are often connected, for example, in the literary topos of the strange woman: the foreign woman who tempts Israelite men to follow other gods through sexual attraction (e.g., Jezebel, 1 Kgs 21:25–26) and the prophetic image of personified (female) Israel/Jerusalem who whores after other (male) gods (see, e.g., Hos 3:1–4).[27] I will discuss how Rufina serves as an embodiment of such a literary type below, when I treat the fall of Simon.

None of these women have a voice in the narrative. Rufina is even explicitly made mute, thus she cannot talk back or oppose the apostle's version of her story. Peter's daughter says nothing but obeys her father silently when he bids her to stand and when he bids her to lie down again. Women's speech was often ridiculed as gossip and old wives' tales—unimportant and annoying.[28] The silence and passivity of these women is in line with common expectations of female behavior in antiquity, and also with the specific Pauline and deutero-Pauline admonitions that urge women to silence (1 Cor 14:33b–36; 1 Tim 2:11–12).

---

26. Horn, "Suffering Children, Parental Authority," 136.
27. Gail Corrington Streete, *The Strange Woman: Power and Sex in the Bible* (Louisville: Westminster John Knox, 1997), 7–8.
28. Marianne Bjelland Kartzow, *Gossip and Gender: Othering of Speech in the Pastoral Epistles*, BZNW 164 (Berlin: de Gruyter, 2009), 115.

The description of the Ethiopian demon is also worth a closer look. This demon, who is mutilated and killed, is described according to gender, class, and ethnic stereotypes. She is Other and inferior to the Christ/Peter figure in every possible way, according to Greco-Roman kyriarchal ideas. This becomes clear in Marcellus's description of his vision:

> In my sleep I saw you sitting in an elevated place and before you a great multitude and a very ugly woman in appearance an Ethiopian, not an Egyptian, but very black, clad in filthy rags, who danced with an iron chain about the neck and a chain on her hands and feet. When you saw her you said to me with a loud voice, "Marcellus, this dancer is the whole power of Simon and of his god; behead her." (Act. Verc. 22)

Simon is explicitly likened to this female demon. His source of power, Satan, is in this figure. In the vision, Peter tells Marcellus to behead her, but Marcellus hesitates, arguing that he is a senator and has never before killed anyone, not even a sparrow. So Peter calls out for Christ to implement the execution, and at once a man appears who looks like Peter and cuts the demon into pieces with his sword.

The demonic figure is identified according to her ethnicity, as an Ethiopian with black skin. It was common in antiquity to describe demons as black.[29] Early Christian writers took over this Greco-Roman trope and often connected blackness in general, and Ethiopians in particular, with demons and the devil.[30] That the woman demon is explicitly Ethiopian, not Egyptian, emphasizes the distinction between Ethiopia and Egypt, namely, that Ethiopia was outside the Roman Empire. Ethiopia was the end of the world—barbarian and mythic.[31]

The figure is further described as dirty, scantily clad in filthy rags, chained, and dancing. It was slaves, criminals, and war captives who were chained. The figure is, then, clearly also inferior to Marcellus in terms of class. In contrast to this Roman senator, who is powerful, free, and well dressed, this slave figure is completely degraded. For a slave to have been chained, she must have been either recently captivated or a runaway who needed to be chained not to escape again. That she is filthy and dressed in rags signals that she is not that valuable to her owner. Why is she dancing?

---

29. Bremmer, "Aspects of the Acts," 8.

30. Gay L. Byron, *Symbolic Blackness and Ethnic Difference in Early Christian Literature* (London: Routledge, 2002), 44–45.

31. Byron, *Symbolic Blackness and Ethnic Difference*, 31.

Perhaps she is presented as the lowliest of slaves, the slave prostitute, the *pornē*.³² Prostitutes were commonly associated with dancing and nudity.³³ Among the ethnic stereotypes about Ethiopians and other dark-skinned people was their sexual license, and they were used as symbols of sexual vice.³⁴ Again we see the image of the foreign seductress surface in this text. The sexual power of this female demon is so dangerous it needs to be entirely eradicated. In addition to the Hebrew Bible figures I have already mentioned, perhaps the narrator also draws on the imagery of the great whore of Babylon (Rev 14:8; 16:19; 17:5; 18:2; 19:2) to create this demon image.³⁵ The stereotype of the foreign seductress is also found in Roman literature. Shelley P. Haley argues that the representations of foreign women in writers such as Virgil and Livy reveal the fear in Roman ruling class men of powerful women and "reinforced the need for patriarchal control of female sexuality, whether domestic or foreign."³⁶

In all these three disabled women—the lame virgin, the paralyzed adulteress, and the mutilated prostitute—there is a connection between sexuality and mobility impairment. All three women are inflicted with disability to reduce their sexual power. Peter's daughter is an involuntary seductress. She cannot help it, but her beauty drives men to extremes, and her disability rescues her from the consequence—the loss of her virginity. Rufina is exposed and humbled before the Christian community because she dares to defile the entire congregation by seeking the Eucharist after her sexual transgression, and the dancing Ethiopian is mutilated and killed to subdue the demonic power of her sexuality.

The disabled (and ultimately dead) body of Simon is also clearly connected with sin. But, as noted, it is not sexual transgression but rather deviant worship and deception of the Roman Christians. However, there are several similarities between the story of Simon and the three female

---

32. Avaren Ipsen, *Sex Working and the Bible* (London: Equinox, 2009), 126.

33. Elaine Fantham et al., *Women in the Classical World: Image and Text* (New York: Oxford University Press, 1994), 23.

34. Byron, *Symbolic Blackness and Ethnic Difference*, 35.

35. Glancy and Moore argue that the great whore is a *pornē* rather than a *hetaira*. See Jennifer A. Glancy and Stephen D. Moore, "How Typical a Roman Prostitute Is Revelation's 'Great Whore'?," *JBL* 130 (2011): 551–69.

36. Shelley P. Haley, "Be Not Afraid of the Dark: Critical Race Theory and Classical Studies," in *Prejudice and Christian Beginnings: Investigating Race, Gender and Ethnicity in Early Christian Studies*, ed. Elisabeth Schüssler Fiorenza and Laura Salah Nasrallah (Minneapolis: Augsburg Fortress, 2009), 34.

stories that serve to effeminize him and link his transgression to the biblical model of idolatry = adultery. Simon is called a seducer (*seductor*, Act. Verc. 7), and the verb *seduco* is used about his actions (9, 10).[37] As a seducer of the faithful, Simon resembles an adulterous woman. His character has similarities to Rufina and the demon (and the biblical imagery), and thus is feminized vis-à-vis Peter.

The ability to speak and its opposite, muteness, is likewise employed in the narrative to illustrate the power of the apostle (either Paul or Peter) and the weakness of his adversaries. According to ancient protocols of masculinity, manliness and virtue were closely tied to the ability to control oneself and one's own body.[38] Proper speech was an important part of male comportment and self-fashioning.[39] Speech was power, and the mute was rendered powerless, as noted concerning Rufina and Peter's daughter. Simon's speech is ridiculed at several points in the story, and his voice is called "weak and useless" (Act. Verc. 12). According to ancient physiognomic treatises, a high-pitched voice was a sign of cowardice. Flaws in vocal control signaled lack of sexual self-control, which was considered a feminine trait.[40] The accusation that Simon is a seducer thus plays on the same notion as the references to his inadequate voice, that Simon is an effeminate, weak character.

Simon is ridiculed and shamed by his resemblance to Rufina and the demon. It insinuates that he is effeminate, an adulterer, nothing more than a gyrating slave. Judith Perkins has argued that the Acts of Peter reveals "a certain sympathy for the sensibilities of slaves."[41] She points to the scene in which Marcellus's slaves harass Simon and to Peter's argument for the manumission of the raised senator's slaves (Act. Verc. 14; 28). The image of the dancing Ethiopian, however, is an image of some-

---

37. These terms can also be found in the Vulgate version of Revelation and 2 John, where they are used about Satan, antichrist, and the beast.

38. Craig A. Williams, *Roman Homosexuality: Ideologies of Masculinity in Classical Antiquity* (Oxford: Oxford University Press, 1999); Fredrik Ivarsson, "Vice Lists and Deviant Masculinity: The Rhetorical Function of 1 Corinthians 5:10–11 and 6:9–10," in *Mapping Gender in Ancient Religious Discourses*, ed. Todd C. Penner and Caroline Vander Stichele (Leiden: Brill, 2007), 165–66.

39. Maud W. Gleason, *Making Men: Sophists and Self-Presentation in Ancient Rome* (Princeton: Princeton University Press, 1995).

40. Gleason, *Making Men*, 83.

41. Judith Perkins, *The Suffering Self: Pain and Narrative Representation in the Early Christian Era* (London: Routledge, 1995), 139.

one altogether Other in race, class, gender. There is no identification or sympathy with this figure.[42] Disfigurement—even complete bodily disintegration—seems necessary.

4. The Uses of Disability

There are several quite different uses of disability in the Acts of Peter: it is a protection against evil in Peter's daughter's case, a punishment for sin as well as a sign of a bad moral state in Rufina's and Simon's cases. Healing is, moreover, a sought-after and valued good, as we see in the story about the blind widows (Act. Verc. 20–21) and in the summary statements that healing was an important part of Peter's ministry (BG 4, 128.10–17; Act. Verc. 29). To understand how these different uses interconnect, we need to ask about the purpose of miracles in general in the Acts. Why are miracles performed?

Miracles inevitably induce faith in the Acts of Peter. The competition between Simon and Peter is a competition in deeds even more than words. When Simon arrives in Rome, flying over the gates, the Christians turn away from their beliefs and worship Simon. Peter's first miracles make people turn back to Christ again. The people cry out to Peter: "Show us another miracle that we may believe in you as a servant of the living god, for Simon too did many wonders in our presence, and on that account we followed him" (Act. Verc. 12). What the miracle consists of does not seem to matter much to the crowd. Peter holds up a smoked fish and asks them if they will believe if he makes it swim. This miracle is an absolute success: "Very many who had witnessed this followed Peter and believed in the Lord," the narrator asserts (Act. Verc. 13).

The miracles in the Acts are, I argue, part of the power game. They serve to prove that God is stronger than the devil, that Peter is right and Simon is wrong. Thus, it is no paradox that the power of the so-called living god (Act. Verc. 17; 23) can be proven with miracles that go from unhealed to healed as well as the other way around. On the one hand, Peter raises three dead men in the forum as the climax of Peter's wonder-working among the people of Rome. On the other, death by divine action

---

42. Callon has also critiqued Perkins's assessment of a "slave perspective" in the Acts of Peter. She does not, however, include the Ethiopian demon in her discussion. See Callie Callon, "Secondary Characters Furthering Characterization: The Depiction of Slaves in the Acts of Peter," *JBL* 131 (2012): 800 n. 5.

is the demon and also Simon's ultimate fate. Whether good or bad, healing or unhealing, miracles prove God's power and induce faith in the Acts of Peter.

In other words, human disability is an important narrative device in the Acts of Peter, since characters with different impairments are used to prove God's power. Disability scholars David Mitchell and Sharon Snyder argue that literary representations of people with disabilities often carry the weight of a narrative: "disability has been used throughout history as a crutch upon which literary narratives lean for their representational power, disruptive potentiality and analytical insight."[43] They call this phenomenon "narrative prosthesis": in the same way as a prosthetic leg supports the person using it, representations of disability carry a key function in many narratives. Rebecca Raphael has used Mitchell's and Snyder's narrative prosthesis in her analysis of disability in the Hebrew Bible. Raphael argues that in Genesis, disability is used to underline a major theological point, namely, God's power and providence. Thus, she argues that God needs human disability as a narrative prosthesis: "The text requires human disability in order to make its point about God's power."[44]

I argue that we see the same in the Acts of Peter. God's power is demonstrated through disabled characters and through a disabling of able-bodied characters. In the story of Peter's daughter, the girl's mobility impairment instigates the narrative. Her physical features seem to demand an explanation and provide the opportunity to address an important question for the community: Why, if we believe in a powerful God, are some healed and not others? How can Peter, who has healed so many, neglect his own daughter? Peter's answer underlines the power but also the inscrutability of God: "It is apparent to God alone why her body is not healthy. Know, then, that god is not weak or unable to give his gift to my daughter" (BG 4, 129.10–16).

According to Mitchell and Snyder, disability sometimes also functions as a metaphorical device.[45] In the Acts of Peter, lameness as well as muteness become metaphors for powerlessness and feminization. Rufina's and Simon's physical falls are connected with their fall from grace and power.

---

43. David T. Mitchell and Sharon L. Snyder, *Narrative Prosthesis: Disability and the Dependencies of Discourse* (Ann Arbor: University of Michigan Press, 2001), 47.

44. Raphael, *Biblical Corpora*, 62.

45. Mitchell and Snyder, *Narrative Prosthesis*, 57–58.

And the women's silence, as well as Simon's inadequate voice, connects muteness with a feminine character.

5. Conclusion: A Narrative Strategy of Violence

In an essay on violence in the canonical book of Acts, Todd Penner and Caroline Vander Stichele make some interesting observations about violence as a narrative strategy. They observe that in Acts, violence by outsiders is represented as unjustified, whereas insider violence is just: "The negative characterization of the violent outsider not only creates a foil to heighten the virtue of the insider, but also endorses as 'fair' and 'just' any action of violence taken against the outsiders by those on the inside."[46] This pattern of violence is gendered, and Penner and Vander Stichele argue that in Acts both the perpetrators and victims of violence are male.[47]

I find a similar narrative strategy of violence in the Acts of Peter. In the stories of unhealing, the infliction of disability is a form of narrative violence. Here, too, outsider violence is unjustified, but insider violence is just. When Simon injures and kills people it is unjustified (Act. Verc. 17; 25). When Peter does the same, it is acceptable—even beneficial. The gendering of violence, however, is somewhat different in the Acts of Peter compared to the canonical Acts. Women are the victims of the narrative violence in the Acts of Peter, not men. It is two women who suffer from Peter's and Paul's just infliction of disability. Simon, the third victim, is feminized through the imagery of the Ethiopian demon.

The stories about unhealing also prop up the masculinity of Peter, by enhancing his power in word and deed. The competition between Peter and Simon takes place in public spaces. In the forum, the marketplaces, and the holy sites of Rome, the two men compete for power. In this contest their masculinity is at stake. Peter proves himself the better man, while Simon is effeminized. Simultaneously, these stories also function as a domestication of women. The women we encounter all belong to the semiprivate

---

46. Caroline Vander Stichele and Todd C. Penner, "Gendering Violence: Patterns of Power and Constructs of Masculinity in the Acts of the Apostles," in *A Feminist Companion to the Acts of the Apostles*, ed. Amy-Jill Levine with Marianne Blickenstaff, FCNTECW (London: T&T Clark, 2004), 198.

47. Vander Stichele and Penner, "Gendering Violence," 199. There is, however, at least one example of a woman being victim of male apostolic violence, Sapphira in Acts 5:7–11.

space of the Christian community. They are inside patrons' houses, attending worship services. The paralyzed female body in both Peter's daughter's and Rufina's case becomes a symbol of God's great power, even though in the first case the woman's body represents innocence and chastity, and the other she represents unchastity. God's people should not be fornicators, like Rufina, but stay holy and uncorrupted, like Peter's daughter. Women who either succumb to such vices or through their beauty awaken lust in men may be disabled for the benefit of the community.

Part 3
Female Voices in Ancient Texts?

Perpetua, Her Martyrdom, and Holy Scriptures

Anna Carfora

1. Introductory Note on Passio Perpetuae et Felicitatis

The source from which we know the story of Perpetua is the Passio Perpetuae et Felicitatis, a narrative of certain catechumens and their catechist who were martyred on 7 February 203 CE in Carthage. The final version of the document must have been written soon after the actual events, during the first decade of the third century.[1] The document is a composite text where it is possible to distinguish at least three elements. First, there is an editorial part, introducing the events—with a theologically elaborated preface and a chronicle that narrates the events, also including the story of Perpetua's martyrdom; second, an account attributed to the catechist Saturus, who tells about his dreamlike vision he supposedly had in prison, with Perpetua as the protagonist; and finally, Perpetua's diary.[2]

The Passio Perpetuae is one of the most interesting and most widely studied examples of martyrological literature. Scholars of varied disciplines have dedicated themselves to the text, which shows great evocative and heuristic potential.[3]

---

1. Tertullian knows and cites the Passio in *De anima*, written between 208 and 211 CE; see Tertullian, *An.* 55.

2. For details concerning the text, see Anna Carfora, *La Passione di Perpetua e Felicita: Donne e martirio nel cristianesimo delle origini* (Palermo: L'Epos, 2007), 47–64 and the bibliographic notes in the text.

3. The Passio Perpetuae et Felicitatis was the topic of a conference and a subsequent publication. See Jan N. Bremmer and Marco Formisano, eds., *Perpetua's Passions: Multidisciplinary Approaches to the Passio Perpetuae et Felicitatis* (Oxford: Oxford University Press, 2012). The volume contains contributions by scholars representing various disciplines, some of whom did not even have the opportunity to acquaint themselves with the text in advance.

2. Perpetua's Diary

According to the scholarly majority, the edited diary included in the Passio can be attributed to Perpetua herself.[4] Who was Perpetua? She was a young woman of twenty-two years and a mother of a small child, introduced by the editor of the Passio as "honeste nata, liberaliter instituta, matronaliter nupta" (see Pass. Perpet. Felicit. 2.1). A member of the *gens* Vibia, she was a Roman citizen and belonged to the social class of *honestiores* and, thus, to the upper ranks. Her education was higher than the average, although it cannot be established with certainty what it consisted of and what the level of her cultural training was.[5] She was married to a man of a high social level, which conferred her the status of *matrona*.

When Perpetua is arrested together with her companions, she is a catechumen and will be baptized in prison (see Pass. Perpet. Felicit. 3.5). During her detention, she describes in her diary her imprisonment and the events related to it, as well as four dream visions she had before her martyrdom. The diary is an extraordinary text that provides more information on this woman, her mentality, her faith, and her culture than the introductory remarks of the editor of the Passio could ever do. I only briefly point out the exceptional value of a source such as this, an example of ancient Christian women's literature from the prisons of the Roman Empire. As a text written in prison, it belongs to the genre of prison literature,[6] and as such, it is also a testimony that preserves and passes on the voice of the victims. It is a story told by those who were defeated and not by the winners.

The diary has two parts: the chronicle and the dream visions. The chronicle of the events has at least two principal narrative threads: on the one hand, Perpetua's motherhood and the conditions of her imprisonment, and, on the other hand, her relationship with authority, be it public or paternal. While both of these spheres are extraordinarily rich and inter-

---

4. See Carfora, *La Passione di Perpetua*, 27–33.
5. See Paul Mckechnie, "St. Perpetua and Roman Education I A.D. 200," *AC* 63 (1994): 279–91; Walter Ameling, "Fermina Liberaliter Instituta: Some Thoughts on a Martyr's Liberal Education," in Bremmer and Formisano, *Perpetua's Passions*, 78–102.
6. It is with good reason that Perpetua's text is included in the anthology of writings of women in prison. See Judith A. Scheffler, ed., *Wall Tappings: An International Anthology of Woman's Prison Writings 200 to the Present* (New York: Feminist, 2002), 42–46. See also Marco Formisano, "Perpetua's Prisons: Notes on the Margins of Literature," in Bremmer and Formisano, *Perpetua's Passions*, 329–47.

esting, it is not possible to discuss them in detail here. It will be sufficient to refer to certain basic aspects. First, Perpetua demonstrates a link between motherhood and martyrdom that later gets lost in religious thinking and martyrological literature, as the strong link between virginity and martyrdom is established.[7] Second, while in discussion with the prosecutor who interrogates her and with her non-Christian father—who tries to persuade her to renounce her faith using multiple strategies—Perpetua shows the determination and independence of a person who can truly be recognized as a conscious actor responsible for her own choices. In the context of early Christian history, these aspects make Perpetua's text extremely interesting from the women's history perspective, in particular in relation to the questions of submission and/or emancipation both before and after the spreading of the new faith.[8]

Perpetua's visions constitute richly elaborated depictions she developed during her martyrdom. This exceptionally important material is the objective of the present study: Perpetua, her martyrdom, and Holy Scriptures. Perpetua's hard and painful encounters with her father and the prosecutor Hilarianus contain the basic elements typical of a martyr's experience and of the literature that passes it on to us, the *sequela Christi*. They include the deconstruction and redefinition of identity and belonging in the light of the new Christian identity and membership,[9] the exercise of παρρησία (bold speech) and of other relational modalities, such as ὑπομονή (patience) and ἱλαρότης (cheerfulness). Thus, the analysis of the dream visions offers a privileged perspective through which we can approach our topic and find new aspects in it.

Perpetua's dream visions are indeed genuine dreams that reveal the profound ways in which she understands and interprets her experiences and prepares herself to face her martyrdom.[10] However, they are also quite

---

7. It is sufficient to think about the construction of the image of the martyr Agnes by Ambrose in *Virg.* 1.2–11 and by Prudentius in *Per.* 14 (PL 60:580–90). "For virginity is not praiseworthy because it is found in martyrs, but because itself makes martyrs" (Ambrose, *Virg.* 1.3.10, PL 16:191; trans. *NPNF*²).

8. See Hanne S. Nielsen, "Vibia Perpetua: An Indecent Woman," in Bremmer and Formisano, *Perpetua's Passions*, 103–17.

9. See M. Eleanor Irwin, "Gender, Status and Identity in a North African Martyrdom," in *Gli imperatori Severi: Storia, archeologia, religione*, ed. Enrico Dal Covolo and Giancarlo Rinaldi (Rome: LAS, 1999), 251–53.

10. See Marie Louise von Franz, *Passion of Perpetua: A Psychological Interpretation of Her Dreams*, SJPJA 110 (Toronto: Inner City Books, 2004).

typical ancient visions, in the context of both Greco-Roman and Jewish-Christian antiquity.[11] In fact, the psychological-existential dimensions are closely intertwined with the prophetic-predictive significance, and it is this weave that contains the biblical references.

3. The Bible and Martyrdom in Perpetua's Dream Visions

It is possible to approach the question of women and the Bible from two angles: women's relationship with the Scriptures, in other words, the exegetic-cultural encounters of women with the Bible, and the relationship of the Bible to women, namely, the ways in which women appropriate the text, letting it to fertilize their existence and liberate them in creative ways. Perpetua's relationship to the Scriptures, mediated and fecundated by the martyrdom experience, is part of the latter.

Perpetua's text offers a rich variety of biblical references. However, the search for these references cannot be done by detecting exact correspondences or recurring to allegorizing interpretations. It is not possible to trace individual biblical elements in individual elements of the visions or even to use the symbols contained in the dream visions to explain the vision itself, as if it were about deciphering of an encrypted dream-visionary code and translating it into plain text. Such methods are oversimplifying and derogatory in view of Perpetua's constructive synergies, which combine the Scriptures, her cultural origins, and her experience of martyrdom.

It has been claimed, for example, that Perpetua's dreams seem "still pregnant with the culture that she had disdainfully denied, putting her own life at stake."[12] The Greco-Roman culture, however, is not something to do away with, a heap of waste requiring detoxification. The whole concept of the so-called pagan remains, as if we were dealing with an incomplete conversion to Christianity, can only be maintained with hindsight, as something later attached to the early Christian mentality. Traces of the resistance and survival of pre-Christian culture can still be found

---

11. See Patricia Cox Miller, *Dreams in Late Antiquity: Studies in the Imagination of a Culture* (Princeton: Princeton University Press, 1994); Simon R. F. Price, "The Future of Dreams: From Freud to Artemidorus," in *Before Sexuality: The Construction of Erotic Experience in the Ancient Greek World*, ed. David M. Halperin (Princeton: Princeton University Press, 1999), 365–88.

12. Francesco Corsaro, "Memorie bibliche e suggestioni classiche nei sogni della *Passio Perpetuae et Felicitatis*," in Dal Covolo and Rinaldi, *Gli imperatori Severi*, 272.

in medieval Christianization processes. In any case, there existed no clear procedures of becoming a Christian in Perpetua's times. They were only found later, when Christianity became an official religion. The idea of the persistence of pagan remains does not pay sufficient attention to the fact that even if Perpetua and many of her fellow sufferers embraced the Christian faith uncompromisingly in their world, it does not follow that they would have abandoned all their precedent cultural features. On the contrary, martyrdom—even though it was characterized by a conflict with the empire, and the Christians succumbed in the hands of the imperial authority—was also a part of the enculturation process found in diverse forms in the Christianity of the time.

The link between biblical meanings and references to the Greco-Roman world is obvious in Perpetua's first dream vision, in which she has to ascend a long and narrow ladder, lined with sharp instruments:

> I saw [writes Perpetua] a ladder of tremendous height made of bronze, reaching all the way to the heavens, but it was so that only one person could climb up at a time. To the sides of the ladder were attached all sorts of metal weapons: there were swords, spears, hooks, daggers, and spikes; so that if anyone tried to climb up carelessly or without paying attention, he would be mangled and his flesh would adhere to the weapons. (Pass. Perpet. Felicit. 4.3)[13]

The ladder has a biblical counterpart in Jacob's ladder in Gen 28:12–17. While Jacob's ladder shows angels climbing up and down, here it is Perpetua herself who has to climb the ladder. How to explain the incomplete agreement between the dream and the biblical text?[14] Indeed, the contact between heaven and earth, which in the biblical symbolism is secured through the passage of the angels, is made difficult and unsecure by the presence of elements that do not derive from the biblical background but from Perpetua's experience. The weapons at the sides of the ladder—a description of the *catasta* with typical instruments of torture used in

---

13. English translation from Herbert Musurillo, *The Acts of the Christian Martyrs* (Oxford: Clarendon, 1972), 111.

14. The representation of a difficult ascension in the form of an impassable ladder can also be found in the pagan world. See Peter Dronke, *Women Writers of the Middle Ages: A Critical Study of Text from Perpetua to Marguerite Porete (1310)* (Cambridge: Cambridge University Press, 1984), 7. From a psychological point of view, the ladder also represents a process of progressive awareness; see Franz, *Passion of Perpetua*.

combat in the arena—make the passage narrow and difficult to pass without hurting oneself. Rather than guaranteed in any way, the passage is uncertain! It is here that the biblical reference becomes personal, and if it is true that at the end of her ascent Perpetua reaches paradise, the biblical reference is extensively reinterpreted, embedded in Perpetua's circumstances and correlated with her martyrdom experience.

The analysis of this first element already shows how biblical reminiscences appear in Perpetua's dream visions; we are dealing with a sort of absorption of Scriptures. The scriptural elements are reelaborated and even rewritten in light of and in relation to Perpetua's own experience. This rewriting also makes use of the cultural mediation of her Greco-Roman background.

In Perpetua's dream vision, a dragon appears at the foot of the ladder: "At the foot of the ladder lay a dragon of enormous size, and it would attack those who tried to climb up and try to terrify them from doing so.... Slowly, as though he were afraid of me, the dragon stuck his head out from underneath the ladder. Then, using it as my first step, I trod on his head and went up" (Pass. Perpet. Felicit. 4.4, 7).[15] In this case, we are also dealing with multiple references: most notably with Gen 3:15 but also with Rev 12 and the serpent whose head is bruised by the woman with her heel—and thus with the images of Eve and Mary, the themes of woman and sin. The Eve-and-Mary line continues in Perpetua with her identification with the one who bruises the dragon's head and climbs the ladder. What we have here is a new type of relationship between the female and the original sin, where redemption takes place precisely through martyrdom. Facing her martyrdom, Perpetua—just like Mary—takes the shape of the new Eve. As already mentioned, the fact that Perpetua's maternity, unlike that of Mary, is not virginal seems to be important. However, this does not diminish the redemptive character of her martyrdom, even though the model of the virgin martyr later overshadows this aspect. As we will see later, the fourth vision gives a sufficient reason to read the passage in this manner. However, the meanings embedded in the dream vision are by no means exhausted, for the emperor is also depicted on coins squashing the head of a dragon with his heel. Thus, the biblical element has also a point of reference in Greco-Roman representations. It is possible to speculate that, by using this image, Perpetua places herself in

---

15. Trans. Musurillo, *Acts of the Christian Martyrs*, 111.

antithesis to the power represented by the emperor and, moving on from there, she appropriates the biblical identity of Eve-Mary, as an authority in relation to the male power that does not come from God.[16]

The second part of the vision is also charged with biblical and other references. When Perpetua has reached the top of the ladder, she finds herself in a garden where a shepherd is meeting her to offer her milk.[17]

> Then I saw an immense garden, and in it a grey-haired man sat in shepherd's garb; tall he was, and milking sheep. And standing around him were many thousands of people clad in white garments. He raised his head, looked at me, and said: "I am glad you have come, my child." And he called me over to him and gave me, as it were, a mouthful of the milk he was drawing: and I took it into my cupped hands and consumed it. (Pass. Perpet. Felicit. 4.8–9)[18]

The first element to consider here is the garden. Having overcome the difficulties related to the climb, in other words, having faced and consummated the martyrdom, Perpetua gains access to this place that certainly bears eschatological connotations. Which paradise is it? It does not match the place and the eschatological conditions described in Rev 7, which reads:

> And I heard the number of those who were sealed. One hundred and forty-four thousand of all the tribes of the children of Israel were sealed.... After these things I looked, and behold, a great multitude which no one could number, of all nations, tribes, peoples, and tongues, standing before the throne and before the Lamb, clothed with white

---

16. Following a psychological reading, the dragon is also connected to Perpetua's father insofar as he exercises coercion over the daughter, but Perpetua manages to overcome him.

17. This element has been interpreted in different ways; one way of reading it sees here a reference to an early baptismal rite where milk and honey represent the foretaste of the promised land (see Musurillo, *Acts of the Christian Martyrs*, 113 n. 8). According to another reading, the shepherd gives Perpetua cheese (*caseo*), which is then connected to the Eucharist, in two variations: either as a reference to the use of cheese in the eucharistic meal of the Artotyrites (Dodds) or as the solid food preparing the Christians for martyrdom (Corsini). See Eric R. Dodds, *Pagan and Christian in an Age of Anxiety: Some Aspects of Religious Experience from Marcus Aurelius to Constantine* (Cambridge: Cambridge University Press, 1990), 51–52; Eugenio Corsini, "Proposte per una lettura della 'Passio Perpetua,'" in *Forma Futuri: Studi in onore del card. Michele Pellegrino*, ed. Maria Bellis (Turin: Bottega d'Erasmo, 1975), 498 n. 36.

18. Trans. Musurillo, *Acts of the Christian Martyrs*, 111, 113.

robes, with palm branches in their hands.... "These are the ones who come out of the great tribulation, and washed their robes and made them white in the blood of the Lamb. Therefore they are before the throne of God, and serve Him day and night in His temple. And He who sits on the throne will dwell among them. *They shall neither hunger anymore nor thirst anymore; the sun shall not strike them, nor any heat; for the Lamb who is in the midst of the throne will shepherd them and lead them to living fountains of waters. And God will wipe away every tear from their eyes."* (Rev 7:4, 9, 14–17)[19]

It does not match since Perpetua's garden has pronouncedly bucolic characteristics, even though there is a reference to a great number of people dressed in white. Instead, there are analogies with a passage in the Sibylline Oracles:

But as for the others, as many as were concerned with justice and noble deeds, and piety and most righteous thoughts, angels will lift them through the blazing river and bring them to light and to life without care, in which is the immortal path of the great God and three springs of wine, honey, and milk. The earth will belong equally to all, undivided by walls or fences. It will then bear more abundant fruits spontaneously. Lives will be in common and wealth will have no division. (Sib. Or. 2.313–321)[20]

Perpetua's paradise probably resembles the gardens of Carthage she knew very well. The shepherd in this vision certainly refers to the image of the good shepherd (see Ps 22 LXX), but it differs from the typical early Christian image of a young and standing shepherd, as here he is old and sitting down. As a matter of fact, the shepherd symbol is transcultural. It often appears in the pagan world; it is sufficient to think, for example, about Poimandres in Corpus Hermeticum. In the Christian world, leaving the iconography aside, it is central also in the Shepherd of Hermas.

I would like to comment here on a particular point: biblical references to texts that later became canonical appear side by side with references to apocryphal texts and to texts that were first considered canonical but later left aside. Even though Perpetua's diary or the Passio or other writings on martyrdom do not provide us with direct evidence on the formation of the canon, a certain knowledge of other types of Christian literature, of their

---

19. Unless otherwise noted, biblical quotations follow the NKJV.
20. Translated in *OTP* 1:353.

use and circulation, is fairly clearly attested. References are made to texts without a clear distinction between those texts that later became canonical and those that were not included in the canon.

The second and the third vision are also rich in biblical references that are similarly ambiguous to the previous ones. For example, we can think of the cup used by Dinocrates, Perpetua's brother, who had died of facial cancer. In Perpetua's dream, he is first thirsty and suffering but becomes healed and able to drink to satisfy his thirst.

> I saw Dinocrates coming out of a dark hole, where there were many others with him, very hot and thirsty, pale and dirty. On his face was the wound he had when he died…. Then I woke up, realizing that my brother was suffering…. And I prayed for my brother day and night with tears and sighs that this favour might be granted me…. And the pool I had seen before now had its rim lowered to the level of the child's waist. And Dinocrates kept drinking water from it, and there above the rim was a golden bowl full of water. And Dinocrates drew close and began to drink from it, and yet the bowl remained full. And when he had drunk enough of the water, he began to play as children do. Then I woke, and I realized that he had been delivered from his suffering. (Pass. Perpet. Felicit. 7.4, 9; 8.3–4)[21]

The cup that quenches the thirst of the recovered child refers to elements from the classical world but also that of the Old and the New Testament. "You shall make its dishes, its pans, its pitchers, and its bowls for pouring. You shall make them of pure gold," we read in Exod 25:29. A quote from Ps 16:5 says, "Lord, you are the portion of my inheritance and my cup."

"They shall drink and roar as if with wine," says Zech 9:15. Revelation 5:8 presents "golden bowls full of incense, which are the prayers of the saints."[22] There is also another peculiarity worth our attention: the cup makes one think of the chalice (Luke 12:50; Mark 10:35–40; Matt 20:20–23), more precisely, the chalice of martyrdom.[23] According to a shift typical of the dream rhetoric, it could point to the chalice that Perpetua is

---

21. Trans. Musurillo, *Acts of the Christian Martyrs*, 115, 117.

22. Jacqueline Amat, *Songes et visions de l'au-dela dans la litterature latine tardive* (Paris: Etudes Augustiniennes, 1985), 130.

23. The healing is "not the result of the cup of eternity drank by Dinocrates but that of his sister's prayers and sufferings. What is thus asserted here is not a baptismal symbolism but the power of the intercession by the martyr." See Michel Meslin, "Vases sacres et boisson d'eternité dans les visions des martyrs africains," in *Epektasis:*

drinking from. In doing so, she transfers the effects of the chalice to little Dinocrates, who is thereby cured. Thus, the martyrdom experience and the biblical reminiscence meet and produce additional meanings.

Perpetua's last dream vision is the most well known and has been the object of varied interpretive exercises. It is the dream in which Perpetua is transformed into a man to fight with an Egyptian, against whom she is able to win.[24]

> The day before we were to fight the beasts I saw the following vision. Pomponius the deacon came to the prison gates and began to knock violently. I went out and opened the gate for him. He was dressed in an unbelted white tunic, waring elaborate sandals. And he said to me: "Perpetua, come; we are waiting for you." Then he took my hand and we began to walk through rough and broken country. At last we came to the amphitheatre out of breath, and he led me into the centre of the arena. Then he told me: "Do not be afraid. I am here, struggling with you." Then he left. I looked at the enormous crowd who watched in astonishment.

Mélanges patristiques offerts au Cardinal Jean Daniélou, ed. Jacques Fontaines and Charles Kannengiesser (Paris: Beauchesne, 1972), 147.

24. On the common conception of the manly women in patristic literature, see Paola F. Moretti, "La Bibbia e il discorso dei Padri latini sulle donne: Da Tertullian a Girolamo," in *Le donne nello sguardo degli antichi autori cristiani: L'uso dei testi biblici nella costruzione dei modelli femminili*, ed. Kari E. Børresen and Emanuela Prinzivalli (Trapani: Il pozzo di Giacobbe, 2013), 137–73. On the transformations into man in the martyr narratives see Giuliana Lanata, "Sogni di donne nel primo cristianesimo," in *Donne sante, sante donne: Esperienza religiosa e storia di genere*, SIDS (Turin: Rosenberg & Sellier, 1996), 77–98; Rachel Moriarty, "'Playing the Man': The Courage of Christian Martyrs, Translated and Transposed," in *Gender and Christian Religion: Papers Read at the 1996 Summer Meeting and the 1997 Winter Meeting of the Ecclesiastical History Society*, ed. Robert N. Swanson (Rochester, NY: Boydell, 1998), 1–10; Antti Marjanen, "Male Women Martyrs: The Function of Gender Transformation Language in Early Christian Martyrdom Accounts," in *Metamorphoses: Resurrection, Body and Transformative Practices in Early Christianity*, ed. Turid Karlsen Seim and Jorunn Økland (Berlin: de Gruyter, 2009), 231–47 (see especially 246–47 on Perpetua's vision). On the transformation into man and its dramatic-communicative dimensions see Anna Carfora, *La Passione di Perpetua e Felicita*, 151–53 in particular. "Perpetua puts on the male armor but does not become a man; she interprets the figure of a fighter to be able to interpret herself. This corresponds to what Christians do in the context of martyrdom in the arena; they enter fully in the role of the *damnati*, accepting the communicative rules of the gladiator games, and transform them from the inside, playing the part themselves. This element gives a strong communicative dynamism to the martyrdom" (153).

I was surprised that no beasts were let loose on me; for I knew that I was condemned to die by the beasts. Then out came an Egyptian against me, of vicious appearance, together with his seconds, to fight with me. There also came up to me some handsome young men to be my seconds and assistants. My clothes were stripped off, and suddenly I was a man. My seconds began to rub me down with oil (as they are wont to do before a contest). Then I saw the Egyptian on the other side rolling in the dust. Next there came forth a man of marvelous stature, such that he rose above the top of the amphitheatre. He was clad in a beltless purple tunic with two stripes (one on either side) running down the middle of his chest. He wore sandals that were wondrously made of gold and silver, and he carried a wand like an athletic trainer and a green branch on which there were golden apples. And he asked for silence and said: "If this Egyptian defeats her he will slay her with the sword. But if she defeats him, she will receive this branch." Then he withdrew. We drew close to one another and began to let our fists fly. My opponent tried to get hold of my feet, but I kept striking him in the face with the heels of my feet. Then I was raised up into the air and I began so to pummel him without as it were touching the ground. Then when I noticed there was a lull, I put my two hands together linking the fingers of one hand with those of the other and thus I got hold of his head. He fell flat on his face and I stepped on his head. The crowd began to shout and my assistants started to sing psalms. Then I walked up to the trainer and took the branch. He kissed me and said to me: "Peace be with you, my daughter!" And I began to walk in triumph towards the Gate of Life. Then I awoke. I realized that it was not with wild animals that I would fight but with the Devil, but I knew that I would win the victory. (Pass. Perpet. Felicit.10.1–14)[25]

The oil rubbed on Perpetua's body, transforming her into a man in order to face the *pancratium*, is again full of references from the prophetic and kingly unction in the Old Testament to the baptismal unction, but it is also the oil with which athletes and fighters rubbed themselves before contests. The entire athletic metaphor in the vision is a recurrent topos of martyrdom[26] and points to Pauline writings as well as to the pagan world. It is well known that Paul uses explicit allusions to contests (1 Cor 9:24–26);

---

25. Trans. Musurillo, *Acts of the Christian Martyrs*, 117, 119.
26. See Zeph Stewart, "Greek Crowns and Christians Martyrs," in *Mémorial André-Jean Festugière: Antiquité païenne et chrétienne*, ed. Enzo Lucchesi and Henri D. Saffrey (Geneva: Cramer, 1984), 119–24.

there is a prize to be won, a crown, like the martyr's crown (Phil 3:12–14).[27] In Perpetua's vision, there is also a reward: the branch that is given to her after the victory. Many references can be identified for the branch: from the fruit in the garden of Eden in Genesis to the apple in the garden of the Hesperides as well as to a sort of synecdoche of paradise.[28]

The image of the Egyptian, who represents the athlete par excellence in the Roman world, bears demonic shades of meaning.[29] Perpetua squashes his head with her heel as she had crushed the head of the dragon at the foot of the ladder in her first vision. Squashing the head of the adversary with her feet, Perpetua does not actually compare to a male model but Eve and the woman of Revelation.[30] The success she attains, seen as the victory over sin and thus the annihilation of the consequences of original sin, contradicts what Tertullian—who was long considered (in my opinion wrongly) as the editor of the Passio and who acted in the same environment and at the same time—suggests, that is, that the consequences of original sin persist in women.[31]

> I think, rather, that you would have dressed in mourning garments and even neglected your exterior, acting the part of mourning and repentant Eve in order to expiate more fully by all sorts of penitential garb that which woman derives from Eve—the ignominy, I mean, of original sin and the odium of being the cause of the fall of the human race. "In sorrow and anxiety, you will bring forth, O woman, and you are subject to your husband, and he is your master." Do you not believe that you are [each] an Eve? The sentence of God on this sex of yours lives on even in our times and so it is necessary that the guilt should live on, also. You are the one who opened the door to the Devil, you are the one who first plucked the fruit of the forbidden tree, you are the first who deserted the divine law; you are the one who persuaded him whom the Devil was not strong enough to attack. All too easily you destroyed the image of God,

---

27. On Paul's use of the agonistic language, see Victor C. Pfitzner, *Paul and the Agon Motif: Traditional Athletic Imagery in the Pauline Literature* (Leiden: Brill, 1967).

28. See Amat, *Songes et visions*, 80.

29. See Joyce E. Salisbury, *Perpetua's Passion: The Death and Memory of a Young Roman Woman* (New York: Routledge, 1997), 110.

30. See Clementina Mazzucco, "*E fui fatta maschio*": *La donna nel cristianesimo primitivo (secoli 1–3)* (Florence: Le Lettere, 1998), 174.

31. Carfora, *La Passione di Perpetua*, 148–49.

man. Because of your desert, that is, death, even the Son of God had to die. (Tertullian, *Cult. fem.* 1.1.1–2)[32]

This confirms the conclusion made regarding the first vision. The biblical Christian elements originating in Perpetua's native culture, as well as the biographical and existential references—as the figure of the Egyptian also refers to the paternal figure[33]—are combined by Perpetua in a new and powerfully meaningful sense. This new sense takes on a particular relevance in Perpetua's path toward liberation and the fulfillment of an authentic female self-awareness. Without fear of exaggeration, I would say that such a female figure did not have space to prevail in the Christian mentality and theology—not at that time, and never since.[34]

---

32. Translated by Edwin A. Quain in *Tertullian, Disciplinary, Moral and Ascetical Works*, FC 40 (Washington, DC: Catholic University of America Press, 1959), 117–18.

33. Mary R. Lefkowitz, "The Motivations for St. Perpetua's Martyrdom," *JAAR* 44 (1976): 419.

34. Thecla, the young heroine of the Acts of Paul and Thecla who dedicates herself to virginity and follows Paul, wears men's clothing precisely to guard her virginity. She was certainly more famous than Perpetua, and in the later centuries, there are other, more emblematic virgin and martyr figures, such as Agnes. Also the image of Perpetua underwent revisions as time went by. As suggested by Emanuela Prinzivalli, we encounter a "normalization" of Perpetua in later acta, where her story is modified. See Prinzivalli, "Perpetua, la martire," in *Roma al femminile*, ed. Augusto Fraschetti (Rome: Laterza, 1994), 153–86. In them, "it would be difficult to deny the ideological dimensions of these modifications" (180). According to Prinzivalli, Augustine was the originator of these changes in his sermons dedicated to Perpetua and Felicitas. In *Sermo* 280, using the play of words based on the names of the two women (*Perpetua et Felicitas coronis martyrii decoratae, perpetua felicitate floruerunt*), he walks a "long path that starts with the concrete women and ends with the strong transparency of the names" (Prinzivalli, "Perpetua, la martire," 181). For a different take on Augustine's view on the femininity of Perpetua and Felicitas, see Katherine E. Milco, "*Mulieres viriliter vincentes*: Masculine and Feminine Imagery in Augustine's Sermons on Sts. Perpetua and Felicity," *VC* 69 (2015): 276–95.

Genesis according to Proba and Eudocia

María José Cabezas Cabello

Through their works and lives, the poets Faltonia Betitia Proba and Athenais Eudocia changed both the religious teaching and the society in which they lived (fourth and fifth centuries CE).[1] In this study, I set out a brief biography of these women and offer an introduction to the Genesis creation stories through their eyes. Both of these poets composed poetry using the same literary form, the cento (which I will explain in more detail below), and on the same topic—the Bible.

1. Faltonia Betitia Proba

One of the first female Christian poets, if not the very first, Faltonia Betitia Proba was a Roman noblewoman who lived between 320 and 370 CE. Her surviving work *Cento vergilianus de laudibus Christi* deals with selected episodes from the Old Testament and the life of Jesus.

Proba's family, the gens Petronia, was educated in the ancient classical tradition. Her father, Petronius Probianus, was in correspondence with the Christian author Lactantius, with whom he shared an interest in poetry, and Symmachus dedicated verses to him.[2]

Sometime after 353 CE, Proba wrote a poem, now lost, addressing cruel wars and battles between the powerful, as she herself describes in the

---

1. See the master's thesis of Cătălina Mărmureanu, Gianina Cernescu, and Laura Lixandru, "Early Christian Women Writers: The Interesting Lives and Works of Faltonia Betitia Proba and Athenais Eudocia" (University of Bucharest, 2008).

2. See Hagith Sivan, "Anician Women, the Cento of Proba and the Aristocratic Conversion in the Fourth Century," *VC* 47 (1993): 140–57; Arnold H. M. Jones, John R. Martindale, and John Morris, *A.D. 260–395*, vol. 1 of *The Prosopography of the Later Roman Empire* (Cambridge: Cambridge University Press, 1971).

preface of *Cento vergilianus*. She then wrote the *Cento vergilianus*, whose exact date is disputed. The theory I find most convincing is that of Elizabeth Clark and Diane Hatch, who follow Aurelio Giuseppe Amatucci in dating the poem to the occasion of the edict of Julian (362 CE), which prohibited Christian teachers from teaching classical texts.³

1.1. The Cento

The Latin word *cento*, κέντρων in Greek, had several meanings in classical antiquity. It originally referred to a patchwork robe sewn together from various pieces of fabric that the poor and the peasants used to clothe themselves.⁴ The word thus evokes the idea of a unity composed of multiple elements. The semantic shift to the literary level can be easily understood on the basis of the usual meaning of cento as a cloth made out of materials in different quality and color. In the same way, shapes are put together from bits and pieces taken from one or more poems and linked together. In its literary meaning, then, the cento designates a poem built from words, half-verses, or entire verses from other poems, especially by Homer, Virgil, and Ovid, to create a new one.

---

3. Elisabeth A. Clark and Diane F. Hatch, *The Golden Bough, the Oaken Cross: The Virgilian Cento of Faltonia Betita Proba*, AARTTS 5 (Chico, CA: Scholars Press, 1981), 98–99; Aurelio Giuseppe Amatucci, *Storia della letteratura latina* (Bari: Laterza, 1929), 147. The edict is Julian, *Ep.* 42 (in Friedrich Hertlein's edition, *Iuliani Imperatoris quae supersunt: Praeter reliquias apud Cyrillum omnia*, 2 vols. [Leipzig: Teubner, 1875–1876], of Julian's works). Some patristic writers also refer to it; see, e.g., Ammianus Marcellinus, *Res Gest.* 22.10.7. Latin text and ET in Ammianus Marcellinus, *History*, vol. 2, *Books 20–26*, trans. John C. Rolfe, LCL (Cambridge: Harvard University Press, 1940), 256–57. See also Paulus Orosius, *Hist. pag.* 7.30. ET in Irving W. Raymond, *Seven Books of History against the Pagans: The Apology of Paulus Orosius*, ACLS (New York: Columbia University Press, 1936), 369. Amatucci suggests that v. 23 of the cento (*Vergilium cecinisse loquar pia munera Christi*) was a direct quote of Julian's decree (*Storia della letteratura latina*, 147). The connection between the cento and the edict is also supported by Caterina Cariddi, *Il centone di Proba Petronia: Nobildonna dei IV secolo della letteratura cristiana* (Napoli: Loffredo, 1971), 18. See also Glenn W. Bowersock, *Julian the Apostate* (London: Duckworth, 1978).

4. Egidio Forcellini and Vincenzo De Vit, *Totius Latinitatis Lexicon*, vol. 2 (Prati: Aldiniani, 1861), s.v. *cento*: "vestis stragula crassior et vilis ex variis pannis veteribus ac diversis coloribus consuta, qua pauperum lecti sternuntur et ipsique pauperes et rustici amiciuntur." See also Charles V. Daremberg and Edmond Saglio, *Dictionnaire des Antiquités grecques et romaines 1, tome 2* (Paris: Hachette, 1887), 1013.

Greek *centones* already existed before the Christian era. However, there is no evidence of Latin *centones* until the end of the second century.

1.2. Genesis in Proba's *Cento vergilianus de laudibus Christi*

Proba's cento, in the form we know it, comprises 694 verses written in dactylic hexameter and divided into two parts of equal length. Part 1 (vv. 1–332) deals with Old Testament stories, while part 2 (vv. 333–694) tells of the life of Jesus Christ.

As a sacred epic, Proba's work closely follows the traditional schema of this literary genre. It contains a *propositio*, an *invocatio*, and a *narratio*. The contents can be summarized as follows:[5]

- Verses 1–55: introduction and invocation (naturally, to God)
- Verses 56–332: Episodes from the Old Testament (creation, paradise, Adam and Eve, Cain and Abel, the flood)
- Verses 333–688: Episodes from the New Testament (nativity, infanticide, John the Baptist, the temptation of Christ, the Sermon on the Mount, the encounter with the rich young man, the cleansing of the temple, the Last Supper, the betrayal of Judas, crucifixion, resurrection, ascension)
- Verses 689–694: epilogue

Proba dedicated practically half of her 694 verses to the Old Testament. However, these 332 verses only tell the story of the first twelve chapters of Genesis and make some isolated references to Exodus. The literary cento is, of course, always selective. Proba did not intend to tell the entire history of salvation, nor did Eudocia (see below). Both poets omit some quite important biblical episodes and instead focus their attention on those characters and biblical stories they choose to emphasize.

In order to explain why Proba dedicated so much time to the creation and the original sin, we must look to theological motivations, as set out by Antonia Badini and Antonia Rizzi. In their words, "What is set out in Genesis comprises convincing arguments against gnostic and, above all,

---

5. See Antonio Arbea, "El carmen sacrum de Faltonia Betitia Proba, la primera poetisa cristiana," in *Textos del Coloquio Mujeres de la Edad Media: Escritura, Visión, Ciencia* (Santiago de Chile: Facultad de Filosofía y Humanidades, 1999).

Manichean ideas that assume an ambiguous or outright diabolic origins of the material world."[6]

Stanislas Gamber already pointed out that the reason why many biblical poets writing in Latin concentrate on the book of Genesis as their polemic or apologetic intention. Broadly speaking, the exegetical traditions in epic biblical poetry relate to two basic Christian ideas: God and the created world. Gamber also maintains that poets were seeking support from the heroic myths of pagan epic poetry.[7] It is therefore understandable that Proba, coming from a pagan background, focused on biblical texts that deal with the prehistory of humanity and Israel's history (Gen 1–12).

1.2.1. Creation (vv. 56–171; cf. Gen 1–2)

First, it must be emphasized that Proba treats the contents and order of the Bible fairly liberally, omitting major theological points and adding elements of literary beauty, both of which were totally normal and natural in poetry production. What she created was her own perspective on the origins of the world.

The Bible contains two accounts of creation, the first in Gen 1:1–4a (in *Cent. verg.* 56–114), which is a schematic and reflective representation highlighting God's transcendence in the whole creation, and the second in Gen 2:4b–25 (in *Cent. verg.* 115–146), a descriptive, anthropomorphic, and popular report.

1.2.1.1. The First Creation Account (Gen 1:1–2, 4a; *Cent. verg.* 56–114)

Proba keeps everything that is in the Bible but tells the story using her lovely poetry. The poem begins with "in the beginning, heaven and earth and flowing Sea, moons glowing sphere, sun's honest toil the Father himself established" (56–57).[8] However, she uses *statuit* and not *creavit*, like

---

6. Antonia Badini and Antonia Rizzi, *Proba, Il centone*, BP 47 (Bologna: EDB, 2011), 42.

7. Stanislas Gamber, *Le livre de la "Genèse" dans la poésie latine au Ve siècle: Versions françaises et provençales de la Genèse au moyen âge* (repr., Geneva: Slatkine, 1977), 60.

8. The English translation here and elsewhere is that of Clark and Hatch in *Golden Bough*. See also the new edition: Alessia Fassina and Carlo M. Lucarini, *Faltonia Betita Proba, Cento Vergilianus*, BSGRT (Berlin: de Gruyter, 2015).

the Vulgate ("In principio creavit Deus caelum et terram"), as the Hebrew ברא (bārā') can also be translated. Therefore, the idea of a *creatio ex nihilo* is not entirely clear in the poem.

Proba speaks of the world's "clearest lamps" (v. 58), the "night jet-dark conveyed by chariot" (v. 61), "chaos plunged down in sheer descent to gloom" (v. 62), "the silent sky" (v. 67), "the southern heat" (vv. 68–69); the seasons: "heat waves, rain and winds that bring the cold" (vv. 72–73), "spring requiring fruitful seed" (v. 75), "in middle summer's heat … the parched grain" (v. 76), "autumn [and] its many-colored fruits" (v. 77), "dark winter [when] olives are ground in the olive press" (v. 78); "fertile falling rain" (v. 80), "the solid ground" (v. 84), "huge leviathans" (v. 86), "vast ocean's moist tribe" (v. 88), "leafiness and bird-haunts" (v. 93), "tuneful birds" (v. 96); various monstrous predators such as "dangerous tiger," "scaly snake," "red-maned lioness," and "giant wolves" (vv. 99–104); and herds grazing through green fields, flocks around abundant water and foraging (vv. 105–106).

As the Father contemplates all these great marvels—"the lands, the sea's expanse, and the depthless sky" (v. 111)—he is thrilled and chooses to create the human being to rule over what he has created (vv. 107–14). Proba's description of creation is extremely positive both from a literary and a theological perspective. She attributes all creation to the "intellect divine" (v. 108).

1.2.1.2. The Second Creation Account (Gen 2:4b–25; *Cent. verg.* 115–146)

The creation of Adam and Eve that is next related is a detailed duplicate of Gen 1:27, where God creates the human being in the duality of male and female in an inseparable unity. The second report reads: "And the LORD God formed man of the dust [אדמה] of the ground, and breathed into his nostrils the breath of life; and man [אדם] became a living being" (Gen 2:7).[9]

After this, "the LORD God planted a garden eastward in Eden, and there He put the man whom He had formed" (2:8), to "tend and keep it" (2:15). Proba describes all this in words from Virgil that, assembled according to her will, convey a completely different meaning from what Virgil had written, but whose beauty and art are in no way inferior to

---

9. Unless otherwise noted, biblical quotations follow the NKJV.

the original. Proba shows great freedom in the interpretation of the biblical text. She presents a God who is thrilled (*Cent. verg.* 110) when he contemplates the wonders he has created with his hands, with eight exclamations of "Let it be done!" She also describes a God who meditates ("secum volutat"; v. 112); an expression reminiscent of the Virgilian words "mecum ipse voluto."[10] After reflecting on himself, an idea arises (v. 115): he has to create a being to represent him and to manage all that he has created. He is the human being formed out of the earth: "He pulled plump clay and gave it shape by kneading on the spot the fertile ground" (vv. 116–117). This first human has a close bond with the earth out of which he is created, and yet is similar to God himself (v. 120). In these verses, Proba merges once again the classical and the Christian worlds. This time her words resemble Ovid's verses that describe the creation of humans by Iapetus, one of the titans and the father of Prometheus (a classical creator god) but also the theology of Irenaeus and Tertullian. Comparing God, who creates human beings who resemble him, to an artist who shapes his work, Proba shows knowledge of Irenaeus's theology of the future incarnation.[11]

The phrase "the image of such holiness" (v. 118) can be found in Virgil's Aeneid ("si te nulla movet tantae pietatis imago"; 6.405). These are the words the Sibyl speaks to Charon when he tells her about Aeneas's descent into the underworld. While the term *pietas* in Virgil's text refers to filial love, Proba's reference is the love of God. According to Maria Cacioli, the *pietas* in Proba's cento means God's infinite love for humans, manifested in creation.[12]

Proba makes no reference to the "breath of life," in which theologians have seen the creation of the immortal soul that gives life to the human body. As for the creation of the woman, Proba says the following: God looks for a companion for the man from all the created creatures but does not find one (*Cent. verg.* 122). So he turns to the man himself and makes the woman "unparalleled in figure and in comely breasts, now ready for a husband, ready now for wedlock," "a wondrous gift" for the man. Again, the expression ("mirabile donum") is borrowed from Virgil, from a passage where Aeneas orders the treasures brought from Troy to be unloaded from the ship to be given to Dido as a thank-you for her hospitality (Virgil,

---

10. They appear in the words of Moeris in Virgil, *Ecl.* 9.37.
11. See Badini and Rizzi, *Proba, Il centone*, 163.
12. See Badini and Rizzi, *Proba, Il centone*, 164.

Aen. 1.652). They are objects that belonged to Helen and that carry the seeds of destruction for the new owners. The wondrous gift that is woman in Proba's work is therefore also a sign of danger and risk.[13]

The man, astonished by the divine power and the creation of such beauty from his bones and limbs, calls her a woman and joins with her in the first embrace of history: "Dazed by the will divine, he took and clasped her hand in his, folded his arms around her" (*Cent. verg.* 134–135). Much has been written about the nature of the union of Adam and Eve. It should be remembered that the act of holding hands was and is a part of the marriage ritual. Charles Witke notes this verse as "the only romantic treatment I know of the encounter between Adam and Eve."[14] Jeremiah Reedy translates the verse into English as follows: "He embraced her, took her hand, / and clung to her in love,"[15] which suggests an erotic context. I agree with Badini and Rizzi that Proba values sexuality positively. The marital act takes place before the fall and is blessed by God. "For Proba, the Fall is not a sexual sin as for Theophilus of Antioch (*Autol.* 2.25), Irenaeus of Lyon (*Haer.* 3.22.4) or Clement of Alexandria (*Strom.* 3.14.94.3), but must be interpreted as disobedience, as a claim of human autonomy to live in complete independence from God. In any case, Proba very likely considered sexuality to be part of the God's plan for human beings."[16]

Proba reproduces the content of the second creation account, following the biblical story but going beyond the literal meaning:

- Man is created from the earth. He is dust and will become dust again.
- The man and the woman are created for each other to complement each other (Gen 2:23).
- God uses the man to create the woman, which means that the two are of the same nature and enjoy the same equality and dignity. Neither is superior to the other.

---

13. See Stratis Kyriakidis, "Eve and Mary: Proba's Technique in the Creation of Two Different Female Figures," *MDATC* 29 (1992): 129.

14. See Charles Witke, *Numen litterarum: The Old and the New in Latin Poetry from Constantine to Gregory the Great*, MST 5 (Leiden: Brill, 1971), 198.

15. See Patricia Wilson-Kastner, *A Lost Tradition: Women Writers of the Early Church* (Lanham, MD: University Press of America, 1981), 49.

16. Badini and Rizzi, *Proba, Il centone*, 167.

- By using adjectives such as *mirabile*, *ingens*, and *insignis*, Proba wants to demonstrate the power of God, whose creation is the irrefutable proof of his greatness.[17]

Proba emphasizes the physical bloom of the young woman in a discourse that is reminiscent of the expression of classic epithalamium, especially the anaphor "iam matura viro, iam plenis nubilis annis" (v. 132; "ready for a husband, ready for wedlock").

1.2.2. Sin and Punishment (vv. 136–277; cf. Gen 3)

1.2.2.1. Temptation

Proba dedicates 141 verses of the cento to the topic of temptation, which indicates that she felt it was important. This is where the snake comes in. In Proba's words, it does not "leave a mite of sin or craft undared, untried" (v. 181); it is constantly in conflict with God's plans and with God himself (vv. 432–435). He is the originator of bitter wars (v. 177); his "sin looms large beyond the rest" (v. 246); he is "sin-inciter, serpent, feeding on harmful herbs" (v. 248). He is full of "impassioned sin" (v. 430) and "prideful speech" (v. 434); he spits "bloody froth" (v. 454). He is baneful and ill-willed (v. 173), the embodiment of all the forces of evil. The serpent is the devil, the nefarious character. "When he speaks a lie, he speaks according to his own nature for he is a liar and the father of it" (John 8:44 NRSV). The serpent even dares to tempt the Son of God, and God himself (*Cent verg.* 430–431).

In the dialogue with the woman, Proba moves away from the biblical text, exaggerating God's prohibitions and praising the gifts that Adam and Eve will receive if they eat the fruit from the forbidden tree. The serpent insists that God is unjust to have created them mortal, for this means that they will be unable to know and possess the marvels of "the second part of your estate" (v. 190). They will attain divine knowledge; they will be like God and know both good and evil.

---

17. See Sophie Malick-Prunier, "Le corps féminin et ses représentations poétiques dans la latinité tardive" (PhD diss., Université Paris-Sorbonne, 2008).

1.2.2.2. Sin

In spite of everything, the woman relents, and as soon as she tastes the fruit of the forbidden tree with her lips, she experiences what evil is (v. 202). As a slave to evil, she begins to do evil, "a greater sinful deed": with the power she has over her husband, as the serpent assured her (v. 194), with the force of feminine sweetness, she changes the mind of the wretched Adam and convinces him to follow her example (vv. 204–205).

The serpent said to them: "Your eyes will be opened, and you will be like God, knowing good and evil" (Gen 3:5). Indeed, their eyes are opened, but only to shame they feel because of their nakedness (Gen 3:7). Before that, they had felt no shame, which indicates their former state of bliss.

1.2.2.3. The Punishment

Following the biblical account, Proba makes God condemn the serpent to spend the rest of his life crawling on his belly and casts him out (*Cent. verg.* 249–250). Adam is also condemned: all of his life will be worn by working the earth (vv. 253–254); and so is the woman: "most remorseless wife" (v. 263), "you shall atone for your egregious sins" (v. 265); "now die, deserving death" (v. 267).

When rendering the curse of the human couple after the fault committed, Proba modifies the biblical text (Gen 3:16). Despite the terrible names and curses on the woman (*Cent. verg.* 263–267), Proba's poem does not mention the curse that the woman will become subject to the man. This omission was certainly not a coincidence: there are numerous scenes in the *Aeneid* in which one person or group is subjected to another, so Proba would have had no trouble finding words of Virgil that would curse Eve, and through her all women. Nor does Proba mention another curse, namely, the pain the woman will suffer when giving birth to her children (Gen 3:16).

Proba does not shy away from describing herself as *vatis* (a poetess; *Cent. verg.* 12). Indeed, she is the first female Christian poet whose work has been preserved—and who has allowed herself certain licenses, such as the significant omission of God's curse on the woman when the first human beings are expelled from paradise, which would refer to her submission to the man.

2. Athenais Eudocia

Eudocia is one of the most important but least-known figures of late Greek poetry (fifth century). Her life has been handed down in many legends, which makes the distinction between myth and reality a complex one. Athenian by birth, she was the daughter of the sophist Leontius. After converting to Christianity, she married Emperor Theodosius II.

A lover of culture, Eudocia gathered a group of Christian and pagan intellectuals at the court in Constantinople. Around the year 443, she left the Byzantine court because of a rivalry with her sister-in-law Pulcheria and moved to Jerusalem, where she led a religious life and devoted herself to writing and helping the poor, both Christian and pagan.

2.1. *Homerocentones*, or Homeric Centos

The question of whether Eudocia is the true author of this work has been the subject of a heated debate in the past century, especially since there are various versions of the poem. Rocco Schembra concludes that Eudocia had an existing version of a Homeric cento, which she modified and rewrote, as she herself describes in the proem to her poem (see below).[18]

The exact date of these poems is unknown, but there is a consensus that they were written during Eudocia's stay in Palestine (444–460). Her Homeric cento totals 2,354 verses and reproduces some fifty biblical episodes.[19] However, only few of these episodes are from the Old Testament, and they all appear within the first one hundred verses, that is, in less than one-tenth of the entire work. They include, for example, the creation, the serpent's temptation, and the fall. In contrast, the New Testament is well represented in the cento.

2.2. Genesis according to Eudocia

In only seven verses, Eudocia starts to tell the story of creation:

> Listen, countless nations of humans who live around the world,
> all mortals who are now on earth and eat bread,

---

18. Rocco Schembra, *Homerocentones*, CCSG 62 (Turnhout: Brepols, 1977), v; see also Brian P. Sowers, *Eudocia: The Making of a Homeric Christian* (Cincinnati: University of Cincinnati Press, 2006).

19. See the critical edition: Mark D. Usher, ed., *Homerocentones Eudociae Augustae*, BSGRT (Stuttgart: Teubner, 1999).

both all who live toward the dawn and sun,
and all behind toward the murky darkness,
while I say what the spirit in my chest commands me,
so you may well discern both God and also man,
who is king over all mortals and immortals. (vv. 1–7)[20]

The most important point in Eudocia's proem is, in my opinion, that of the dual nature of Christ (v. 6, "both God and also man"). This was a topic of great importance in Eudocia's time. It had by then been hotly debated for more than a century as part of the Arian controversy. The conflict between Nestorianism (two natures and two persons) and monophysitism (only one nature, the divine), which was not only religious but also political, with the patriarchal support of Constantinople for Nestorianism and Alexandria for monophysitism, obliged Pope Celestine I to convene a synod in Rome in 430. Nestorius's teaching was condemned and Cyril's confirmed. According to the latter, there is only one person in Christ, in whom the two natures are united.

Eudocia wrote her *Homerocento* under these circumstances. It is not clear why she propagated monophysitism among the Christians in Palestine, whether out of vengeance, or to contradict her sister-in-law Pulcheria, or because she sincerely believed so.[21] In any case, in her poem, she exalts the figure of Christ, God and man.

2.2.1. The Creation of the World and the Human Being (vv. 8–33)

From verse 8 on, Eudocia starts to tell the story of creation, culminating in the creation of the human being in verse 33. In her poem, she only needs twenty-five verses for what Proba recounts in 113. Eudocia only briefly describes the creation of the world and the human being and then the fall (vv. 34–91), so that in the rest of the poem (vv. 92–2354) she can devote herself in detail to the figure of Christ, the model for human salvation.

Eudocia presents the creation of the world as follows. First, she describes the creation of the earth, the sky, the sea, and the stars (vv. 8–10), without specifying the days of creation or following the order of

---

20. All English translations of the *Homerocento* are by Brian Duvick, who is currently preparing a publication of Eudocia's cento in English.
21. Ana Martos, *Papisas y teólogas: Mujeres que gobernaron el reino de Dios en la tierra*, HI (Madrid: Nowtilus, 2008).

the biblical account. It seems that God "who is king over all mortals and immortals" first created the earth, the heavens, the sea, the untiring sun and full moon, and all the constellations that crown heaven. Eudocia uses six verses from the *Iliad* to explain the first moment of creation (vv. 8–13). These Homeric verses describe how the god Vulcan creates a large shield for the hero Achilles:

> Five were the layers of the shield itself; and on it he made many adornments with cunning skill. On it he fashioned the earth, on it the heavens, on it the sea, and the unwearied sun, and the moon at the full, and on it all the constellations with which heaven is crowned—the Pleiades and the Hyades and mighty Orion. (Homer, *Il.* 18.481–486 [Murray and Wyatt])

Eudocia, who was Greek, probably read the Bible in the form of the Septuagint, especially since this was also a prerequisite for converting to Christianity. Without a doubt, she knew the two accounts of the creation in the first two chapters of Genesis, so she followed the scheme of Gen 1, the appearance of heavens and their ornamentation. In the creation account of the Bible, the heavens are created in three days; Eudocia, however, allows everything to emerge at the same time, including the sun, the moon, and the stars of the firmament of the heavens that are part of the "ornament" in Gen 1:11–31. Elements of Greek mythology also appear in Eudocia's sky, for example the Pleiades (the seven-star), the Hyades, and the strong Orion, which are only listed as "stars" in Gen 1:16. It is very likely that the poet wanted to recall the verses of the book of Job, in which Job, recognizing the greatness and righteousness of God, describes God as follows: "He made the Bear, Orion, and the Pleiades, and the chambers of the south" (Job 9:9). Or she might have had in her mind Job 38:31, where God addresses Job and asks him: "Can you bind the cluster of the Pleiades, or loose the belt of Orion?" As Schembra notes,[22] the Pleiades inspired numerous Greek and Latin poets, which is why Eudocia knew this tradition and therefore presented the short biblical quotation in much greater detail.

Another example of the agreement between the text written by Eudocia and the Bible is the words τὰ κήτη τὰ μεγάλα (the great sea creatures) in Gen 1:21 and μεῖζον … κῆτος in verses 16–17 of Eudocia's cento. In these

---

22. Rocco Schembra, *La prima redazione dei centoni omerici: Traduzione e commento*, Hellenica 21 (Alexandria: Ediciones dell'Orso, 2006), 90.

verses, we encounter the same categories of animals that are created on the fifth day according to the biblical account, namely, sea animals and birds.

Then follows a list of the creatures of the earth, without a reference to a specific day: "and horses and mules and stout head of oxen, bears and wild boars and bright-eyed lions, all things that breathe and crawl the earth" (vv. 18–20). The list resembles to a large extent to a large extent the account of Gen 1:24–25, at the end of the fifth day: "Then God said, 'Let the earth bring forth the living creature according to its kind: cattle and creeping thing and beast of the earth, each according to its kind'; and it was so. And God made the beast of the earth according to its kind, cattle according to its kind, and everything that creeps on the earth according to its kind. And God saw that it was good."

Only after God has created animal does Eudocia make him create plants and the water, thus reversing the logical sequence of the biblical creation story. Again using verses from the *Iliad*, Eudocia describes how "under them the radiant earth grew new sprouted grass and dewy lotus and crocus and hyacinth" (vv. 21–22; see Homer, *Il.* 14.347–348).

In verses 29–32, Eudocia speaks of water, the fundamental element for the survival of animal species. In verse 25, however, she has already indicated that there is water, which is necessary for life. She equates Homer's "four springs in a row" that "flowed with white water" (see Homer, *Od.* 5.70–71) with the biblical verse "Now a river went out of Eden to water the garden, and from there it parted and became four riverheads" (Gen 2:10).

Eudocia describes the creation of man in only one verse: "He created in the last place, the man who is far the best, marvellously like his very self" (v. 33).[23] This is a combination of two Homeric verses (*Il.* 23.536 and 107). This book of the *Iliad* is about the funeral ceremonies for Patroclus and the games (chariot races) that are held in his honor. Verse 536 reads: "*In the last place* drives his single-hoofed horses *the man who is far the best*," while verse 107 is about the appearance of Patroclus's soul, "was *marvelously like his very self*" (the words Eudocia adopted from Homer are italicized).

Eudocia combines these two verses masterfully so that the new verse resembles the creation of man in Gen 1:26: "Let us make man in Our image, according to Our likeness." Eudocia's selection of words has a high

---

23. Here the Homeric wording is maintained (trans. Murray and Wyatt). Duvick translates: "At last a man was defined but mysteriously like himself."

theological content, since it underlines that the similarity between man and God is the same as there is between the "shadow" (in which Patroclus appears to Achilles) and the corresponding body. Furthermore, the verbal adjective θέσκελον, which is etymologically close to θεός, has undergone a semantic change with respect to Homer's poem and has here the meaning "God-like," that is, God's image. Nonnus of Panopolis (fifth century) also affirms that this adjective means "divine" (*Paraph.* 1.76).

Thousands of pages have been written on this biblical verse. I would like to emphasize here that Eudocia uses the word ἀνήρ (man), while the Bible refers to the human being, man and woman, as God's representatives and his stewards who continue his work. Eudocia could just as easily have used the generic ἄνθρωπος (human being), without specifying the gender, as is the case in Genesis. By using the word "man," she excludes the woman and, quite surprisingly, does not mention her until she meets the serpent.

2.2.2. Temptation and Original Sin (vv. 34–91)

Next, Eudocia describes the serpent, the symbol of evil, who is capable of bringing many people to death:

> Then appeared a great sign: a serpent with blood-red back,
> dread and dire and wild, not to be resisted,
> who worked many evils, more than all the others together,
> and by allure stole the sense of even the prudent.
> He was so great and put many men on the grievous pyre. (vv. 34–38)

The snake is the symbol of deceit and sin in many cultures. Eudocia next gives the serpent a lengthy speech that is addressed to the woman. In the poem, the serpent begins to speak "with a human voice" and describes what Hesiod calls "the golden age":

> There life is easiest for men,
> no snow nor heavy winter nor ever storm
> but always bursts of the whistling west wind,
> issuing swelling gusts of every sort.
> Neither do they plant with hands nor plow,
> but all things grow unsown and unplowed.
> Famine never enters the land, nor does any other
> hateful illness fall on miserable mortals.
> There lovely trees grow plump

and sweet figs and plump olives
and many other things besides. (vv. 47–57)

Like the book of Genesis, Eudocia presents an idyllic vision of the world before the humans sinned. It is what God wanted in creating humanity: a living being in harmony with himself, with his Maker, with his neighbor, with the earth, and with the animals. Proba also describes the delights of paradise (vv. 157–169). Eden represents for her the ideal place for people's lives, especially from the climatic point of view: there is no snow, no cold, and no rain, but the mild west wind always blows. Eudocia's model is the *Odyssey* and its description of the Elysian fields, the pagan counterpart of the Christian paradise (Homer, *Od.* 4.565–567).

But behold, the serpent tempts the woman. The words of the serpent are pleasing to her. She opens her eyes and reflects on the promise: the gods neither age nor die. Eudocia uses Homer's verse where Calypso speaks to Hermes Argeïphontes concerning Odysseus (*Od.* 5.136). She has looked after him ever since he landed on her shores, loving him, feeding him, and promising to make him immortal if he stays with her. Odysseus, however, cannot stop thinking about his wife, Penelope, and his son, Telemachus. Whereas Odysseus rejects immortality, Eve chooses it.

The serpent, however, tempts the woman in the *Homerocento* even more, with "husband, home, and concord fine"—again, a Homeric phrase (*Od.* 6.181–185). It is the desire that Nausicaa feels when she sees Odysseus. Was this the ideal that Eudocia desired in her lifetime (fifth century)? As is well known, Eudocia was drawn into a plot that resulted in a marriage to Emperor Theodosius II. After living with him for about twenty years, she separated from him—it is not entirely clear whether due to the circumstances (which also involved an apple!)[24] or willingly—and moved to the Holy Land, where she spent the rest of her life.

In its version of the fall, Eudocia's cento offers us an interesting starting point for considering the responsibility and the impact of guilt on the female gender. It uses only one verse (v. 67) to establish a sin that will be passed down from generation to generation for eternity.

---

24. Since the Trojan War, the apple has been a topos in legends that have been transmitted through the fairy tales of the Arabian Nights. See Nancy Calvert-Koyzis and Heather E. Weir, *Breaking Boundaries: Female Biblical Interpreters Who Challenged the Status Quo*, TTCLBS (New York: T&T Clark, 2010).

The recklessness of the woman is softened by reminding the reader of what the nature of the woman is like, namely, forgetful and inattentive, but not prone to evil. According to Schembra, the attitude is not misogynistic, but this reflection is carried out from a feminine point of view.[25] He justifies his view with the evidence he finds in the following verses. In verse 77, the song that men produce to criticize and reproach Eve's transgression is described with the adjective στυγερή (hateful): "she will bring hard repute on more gentle women, even on her who does good works, women who now are and who will later be" (vv. 78–80; see *Od.* 24.201–202). The next verse reads, "there is nothing more dreadful and bitchy than a woman" but immediately continues that it was Eve "who has such deeds in mind" (v. 82). This shows that the poet did not generalize the punishment for all women but wanted to limit it to the one who allowed this disaster to happen. Finally, verse 84 gives the reader a sense of solidarity with women: she "did a great deed in ignorant thought" (see *Od.* 11.272). This leads Schembra to conclude that the final author is a woman, Eudocia, who based her work on a text of bishop Patricius.[26] Clark and Hatch, on the other hand, claim that the poem reflects similar misogynistic ideas of Eve as in the texts of patristic authors and that there is no proof that the text was written by a woman.[27]

2.2.3. The Punishment (vv. 85–87)

"Lost woman, who gave many evils to men and sent many strong souls to Hades, put pain on all and set troubles on many" (vv. 85–87; see *Od.* 17.287; *Il.* 1.3; 21.87). When choosing these Homeric verses, Eudocia is well aware that the evil deed of a single woman (Eve) has extended the disastrous reputation to all women around the world. This is dreadful, as she knows through her firsthand experience (she had to leave the court in Constantinople and go into exile in Palestine, accused of adultery).[28]

In conclusion, I would like to point out that in this context, Hades should be understood as the place where all souls, both the just and the

---

25. Schembra, *La prima redazione*, 103. For a different opinion, see Gérard-Henry Baudry, "La responsabilité d'Eve dans la chute: Analyse d'une tradition," *MScRel* 53 (1996): 293–320.

26. Schembra, *La prima redazione*, 104.

27. Clark and Hatch, *Golden Bough*, 151–52.

28. See Schembra, *La prima redazione*, 103.

ungodly, meet before the last judgment (see Irenaeus, *Haer.* 5.31.2). After making it clear that all evil came to the paradise created by God because of a woman, Eudocia goes on to present the redemption of all evil by the Son of God.

3. Conclusion

Two great poems, Proba's Vergilian *Cento vergilianus de laudibus Christi* and Eudocia's Homeric cento, were created a century apart: the first in the middle of the fourth century, the latter in the fifth century. They were both written in the same literary genre, the cento. We recall that, for early writers, the idea of imitation was vastly different from what we now have. Using another writer's material was a compliment, an homage, rather than plagiarism. What had to be justified was not being inspired by another author, not imitating.[29]

There is no doubt that Eudocia had read Proba's work, as can be deduced from the foreword to her poem, written by an anonymous scribe who invites the Eastern Roman emperor Flavius Arcadius (383–408) to read and preserve her work, to give it to his children, and to pass it on to his grandchildren, so that the entire imperial family (*augusta propago*) will know the Christian teaching.

Indeed, both poems represent a reconciliation of classical and biblical cultures, the transition from paganism to Christianity, the connection between the old and the new.[30] Two educated women, a Roman and a Greek, both well versed in the classical works of Latin and Greek literature (Virgil and Homer), managed to find their female work a place in a tradition dominated by men. It suffices to note Proba's influence on Paulinus, Prudentius, and Damasus.[31] In the case of Pope Damasus, for example, many of the ideas expressed in his poems recall Proba's work. As Roger Green shows, the language and logic of the Roman poet Lucan (39–65 CE) can be found in the works of both Proba and Damasus. Nevertheless, when the chronological data and the style of the two are explored, it becomes evident that Lucan's language and logic dominate in Proba, while

---

29. See Antonio Arbea, "El centón homérico de Eudoxia (s. V d. C)," *TV* 43 (2002): 97–106.

30. See Karl Olav Sandnes, *The Gospel "according to Homer and Vergil,"* NovTSup 138 (Leiden: Brill, 2011).

31. Mărmureanu, Cernescu, and Lixandru, "Early Christian Women Writers," 9.

Damasus, who had read and known little of the classic authors, is likely to have found them in Proba's work.[32] Hundreds of years later, Giovanni Boccaccio, in his work *De mulieribus claris*, from 1362, presents Proba as a woman who should be remembered not only because of her knowledge of the Holy Scriptures but also because of her knowledge of classical literature. In the portraits of Proba that have survived from this period, she is depicted surrounded by books and teaching others. No less can be said about Eudocia. Her works that survive today (*The Martyrdom of Saint Cyprian* and *Homerocentos*) show her profound education and great piety.

Nevertheless, there are also some differences between the two poets. Proba, who followed a compositional technique, the cento, that had been used before, was the first woman to write a biblical-Christian cento in Latin. Eudocia, on the other hand, as discussed above, adopted a poem written in Greek by a bishop, about whom we know practically nothing apart from his name, Patricius. She rewrote the poem as she liked and inserted in it, among other things, the creation account, including the fall, and God's decision to send his Son into the world.

Both women, Proba and Eudocia, established a feminine discourse in a tradition dominated by men. Their words have become a testament for the collective consciousness but have been long neglected in the male-dominated world.

---

32. Roger P. H. Green, "Proba's Cento: Its Date, Purpose and Reception," *ClQ* 45 (1995): 561.

Pilgrim of the Word:
The Bible and Women in Egeria's *Itinerarium*

M. Dolores Martin Trutet

1. A Single Manuscript from a Unique Author

"Ostendebantur iuxta Scripturas."[1] These three words that open the diary of Egeria are absolutely programmatic.

1.1. A Unique Manuscript

In 1884, historian Gian Francesco Gamurrini discovered a manuscript in the Confraternità del Laici library in Arezzo. He instantly recognized its importance, even though it was partly damaged, which rendered the establishment of its title, original preface, date, and author more complicated. Following three years of study, it was published in 1887. The text told the tale of a Western pilgrimage to the Christian East, through the medium of a long letter, a report. It has two clearly distinct parts: a detailed travel journal and a detailed description of the liturgy of Jerusalem.

Another milestone in the research of this text was reached when Bollandist Paul Devos managed to establish the date for the author's stay in Jerusalem: the pilgrim arrived just before Easter 381 and left on Easter Monday 384.

So far, no other copies of this text have been found. This single manuscript is unique, and even though it is short, the bibliography of studies

---

1. "Shown according to the Scriptures" (Egeria, *Itin.* 1.1). The critical text is from the edition of Ezio Franceschini and Robert Weber, *Itinerarium Egeriae*, CCSL 175 (Turnhout: Brepols, 1981). The English translation is from George E. Gingras, *Egeria: Diary of a Pilgrimage*, ACW 38 (Mahwah, NJ: Newman, 1970). See also the translation of John Wilkinson, *Egeria's Travels to the Holy Land* (Wiltshire: Aris & Phillips, 1999).

devoted to it reaches around five hundred publications.[2] Hélène Pétré, the first translator and commentator on the text for the Sources chrétiennes series, called it "a veritable gold mine," referring both to its contents and to its author and readership.[3] It is the earliest work from early Christianity that shows "feminine thinking throughout."[4]

1.2. "An Eager Reader of All the Books of the Old and the New Testament"

The author of the travel journal was a mysterious figure and to a certain extent still remains such. Both her geographical origin and her social and religious status are still debated by scholars.

Gamurrini called the work *Sanctae Silviae Aquitanae peregrinatio ad Loca Sancta*. The author's level of education, the respect she received from civil and religious authorities, and the length and cost of the pilgrimage all pointed in his view to the identification of the author with Saint Silvia, the

---

2. The classical bibliographies by Baraut and Starowieski have been updated by Sebastià Janeras. See Cipriano Baraut, "Bibliografia egeriana," *HispSac* 7 (1954): 203–15; Marek Starowieski, *"Bibliografia Egeriana," Aug* 19 (1979): 297–318; Janeras, "Contributo alla bibliografia egeriana," in *Atti del Convegno Internazionale sulla Peregrinatio Egeriae: Nel centenario della pubblicazione del "Codex Aretinus 405," già "Aretinut VI,3," Arezzo October 23–25, 1987* (Arezzo: Academia Petrarca, 1990), 355–66. See also Janeras's supplements: "Bibliografia egeriana recent," *RCT* 28 (2003): 231–40; "Addenda," *RCT* 28 (2003): 507–10; "Noves publicacions sobre Egèria," *MLC* 19 (2011): 23–30.

3. See Hélène Pétré, *Journal de voyage*, Sources chretiennes 21 (Paris: Cerf, 1948). A newer edition in the same series is Pierre Maraval, *Égérie, Journal de voyage (Itinéraire)*, SC 296 (Paris: Cerf, 1982).

4. This is how Elena Giannarelli puts it in her introduction to the Italian translation, *Egeria, Diario di viaggio* (Milan: Edizioni Paoline, 1992). See also Giannarelli, "Antiche lettrici della Bibbia: Dame, martiri, pellegrine," in *La Bibbia nell'interpretazione delle donne*, ed. Claudio Leonardi, Francesco Santi, and Adriana Valerio, CSPFF (Napoli: SISMEL edizioni del Galluzzo, 2002), 23–48; Giannarelli, "Women and Travelling in Early Christian Texts: Some Aspects of a Problem," in *Gender and Religion*, ed. Kari Elisabeth Børresen, Sara Cabibbo, and Edith Specht (Rome: Viella, 2001), 155–74; Giannarelli, "Il pellegrinaggio al femminile nel cristianesimo antico: Fra polemica e esemplarità," in *Donne in viaggio: Viaggio religioso, politico, metaforico*, ed. Maria Luisa Silvestre and Adriana Valerio (Rome: Edizioni Laterza, 1999), 27–54. For the few surviving writings from Christian antiquity that were written by women, see Kari Elisabeth Børresen, "Ancient and Medieval Church Mothers," in *Women's Studies of the Christian and Islamic Traditions: Ancient, Medieval and Renaissance Foremothers*, by Kari Elisabeth Børresen and Kari Vogt (Dordrecht: Kluwer, 1993), 245–75.

sister of Rufinus of Aquitaine, a high-ranking official in Constantinople during the Theodosian era.

This attribution was accepted until 1903, when French Benedictine Marius Férotin saw the link of the text with the *Epistula Beatissime Egerie laude*, written by seventh-century Visigoth monk Valerius of Bierzo to his brothers. Valerius's text clearly indicates that he had access to the complete manuscript of the *Itinerarium* and suggests that he considered the author as his compatriot. The thesis of the Galician origin of Egeria is currently the majority opinion. Even if the identification with Silvia of Aquitaine is ruled out, the hypothesis of the author's friendship or kinship with the emperor Theodosius can be maintained, for Theodosius shared the same roots as Egeria. Between 375 and 378, he retired to his properties in Galicia to lead a life of a provincial aristocrat.

1.3. *Beatissima Sanctimonialis*?

Valerius of Bierzo affirms that Egeria is a *beatissima sanctimonialis*, and some medieval manuscripts designate her as an abbess. For some commentators, there can be no doubt that Egeria and her interlocutors belonged to the monastic movement. She has been described as an "itinerant nun," whose asceticism consisted of being uprooted and on the go. Alternatively, she has been taken as a member of a Galician monastery.[5]

Some scholars are more cautious. In their view, the most that can be said is that Egeria "belonged to a group of rich and aristocratic families with certain community links between them."[6] Elena Gianarelli, following Christine Mohrmann,[7] speculates that Egeria was a widow who

---

5. See Maribel Dietz, *Wandering Monks, Virgins and Pilgrims: Ascetic Travel in the Mediterranean World, A.D. 300–800* (University Park: Pennsylvania State University Press, 2005). The same idea was already brought up by Anscario Mundó, "Il monachesimo nella penisola iberica fino al s.VII: Questioni ideologiche e letterarie," in *Il monachesimo nell'alto Medioevo e la formazione della civiltà occidentale: Atti della IV settimana di studio dall'8 al 14 aprile 1956* (Spoleto: CISAM, 1957), 78–79.

6. So formulates Antonio Linage Conde in his chapter on the Hispanic pre-Benedictine monasticism. See Conde, *Los orígenes del monacato benedictino en la península ibérica I* (León: Centro de Estudio y de Investigación San Isidoro, 1973), 1:221.

7. See Christine Mohrmann, "Égérie et le monachisme," in *Corona Gratiarum: Miscellanea patristica, historica et liturgica Eligio Dekkers XII lustra complenti oblata* (Bruges: Nijhoff, 1975), 1:163–80.

sympathized with the monastic world and was attracted to it, while not necessarily belonging to it.

There are two possible reasons why Valerius of Bierzo identifies Egeria as a nun. Thanks to his geographical and cultural proximity, he might have had information that we do not—neither the *Itinerarium* nor any other source tells us whether Egeria was able to return home from Constantinople and to rejoin her community, if there was a community and not just an informal circle of women united by their common spiritual and cultural interest. The other theory is that the Visigoth monk has anachronistically given Egeria features from his own world. If Gianarelli is correct in maintaining that, from the first Christian communities up to the end of the fourth century, widows had a leading role, secured opportunities for influence, and took initiatives from their new empowerment, by Valerius's time things had changed. Visibility, respectability, power, and initiative were linked with the figure of an abbess, while informal ascetic circles had practically disappeared, in favor of institutionalized monasticism.

2. Textual and Ritualistic Pilgrimage

Egeria characterizes her pilgrimage as a "desire" (*desiderium*, also as *curiositas*, "curiosity") that pushed her to visit holy sites. The same language is used of another contemporary pilgrimage, that of Melania, whose biographer, Gerontius, says that her motivation for pilgrimage is "the desire to venerate holy sites" (*Vit. Sanct. Mel.* 2.34).[8] It is significant that the world *peregrinatio* to designate what we call a pilgrimage never appears in the *Itinerarium*. Instead, we find the expression *orationis gratia*, which literally means "for the sake of prayer" and is the Latin equivalent of the Greek εὐχῆς ἕνεκεν, an expression used in *Historia Lausiaca*.

For Egeria, the Bible is the inspiration and guide for her entire journey, so much so that we can call her journey a textual pilgrimage. The Holy Scriptures guide her interests, mark her journey, and even define the exact route of her pilgrimage.

Valerius of Bierzo reports that Egeria had prepared her journey with the Bible in her hand and studied the places she intended to visit. She also had a specific goal: to create a precise topography of salvation history.[9]

---

8. See Denys Gorce, *Vie de sainte Mélanie*, SC 90 (Paris: Cerf, 1962).

9. Glenn Bowman's expression "mapping history's redemption," which he uses in relation to the Bordeaux pilgrim, also applies to Egeria. See Bowman, "Mapping

The Bible was her compass and determined her route. Although Egeria generally used the main connecting roads of the time, she did not hesitate to embark on more difficult and dangerous expeditions (she was even in need of a military escort). The existing text of her *Itinerarium* starts at Mount Sinai. Egeria is truly aware that she is following in the footsteps of Moses and the Israelites and she tries to pinpoint carefully each of the biblical episodes. She is a real pioneer and the first to describe these places in detail; her curiosity and desire to learn about local traditions, and the persistence with which she searches for precise topographical details, result in more information than the pilgrims before her have offered. Egeria visits, identifies, and carefully records the various stages of the exodus, and she does the same with the traces of the patriarchs on other expeditions.

Frequently Egeria points out that the places, which she normally visits accompanied by a retinue of local monks or clergy, are sites that "I was forever seeking out, following Holy Scripture" (e.g., Egeria, *Itin.* 5.12).[10] She visits them as illustrations of texts that are for her the primary source of authority and divine power. The sacred geography outlined by the *Itinerarium* is significant in the manner it illustrates the biblical text. For Egeria, it was about checking in situ the correspondence between the textual sacred place, the biblical passages, and the physical sacred place.

This plan and this motivation of the pilgrim logically guide her reading of the Scriptures. A literal reading dominates, while the *Itinerarium* does not offer examples of allegorical and typological readings or mythical and spiritual musings. Nevertheless, the text reflects an authentic spirituality. For Egeria, the geographical locations of the *ipsissima loca* that construct a sacred topography are also a spiritual experience, lived through prayer. She indicates this experience with tender brushstrokes (*Itin.* 5.12): "In nomine Christi Dei nostri profecta sum ... in nomine Dei perveni"; "In the name of Christ our God, I set out.... in the name of God, I arrived" (18.1–2).[11]

What is striking is the indifferent or distant attitude that she shows toward the acquisition of relics, at a time when this practice and form of popular piety was booming. Egeria is clearly willing to give the biblical text a central position, which she expresses with a whole series of formulations:

History's Redemption: Eschatology and Topography in the *Itinerarium Burdigalense*," in *Jerusalem: Its Sanctity and Centrality to Judaism, Christianity, and Islam*, ed. Lee I. Levine (New York: Continuum, 1998), 163–87.

10. Trans. Gingras, *Egeria: Diary of a Pilgrimage*, 58.
11. Trans. Gingras, *Egeria: Diary of a Pilgrimage*, 76.

"Scripturae sanctae" (5.12; 48.2), "libri sancti" (5.8), "scripturae Dei" (20.13), "scriptum est" (2.5; 5.6; 6.3; 7.5; 10.3; 12.2; 20.10), "locutus est Deus dicens" (4.2), "dixit Deus" (4.7; 5.1), "iussit Deus dicens" (10.1). As Joseph Ziegler puts it, for Egeria the Bible is more than a travel guide; it is her favorite book, her guide of spiritual life.[12]

2.1. Biblical Passages

This central position of the Bible is also manifest in the numerous biblical quotations in the *Itinerarium*. In the part that has survived of Egeria's work, there are more than one hundred explicit or implicit quotes from the Bible. In addition, there are innumerable allusions to single words, historical or geographical names, or other characteristics of the Vetus Latina translation. Angelo Tafi estimates that the work was four or five times larger than what remains of it today, which means that the total number of biblical quotations and other references can be multiplied.[13]

Since the text is damaged and a large part of the account of New Testament sites is missing, it is difficult to assess the true balance between Old and New Testament references. As Egeria was concerned about a sacred topography, she directed her attention mainly to the Pentateuch and Historical Books, rather than prophetic or sapiential literature.

Visiting biblical sites gives Egeria an opportunity to make a special link to the biblical text. The *lectio divina* that she undertakes along the way makes her pilgrim of the Word.[14] Egeria shapes this re-actualization and

---

12. Joseph Ziegler, "Die Peregrinatio Aetheriae und die hl. Schrift," *Bib* 12 (1931): 163–64.

13. Angelo Tafi, "Egeria e la Bibbia," in *Atti del Convegno Internazionale*, 168. Obviously, there is no complete agreement among scholars on the exact number, due to various methodologies used. Moreover, in the section on the liturgy of Jerusalem, it is necessary to rely on the Armenian lectionary to clarify and specify the biblical readings to which Egeria refers, while she only indicates that the reading is done "according to the custom," or "as it is fixed," or "just as we (in the West) do."

14. See Mariella Carpinello, *Données à Dieu: Figures féminines dans les premier siècles chrétiens* (Bégrolles-en-Mauges: Abbaye de Bellefontaine, 2001), 342: "Among the women who display love of studying the Bible, each one follows a distinctive itinerary. Olympia is influenced by Origen; Marcella seeks to defend the absolute truth through an intellectual effort; Paula and Eustochium have Jerome as their commentator of scripture in their great adventure; Melania the Younger reads all texts three or four times a year. Egeria instead builds a real tour. That is why her pilgrimage, in which

internalization of the Scriptures throughout her journey with the help of some rituals, which she records with meticulous precision.

2.2. Egeria's Rituals

At each stage of her pilgrimage, Egeria organizes a prayer service. It is striking that, although surrounded by monks and clerics, she is the one who takes the initiative and oversees the selection of the texts. She is not a tourist who is simply shown around but rather an astute observer, organizer, and instigator of personal liturgy.

The passage in which Egeria describes her descent from Mount Sinai and her visit to Mount Horeb is paradigmatic (*Itin.* 4.1–3). It contains all the fundamental elements of her pilgrimage experience and the typical way of approaching the holy places. First, the longing to see the place in question; then the identification of the physical site with the one in the biblical text; the presence of monks, who act as guides; and a reading of the Scriptures as an expression of the sanctity of the place.

The place, Elijah's grotto, is shown to Egeria (*ostenditur*) by the monks and priests. The experience of the divine is made tangible thanks to the meditation of the senses, especially that of sight. It is not just a matter of "looking" but rather "looking deeply" (*pervidere*, 7.1) which underscores the intention of seeking the deepest knowledge possible.

But the experience of the holy place is not limited to seeing. It occurs through a ritual that repeats itself every time Egeria visits a place associated with a biblical event outside the city or the outskirts of Jerusalem. The ritual consists of four basic elements: a prayer, the reading of a biblical passage linked with the site, the recitation of an appropriate psalm, and a second prayer (10.7; 14.1). The ritual is sometimes shortened and simplified. When a bishop is present, he offers a blessing. On some occasions, the Eucharist is also celebrated. Egeria summarizes the structure, content, and purpose of the ritual in a programmatic text:

> On arriving in this plain we proceeded to this very place; there we said a prayer and read a certain passage from Deuteronomy, as well as the canticle and the benediction which Moses had said over the children of Israel. We said a second prayer after the reading from scripture, and, having

---

she invests all her religious sensation, is more captivating than any other devotional itinerary of the time."

given thanks to God, we moved along. Whenever we were empowered to reach our destination, it was always our custom first to say a prayer, then to read a passage from the Bible, sing a Psalm fitting the occasion, and finally say a second prayer. We always observed this custom whenever, God willing, we were able to reach our destination. (*Itin.* 10.7)[15]

2.3. Egeria's Bible

Egeria states that they read "a passage from the Bible."[16] In her homeland, the Vetus Latina was used, which follows the LXX very closely. For obvious reasons, the quotes cannot be from the Vulgate, because Jerome published his translation sixteen years after Egeria had ended her pilgrimage. Despite the numerous quotes from and references to the Vetus Latina in the *Itinerarium*, it is not possible to identify with any certainty whether the version used was a Galician or a Hispanic one, because the references are too short. On her pilgrimage Egeria is constantly surrounded by people from the Greek culture. Even though she does not prove to be a perfect Hellenist, the vocabulary she uses in the *Itinerarium* suggests that her basic knowledge of Greek was sufficient to get along. Perhaps it was good enough to allow her to read the biblical text and other reference works such as the *Onomasticon*[17] and the *Church History* of Eusebius, the Latin translation of which was not published until several years after the pilgrimage. Bible readings for the devotions she arranged may have been read directly from the LXX, which she might have bought in Constantinople or borrowed from the episcopal library in Jerusalem, which, together with the one in Caesarea, was the best-stocked library in Palestine. However, her linguistic world was undoubtedly that of the Vetus Latina.

2.3.1. Bible and Classical Culture

Linguists have noticed that her means of expressing herself, writing, narrating, her use of vocabulary, and style are entirely based on the biblical

---

15. Trans. Gingras, *Egeria: Diary of a Pilgrimage*, 66.
16. "*Deinde legeretur lectio ipsa de codice.*"
17. Ziegler argues that she had a Latin translation at her disposal, but his arguments are not very compelling. See Joseph Ziegler, "Die Peregrinatio Aetheriae und das Onomastikon des Eusebius," *Bib* 12 (1931): 70–84.

text of the Vetus Latina.[18] Mercedes González-Haba goes further; in her view, Egeria is an example of the complete and deliberate ignorance of the values of classical culture.[19] Celestina Milani, however, has shown that this statement requires some nuancing, detecting some rhetorical patterns and classical parameters within the *Itinerarium*.[20]

2.3.2. An Imperialist Discussion?

North American scholar Andrew Jacobs believes that Egeria's idea was to create, using textual construction of the religious landscape of Palestine, an exclusively Christian space for practicing piety and religious authority.[21] Her report would testify to Theodosius's political project to establish an homogeneous orthodox Christian empire. The Edict of Thessaloniki was issued in 380, one year before Egeria started her journey to the holy places. For Jacobs, Theodosius's intention was Christian imperialism, since he wanted to erase all differences and diverse identities. This is what Egeria does; by grounding her writing in the totalizing system of Christian Scriptures, she erases alternative viewpoints.

The theoretical frameworks of González-Haba and Jacobs maybe too rigid and reductionist, but they do contain some truth. Egeria was certainly a representative of the emerging new imperial Christian culture, which aimed at substituting pagan Roman traditions with biblical traditions and a theologically conceived story of salvation. Following the steps of the patriarchs and of Moses, Egeria could identify with the experiences of the chosen and liberated people of Israel through her own experience as a pilgrim. Each pilgrimage contained an element of personal vocation and exodus, and Egeria could connect this with her theological vision that

---

18. See Veikko Väänänen, *Le journal-épître d'Égérie: Étude lingüistique* (Helsinki: Suomalainen Tiedeakatemia, 1987).

19. Mercedes González-Haba, "El Itinerarium Egeriae: Un testimonio de la corriente cristiana de oposición a la cultura clásica," *EstCl* 20 (1976): 123–31.

20. Celestina Milani, "Studi sull' Itinerarium Egeriae: L'aspetto classico della lingua di Egeria," *Aev* 43 (1969): 381–452.

21. Andrew S. Jacobs, *Remains of the Jews: The Holy Land and Christian Empire in Late Antiquity* (Stanford, CA: Stanford University Press, 2004). In the fourth chapter, Jacobs describes the *Itinerarium* of Egeria, as well as the text of the pilgrim of Bordeaux and that of the pilgrim of Piacenza, as imperialist discourses that use historization, textualization, aestheticization, and ritualization to try to erase the presence of Jews and pagans.

the Old Testament prophecies have been fulfilled in Christ, and with the conceptualization of history as liberation, from persecution to the establishment of the Christian empire.

2.4. The Biblical Women in the *Itinerarium*

Within her journey through the paths of the Old Testament, several allusions to female biblical characters appear repeatedly in Egeria's work. Two sections deserve special mention: the pilgrimage to Mount Nebo (ch. 12), in which Egeria tells of her previous visit to the shores of the Dead Sea, and the expedition in the footsteps of the patriarchs to Osrhoene and Mesopotamia (chs. 20–21).

2.4.1. Lot's Wife

The first female character referred to by Egeria is Lot's wife.

> We were also shown the place, and this place is even mentioned in Scripture, where the pillar of Lot's wife stood. Believe me, reverend ladies, the pillar itself is not visible now, although its location is shown; but the pillar is said to have been covered by the Dead Sea. Indeed we saw the place, but we did not see any pillar, and on this matter I cannot deceive you. (*Itin.* 12.6–7)[22]

The relic of Lot's wife, who turned into a pillar of salt at the sight of the destruction of Sodom and Gomorrah (Gen 19:26), aroused the curiosity of the pilgrims. A series of legends, perhaps inspired by Jewish traditions, attributing special powers and extraordinary phenomena, were linked to the petrified salt columns that the pilgrims saw. Flavius Josephus mentions the existence of the stela without adding any narrative to it. Nevertheless, at the end of the second century, when Irenaeus established a parallel between Lot's wife and the church, which "has been left behind within the confines of the earth … and while entire members are often taken away from it, the pillar of salt still endures" (*Haer.* 4.31.3),[23] the crescendo of legends had already begun.

---

22. Trans. Gingras, *Egeria: Diary of a Pilgrimage*, 69.
23. Trans. from *ANF* 1.

At the time when Egeria journeyed to the Christian East, the poet Prudentius, who came from Hispania, like her, was thirty years old. The final edition of his poetic work includes a poem on the origin of sin, *Hamartigenia*. It states that the pillar perfectly replicates the physical form of Lot's wife: her beauty, her dress, her eyes, and her hair. The anonymous author of the poem *De Sodoma*, from the same period, is even more explicit: though she is "in a different body," Lot's wife "still has her period" (Pseudo-Cyprian, *Sod.* 125–126).[24]

In the Genesis narrative, Lot's wife's turning to salt fulfils the same narrative function as the yearning of the "meat pots of Egypt" in the book of Numbers or the attitude of those who do not wish to "leave Babel" in prophetic literature. In Egeria's time, however, a layer of legends lay over the story, with an emphasis on corporeality. The pillar of Lot's wife appears as a mysterious and strange gendered body. It is implied that her sin was not looking back, but rather had to do with her being a woman. Egeria's sober report of the precise location indicates, at the risk of disappointing her readers, that nothing else can be seen. This is not a case of demythologization but rather about asserting the primacy of the biblical text and the facts.

2.4.2. The Matriarchs

Other female biblical characters who appear in the *Itinerarium* are the biblical matriarchs. They turn up frequently in Egeria's sacred topography.

> And the holy bishop said to us: "Here is the well from which the holy woman Rebecca watered the camels of Abraham's servant Eliezer." (20.4)

> The saintly bishop [of Edessa] then said to me: ... "For the Scriptures indeed testify that the servant of the holy man Abraham came here to take away the holy woman Rebecca; and later the holy man Jacob came here when he took the daughters of Laban the Syrian." (20.11)

> After I had spent two days there, the bishop guided us to the well where the holy man Jacob had drawn water for the flocks of the holy woman Rebecca. This well is about six miles from Carrhae [= Haran]; and in

---

24. *Dicitur et uiuens alio iam corpore sexus / munifico solitos dispungere sanguine menses.* See Josep M. Escolà i Tuset, *Pseudo-Cebrià, Poemes*, EC (Barcelona: Fundació Bernat Metge, 2007), 53.

honor of this particular well, the holy church, very large and beautiful, has been built beside it. (21.1)

He showed me in the village the tomb of Laban the Syrian, Jacob's father-in-law; and I was also shown the place from which Rachel stole the idols of her father. (21.4)[25]

The account is revealing in two senses. On the one hand, it reflects Egeria's personal interest in the female figures such as Sarah, Rebecca, Rachel, and Leah. Her narration does not leave them in the shade of the patriarchs. Implicitly, Egeria indicates that they are not a mere anecdote but rather have a decisive role in salvation history.[26] On the other hand, it also testifies to a Jewish tradition of veneration and memory, presumably rooted in the vivid memory of women, taken up by the local Christian community and by the pilgrims who give the matriarchs the title of "saints," similar to the "saintly" Abraham, Isaac, and Jacob.

2.4.3. The Pilgrim of Bordeaux

Some fifty years before Egeria, the pilgrim of Bordeaux, an anonymous author of the earliest surviving report of a Jerusalem pilgrimage, dated around 333, also named places related to biblical women. Compared to Egeria's lively description, the *Itinerarium Burdigalense* contains a rather flat report of the distances between the stages of the pilgrimage and the best places to stay along the route. Such *itineraria* were originally intended to replace or supplement the maps of the Roman army; however, while the center from which the distances to the locations of the military camps were calculated was Rome, the Bordeaux pilgrim places Jerusalem as the symbolic center of the Christian empire.[27] Only when getting closer to the goal does the pilgrim begin to insert details and biblical places that indicate more than a simple logistical interest. What Laurie Douglass considers particularly striking in this regard is the atten-

---

25. Trans. Gingras, *Egeria: Diary of a Pilgrimage*, 82–86.
26. On the role of the biblical matriarchs in the book of Genesis, see Irmtraud Fischer, *Gottesstreiterinnen: Biblische Erzählungen über die Anfänge Israels* (Stuttgart: Kohlhammer, 2006).
27. Jas Elsner, "The Itinerarium Burdigalense: Politics and Salvation in the Geography of Constantine's Empire," *JRS* 90 (2000): 181–95.

tion that the *Itinerarium de Burdigalense* pays to certain biblical women.[28] It reports where the prophet Elijah asked the widow of Zarephath for a piece of bread; where Dinah, the daughter of Jacob, was raped—none of the other early Christian pilgrims mention this incident; the location of Jacob's well, where Jesus met the Samaritan woman; and the house of Rahab the prostitute. For Douglass, this less androcentric viewpoint could indicate that the author was a woman. In her rejoinder, Susan Weingarten claims that Douglass's arguments are inconsistent.[29] The places mentioned in the *Itinerarium* are connected with the stages of the *cursus publicus*, and any pilgrim could visit them without any particular interest in them.

Be that as it may, the *Itinerarium Burdigalense* and Egeria's diary are evidence that the memory of biblical women in the Christian East of the fourth century was not insignificant. Christian communities adopted Israel's spiritual heritage and Jewish traditions around the matriarchs and other female figures from the Old Testament and incorporated them in their sacred geography and their devotional world.[30] These devotional forms continued throughout the Middle Ages, sometimes provoking conflict, as the question was not only about adopting but rather monopolizing, as Jacobs has emphasized (see above). A twelfth-century Jewish traveler, Petachiah of Regensburg, reports how some Christian monks tried in vain to move the marble stone covering Rachel's tomb, half a day's journey from Jerusalem, in order to place it in their own holy place.[31] The *Itineraria* of Egeria and the Bordeaux pilgrim are more concerned with accommodating the matriarchs and giving visibility to them than of monopolizing them. Biblical women find space and meaning in Egeria's textual pilgrimage, in her spirituality, and in the cartography of salvation.

---

28. Laurie Douglass, "A New Look at the Itinerarium Burdigalense," *JECS* 4 (1996): 327–29.

29. Susan Weingarten, "Was the Pilgrim from Bordeaux a Woman? A Reply to Laurie Douglass," *JECS* 7 (1999): 291–97.

30. Marcel Simon, "Les saints d'Israël dans la dévotion de l'Église ancienne," in *Recherches d'histoire judéo-chrétienne* (Paris: Mouton, 1962), 154–80.

31. This example is from Joseph Shatzmiller, "Récits de voyages hébraïques au Moyen-âge," in *Croisades et Pélerinages: Récits, chroniques et voyages en Terre Sainte*, ed. Danielle Régnier-Bohler (Paris: Bouquins, 1997), 1290.

3. Monastic Approaches to Scripture

For Egeria, it is not only the Word but also the people who make up the holy places. Significantly, she uses the word *sanctus* not only to describe the books of the Bible or places mentioned in the Scriptures (such as "the holy mountain" to mean Mount Sinai) or biblical characters, but also of the guardians of the holy places. The sanctity of the sites she visits is always the result of historization and humanization. The place is always part of a story, and its sacred dimension is conveyed by a human mediator, usually monks.

3.1. Monastic Icons

This monastic presence unfolds in various dimensions. The first, the most external, graphic, and visual dimension, presents monks as a sort of biblical icons, who populate the landscape, recalling the figures of patriarchs and prophets who lived in the same places.[32] On her arrival in Salem, Egeria meets a monk who resembles Melchizedek (see *Itin.* 14.2), who lives a holy life and embodies the historical memory of the place and in-depth knowledge of the Scriptures. This final dimension is one that Egeria frequently emphasizes. For example, she tells of the bishop of Arabia that "this saintly bishop is a former monk, who had been raised from childhood in a cell, and is therefore as learned in the Scriptures as he is above reproach in his way of life" (9.2). She also says to her addressees, "For I do not want Your Charity to think that the conversations of the monks are about anything except the Divine Scriptures and the actions of the great monks" (20.13).[33]

3.2. Monastic Practice

What were the characteristics of this monastic training in the Scriptures that so attracted Egeria's attention? The example of Egyptian monasticism is paradigmatic to understand it. The damaged text of the *Itinerarium*

---

32. We know that in the original autograph manuscript, Egeria had sketched for her companions some drawings of the buildings she saw on her way: "facta est ista ecclesia, quam videtis" (*Itin.* 16.6). She is not only "curious," as she humorously says, but also extremely attentive observer, and throughout the story she outlines some almost "photographic" snapshots, as in *Itin.* 1.4.

33. Trans. Gingras, *Egeria: Diary of a Pilgrimage*, 63, 85.

means that the story of Egeria's journey to Egypt, which she undertook probably after Easter of 382, is lost. She wanted to get to know Alexandria and the monasteries and hermitages of the Nile Delta and the Thebaid, as Melania the Elder and Rufinus of Aquileia had done before her, and Jerome and Paula were to do shortly after her.[34] Unlike these famous pilgrims, Egeria does not appear in the company of Western clerics or monks. Since we do not have Egeria's text, we have to rely on other contemporary sources to get a picture of the practices of Scripture reading that Egeria observed among the anchorites and the cenobitic monks of Egypt. While there are far fewer sources that tell about female anchorites and cenobites, whom the Western pilgrims also visited, some texts allow us to understand their ways of approaching the Scriptures.

In the desert, the Scriptures formed an essential element of the spirituality of the monks. Their religious culture was very much nourished by the encounter with the Word. However, attitudes to the written text were ambivalent, partly due to sociological factors, such as a high illiteracy rate, partly to spiritual factors that emphasized that the Word should not become a dead letter. The Scriptures were to be put into practice and incorporated into the fabric of the daily life as a continuous presence.[35]

We find the same practice among the desert mothers. The Life of Saint Syncletica, wrongly attributed to Athanasius, whose author remains unknown, is a good example of this semi-eremetic female monastic environment at the end of the fourth century.[36] Alongside the *Life of Saint Macrina* by Gregory of Nyssa, it is one of the oldest hagiographic stories after the martyrs' acts. The author of the Life of Saint Syncletica underlines throughout the text how the spirituality and the teaching of the desert

---

34. According to some commentators, the epistolary genre of the *Itinerarium* suggests that on her trip to Egypt, she might not have been content with a detailed account but wanted to write a "monographic supplement" on Egyptian monasticism, in the same way as she had dedicated such a work on the liturgy of Jerusalem to her recipients.

35. On this subject, the decisive work is Douglas Burton-Christie, *The Word in the Desert: Scripture and the Quest for Holiness in Early Christian Monasticism* (New York: Oxford University Press, 1993).

36. Odile Bénédicte Bernard, Jean Bouvet, and Lucien Regnault, eds., *Vie de sainte Synclétique* (Bégrolles-en-Mauges: Abbaye de Bellefontaine, 1991). For an English translation, see Laura Swan, *The Forgotten Desert Mothers* (Mahwah, NJ: Paulist, 2001).

ammas was deeply rooted in the Scriptures and how masterfully she quotes the Bible.[37]

Egeria also encountered the other pole of monasticism, the cenobitic life.[38] It is likely that, as was customary among Western pilgrims of her era, she stayed in one of the female monasteries during her journey. With the Pachomian rule, there is no question of the ambivalence found among the *abbas* and *ammas* of the desert; on the contrary, literacy was obligatory as a prerequisite of accessing the Scriptures, and there was a regulated curriculum (precepts 139–40).[39]

While the Pachomian nuns are known to have led a life similar to monks, we know little of their level of literacy or their intellectual and scriptural training. Recent studies by María Jesús Albarrán Martínez that take into account private letters and other documentary papyri as well as Coptic ostraca in addition to patristic sources offer us some limited answers to these questions.[40] It appears that it was not only the superiors and other women in important positions who were educated but that every nun in the religious community had a basic level of literacy in order to take part in the spiritual and liturgical life. Female monasteries owned libraries, and there is evidence that women linked to monastic centers were involved in copying, binding, and decorating of books, particularly the holy books. This was the reality and practice that Melania the Elder, Egeria, and other

---

37. The etymology of her name has led some scholars to suspect that she is a fictional, synthetic saint, a representation of an ideal portrait of Egyptian female asceticism. However, the possibility of an authentic historical nucleus cannot be ruled out. In the Apophtegmata Patrum collections, twenty sayings attributed to her are preserved. See Maria Sira Carrasquer Pedrós and Araceli de la Red Vega, *Matrología 1: Madres del desierto* (Burgos: Monte Carmelo, 2000), 168–69.

38. On the different currents of female ascetic life that Egeria encountered during her journey and on the relationship between *parthenoi*, widows, and deaconesses, see Susanna Elm, *Virgins of God: The Making of Ascetism in Late Antiquity* (Oxford: Clarendon, 1996).

39. See A. Veilleux, ed. and trans., *Pachomian Chronicles and Rules*, vol. 2 of *Pachomian Koinonia: The Lives, Rules and Other Writings of Saint Pachomius and His Disciples*, CS 46 (Kalamazoo, MI: Cistercian Publications, 1981), 166.

40. María Jesús Albarrán Martínez, *Ascetismo y monasterios femeninos en el Egipto tardoantiguo: Estudio de papiros y ostraca griegos y coptos* (Barcelona: Abadia de Montserrat, 2011). On the literacy of women in Byzantine Egypt, see Albarrán Martínez, "Letradas e iletradas en el Egipto bizantino," in *Mujer y cultura escrita: Del mito al siglo XXI*, ed. María del Val González de la Peña (Gijón: Trea, 2005), 29–45.

Western pilgrims encountered when they passed through the monasteries of the Christian East.

4. Privileged Witness to the Practices of the Church of Jerusalem

The monographic supplement on the liturgy of Jerusalem is of first-class importance as a source for the liturgical history. It shows a liturgy that is completely rooted in the biblical text. During her long stay in the city, Egeria immersed herself in the life, customs, and rituals of the ecclesial community. Thus, she became a privileged witness to the ways in which the liturgical celebration unfolded, the constitution of the biblical lectionary, preaching, catechesis, and the establishment of canon at a time of particular activity and creativity.

4.1. Biblical Icons

Egeria was able to capture the particular style and theological character of the Jerusalem liturgy and knew how to translate it for her audience. This liturgical style was characterized by encounters with the historical Jesus, the Holy Scripture, the popular spirit, and the importance of gestures and symbols.[41] The liturgical celebration used theatrical elements to bring scenes from the gospels to life. Egeria describes the actors of the celebration: the bishop, who represents Christ, and the people, who also have an essential role. She notes the active presence of the laity;[42] men and women ("viri aut mulieres"), even children; pilgrims of both sexes, lending the local church a cosmopolitan element. The male and female monastics ("monazontes et parthenae"), both domestic and from abroad, prevent the monopoly of the clerics.[43] The images that Egeria creates are rich in detail and full of life. The procession of consecrated women in the Sunday cel-

---

41. Carmelo García Del Valle, *Jerusalén: La liturgia de la iglesia madre* (Barcelona: CPL, 2001).

42. On the creation and development of the term *laity* in the church in the first centuries and on the role of women in the various stages of the development of the institutional system, see Alexandre Faivre, *Ordonner la fraternité: Pouvoir d'innover et retour à l'ordre dans l'église ancienne* (Paris: Cerf, 1992).

43. In Egeria's detailed listing, there is a striking absence: deaconesses do not appear. In the church of Jerusalem, some of their functions may have been taken over by the numerous groups of ascetic women. As for catechesis, it was taken care of by the bishop. Nor do they seem to have been involved in baptismal rites. This fact also

ebration of the resurrection, accompanied by townsfolk who descended to the Anastasis at dawn amid the perfume of incense, is like a biblical picture of the anointing women (see *Itin.* 24.1). In the Jerusalem liturgy, with its popular and monastic icons, the presence of women was very visible and vital. "On the way from Jerusalem to the Lazarium, at about a half mile from that place, there is a church along the road at the very place where Mary, the sister of Lazarus, came forth to meet the Lord.... And the proper passage from the Gospel is read, describing how Lazarus's sister met the Lord" (*Itin.* 29.4).[44] However, in the case of catechesis, at no time does this presence cross over to a public role.

4.2. Liturgical Celebrations and the Constitution of the Lectionary

In this section, it is not Egeria who gets to choose the biblical passages that match the sites she visits; rather, she follows a lectionary that was already established or was in the process of creation and fixation. The rite itself is a pilgrimage of the entire Christian community, following the traces of Jesus Christ and listening to the accounts of the gospels. Egeria's report testifies to the transition from the private liturgy of the pre-Constantinian era to the public liturgy of imperial Christianity, and it reflects the overlap of the temporal with the spatial.[45] It is about a fundamental development in the history of Christian liturgy, now that the essentially temporal essence of the Jerusalem liturgy can be exported to other places. Egeria's interest in the Jerusalem literature allows us to think that, for the pilgrim, this ritual has a paradigmatic value that must be known by the women to whom it is directed (*Itin.* 24.1). This is an important development in the history of Christian liturgy, since the essentially temporary Jerusalem liturgy could be exported elsewhere. Egeria's interest in the Jerusalem liturgy suggests that this ritual had a paradigmatic value for her, and it must have been also known to the group of women for whom she wrote. She is not mistaken in her esteem and actively contributed to the spreading of the autochthonous Jerusalem liturgy with its biblical lectionary, which has played a decisive

---

caught the attention of Martimort. See his classic study: Aimé Georges Martimort, *Les diaconesses: Essai historique* (Rome: Edizioni Liturgiche, 1982), 121, 128–29.

44. Trans. Gingras, *Egeria: Diary of a Pilgrimage*, 102.

45. This is emphasized by Jonathan Z. Smith, *To Take Place: Toward Theory in Ritual* (Chicago: University of Chicago Press, 1987), 88–94.

role in the development of the liturgical cycle and the theological sanctification of time, both in the East and in the West.

4.3. Catechesis

In Jerusalem, Egeria also discovered the catechesis of Cyril of Jerusalem,[46] who promoted a structuring of the Christian initiation along a line of demand and prestige, more than a quarter-century ahead of other churches (Carthage, Antioche, Milan, Rome, etc.). Egeria recognizes the importance of this catechesis, founded on and nourished by the Scriptures. It represents the theological method used in catechesis, moving from the literal sense (*carnaliter*) to the spiritual sense (*spiritaliter*); that is, it proposes a way of Christian life according to the Spirit, where one moves from narrating the events (*narrante*) to discussing (*disputante*) their significance for salvation. It also highlights the secure pedagogy of the bishop in the mystagogical process (*Itin.* 46.2, 47.2).

In the Jerusalem church, the catechumenate was mixed; candidates of both genders, presented by their godparents, came to the same catechesis taught by the bishop. On the whole, men and women received the same instruction and, therefore, were equally equipped biblically, dogmatically, and spiritually. However, the transcription of the catechesis indicates that Cyril went on to impose different requirements based on sex.

> Let the men sit together and have a good book; one man can read and the rest listen. If there isn't a book available, one man might pray, and another speak a few helpful words. The unmarried women should be kept together in the same way, either singing or reading silently, so that their lips move inaudibly, "for I do not allow a woman to speak in church." Married women should observe the same practice, praying and moving their lips silently.... I shall observe each man's earnestness and each woman's devotion. (Cyril of Jerusalem, *Catech.* prol. 14–15)[47]

Cyril demands and encourages participation from men: they should express their interest, that is, show a proactive attitude. Women, by contrast, are called to meditate on the same content in silence and receptive

---

46. Pierre Maraval, "Les Catéchèses baptismales de Cyrille de Jérusalem et le témoignage d'Égérie," *CPE* 91 (2003): 29–35.

47. Translation from Edward J. Yarnold, *Cyril of Jerusalem* (London: Routledge, 2000), 84.

prayer. Egeria, who knows how to move in a mixed world and, thanks to her letters of recommendation, is received with honor by bishops wherever she goes, may not have done very well in the categories instigated for the catechumens.[48]

4.4. The Canon

Egeria was also a witness to the canonization process in the Jerusalem church. The fourth catechesis of Cyril adds a final section on the Scriptures. The bishop set out the Old and New Testaments, reading the catechumens the legend of the origins of the LXX, which he took to present a historical fact. He then immediately gave a list of the canonical writings permitted in the Jerusalem church alongside a series of warnings on the apocrypha (Cyril of Jerusalem, *Catech.* 4.33–36). This shows that the canon was still in the process of being fixed; Cyril makes no mention of the book of Revelation. Like him, Egeria appears firmly convinced of the continuity between the Old and New Testament and is familiar with the concept of canonicity; she uses the technical term *canonical scriptures* in her conversation with the bishop of Edessa (*Itin.* 20.10). After her long stay in Jerusalem, she must have been familiar with the list of books that Cyril considered canonical; nevertheless, she acts with great freedom in her readings, without being completely restricted by the bishop's admonitions and without feeling this as a betrayal of the Scripture she so loved.

5. Beyond the Canon: An Open Spirituality

Before she started her return from Jerusalem to Constantinople, Egeria received a copy of the correspondence between Jesus and King Abgar from the bishop of Edessa; she also mentions that her circle of women already had a shorter copy of the text in their library (*Itin.* 19.2).[49] She also read "some passages concerning Saint Thomas" ("aliquanta ipsius Sancti Thomae"), possibly an extract of the Acts of Thomas, at

---

48. The fears and reservations that Gregory of Nyssa expresses regarding the appropriateness of pilgrimages for women are completely foreign to her. See Pierre Maraval, "Égérie et Grégoire de Nysse," in *Atti del Convegno Internazionale*, 315–31.

49. On this text and the legend of Abgar, see Marlène Kanaan, "Jésus et le roi Abgar," *CPE* 94 (2004): 12–20.

the apostle's tomb (19.16–19). Finally, in Seleucia she read the Acts of Thecla in the church where she was buried (23.5). Egeria does not view these readings as an alternative to the canonical texts but as an addition to them.

5.1. Egeria's Naïveté?

Among some commentators, it is popular to attribute to Egeria a certain degree of naïveté. Remo Gersolomino disagrees with this evaluation: "There is nothing gullible or naïve about Egeria. In my opinion, behind her enthusiasm there is always an element of prudence and caution."[50] Other observers like to point out Egeria's lack of classical education or theological training. She certainly did not meet the standards that Jerome required of the intellectual elite of the "ladies of Aventine,"[51] but in her historical context she did demonstrate a breadth of knowledge and solid cultural preparedness. Attributing Egeria's use of apocryphal texts to a deficient theological training or a love of romantic novels does not sufficiently explain her attitude and use of the apocrypha. We have to look to other directions, one of which is Priscillianism.

5.2. Egeria and Priscillianism

The temporal coincidence with the emergence of Priscillianism in Galicia, Egeria's belonging to the provincial aristocracy, and her relation to and involvement in the female ascetic-monastic movement have together brought up the idea of locating Egeria among the followers or sympathizers of Priscillian. The movement had a number of female followers, but there is no direct link to Egeria.[52] However, if Priscillianism was a radical reformist reaction against post-Constantinian Christianity and its power hierarchy, Egeria appears far more convincingly as a representative and

---

50. Remo Gelsomino, "Egeria, 381–384 d.C.: dalle radici romane alle radici bibliche," in *Atti del Convegno Internazionale*, 268.

51. See the derogatory remarks of Gabriel Sanders, "Égérie, saint Jérôme et la Bible: En marge de l'Itin. Eg. 18, 2, 39, 5 et 2, 2," in *Corona Gratiarum*, 181–99.

52. Diego Piay Augusto, "Acercamiento prosopográfico al priscilianismo," in *Espacio y tiempo en la percepción de la antigüedad tardía*, ed. Elena Conde Guerri, Rafael Gonzáles Fernández, and Alejandro Egea Vivancos, AC 23 (Murcia: Universidad de Murcia, 2006), 601–26.

promoter of Theodosian imperial Christianity and in no way as an advocate of any form of radical asceticism or charismatic exaggeration.[53]

5.3. An Open Spirituality

Egeria's position cannot be easily labeled. As far as we can tell today, her approach was eclectic, and her intellectual and spiritual journey was independent and anticonformist. Her natural curiosity results in an open spirituality. The episode of Abgar's letters can perhaps be explained as belonging to the context of Egeria's discovering the local church in Edessa, but her reading of the Acts of Thecla in Seleucia is more significant. It reminds us that, in the *Itinerarium*, in addition to the above-mentioned biblical women, Egeria names three emblematic figures for the spirituality of Christian women of her time: Helena, Thecla, and Euphemia. To these three should be added Marthana, the only person Egeria encountered during her pilgrimage whom she mentions by name.

5.4. Models of Female Empowerment

In her account of her encounter with Marthana, Egeria uses two semantic registers: first is the warm and loving tone typical of sisterhood; it is the same register she uses when she addresses the recipients of her text, calling them, for example, "*dominae animae meae, dominae, lumen meum.*" The other register, however, is shown in the description of the "person to whose way of life everyone in the East bears witness, the holy deaconess Marthana" (*Itin.* 23.3).[54] In an identical way, she describes monks and bishops as icons of holiness and testimonies to the Christian life, and identifies them with the Word. In her friend Marthana, we see a practice common in various churches in Asia Minor, in which the title and the function of the deacon went together with the leadership of the monastic community.

It is not insignificant that "innumerable monasteries of men and women," including the communities run by Marthana, were in the vicinity of the cathedral of Saint Thecla. It is there that Egeria read the Acts of Thecla in its entirety, ending her reading with a deeply emotional thank-

---

53. Francisco Javier Fernández Conde, *Prisciliano y el priscilianismo: Historiografía y realidad*, EHO (Gijón: Trea, 2008). See also Mohrmann, who emphasizes that Egeria is far from any ascetic radicalism ("Égérie et le monachisme").

54. Trans. Gingras, *Egeria: Diary of a Pilgrimage*, 87.

you. If the apocryphal acts as a whole can be taken to represent a feminine vindication and an affirmation of the role of women in early Christianity, the Acts of Thecla are surely the major exponent of this movement.[55] Therefore, the author of the Life of Syncletica calls her a "genuine disciple of the blessed Thecla, following the same teachings." There are also constant references to Thecla in the *Life of Saint Macrina*.[56]

At the end of the fourth century, when Egeria undertook her pilgrimage, there were various portrays of Thecla.[57] The oldest and most subversive version of the Acts of Thecla, which Egeria read, depicts her breaking the traditional female roles, and the light version, which became the most popular one in the fifth century, portrays her as a miracle-working virgin whose life Basil of Seleucia wrote of in his *Life and Miracles of Saint Thecla*. There is no doubt that Egeria's preferences lean toward the first version.

On her return trip to Constantinople, Egeria stopped at Chalcedon, "because of the very famous shrine of Saint Euphemia, already known to me from before" (*Itin.* 23.7).[58] Likewise, in the section dedicated to the Jerusalem liturgy, there is a reference to the empress Helena. Her presence in the *Itinerarium* is hardly surprising, given that her pilgrimage to Jerusalem and her stay there in 325 inspired new pilgrims to the Holy Land. Unlike Eusebius in his *Vita Constantini*,[59] Egeria, based on solid local tradition, emphasizes the role of Helena in the construction of the churches of Anastasis and Martyrium (*Itin.* 25.9).

---

55. See Amy-Jill Levine and Maria Mayo Robins, ed., *A Feminist Companion to the New Testament Apocrypha*, FCNTECW 11 (London: T&T Clark, 2006); similarly, Stevan L. Davies, *The Revolt of the Widows: The Social World of the Apocryphal Acts* (Carbondale: Southern Illinois University Press, 1980); Virginia Burrus, *Chastity as Autonomy: Women in the Stories of Apocryphal Acts*, SWR 23 (Lewiston, NY: Mellen, 1987). See also Kim Haines-Eitzen, "Women's Literature? The Case of the Apocryphal Acts of the Apostles," in *The Gendered Palimpsest: Women, Writing and Representation in Early Christianity* (Oxford: Oxford University Press, 2012), 53–64.

56. On the Thecla reference in the Life of Syncletica, see Carrasquer Pedrós, *Matrología 1*, 162–63. On the meaning of the reference to Thecla in the *Life of Macrina*, see Jostein Børtnes, "Schwestern in Jungfräulichkeit: Gorgonia und Makrina in der Erinnerung ihrer Brüder," in *Christliche Autoren der Antike*, ed. Kari Elisabeth Børresen and Emanuela Prinzivalli, BF 5.1 (Stuttgart: Kohlhammer, 2015), 100–117.

57. See Elena Giannarelli, "Da Tecla a santa Tecla: Un caso de nemesi agiografica," *Sanctorum* 4 (2007): 1–16.

58. Trans. Gingras, *Egeria: Diary of a Pilgrimage*, 88.

59. See Pierre Maraval, "La découverte de la croix au IVe siècle," *CPE* 89 (2003): 10–14.

Thus, roaming through places and texts that were important for the spirituality of Christian women, Egeria offers us various icons of female empowerment in the *Itinerarium*. These include a female apostle, hard to classify; a radical martyr; a builder empress; and a deaconess-abbess. To these we can add one more: Egeria herself, the pilgrim of the Word.

6. Conclusion

In the course of her journey in the Christian East, Egeria introduced various practices of reading the Bible. She herself organized rituals in which the Bible functioned as the compass of her efforts to map salvation history and her spiritual experience. She also demonstrated her knowledge of monastic approaches to the Scriptures and witnesses of the reading practices of the Jerusalem church. When planning her journey, she took into account the places of particular significance for the Christian women of her time. Egeria moved around skillfully in a patriarchal world where monks and bishops demonstrated the connections between biblical texts and holy places. She subverted this order by her independence, her initiative, and her determination to put her discoveries into words using her own voice. To her sisters in faith, her original audience, and also to us today, Egeria appears a fearless, determined, and cheerful reader.[60] An exceptional work written by a woman for a group of women, the *Itinerarium* builds bridges between East and West and offers an original contribution to the Christian culture that was emerging at the end of the fourth century.

---

60. This is how Valerius of Bierzo characterizes her in his *Epistola de laude Aetherie virginis*. A translation of his letter has been published by Consuelo María Aherne, *Valerio of Bierzo: An Ascetic of the Late Visigothic Period* (Washington, DC: Catholic University of America Press, 1949).

Mixed Doubles:
The Epithalamium of Paulinus and Therasia

Cristina Simonelli

At the end of the poem numbered 25 in the letter collection of Paulinus of Nola—an epithalamium for the wedding of Titia and Julian, the future bishop of Eclanum—appear the names of its donors: Paulinus and his wife, Therasia. Studies that focus on the poem only rarely mention this fact, although it is supported by the manuscript tradition and its authenticity has never been questioned in critical editions. In my view, it is incorrect to dismiss its relevance. While it is true that the mention of both names here *merely* shows who the benefactors are, in the tradition of classical epithalamium poems—which also serves as inspiration here—the name of the benefactor, when quoted or alluded to, is important and corresponds to the name of the author.

The inclusion of the wife's name is unusual and went against the practice of the time. Thus, the presence of the name should at least be evaluated according to what in exegetical studies is often referred to as "resistance to tendencies."

The absence of Therasia's name in scholarly discussions reflects the deep-rooted and unrepentant habit of ignoring women's names in ancient texts. This is based on the presumption that texts attributed to women, even those bearing a woman's name, must either be based on a man's idea or be written by a male hand. This is the case of Macrina and her brother Saint Gregory of Nyssa (*Life of Saint Macrina* and *On the Soul and the Resurrection*) and also applies to the controversy over the attribution of the *vexilla crucis* to Radegund of Poitiers. Even though the hymn contains her name, authorship has been suggested to belong to her friend Venanzio Fortunato. The same happens with the names of the *ammas* (desert mothers) in the alphabetical series of the Apophthegmata Patrum and to the signature of Paula in Jerome's letters, and in the fourth letter of Salvian of Marseille, despite the fact that it also bears the name of his wife, Palladia, and that of their little daughter, Auspiciola.

This attitude is seemingly scrupulous, being critical of the assumed pseudonymity. Often, however, it is simply superficial, as suggested by many researchers on women's history, such as Nicole Loreaux, Luisa Muraro, Annarosa Buttarelli, and historians focusing on women in Christianity, such as Adriana Valerio and Cettina Militello. What we need is particular care and dedication in the search for gaps and allusions to the presence of figures who are habitually excluded.[1] If this is true in the case of persons with symbolic importance, it is even more so for historical people.

In addition to these general considerations, I would like to point out that mentioning Therasia's name in poem 25 is not an isolated case in the works of Paulinus. A total of eleven letters of his letter collection contain a similar double signature, and still others, as we will see, are addressed to couples. Alongside poem 25, other poetic passages also mention Therasia's name.

Having thus set the question, I will discuss the contents of the epithalamium and, in particular, the biblical references it contains. They seem extremely original, particularly with regard to marriage and the relationship between men and women. Could this specific form, with its respectful attention to the *female*, be attributed to Therasia's inspiration? In any case, the wife of Paulinus, mentioned by her own name, should not be ignored. Therefore, let us play a game of mixed doubles!

1. Historical and Biographical Framework

Paulinus was born in Burdigala (Bordeaux) in Aquitaine. His literary competence developed in the school of the poet Ausonius, with whom he remained in contact throughout his life despite the choices that led

---

1. See Annarosa Buttarelli, *Sovrane: L'autorità femminile al governo* (Milan: Il Saggiatore, 2013), 60. She quotes Nicole Loreaux and Maria Zambrano. See further Luisa Muraro, *Il Dio delle donne* (Milan: Mondadori, 2003); Adriana Valerio, *Cristianesimo al femminile* (Napels: D'Auria, 1990); and many other books in this series; Cettina Militello, *Il volto femminile della storia* (Casale Monferrato: Piemme, 1995). Particularly relevant is the study of Militello on Paulinus and Therasia. See Cettina Militello, "Un'avventura coniugale," in *L'amicizia tra uomo e donna nei primi 13 secoli del cristianesimo*, ed. Clementina Mazzucco, Cettina Militello, and Adriana Valerio (Milan: Paoline, 1990), 168–90.

him to other places and other assignments. He was also a Roman official (*aedilis*, *praetor*, and *senator*), and came to Campania while working as governor from 379 to 381. He became particularly enchanted by the town of Cimitile near Nola. He then moved to Spain, where he met and married Therasia, who already was a committed Christian. Paulinus was baptized in his native town and was later ordained presbyter in Barcelona, but Ambrose seems to have considered him as part of his clergy, probably in a spiritual sense:

> For though I was baptised at Bordeaux by Delphinus, and ordained at Barcelona in Spain by Lampius, when the people there were suddenly fired to put compulsion on me, yet I have always been nurtured in the faith by Ambrose's affection, and now that I am ordained priest he cherishes me. In fact, he wanted to claim me as one of his clergy, so that even if I live away from Milan I may be regarded as a priest of his. (Paulinus, *Ep.* 3.4 [to Alypius])[2]

In Milan, Augustine and his son Adeodatus were catechumens and were baptized. However, the correspondence between Paulinus and Augustine started only later, through the mediation of Alypius, who at that time was the bishop of Thagaste and lasted for a long time. In this correspondence, a letter sent to Augustine by Paulinus and his wife is of special interest:

> The sinners Paulinus and Therasia send their greetings to Lord Augustine, their holy and loving brother ... my spiritual brother who judges all things.... We are together though apart, and acquainted though unknown to each other, for we are members of the one body, we have the one Head, we are steeped in the one grace, we live on the one Bread, we tread the same path, we dwell in the same house.... We have one heart and one soul in the Lord [*sunt enim unum cor et una in Domino anima nobiscum*]. (Paulinus, *Ep.* 6.1–3)[3]

---

2. English translation by Patrick G. Walsh in *Letters of St. Paulinus of Nola*, ACW 35–36 (Westminster, MD: Newman, 1966), 1:46. For the Latin text, see Giovanni Santaniello, ed., *Paolino di Nola: Le lettere* (Naples: LER, 1992). This also includes a thorough introduction to his life and to the principal themes of the letter collection. All letters cited in this paper are from this edition. The correspondence with Ambrose is not preserved, but Ambrose refers to both Paulinus and Therasia in a letter to Sabinus (Ambrose, *Ep.* 27.1–2).

3. Trans. Walsh, *Letters of St. Paulinus*, 1:70–72. This letter and Augustine's reply to it also belong to Augustine's letter collection (Augustine, *Ep.* 30–31). The reply is

After the wedding, the two set off on an increasingly demanding Christian life, giving away, among other things, a considerable part of their enormous wealth. Their marriage was burdened by difficult pregnancies and, above all, by the death of their only son just a few days after his birth. Paulinus and Therasia decided to retire gradually to a monastic life. They were not the only couple recorded to have made such a choice, often after having had children. In his poem 21, Paulinus refers to others who settled in Cimitile of Nola together with him and his wife. They include Albina, the widow of Publicola and, thus, the daughter-in-law of Melania the elder; her daughter Melania and her husband, Pinianus, who had married at the respective ages of seventeen and fourteen and whose two children had died in infancy; Avita and Turcius Apronianus, with their children Eunomia and Asterius; and Emilius, the bishop of Benevento, who is presented as the father of the bride in the epithalamium we are here discussing.

Other couples were also linked through correspondence to this company, for example, Eucherius and Galla, who lived on the island of Lero, close to Lérins:[4]

> They [the bearers of the letter] said they had left you through God's kindness in good health, and that you were carrying out the activities of your admirable calling, working at your studies and aiming at heaven with the same harmony with which you left behind worldly matters. (Paulinus, *Ep.* 51.1)[5]

---

addressed "to Paulinus and Therasia," and Augustine congratulates the couple, the meek and humble-hearted disciples of Christ, and says that in their marriage both sexes have overcome pride (*Ep.* 31.6).

4. A fundamental work on monasticism in Lérins is Salvatore Pricoco, *L'isola dei santi: Il cenobio di Lerino e le origini del monachesimo gallico* (Rome: Edizioni dell'Ateneo & Bizzarri, 1978). For more information on these couples, see Christina Simonelli, "Introduzione," in *Il Commonitorio*, by Vincenzo di Lérins (Milan: Paoline, 2008), 24–29. This work contains a more extensive bibliography. Salvian, known as the presbyter of the church of Marseilles, also resided at the same time in Lérins with his wife, Palladia, and daughter Auspiciola, at least for a short time. See Salvian of Marseilles, *Ep.* 4: "Salvian, Palladia and Auspiciola to the parents Hippasus and Quieta" (PL 53:160).

5. Trans. Walsh, *Letters of St. Paulinus*, 2:293. In the end of the letter, Paulinus wishes that their friendship would continue, precisely because it has emerged from the depths of Christ's charity. He adds: "Therefore between our hearts there must inevitably abide that perennial harmony which was joined at Christ's instigation, for what force or forgetfulness can separate what God has joined together?" (*Ep.* 51.3; trans.

May the Lord bless you out of Sion with the blessing *by which the man is blessed that feareth the Lord.* May he bless you who are man and wife forever, and not only you who are parents but also the holy God-sent offspring of your most eminent sanctity. (Paulinus, *Ep.* 51.4)[6]

In this context, the double dedication of the epithalamium poem is not at all isolated. As mentioned above, as many as eleven letters are signed by both Paulinus and Therasia, and her name also appears in other poems.[7] Among these, particularly worth mentioning are *Letter* 24, a true guide of spiritual life,[8] and poem 31, dedicated to a couple who, like Paulinus and Therasia, had lost a child named Celsius. The 632 verses in elegiac distich of this poem represent a new Christian interpretation of the classic *consolatio* in light of the resurrection.

It is significant that Therasia's name appears in this context, and the memory of their infant son is also mentioned (v. 601). *Letter* 13 must also be mentioned as part of this brief overview. It is a *consolatio* offered to Pammachius on the death of his wife, Paulina.[9] The letter is signed by Paulinus alone, but the delicate and affectionate way in which he writes about the spouses is, once again, also characteristic of his relationship with Therasia:

Walsh, *Letters of St. Paulinus*, 2:295). Even if he is talking about the friendship between the couple and Paulinus, we can safely think that the use of biblical terms related to matrimony in connection with the friendship was something inspired by the their mutual experiences of marriage. In addition, *Letters* 42, 45, 80, and 149 are addressed to Eucherius and Galla.

6. Trans. Walsh, *Letters of St. Paulinus*, 2:295. Important in this context are also the words that Paulinus asks to be engraved in the basilica of Primuliacum, built by his friend Suplicius Severus: "In your kindness receive these prayers of sinners who ask you to be mindful of Paulinus and Therasia. Love these persons entrusted to you by the mediation of Severus.... Let the love of a friend held in common kindle in both of us an eternal covenant.... You cannot separate men who are united.... So, embrace Severus and Paulinus together as brothers indivisible. Love us and join with us in this union" (Paulinus, *Ep.* 32.6; trans. Walsh, *Letters of St. Paulinus*, 2:140–41).

7. In addition to *Carm.* 25.240, see 10.190 (referred to as Lucretia); 21.281; 31.626.

8. See further Christina Simonelli, "Il tesoro e la perla: Unificazione e comunione nell'ep.24 di Paolino e Terasia," in *Frammentazione dell'esperienza e ricerca di unità*, ed. Cristina Simonelli, Francesco Botturi, and Patrizio Rota Scalabrini (Milan: Glossa, 2010), 31–51.

9. Both also appear frequently in Jerome's letters: Paulina is one of the daughters of Paula, the spiritual companion of Jerome, who came with him to Bethlehem.

> Therefore, I embrace you with this love, and reverence you as Christ's member. I love you as a fellow member.... In reflecting on your emotions I feel my own heart torn by your sighs, and the limbs which truly belong to both of us pierced by the pain of your wound.... For I have heard not only of my holy sister being called to God, but also of your devoted piety in Christ. For the father of the household of your wise, holy, and true love for your wife, since unlike most men you accompanied her to burial with her tribute of tears, and unlike those deprived of Christian hope, without empty pomp and honour.... For the father of faith [Abraham] mourned his wife Sara, the mother of our calling, not because he had any doubt that she would be reunited with him, but because he missed her when she went before him [*praegressae desiderio*].... Jacob, too, honoured the much beloved and eagerly awaited (*dilectam illam et espectatam*) Rachel.... So the duty of burial is good, and so are the tears of love with which father Abraham buried the mother of our pledge.... As she always was, so shall she be *a crown for her husband for ever*, and *her lamp shall not be put out*.... Hence she is more worthy of tears than of lamentation; it is better that you should long for her continually than grieve for her. (*Ep.* 13.3–5)[10]

Paulinus is also the addressee of a joint letter by Augustine and Alypius. The tone of the letter is not exactly friendly, since it is written to dissuade him from every remotest form of support to the Pelagian position (see Augustine, *Ep.* 186).[11] An extensive network of people was involved in these debates over mercy, freedom, and human nature, conducted at different levels of confrontation. Among them is also Julian of Eclanum, son of the bishop Memor and the husband of Titia, to whom the wedding poem that concerns us here is dedicated. In the period after the intervention of Pope Zosimus and his his *Epistola tractoria* (circular letter) in 418, Julian is often named as the main opponent of Augustine.

In his argumentation, Julian also refers to the topic of marriage. While this topic may not be a central element of the debate, it is nevertheless important for the effective history of the entire debate on mercy. The bishop of Eclanum wants to praise God as the maker of the good in creation and, therefore, also wants to praise marriage.[12] Questions pertaining

---

10. Trans. Walsh, *Letters of St. Paulinus*, 1:119–22.

11. The movement bears the name of one of its early promoters, the British monk Pelagius. The debate was over the question of the extent to which free will and thus the possibility of doing good are part of the human nature, and to which extent they are a gift of God, in other words, a result of mercy.

12. Augustine's version of the entire debate can be found in his *C. du. ep. Pelag.*

to sexuality and marriage were highly controversial in those years, with Jovinian as the central figure.[13] Jovinian was a monk who in the 390s suggested that the effects of baptism would extend to all realms of life. Jerome attacked him fiercely, and the synods of Rome and Milan censored him (Siricius, *Optarem*).[14] The remains of his manifesto, which was written in the name of a larger Italian party to oppose the encratite propaganda and exaggerated forms of asceticism, implies that the debate was more extensive and more widely spread than generally assumed.

The picture that emerges when one reads the full documentation of these events shows that, side-by-side with the more well-known men, there were also women involved in the lively debates over marriage. From this perspective, the epithalamium that Paulinus and Therasia gave as a wedding gift to Julian and Titia reveals more than just the aesthetic principles of its poetic form.

2. Poem 25: Classic Tradition and Christian Marriage

The poem in elegiac distich concludes with three verses in pentameter and is listed as poem 25 in Wilhelm von Hartel's critical edition. It has been an object of several studies.[15] In some manuscripts, there is an accompanying

---

4.2.2, where Augustine quotes a letter Julian and other bishops sent to Rufus of Thessalonica. Fragments of the text addressed to Rufus are collected in the Latin series of Corpus Christianorum (CCSL 88:336–40).

13. David Hunter, "Resistance to the Virginal Ideal in Late Fourth Century Rome: The Case of Jovinian," *TS* 48 (1987): 45–64; Yves-Marie Duval, *L'affaire Jovinien: D'une crise de la société romaine à une crise de la pensée chrétienne à la fin du IVe et au début du V e siècle*, SEAug 83 (Rome: Institum Patristicum Augustinianum, 2003).

14. CSEL 8.3:297–99; PL 16:1121–23, preserved as *Ep.* 42 in Ambrose's letter collection (*Recognovimus*). ET available in Mary Melchior Beyenka, trans., *Saint Ambrose Letters 1–91*, FC 26 (Washington, DC: Catholic University of America Press, 1954), 225–30.

15. The critical edition of Wilhelm von Hartel has been reedited by Margit Kaptner, for the same series. See von Hartel, *Paulini Nolani Opera 2: Carmina*, CSEL 30 (Vienna: Tempsky, 1894); Kaptner, *Paulini Nolani Opera 2: Carmina*, CSEL 30 (Vienna: Verlag der Österreichischen Akademie der Wissenschaften, 1999). An English translation has been produced by Patrick G. Walsh, *The Poems of St. Paulinus of Nola*, ACW 40 (New York: Newman, 1975). M. Teresa Piscitelli Carpino has discussed the poem in many of her works, of which I only mention the most recent one. See Piscitelli Carpino, "L'amore coniugale nella poesia Cristiana: L'epitalamio di Paolino di Nola," in *Carminis incentor Christus*, ed. Antonio Vincenzo Nazzaro and Rosario Scognamiglio (Bari: Ecumenica Editrice, 2012), 51–85. Among many other studies,

comment to the poem that is not written by the author.[16] It defines the poem an epithalamium composed by Paulinus to celebrate the marriage of Julian and Titia. This fact is generally accepted in research even though the poem does not include their names but the names of their fathers: Bishop Memor, the father of Julian, and Bishop Aemilius of Benevento, who was either the biological or the spiritual father of Titia.

The poem belongs to the tradition of wedding poetry, which was still widespread in late Christian antiquity. The most famous names of the fourth and fifth centuries are Claudian, who wrote on the wedding of Emperor Honorius to Maria, daughter of Serena and Stilicho; and after him, Sidonius Apollinaris and Venantius Fortunatus. The evaluation of the aesthetic quality of this poetry is not very flattering. This, however, is not the commentary I am to follow here, as it does not belong to my expertise. Moreover, I find the theological and biblical contents so fascinating that it may have an impact on how I enjoy the lyrical form.

The structure of the poem follows the common form of the genre, exemplified by Sappho and codified by Menander,[17] which consists of several elements: A preface encouraging harmony and mentioning pronubial gods and goddesses is followed by a praise of the wedding and a eulogy of the bride and groom. Then comes the actual invitation to marriage, with a prayer of fertility. In certain cases, this leads to *fescennini*, erotic and quite explicit songs about the delights of intimacy about to happen. In the case of the above-mentioned imperial wedding, Claudian divides the poem into a *preafatio* (ch. 9), the epithalamium proper (ch. 10), and four *fescennini* (chs. 11–14). They all refer to the same event but were probably intended for various modes of public proclamation.[18]

---

it must suffice to mention Anna Sbrancia, "L'epitalamio di S. Paolino di Nola (carme 25)," *AFLF* 11 (1978): 83–129; Franca Ela Consolino, "Cristianizzare l'epitalamio: Il carme 25 di Paolino di Nola," *Cassiodorus* 3 (1997): 199–213.

16. "The beginning of the epithalamium by S. Paulinus to Julian, the son of the bishop Memor, and his wife Titia, a woman of noble origins" (see von Hartel, *Paulini Nolani Opera 2*, 238).

17. See the study of Stefania Filosini, *Sidonio Apollinare: L'epitalamio di Ruricio e Iberia*, STT 12 (Turnhout: Brepols, 2014). She traces the genre of the epithalamium to the poetess of Lesbos.

18. Marco Fernandelli, "Cultura e significati della praefatio all'Epitamio per le nozze di Onorio e Maria di Claudiano," in *Il calamo della memoria V: Riuso di testi e mestiere letterario nella tarda antichità*, ed. Lucio Cristante and Tommaso Mazzoli (Trieste: Edizioni Università di Trieste, 2013), 75–125.

All these elements are also found in the epithalamium of Paulinus. His aim, however, is to change the pagan image into a Christian counterpart. This is obvious not only in the dialectic overturning of the themes of the classic form, with the following sequential scansion, but also in the criticism of the poetic forms, made by the above-mentioned contemporary Christian authors. In the ecclesiastical context of Nola, such forms that included, even if only for aesthetic reasons, nymphs and goddesses, must have appeared too close to the pagan model. This careful and even excessive practice of dialectical reversal is also manifested in the paradoxical calls for continence. Certainly, they are emphatically there, but it seems to me that they should be read, at least partially, against this desire to overturn the old meaning and find a new one.

If we then briefly follow the entire sequence, we note that the invitation to unity (*concordes animae*) is expanded to the affirmation that conjugal peace is the peace of the yoke (*iugum*) of Christ. Juno, Cupid, and Venus are absent from the wedding, whereas Christ is present at the ceremony, as he was in the wedding at Cana in Galilee (vv. 151–153; cf. John 2:1–11). The praise of the wedding reflects the relevant passages from the book of Genesis, which are understood as the origin of marriage: "God with his own lips consecrated the course of this alliance and with His own hand established the pairing of human persons" (*Carm.* 25.15–17).[19] The praise of the couple exalts their inner beauty, decorated by their virtues, which also constitute the dowry of the bride and thus replace the riches that were listed in the public reading of the wedding *tabulae* including the spouses' property. The festive procession that accompanies the bride to her new home is replaced by a quiet passage ("no mob dancing on decorated streets"; *Carm.* 25.31);[20] the *dexterarum coniunctio*, which was also performed at the marriage of Honorius and Maria by the *paterfamilias* (Stilicho), is here carried out by one of the two fathers, who in this case is also the bishop. Then follows a benedictory prayer and an *allocution*. Usually this would be an invitation to consummate the marriage and to have children, but in this case, as already mentioned, what follows is the obstinate and paradoxical overturning of the theme, with no erotic overtones, leading to the contradictory request not to consummate the marriage or, at any rate, to have chaste children. The last verses come with a change in the meter, which indicates a break

---

19. Trans. Walsh, *Poems of St. Paulinus*, 245.
20. Trans. Walsh, *Poems of St. Paulinus*, 246.

from the preceding verses. They contain a dedication formula that often is already a part of the *praefatio*, also with a metric change.[21] Here it appears in a play on words involving the name of the *paterfamilias* Memor and the request to remember the donors, Paulinus and Therasia. This double dedication is also a part of the dialectic renewal: in other epithalamia, no women are mentioned, only the poet or the male donor.

The reason to study this poem in the context of the history of Christian marriage has to do with its mention of certain ritual elements that belong to the oldest references among the relatively rare examples.[22] Scholars are in agreement in their interpretation of the final sequence: the bishop Memor, the father of the bridegroom, takes the couple to the altar and prays, while Aemilius, the father of the bride, spreads a veil over their heads and in turn speaks a blessing.[23] The reference to the *velatio* performed over the bridal couple testifies to its closeness to the Jewish ritual, perhaps not directly but transmitted through otherwise unknown ritual forms. In traditional Roman weddings, the orange veil, the *flammeum* with its apotropaic and augural meaning, only covered the bride. In talmudic Judaism, on the other hand, the actual wedding ceremony is the second part after the betrothal. It is called *nesuin* or *chuppah*, after the word for the canopy under which the bride is brought. Sometimes it is symbolized by a cloth stretched over the heads of the couple. This is a highly festive occasion with seven blessings.[24]

---

21. "Typically, the Claudian *praefatio* is the place for the expression of the poetic self" (Fernandelli, "Cultura e significati," 83).

22. Other early examples include Ambrose, *Ep.* 19 (to Vigilius) and Siricius, *Letter to Himerius* (both from the fourth century); the Roman euchology from the fifth century, contained in the *Sacramentarium Veronense* (31.1105–1110; Leo C. Mohlberg, *Rerum ecclesiasticarum documenta*, Fontes 1 (Rome: Herder, 1960), 239–40.

23. "Ipse pater vos benedicat episcopus … duc Memor alme, commendaque santificante manu … ille [Aemilius] iungans capita amborum sub pace iugali velat eos dextra quos prece santificat" (vv. 199–202; von Hartel, *Paulini Nolani Opera 2*, 244–45.)

24. This is the sixth one: "Blessed are You, Lord our God, King of the universe, Who has created joy and gladness, groom and bride, delight, exultation, happiness, jubilation, love and brotherhood, and peace and friendship. Soon, Lord our God, may there be heard in the cities of Judea and in the streets of Jerusalem the sound of joy and the sound of gladness, the sound of the groom and the sound of the bride, the joyous sound of grooms from their wedding canopy and of young people from their feast of song." The text of the blessing is found in the Babylonian Talmud (b. Ketub. 7b); the English translation is taken from Adin Even-Israel Steinsaltz, trans., "Ketubot 7b," William Davidson Talmud, https://tinyurl.com/SBL6010c.

However, none of the prayer or blessing formulas spoken at the wedding of Julian and Titia has survived, and any attempt to fill the gap would be pure speculation, even if it is legitimate to ask whether the many biblical passages quoted in the preceding sections could not have played a role in the rite. The biblical dossier thus built deserves to be taken into consideration, also as a part of the ritual sequence, because it contains passages that are not typical in Paulinus's literary work. Therefore, it is possible that they were used specifically in this context of celebration.

3. Biblical Themes of the Poem

We will now look specifically at the biblical evidence that runs through the various sections of the epithalamium. Taking into account its original character, it is justified, at this point, to return to the dedication with Therasia's name. It seems plausible, to say the least, that this particular biblical horizon was rooted in the couple's joint thinking.

In the passage that speaks about the origins of marriage, the point of reference is the second chapter of Genesis. It places particular emphasis on Adam's words when he sees his equal counterpart, which is not frequently found in ancient texts. Adam sees Eve as his twin, another self that is taken from his side, and thus becomes the "prophet of his own situation":

> God with His own lips consecrated the course of this alliance, and with His own hand established the pairing of human persons. He made two abide in one flesh so that he might confer a love more indivisible. While Adam slept, he was deprived of the rib which was removed from him, and then he obtained a partner formed of his own bone.... Once he beheld this other self sprung from himself in the flesh they shared, he then became the prophet of his own situation, speaking in tongue renewed. "This flesh," he said, "is the flesh of my flesh. I recognise the bone of my bones. She is the rib from my side." (*Carm.* 25.15–27)[25]

In any case, there is no trace of a recognizable reference to Eve's guilt;[26] rather, in another section of the poem we see that "Eve's subservience came to an

---

25. Trans. Walsh, *Poems of St. Paulinus*, 2:45–46.
26. Only in *Carm.* 5.31 it is said: "Let it be enough that the snake destroyed Eve of old, and deceived Adam, too" (trans. Walsh, *Poems of St. Paulinus*, 2:36). According to textual critics, however, the author here is Ausonius, the teacher of Paulinus.

end, and Sara became the free equal of her holy husband. When Jesus' friends were married with such a compact as this he attended as a groomsman, and changed water into wine like nectar." Like Mary, like the church, Titia "will be a companion under the same yoke" (*con-iuge*), which is that of Christ; thus she will be "the Lord's bride and His sister … not subject." We may observe that in this context, there is not yet the idea of a marriage that is *continent* but rather a relationship that is *chaste*, not necessarily in the monastic sense of renouncing sexual intercourse but perhaps in a moral sense of a respectful relationship. Instead of a monastic context, the reference to the church, which, like Mary, is a virgin mother, can relate to baptism. In fact, the theme appears earlier and more often in baptismal literature. Be it as it may, the end of slavery is connected to the release from what is called Adam's heritage, which is stripped off in baptism. This is the background of the entire passage.

This dimension is also important and strongly emphasized in *Letter 24*, which is one of the letters with a double signature:

> This is why Paul said: *So run that you may all obtain*. It is just the opposite in an earthly contest. A wrestling match cannot end without differing outcomes for the contestants; the glory of the one is the shame of the other. But since we, being many, are one in Christ, we all run as one and all share a joint journey to the one good. So we are told: *So run that you may all obtain*. As Paul also says, there cannot be a cleavage in the body whose head is Christ. He is the summit common to all His members, the single structure of which goes with Him. Since the members cannot be at odds with each other, let us run together that we may all obtain, without hostile rivalry and with equal success. Just as in the struggle of the race we are the toil of Christ [*labor Christi*], so when we reach the goal we can be His triumph, and He can bless us *in the crown of the year of His goodness*. (*Ep.* 24.15)[27]

A similar sequence appears in the epithalamium. It includes a meditation on marriage in a baptismal context, referring to Gal 3:28. The only element that is present from this Pauline passage is the opposing pair of man and woman. The potential male superiority is radically downsized and relativized through the common reference to Christ as the head. "This is why the teacher Paul says that in Christ there is no male or female, but one body and one faith, for all of us who acknowledge Christ as Head of our body are one body" (*Carm.* 25.180–183).[28] The idea is that, once reborn

---

27. Trans. Walsh, *Letters of St. Paulinus*, 2:65.
28. Trans. Walsh, *Poems of St. Paulinus*, 2:51.

in baptism, both genders are part of Christ, the perfect *human*, and he, the head of all and all in one, will lead his members to the Father's kingdom. This is a perfect baptismal sequence: to be reborn from God in the church,[29] based on Gal 3:28 and 1 Cor 12:13, 27 (the baptism into one body), and a long quotation of Eph 4:1–16, which gives the basic structure to the sequence. The idea of reaching the fullness of Christ, the distinction between body and head, and the image of getting rid of the old to take on the new all come from this passage. Finally, the sequence ends with a reference to 1 Cor 15:28 and the handing over of the kingdom to the Father.

The theme of being members of one single body,[30] an ecclesiastic and eucharistic topic par excellence, also enters in a dialectical relationship to bridal metaphors from passages such as Eph 5:22–33. The bridal metaphor, which does not appear anywhere else in the Paulinus/Therasia corpus, is both cited and overturned here. While the epithalamium cannot be held responsible for the fatal asymmetry of associating the masculine with the divine, typical of our current reading, it is interesting to note that this asymmetric polarity is put into perspective. Before describing the arrival of the two fathers and the ritual elements discussed above, the epithalamium expresses an appeal, formulated as follows: "As brother and sister hasten together to meet Christ the Bridegroom, so that you may be one flesh in the eternal body. You must be enmeshed with that love by which the Church holds fast to Christ, and by which Christ in turn hugs her close" (*Carm.* 25.195–199).[31]

4. The Game Is Still On

A few words should suffice to complete this exploration, for I hope that what is postulated in the title and affirmed in the introduction has shed

---

29. "The children of this mother comprise equally old and infants; this offspring has no age or sex" (*Carm.* 25.175–76; trans. Walsh, *Poems of St. Paulinus*, 2:51). Numerous parallels can be found in contemporary baptismal homilies.

30. "Remember that there are *diversities of graces* and different measures of gifts. God, who is the sole Steward, arranges these in the limbs of His body, distinguishing the different members by the offices He decides upon. But out of the different limbs he makes one body. He is enriched by the grace of His sacred body if manifold virtues are numbered in the single structure. So *the queen may stand on His right hand with gilded fringes, clother around with variety*" (*Ep.* 24.2; trans. Walsh, *Letters of St. Paulinus*, 2:52). In *Ep.* 28.2, the reference has eucharistic overtones.

31. Trans. Walsh, *Poems of St. Paulinus*, 2:51.

light on the issue. It has been my aim to contribute to the aim of this volume and the whole series of which it is a part. Adopting a different perspective is often enough to make the presence of women—and not just female metaphors—visible, women who have been buried in the stories for a long time. It also shows how this inclusive authorship is characterized by its creative use of biblical passages.

The game is still on, not only because the names of women remain stubbornly in the margins, if anything, in the historiographical and exegetic reconstructions, but also because male and female metaphors—in discourses on God or marriage—are used abundantly but with little gender awareness. Mapping this terrain, as I have aimed to do, is not just a scholarly exercise but has to do with the reality we live in. Thus, women—and men who, like Paulinus, do not feel threatened in their masculinity—we still have an exciting game to play.

Early Christian Female Theologians in Profile: Maximilla's and Quintilla's Visions for the Church

Heidrun Mader

1. Female Theologians in the Early Christianity of Asia Minor

Self-assured female voices resound in Christian circles in Phrygia in the second century after Christ. Prominent among them, a prophetess with the name Maximilla speaks and connects herself with the highest authorities. She is said to have called herself a mediator of the Kyrios himself (Epiphanius, *Pan.* 48.13.1). Maximilla's prophecy fell on receptive ears; she gathered numerous followers around her, and her name was accounted as great in Montanist Christian circles for centuries after her life.[1] Maximilla was *one* voice in a choir of female theologians in early Christianity. Along with her, the polemically named so-called prophetess Jezebel, the four daughters of Philip, and Ammia of Philadelphia are mentioned in early Christian literature in Asia Minor alone.[2] At Maximilla's side stands the prophetess Priscilla, as well as a later prophetess from the same movement by the name of Quintilla (Epiphanius, *Pan.* 48–49; Eusebius, *Hist. eccl.* 5.16–18). If one includes epigraphic evidence, then the choir of female

---

1. Even her bones were kept as relics. They were burned as late as 550 CE in a destructive blow against the Montanists. See William Tabbernee, *Fake Prophecy and Polluted Sacraments: Ecclesiastical and Imperial Reaction to Montanism*, VCSup 84 (Leiden: Brill, 2007), 399.

2. The seer John polemicizes against the prophetess Jezebel and thereby reveals her influence in the congregation at Thyatira (Rev 2:20–23). The four prophetic daughters of Philip, active in Caesarea, are mentioned in Acts 21:9. Eusebius also reports about the extent of their fame and tells that later they were active in Hierapolis (*Hist. eccl.* 3.31.4–5; 37.1).

theologians expands by further voices.³ That feminine-prophetic proclamation resounded particularly powerfully in Asia Minor corresponds to the religious-cultural background of this region, in which the female element was strongly present in the local cultures from time immemorial and was frequently accompanied by prophetic forms.⁴

This essay presents Maximilla, and the somewhat later active prophetess Quintilla, as examples of prominent and popular female theologians of the early Christian second century CE. Her theology and how she expresses herself in the sayings (logia) attributed to her, as well as also her female sex, will be distinguished as factors in her prophetic self-understanding. Thereby, it is methodologically interesting to be able to consider these female theologians' *own* words and not to have to (re)construct the profile of these women from masculine accounts *about* them.

Maximilla and Quintilla, as well as all the other women listed above, are examples of the fact that the proscriptive texts of the New Testament and the ancient church are not representative of ecclesiastical practice, as Ute E. Eisen has shown with her helpful, corrective hermeneutical and methodological premises.⁵ Perhaps surprisingly, Maximilla is not commanded to keep silence in the early texts written against her because she is a woman.⁶ Although Maximilla's opponents gladly refer to Paul (e.g., Epiphanius, *Pan.* 48.1.4; 2.8; 3.1; 8.7–9; 9.10; 10.4; 11.7, 10; 12.5, 12; and the Anonymous in *Hist. eccl.* 5.17.4), they do not cite 1 Cor 14:34 or 1 Tim

---

3. See here the survey by Ute E. Eisen, "Frauen in leitenden Positionen im Neuen Testament und in der frühen Kirche," *BK* 65 (2010): 210–13; and in detail Eisen, *Women Officeholders in Early Christianity: Epigraphical and Literary Studies*, trans. Linda M. Maloney (Collegeville, MN: Liturgical Press, 2000). The prophetess Nanas, from Phrygia, emerged in a prominent role. The veneration paid to her is evidenced in inscriptions.

4. See Vera Hirschmann, *Horrenda Secta: Untersuchungen zum frühchristlichen Montanismus und seinen Verbindungen zur paganen Religion Phrygiens* (Stuttgart: Steiner, 2005), esp. 109–17.

5. Eisen, "Frauen in leitende Positionen," 208. Reference to the silence commands has been made too quickly and methodologically in a dubious way as to indicate a general ecclesiastical practice. Here especially 1 Cor 14:33–36 and 1 Tim 2:11–15 are to be mentioned.

6. Among the earliest texts, also originating in Asia Minor, that are directed against the prophetic trio of Montanus, Maximilla, and Priscilla, as well as against their followers in the subsequent generations, belong the sources of Epiphanius (*Pan.* 48.1.4–48.13.8), the so-called Anonymous, contained in Eusebius (*Hist. eccl.* 5.16–17), and Apollonius in Eusebius (*Hist. eccl.* 5.18).

2:11–15 against her.⁷ Rather, they react negatively to the *content* of what she says.⁸ Epiphanius's claim that there were ordained female officeholders only in heretical groups is too quickly taken as an historical fact (*Pan.* 49.2.2), as Eisen has correctly noted. Epiphanius's description, she says, ought not to be confused with reality; it is rather an expression of gender-ideological interests.⁹ In the case of Maximilla and Quintilla, we are dealing with women from such an anathematized group. However, we also need to consider that Maximilla appears as a leading prophetess *before* the prophetic movement associated with her became an anathematized marginal group, which was denounced subsequently as so-called Montanism.¹⁰ The prophetic group originated first of all within the church, and Maximilla's theology thus must be treated on an equal footing with inner-Christian attacks on it (Eusebius, *Hist. eccl.* 5.16.17).¹¹ The anathematizing process

---

7. Eusebius's Anonymous even lists other women, such as the daughters of Philip and Ammia of Philadelphia, whom he recognizes as legitimate prophetesses and among whom he does not want to class Maximilla and Priscilla (*Hist. eccl.* 5.17.3).

8. Similarly also Eisen, *Women Officeholders*, 73; Anne Jensen, *God's Self-Confident Daughters: Early Christianity and the Liberation of Women* (Louisville: John Knox, 1992), 33.

9. Eisen, "Frauen in leitende Positionen," 208. In light of further sources, she claims that the practice of appointing women to offices in anathematized groups only is highly improbable (212). In more detail see Eisen, *Women Officeholders*, 116–23; see also Tabbernee, *Fake Prophecy*, 375.

10. The Phrygian prophetesses are characterized polemically as "Montanists," and the movement itself as "Montanism" only from the fourth century. See Christoph Markschies, "Montanismus," *RGG* 5:1471, with a reference to Cyril of Jerusalem, *Catech.* 16.8.6; (Pseudo-)Didymus, *Trin.* 3.18.23, 41.

11. Christine Trevett, *Montanism: Gender, Authority and the New Prophecy* (Cambridge: Cambridge University Press, 1996), 151: "Women of earliest prophecy were not heretical." See Epiphanius, *Pan.* 48.2.1; the followers of Montanus, Maximilla, and Priscilla demand that there must be charismata *in the church*. In Eusebius, the anonymous author from Asia Minor writes in 193 CE that the movement had separated from the church only shortly before (πρόσφατος; *Hist. eccl.* 5.16.6). The anathematization of the movement, which is described in more detail in *Hist. eccl.* 5.16.10 by the Anonymous, was at first carried out by local synods and referred to limited regions. Tertullian of Carthage, even though a disciple of the prophetic movement from ca. 208/9 CE, remained in the church of Carthage. There are no indications that there ever were separate Montanist congregations there (see Tabbernee, *Fake Prophecy*, 131). For a description of the process of the anathematizing of the Montanist movement, see Trevett, *Montanism*, 214–23. See also Heidrun Mader, *Montanistische Orakel und kirchliche Opposition: Der frühe Streit zwischen den phrygischen "neuen Propheten" und*

followed only later and was not set in motion by the fact that women took over leading roles in the movement.[12] The anathematizing dealt primarily with *the ecstatic form* of the prophecy.[13]

What is clearly shown by this reaction is the fact that proclamation was exercised on an equal basis by both women and men, especially in the first two centuries of Christianity. Afterwards, the parallel position that wanted to oust women from leadership positions prevailed.[14]

Maximilla's logia are the earliest theological statements that can be attributed with certainty to a woman in Christianity.[15] This merits attention, for, in the production and transmission of early Christian tradition, androcentric dominance must be questioned methodologically. Only a few texts from the first centuries of Christianity are attributed explicitly to women. To the present, four early Christian female authors (second to fourth centuries) have been identified:[16] Perpetua's report of martyrdom,

---

dem Autor der vorepiphaninschen Quelle als biblische Wirkungsgeschichte des 2. Jh. n. Chr. (Göttingen: Vandenhoeck & Ruprecht, 2012), 161–62.

12. Similarly, Eisen, *Women Officeholders*, 72. Beyond Asia Minor, however, the polemic against women began earlier. Origen, at the beginning of the third century CE, cites the well-known Pauline passage that women ought to keep silence in the ἐκκλησία against the female prophets (*Cant. Pauli Cor.* 14.36); see Hirschmann, *Horrenda Secta*, 105–6.

13. See Antti Marjanen, "Female Prophets among Montanists," in *Prophets Male and Female: Gender and Prophecy in the Hebrew Bible, the Eastern Mediterranean, and the Ancient Near East*, ed. Jonathan Stökl and Corrine L. Carvalho, AIL 15 (Atlanta: Society of Biblical Literature, 2013), 141. "In the debate between Miltiades and the Montanists, the aspect of gender is not an issue."

14. See Eisen, "Frauen in leitende Positionen," 211. In regard to women in leadership positions in Montanism, this dynamic is reflected in the argumentation starting from Origen at the beginning of the third century CE and can be found once again in the fourth century CE in the Dialogue of a Montanist with an Orthodox (Dialogus Montanistae et Orthodoxi) and also in Didymus, *Trin.* 3.41.

15. Trevett mentions this almost in passing (*Montanism*, 154). Luke, of course, writing in the first century, lets Mary's voice sound with a theologically dense psalm, but these words are attributed to Luke's redaction. See, e.g., François Bovon, *Das Evangelium nach Lukas (Lk 1,1–9,50)*, EKKNT 3.1 (Neukirchen-Vluyn: Neukirchener Verlag, 1989), 82.

16. Above and beyond this, Adolf von Harnack suggested more than a century ago attributing the letter to the Hebrews to the married couple of Prisca and Aquila, more probably to Prisca. See Harnack, "Probabilia über die Adresse und den Verfasser des Hebräerbriefs," *ZNW* 1 (1900): 40–41. The four texts that can be attributed to women are accessible in Patricia Wilson-Kastner, *A Lost Tradition: Women Writers*

Proba's Bible cento, Egeria's pilgrimage account, and the extant works of the prominent Byzantine empress Eudocia. The logia of the Montanist female prophets cannot compete with these works because of their much shorter length, but they can be incorporated into this group as they allow us to hear the voices of early Christian female theologians.

The logia of the Montanist prophets must be fragments of a larger collection of written works.[17] Unfortunately, we do not know whether they were taken from a longer coherent text or whether they were chosen from a collection of sayings. This is because the works of the Phrygian prophets did not belong to churches' processes of textual transmission but were systematically eliminated by their opponents. Indeed, these texts were available to the early opponents of the female prophets. They, however, chose to quote only those sayings that they needed for their polemical purposes. In doing so, they unwittingly left us a small window open for words that can be almost unquestionably attributed to these prophets whom we know by name.

2. Maximilla, the Interpreter of God's Secrets at the Zenith of the Times

The portrait of Maximilla by her opponents is hostile. She is depicted as a wild, ecstatic woman with a barbaric name who has associated herself, together with the prophetess Priscilla, with the prophet Montanus.[18] Financially, she lives like a lord, drapes herself heavily with jewelry, and wears thick makeup. She left her husband in order to seduce decent Christian people to heresy with her religious madness.[19] According to rumor, she took her own life.[20]

This sample from the polemics directed against heretics shows that Maximilla's opponents had to make a real effort to come up with material with which to discredit this popular prophetess. Maximilla had a large, loyal following. Her theology was rich in content and exerted influence

---

of the Early Church (Lanham, MD: University Press of America, 1981). See also the discussion of the texts in the present volume.

17. The Anonymous cites Maximilla's logion in the book by Asterius Urbanus in *Hist. eccl.* 5.16.17; see Trevett, *Montanism*, 154.

18. So reports the Anonymous in Eusebius, *Hist. eccl.* 5.16.9.

19. This is the polemics by Apollonius, cited by Eusebius, *Hist. eccl.* 5.18.3–14.

20. Even the Anonymous, who reports about her suicide, grants that this may be a rumor (Eusebius, *Hist. eccl.* 5.16.13–15).

over a lengthy period of time. Shortly after her death, her supporters demanded charismata for their church, and thereby were dismissed from the conventional ecclesiastical community (Epiphanius, *Pan.* 48.1.4).[21]

Maximilla's four logia offer a unique opportunity to get a feel for the theology and the theological self-understanding of a female theologian of this early period. Beyond all polemics, Maximilla's own words reveal the following picture of her.

In her first logion transmitted by Epiphanius, Maximilla presents herself explicitly in her prophetic role:

ἀπέστειλέ με κύριος
τούτου τοῦ πόνου καὶ τῆς συνθήκης καὶ τῆς ἐπαγγελίας
αἱρετιστὴν μηνυτὴν ἑρμηνευτήν,
ἠναγκασμένον, θέλοντα καὶ μὴ θέλοντα, γνωθεῖν γνῶσιν θεοῦ.

The Lord has sent me,
as adherent, revealer, interpreter
of this suffering and of the covenant and the promise,
compelled, willingly or not, that the knowledge of God is made known.
(Epiphanius, *Pan.* 48.13.1)[22]

Maximilla conveys the secrets of God, through which God may be known. Maximilla is an interpreter, that is, she recognizes something that she can translate or make accessible. She explains the secrets of God to others. She characterizes the content of these divine secrets as a promise. The revelation of these secrets through prophecy constitutes the age of the new covenant. They lead to the end of the world, which soon will begin. Maximilla sees herself as a person who is the last prophet in a series of prophets before the end of the world: μετ' ἐμὲ προφήτης οὐκέτι ἔσται, ἀλλὰ συντέλεια ("After me there will be no other prophet, but the end"; Epiphanius, *Pan.* 48.2.4). The end will dawn after her death. With the end of the world, all the secrets of God, which previously could be revealed only through the prophecy of the new covenant, will be fulfilled. Thus, there needs to be no more prophecy after Maximilla. Until then, though, Maximilla sees the present time as a period marked by suffering. She does not protest against the experience of suffering but rather devotes herself as its disciple and

---

21. Maximilla died in 179 CE. Her name remained on everyone's lips together with Montanus and Priscilla as long as the successful movement was active.

22. The translations of the logia are my own.

identifies herself with it. In what this suffering consists must remain open. It is conceivable that it refers to social distress.[23] It may also be caused by the inner-Christian oppression of her theological opponents, who want to discredit her as a false prophet. By identifying herself with suffering, Maximilla makes clear that she does not let herself be dissuaded through any resistance from fulfilling her role as a proclaimer of the new covenant. Maximilla experiences this role so intensely that she speaks of being compelled to fulfill it. Her own will is then irrelevant to her.

No resistance keeps her from being devoted to the new covenant, not even inner-Christian persecution. Her opponents judge her to be a false prophet, but Maximilla replies:

διώκομαι ὡς λύκος ἐκ προβάτων,
οὐκ εἰμὶ λύκος, ῥῆμά εἰμι καὶ πνεῦμα καὶ δύναμις.

I am pursued like a wolf, driven away from sheep.
I am not a wolf; I am word and spirit and power. (Eusebius, *Hist. eccl.* 5.16.17)

Her inner-Christian opponents have used Matt 7:15 to characterize her as a wolf pursuing sheep.[24] Maximilla takes up their words and turns the tables on them; even though she is not a wolf, she is forced to leave her sheep, driven away like a wolf. Thereby, she makes allusion to shepherds, ecclesiastical authorities, who want to hinder her in her work as a prophet.[25] Maximilla forcefully opposes the Matthean image with the Pauline words according to which she is not a wolf but rather spirit, power, and the Word (see 1 Cor 2:4). In so doing, she ascribes to herself the highest prophetic attributes; indeed, she identifies herself with them using a formula

---

23. An inscription from Tymion, the neighboring city to Pepouza, goes with this. According to it, the city complained about *exactiones*, i.e., illegal tributes (l. 12). See on this Peter Lampe and William Tabbernee, *Pepouza and Tymion: The Discovery and Archeological Exploration of a Lost Ancient City and an Imperial Estate* (Berlin: de Gruyter, 2008), 61.

24. The image of the predatory wolf stands in early Christian texts for false teachers from within, who have slipped into congregations. It is widespread; see, e.g., Acts 20:29; Did. 16.3; Ign. *Phld.* 2.2; 2 Clem. 5.2–4; Justin, *1 Apol.* 16.13; *Dial.* 35.3; 81.2; Eusebius, *Hist. eccl.* 5.13.4 (Rhodo against Marcion); Epiphanius, *Pan.* 48.3.2.

25. In the context of the logion, it is reported that the neighboring bishops Zoticus of Comana and Julianus of Apamea attempted an exorcism on Maximilla.

of self-presentation. In my detailed exegesis of Maximilla's logia, I have shown that she subtly takes up Pauline language in many occasions.[26] She identifies herself with the apostle in his role as a preacher who, like herself, is persecuted by inner-Christian opponents (Gal 5:11). Further, she sees herself as taking the same course as he in proclaiming the Word of God in the face of all resistance, even against her own will (see Epiphanius, *Pan.* 48.13.1, quoted above, and 1 Cor 9:16–17). In Maximilla's time, the title "apostle" was not frequently used anymore; it belonged to past generations.[27] The title "prophet," with which she designates herself, transports the apostolic title into the period of the coming end of the world.

Maximilla strongly emphasizes her prophetic role in all the logia. Only the wakening call logion points away from herself, but in its relational formulation takes it for granted that she is still present: ἐμοῦ μὴ ἀκούσητε, ἀλλὰ Χριστοῦ ἀκούσατε ("Do not hear me, but rather hear Christ!"; Epiphanius, *Pan.* 48.12.4). This logion introduces the christological aspect of Maximilla's theology, not yet addressed. Maximilla understands Christ as the speaker of the proclamation of the secrets of God. When she speaks as the spirit of God, she transmits the words of Christ. In addition, Christ as the Kyrios is the one who has sent her out as an emissary.

In none of the extant logia does Maximilla emphasize her gender. On the contrary, it is striking that she employs masculine grammatical forms. For example, in the logion in *Pan.* 48.2.4, she says that there will be no more προφήτης after her. The corresponding feminine form would be προφῆτις. This latter usage also appears in some manuscripts, but, in accord with the *lectio difficilior*, the masculine form must be the original one. This finding in regard to the masculine form alone would not yet be

---

26. See Mader, *Montanistische Orakel*, 186–89.

27. In Maximilla's time, there was no longer any firm evidence for the apostolic office. The apostolic title was reserved for the apostles of the past, prominent among them the Twelve and Paul. See Jürgen Roloff, "Apostel/Apostolat/Apostolozität," *TRE* 3 (1978): 440–41; Georg Günther Blum, "Apostel/Apostolat/Apostolizität II," *TRE* 3 (1978): 445–46; David Aune, *Prophecy in Early Christianity and the Ancient Mediterranean World* (Grand Rapids: Eerdmans, 1983), 203, 209. Along with the Twelve, other individual apostles are named, among them the apostle Junia (Rom 16:7) and Mary Magdalene. See, for the patristic witnesses of the latter, Andrea Taschl-Erber, "'Eva wird Apostel!': Rezeptionslinien des Osterapostolats Marias von Magdala in der lateinischen Patristik," in *Geschlechterverhältnisse und Macht: Lebensformen in der Zeit des frühen Christentums*, ed. Irmtraud Fischer and Christoph Heil, EUZ 21 (Münster: LIT, 2010), 164–75.

all that significant since, with this term, Maximilla refers to a prophetic collective, in which masculine candidates would definitely be possible. Yet, in the logion in *Pan.* 48.13.1, Maximilla does not choose feminine forms when she describes her roles as αἱρετιστής, μηνυτής, and ἑρμηνευτής. According to usual Koine Greek usage, she would have had the possibility of feminizing these substantive nouns with a feminine article. Still more striking are the following participles ἠναγκασμένον and θέλοντα, which are masculine in gender. When Maximilla describes herself with masculine attributes, she ascribes strength to herself. This is shown by Silke Petersen's observations of ancient texts, which ("at least mythologically")[28] speak of gender exceeding its limits. Masculinity in them is the desirable, strong condition; femininity is the problematic and vulnerable one.[29] Petersen's citation from Origen (d. 254 CE), in which he understands feminine and masculine as social categories,[30] sums up this attitude:

> For divine Scripture does not know how to make a separation of men and women according to sex. For indeed sex is no distinction, but a person is designated either a man or woman according to the diversity of spirit. How many out of the sex of women are counted among the strong men before God, and how many of the men are reckoned among slack and sluggish women? (Origen, *Hom. Josh.* 9.9)[31]

Maximilla is not the only one to furnish herself with masculine attributes. Others, too—in this case, her inner-Christian opponents—apply the metaphor of the wolf to her (see Eusebius, *Hist. eccl.* 5.16.17, cited above). The wolf does not lend itself especially well as a metaphor proscribing femininity but rather expresses strength and a danger that needs to be taken seriously.[32] A central aspect in the self-image posed by Maximilla against

---

28. Silke Petersen, "Maria Magdalena wird männlich, oder: Antike Geschlechtertransformationen," in *Unbeschreiblich weiblich? Neue Fragestellungen zur Geschlechterdifferenz in den Religionen*, ed. Christine Gerber, Silke Petersen, and Wolfram Weiße, TFE 26 (Münster: LIT, 2011), 130.
29. Petersen, "Maria Magdalena wird männlich," 130–31.
30. Petersen, "Maria Magdalena wird männlich," 121.
31. Latin text: Annie Jaubert, *Origène, Homélies sur Josué*, SC 71 (Paris: Cerf, 1960), 266; English translation Barbara J. Bruce in Origen, *Homilies in Joshua*, FC (Washington, DC: Catholic University of America Press, 1984), 106. Petersen also discusses other ancient Jewish-Christian texts that describe gender transformation, including Gos. Thom. 114; Clement of Alexandria, *Strom.* 6.100.3; Philo, *QE* 1.18.
32. The writer of the book of Revelation does not choose the metaphor of the

the wolf (see above) is the concept of πνεῦμα, which, again according to Petersen's observations, ancient texts directly link with the masculine.[33] In this respect, Maximilla is in no way inferior to her opponents, chief among them the male bishops Zoticus of Comana and Julianus of Apamea. Indeed, Eusebius writes that these men could not subdue her spirit (*Hist. eccl.* 5.16.17).

It is difficult to find comparable statements from the mouths of ancient women who adorn themselves with masculine attributes, since very few self-designations made by females exist in ancient sources. The female prophet in the second book of the Sibylline Oracles (after 180 CE),[34] for example, proclaims woe upon herself and chooses feminine forms for describing herself. The prophet vilifies herself with decidedly feminine attributes as a "poor person" (δειλή), "fool" (δύσφρων), and "female lapdog" (κυνῶπιν), in each case in feminine gender (Sib. Or. 2.339–345).[35] In accord with Petersen's observations of gender transformations, the point at issue here is precisely her weak side.

In the Gospel of Luke, Mary describes herself in her hymn of praise not as a prophet but in her relation to God (Luke 1:48). Luke formulates the self-designation "female slave" (ἡ δούλη) in decidedly feminine form and places it in Mary's mouth (ca. 80–100 CE). Proba, who presents herself as a female seer in her biblical cento (384 CE), chooses the Latin term *vatis* in order to designate herself (Proba, *Cento* 10).[36] *Vatis* is masculine as well as also feminine, a *nomen commune*. On the pagan side, Apollo speaks through the mouth of the priestess Satornila and calls her a "female temple servant" (ζακόρος) in *nomen commune*.[37] The oracle for Didyma about the priestly

---

wolf as a polemic term to use against the woman he deems as a false prophet in the congregation at Thyatira, but rather the name Jezebel (Rev 2:20), a denunciation that has an especially feminine connotation.

33. Petersen, "Maria Magdalena wird männlich," 125. Correspondingly, she observes, the combination is female-corporeal.

34. Ursula Treu, "Christian Sibyllines," in , *Writings Relating to the Apostles, Apocalypses and Related Subjects*, vol. 2 of *New Testament Apocrypha*, ed. Wilhelm Schneemelcher and R. McLeod Wilson (Louisville: Westminster John Knox, 1992), 654.

35. Critical text edited by Johannes Geffcken, *Die Oracula Sibyllina*, GCS 8 (Leipzig: Hinrichs, 1902).

36. Text and English translation in Elizabeth A. Clark and Diane F. Hatch, trans., *The Golden Bough, the Oaken Cross: The Virgilian Cento of Faltonia Betitia Proba*, AARTTS 5 (Chico, CA: Scholars Press, 1981).

37. The oracle is handed down as an honorary inscription from Miletus. In order

office of Artemis is spoken by the "Lord himself" and by the goddess. The "goddess" (θεά) names herself by using the feminine gender.[38] Maximilla, with her decidedly masculine forms, thus remains without parallel among the few sources that contain self-designations by women in antiquity.[39]

Even though it is uncertain whether Perpetua's words can be taken as a self-testimony, I place her at Maximilla's side. Shortly before her martyrdom, in her last vision, which involves a struggle with her aggressor, a great and powerful Egyptian, Perpetua becomes a man ("facta sum masculus") and is able to conquer the Egyptian in a duel (Pass. Perpet. Felicit. 10.7).

Beyond these masculine self-designations, Maximilla's logion in *Pan.* 48.12.4 makes clear that, as a prophet, she can convey the words of the masculine Christ. There are no concrete parallels for this, either, in other early Christian texts. There is only one reference that has to do with a female prophet, given by Tertullian. He tells that she communicates with the angels and, at times, also with the Lord.[40] It is, however, not possible to infer from Tertullian's description whether the Lord also speaks through this prophetess. In pagan oracles, on the other hand, there are several parallels to the idea that a masculine god can speak through a feminine medium, as the example of Satornila, cited above, shows. Through her the masculine god Apollo speaks.

3. Quintilla Sees Christ in the Shape of a Woman

Sometime after Maximilla, the prophetess Quintilla begins to speak. Quintilla stands in the succession of the Montanist prophetic trio of Montanus, Maximilla, and Priscilla. She too is so highly respected that a group within

---

to honor the achievements of their mother, her two sons, both named Marcus Aurelius, focus on her priestly office. For this purpose, they cite Apollo's oracle. The parts of the names and the character of the letters point to a date in the decades after 212. See Christian Oesterheld, *Göttliche Botschaften und zweifelnde Menschen: Pragmatik und Orientierungsleistung der Apollon-Orakel von Klaros und Didyma in hellenistisch-römischer Zeit* (Göttingen: Vandenhoeck & Ruprecht, 2008), 325–26.

38. Oesterheld, *Göttliche Botschaften*, 487.

39. The peculiarity of the male forms can also be taken as a further proof of the authenticity of Maximilla's logia.

40. "Conuersatur cum angelis, aliquando etiam cum domino" (Tertullian, *An.* 9.4). This prophetess receives her visions during the worship service but, as is probably her habit, communicates them after the worship service. See on this Trevett, *Montanism*, 173.

the Montanist movement calls itself Quintillians after her.[41] Epiphanius reports about this group (*Pan.* 49.1.1), although he does not write further about Quintilla, nor do we hear about her in other sources. Epiphanius quotes a logion in this context but says that he is not sure whether it is to be attributed to Quintilla or to Priscilla. Epiphanius cites the logion in order to explain why the Quintillians (or Priscillians—here, too, he is not quite certain) expect the heavenly Jerusalem to be established in Pepouza and why they carry out certain rites there. Two reasons speak in favor of attributing the logion to Quintilla, which is Epiphanius's first suggestion. First, it is more probable that the logion was attributed retrospectively to the more well-known of the two personalities, that is, Priscilla, in order to lend the logion authenticity. The other way around would not have done any good.[42] Further, the early sources do not mention this logion, which would be surprising in the case that Priscilla had spoken it.[43] Quintilla must have appeared at least several decades after the founding trio, since Eusebius's Anonymous and the early source of Epiphanius report that, after the death of these three, no significant prophetic personalities for a time appeared (Eusebius, *Hist. eccl.* 5.17.4; Epiphanius, *Pan.* 48.2.1–2).

Quintilla's logion stands out from the other authentic logia of the Montanist prophets and prophetesses in that it directly brings motifs of femininity to bear upon theology, and in this case even combines motifs of femininity with Christology: Christ as a woman, Wisdom, and Jerusalem. Thus, we clearly have a different perspective on gender than that of Maximilla, with whom no decidedly feminine motifs appear.

Quintilla speaks in the following way:

ἐν ἰδέᾳ γυναικός, ἐσχηματισμένος ἐν στολῇ λαμπρᾷ
ἦλθε πρός με Χριστὸς καὶ ἐνέβαλεν ἐν ἐμοὶ τὴν σοφίαν
καὶ ἀπεκάλυψέ μοι τουτονὶ τὸν τόπον εἶναι ἅγιον
καὶ ὧδε τὴν Ἱερουσαλὴμ ἐκ τοῦ οὐρανοῦ κατιέναι.

---

41. It is also possible that this is a name Epiphanius gave to the group after their founder.

42. See Tabbernee, *Fake Prophecy*, 117–18; Douglas Powell, "Tertullianists and Cataphrygians," *VC* 29 (1975): 44.

43. See Trevett, *Montanism*, 168. Similarly, Marjanen favors Quintilla with the argument that, among the early trio, only Montanus, but not Priscilla, is associated with the descent of the heavenly Jerusalem in Pepouza ("Female Prophets among Montanists," 133).

In the form of a woman dressed in a shining robe,
Christ came to me and threw wisdom into me,
and revealed to me that this place is holy,
and that Jerusalem here/for this reason descends from heaven. (*Pan.* 49.1.3)

Christ's appearance in the form of a woman as the first motif dominates the logion and is unique in early Christian literature.[44] In order to place the motif in the ancient religious world, in early Christianity in particular, with the aid of parallels, two aspects must be emphasized more than has been done previously. First, it is important to take a look at the gender-transformed Christ. Second, the apparition of a female form should be investigated. Too often in the discussions of the logion, only the latter aspect is considered in light of parallels, while the unique and certainly also provocative aspect of Christ's gender transformation finds too little consideration or is interpreted in an overly sexual manner.[45]

A Jewish background is not an option for a divine gender change, because according to the Jewish concept, God is not humanly determined and thus has no gender.[46] In appearances, metaphors, and comparisons, masculine motifs dominate, but significant feminine motifs also come into play for metaphors and comparisons (see, e.g., Isa 42:13–14; 46:3–4; 49:14–15).[47] In the pagan mythological sphere, on the other hand, a divinity with a transformed gender is common. For example, the prominent Olympian goddess Athena at first appears to Odysseus as a young, graceful shepherd, then as a beautiful and tall woman (Homer,

---

44. Similarly, Jensen, *God's Self-Confident Daughters*, 166.
45. See Nicola Denzey, "What Did the Montanists Read?," *HTR* 94 (2001): 438–41; Trevett, *Montanism*, 169; John Poirier, "Montanist Pepuza-Jerusalem and the Dwelling Place of Wisdom," *JECS* 7 (1999): 498. Wilhelm Scheperlen sees a lover's meeting with the heavenly bridegroom. See Scheperlen, *Der Montanismus und die phrygischen Kulte: Eine religionsgeschichtliche Untersuchung* (Tübingen: Mohr, 1929), 145. Frederick C. Klawitter sees at least sexual overtones in ἐνέβαλεν. See Klawitter, "The New Prophecy in Early Christianity: The Origin, Nature, and Development of Montanism, A.D. 165–220" (PhD diss., University of Chicago, 1975), 90–91. In my opinion, the verb belongs to a prophetic-ecstatic language complex, as I show below.
46. See Gerhard Delling, "Geschlechter," *RAC* 10 (1978): 786, 790.
47. Hanne Loland deals in detail with the "gendered God-language" in her book *Silent or Salient Gender? The Interpretation of Gendered God-Language in the Hebrew Bible, Exemplified in Isaiah 42, 46 and 49* (Tübingen: Mohr Siebeck, 2008).

Od. 13.221–440).⁴⁸ In mythology, gender transformation also appears as a part of the human world. Illustrious examples for this are found above all in Ovid's *Metamorphoses*.⁴⁹ Early Christian approaches to a Christ with feminine connotations can be found in Jesus's logion in Matt 23:37, where he compares himself with a mother hen who wants to gather her children under her wings. The Secret Book of John (second century CE) has Christ present himself as a mother between the father and the son (Ap. John [BG 2] 21.19–21).⁵⁰ Eusebius's report about the martyr Blandina in (*Hist. eccl.* 5.1.41) is also interesting. She is bound to a stake presenting the form of the cross. Her fellow martyrs see the crucified Jesus in Blandina's posture, and this is a comfort to them in their final agonies.⁵¹ But Quintilla's vision of the gender-transformed Christ in the form of a woman goes further than these examples and follows more clearly the imagery world of pagan myths.

If one blocks out the gender transformation and takes a look only at the apparition in the form of a woman, one can, of course, find several

---

48. Bernhard Heininger cites this example among others in order to present Greco-Roman visionary forms. See Heininger, *Paulus als Visionär: Eine religionsgeschichtliche Studie* (Freiburg: Herder, 1996), 76.

49. For example, the hero Caeneus was born as a girl. Only after her rape by Neptune did the god of the waters fulfill her wish to be a man from that time on so that she did not have to suffer such things any more (Ovid, *Metam.* 12.170–209). Iphis also goes through a gender transformation. Born as a girl, she is disguised as a boy. Just in time before her wedding with a beautiful girl, with whom she fell passionately in love, her dearest wish to become a man and so to possess her beloved happily is fulfilled by her patron goddess, Isis (*Metam.* 9.666–797).

50. See Petersen, "Maria Magdalena wird männlich," 135–38. She sees another indication of Christ's femininity in this text in the "relationship between the various revelatory speeches of the text" (138). Judith Hartenstein places Jesus's preceding change from a child to an old man in the vision in a religion historical context. See Hartenstein, *Die zweite Lehre: Erscheinungen des Auferstandenen als Rahmenerzählungen frühchristlicher Dialoge* (Berlin: Akademie, 2000), 84–85. This change of form also represents a parallel to the motif of Quintilla's logion. Further connections between Quintilla's logion and gnostic texts are listed by Denzey, "What Did the Montanists," 441–47. Obviously, there is a common interest in the further processing of Judeo-Christian prophetic and wisdom theology, which highlights female elements in theology.

51. Bernadette J. Brooten drew my attention to these parallels in 2014. The relationship between the martyrs of Lyon and the Montanist movement is close. See the summary by Tabbernee, *Fake Prophecy*, 180–81.

parallel examples in early Jewish Christian visionary literature. The parallels frequently mentioned in secondary literature are the vision of the pregnant woman clothed with the sun in Rev 12, the apparition of the old woman in the Shepherd of Hermas (Vis. 2.4.1; 2.1.1–4), and the grieving woman in 4 Ezra 9, whose face becomes luminous.[52] In all these very different apparitions the woman represents the community of salvation. In the Jewish context, she represents Zion; in the Christian context, she is the church. This uniformity in the interpretation of the motif in spite of the diversity in the form suggests an ecclesiological interpretation of the appearance of Christ in Quintilla's logion, too.[53] Thus, if Christ appears in the form of a woman, the feminine Christ can be expected to convey an ecclesiological message. The words of Christ that promise the coming of the heavenly Jerusalem strengthen this thesis. Jerusalem is the central focus of the church, since the gospel emanates from there (see, e.g., Isa 2:3; 1 Cor 14:36; Rom 15:19; Acts 1–2).[54] Further, Jerusalem too is represented metaphorically with feminine archetypes. She is a mother (Gal 4:26), and she is a bride (Rev 21:9–10). The feminine appearance of Christ thus fits in with his/her revelatory content through the ecclesiological connection.

It is worth emphasizing that, in spite of the symbolic connection between Christ as a woman and the church as a feminine apparition, it is bold and unparalleled to describe Christ as a woman. It differs from all parallels discussed above. Whoever imagines Christ as a woman, representing the church, ought all the more to be able to imagine women, too, in authoritative ecclesiastical offices. This conforms to the content of the polemics of Epiphanius, who claims that the group of the Quintillians ordained women (*Pan.* 49.2.2).[55]

We come to the next motif: Christ throws wisdom into the prophet. The prophetic context of the Montanist movement suggests that wisdom is to be understood here in the sense of the first gift of the Spirit that Paul

---

52. A thorough presentation and interpretation is provided by Trevett, *Montanism*, 168–70, who also refers to Powell, "Tertullianists and Cataphrygians," 45–46.

53. Powell and Trevett see here a possible connection with 2 Clem. 14:2 (Powell, "Tertullianists and Cataphrygians," 46 n. 59; Trevett, *Montanism*, 169). Here, the spiritual church (πνευματικὴ ἡ ἐκκλησία) becomes manifest in the flesh of Jesus.

54. See Lars Hartman, "Ἱεροσολυμά Ἱερουσαλήμ," *EDNT* 2:438.

55. καὶ τὴν ἀδελφὴν τοῦ Μωυσέως προφῆτιδα λέγουσιν, εἰς μαρτυρίαν τῶν παρ' αὐτοῖς καθισταμένων γυναικῶν ἐν κλήρῳ. Firmilian reports about a prophetess who administers the sacraments (Cyprian, *Ep.* 75.10.).

lists (1 Cor 12:8).⁵⁶ It is interesting to note that Maximilla attributes to herself the second gift from the same Pauline series: knowledge (Epiphanius, *Pan.* 48.13.1). According to the early source Epiphanius uses in *Pan.* 48.1.4–13.8, one can read that Maximilla's followers claimed gifts of the Spirit for the church. The Pauline list of gifts in 1 Cor 12 certainly played a role here.⁵⁷ If this central concern of the Montanist movement is applied to Quintilla's logion, it shows how the spiritual gift of wisdom is personally transferred to Quintilla. She is made a leading prophet of the inspired congregation by Christ himself, who here, in addition, acts in an ecclesiological role. In this way, the claim of Maximilla's followers is supplemented through Quintilla's vision in an exemplary manner. Since Christ himself throws wisdom into Quintilla, the genuineness of wisdom as a spiritual gift is ensured and understood in christological terms.

In the prelude to 1 Cor 12, Paul had dealt critically with the Corinthians' understanding of wisdom and had refilled the concept with christological content (see, above all, 1 Cor 1–2). This also shows that σοφία is not the personified revealer but a spiritual gift, since here Christ represents a separate entity. Christ does not embody σοφία nor replace her, but rather transmits her.⁵⁸ Neither does Christ represent her in female form, as has been suggested on various occasions.⁵⁹ The verb ἐμβάλλω, which describes the act, fits into a prophetic usage that finds its model in prophetic scenes in LXX. For example, God throws (ἐπιβάλλω) the frenzy of sleep on Adam before he, according to Montanist understanding, utters the first prophecy in the following verses (Gen 2:21). The lyre logion of Montanus makes its central reference to this story (Gen 2:21–24).⁶⁰ The verbs of throwing that

---

56. ᾧ μὲν γὰρ διὰ τοῦ πνεύματος δίδοται λόγος σοφίας, ἄλλῳ δὲ λόγος γνώσεως κατὰ τὸ αὐτὸ πνεῦμα.

57. See Mader, *Montanistische Orakel*, 41–44.

58. This is, in my opinion, different from the notions of gnostic texts, which describe Wisdom as the figure of the Revealer and not as a gift that is transferred by Christ. According to Luke 7:35 and parr., Christ takes the place of the person-like figure of the Revealer and embodies the Wisdom of God. See Harald Hegermann, "σοφία," *EDNT* 3:618.

59. See Jensen, *God's Self-Confident Daughters*, 164.

60. Mader, *Montanistische Orakel*, 197. Further examples in and beyond the LXX are, e.g., the following: God throws the word (ῥῆμα) into the mouth of the prophet Balaam (Num 23:5, 16); God throws a spirit (πνεῦμα) into a human being (Isa 51:53); God throws the ecstasy of sleep (in Gen 2:21). Beyond LXX, the expression finds further parallels. In Prot. Jas. 7.3, in a beautiful scene, God throws grace (in the sense of

express the giving of the Spirit in these texts underline the suddenness of the event that is based solely on the sovereignty of the donor.⁶¹

The last motif of the logion, namely, the promise of the future descent of the heavenly Jerusalem, anticipates that the wisdom, already conferred as a gift on Quintilla and abundantly present in Pepouza, comes into its fullness when the heavenly Jerusalem, in harmony with this gift, comes down in this place.⁶²

4. Maximilla and Quintilla in Profile

Two leading female theologians of the second century have visions for their congregations in which they themselves play a central role.

Maximilla sees the church filled with prophetic charismata. The church finds itself in the last days. Maximilla herself, in her role as a prophet, reveals the secrets of God to her congregational members in this last time by speaking them with the voice of Christ. She sees her own role as closely related to Paul's role as an apostle. Whoever identifies with Paul's apostolic role is not likely to see any limits in the exercise of spiritual tasks in the congregation. Maximilla fulfills her prophetic role, as did Paul, in spite of all suffering, all resistance, and also all the attacks against her from within her own ranks. She does not highlight her femininity in the statements that are attributed to her. On the contrary, she formulates her role in masculine attributes, in order to emphasize her strength. Maximilla brings to focus the content of life in the new covenant, a life that is revealed through prophecy.

---

revelation) on the little Mary, who thereupon dances upon the stairs. Further, in T. Ab. (A) 4.8, God decides to throw a symbolic dream into Isaac's heart about the death of his dear father.

61. See Rainer Stichel, "Die Einführung Marias in den Tempel: Vorläufige Beobachtungen," in *Religionsgeschichte des Neuen Testaments: Festschrift für Klaus Berger zum 60. Geburtstag*, ed. Axel von Dobbeler, Kurt Erlemann, and Roman Heiligenthal (Tübingen: Francke, 2000), 396.

62. John Poirier suggests that Quintilla's vision draws from Sir 24, according to which Jerusalem (here represented by Pepouza) was the residence of wisdom per se ("Montanist Pepuza-Jerusalem," 499–501). The Montanist context speaks in favor of the future eschatological descent of Jerusalem (*Pan.* 48.2.4; *Hist. eccl.* 5.18.2). The presentist eschatological element fits in with Montanus's logia in *Pan.* 48.11.1 and 48.11.9, according to which God lives in, or has come to (ἦλθον), the human being.

Quintilla, on the other hand, who occupied a prophetic leadership role several decades after Maximilla, shifts feminine motifs to the foreground. Whoever can see Christ as a woman can, as a matter of course, also see women in ecclesiastical leadership roles. Quintilla also sees the church in the fullness of the last days. In Pepouza, which is filled with the prophetic gift of wisdom, she can lead the way, as a prophet filled with the Spirit, as a model for the other members of the congregation. When Quintilla describes the prophetic fullness in terms of wisdom and of the descent of the heavenly Jerusalem, both customarily envisioned as feminine, then she, differently from Maximilla, does theology in decidedly feminine language and with feminine symbols.

Quintilla was active several decades after Maximilla. Perhaps it was necessary at that point to emphasize the feminine element in the movement, since it was no longer an integrated part of the Christian world but was under attack from the outside. These two women were certainly not the only ones who exercised a spiritual role. However, they are two of the very few examples of women in leadership roles in the congregations whose own theological statements have been handed down to us.

Early Christian Women in Leadership Positions: The Testimony of Grave Inscriptions

Ute E. Eisen

The epigraphs from antiquity and from the early Middle Ages are still to a great extent an unlocked treasury for women's and gender history.[1] These historical sources are highly significant—just like the documentary papyri, ostraca, and wooden and wax tablets—because they, in contrast to literary sources, offer at first hand special insights into the daily lives of ancient people. These sources are valuable reference bases also in regard to the understanding of the New Testament, as shown by the first annotated source editions of epigraphs, documentary papyri, and ostraca in connection with the New Testament presented by Adolf Deissmann in his works *Bibelstudien* (1895) and *Licht vom Osten* (first edition 1908).[2] This meritorious approach taken by Deissmann was not continued systematically until the 1970s, by Gregory H. R. Horsley in the outstanding series *New Documents Illustrating Early Christianity*. Before the creation of these corpora, the inscriptions were not readily accessible to broader research, which is undoubtedly the reason why they were included within New Testament scholarship relatively late. However, this does not explain why *mainstream* New Testament scholarship has paid so little attention to these significant sources.[3] A commendable step in the analysis of early Christian

---

1. On the relevance of the epigraphs for women's and gender history, see below in detail in section 1.

2. Adolf Deissmann, *Licht vom Osten: Das Neue Testament und die neuentdeckten Texte der hellenistisch-römischen Welt*, 4th rev. ed. (Tübingen: Mohr, 1923); Deissmann, *Bibelstudien: Beiträge, zumeist aus den Papyri und Inschriften zur Geschichte der Sprache, des Schrifttums und der Religion des hellenistischen Judentums und des Urchristentums* (repr., Hildesheim: Olms, 1977).

3. This is less true for the documentary papyri, ostraca, and wooden and wax

epigraphs is taken by the project Inscriptiones Christianae Graece (ICG). Since 2008, it has developed a freely accessible database of early Christian epigraphs from Asia Minor and Greece from the time period between the second and the sixth century.[4]

In the present volume of the series Bible and Women, my task is to inquire about the reception of New Testament women in the inscriptions. It should be noted that explicit Bible citations occur in inscriptions only after the Constantinian turn.[5] Antonio Enrico Felle has offered a first collection of inscriptions with biblical citations. According to him, the Old Testament is cited much more frequently than the New Testament in these inscriptions.[6]

The character of these sources is also probably the reason for their neglect in New Testament research. There is a myriad of inscriptions, which are widely disseminated and of various genres, and they are found on the most diverse array of writing surfaces—for example, stone, bronze tablets, walls of houses, and broken potsherds.[7] They are often damaged and fragmentary, which complicates the reconstruction of the text. In

---

tablets, since the project Papyrologische Kommentare zum Neuen Testament has been in operation for almost a quarter-century. However, it was only in 2014 that the project Epigraphische Kommentare zum Neuen Testament was started at a conference in Vienna. See Peter Arzt-Grabner, "Die Auswertung inschriftlicher Zeugnisse für die neutestamentliche Exegese: Erfahrungen, Chancen und Herausforderungen," in *Epigraphik und Neues Testament*, ed. Thomas Corsten, Markus Öhler, and Joseph Verheyden, WUNT 365 (Tübingen: Mohr Siebeck, 2016), 27. The volume offers a first contribution to the project. A second volume with individual studies that deals with the letters to the Colossians is being prepared by Joseph Verheyden, according to information from Markus Öhler.

4. Cilliers Breytenbach et al., eds., Inscriptiones Christianae Graecae (ICG): A Digital Collection of Greek Early Christian Inscriptions from Asia Minor and Greece (Berlin: Edition Topoi, 2016), http://repository.edition-topoi.org/collection/ICG.

5. So Walter Ameling, "Neues Testament und Epigraphik aus der Perspektive der epigraphischen Forschung," in *Epigraphik und Neues Testament*, 7.

6. See the statistics compiled by Antonio Enrico Felle, *Biblia Epigraphica: La Sacra Scrittura nella Documentazione Epigrafica dell' Orbis Christianus Antiquus (III–VIII Secolo)*, ICIS 5 (Bari: Edipuglia, 2006), 412–25. The inscription concerning the deaconess Maria, with two Bible citations, treated below, is lacking in this collection.

7. See Eva Ebel, "Epigraphik (NT)," in WiBiLex (2009), https://tinyurl.com/SBL6010d. See Ute E. Eisen, *Women Officeholders in Early Christianity: Epigraphical and Literary Studies*, trans. Linda M. Maloney (Collegeville, MN: Liturgical Press, 2000), 18–20.

addition, there are further difficulties with deciphering the text, for many of them are written in *lectio continua* without separation of words or sentences, and contain abbreviations to save space. The texts are frequently short, schematic, and formulated in the vernacular. Dating is only vaguely possible, insofar as the inscriptions themselves contain no dating of their own. To make matters worse, the edited sources are often found in confusing inscription corpora or are scattered, frequently without accompanying translation, in a large number of individual publications that are difficult to survey. Thus, the analysis and assessment of these historical sources demands special skills and knowledge of languages. However, these sources are becoming more accessible, of which the database Inscriptiones Christianae Graece is only one example. Also, one of the most important instruments for analyzing epigraphic sources—the *Guide de l'épigraphiste* in its most current edition—is already available in open access.[8]

In the following, I will first deal with the relevance of the inscriptions for women's and gender history, then analyze two selected inscriptions for deaconesses, through which I treat the question of the reception of the women in the New Testament. A summarizing résumé follows in conclusion.

1. The Relevance of Inscriptions for Women's and Gender History

The investigation of epigraphical sources has shown how insightful inscriptions are for understanding daily life in antiquity and, in this connection, for the reconstruction of women's and gender history. In contrast to literary sources that in many cases reflect androcentric and patriarchal culture, inscriptions give an undogmatic point of view of the lives of ancient people.

Research on Latin and Greek inscriptions from antiquity has shown that women held responsibility in economic matters, politics, religion, and society.[9] In the area of economics, women come up in inscriptions as active in numerous professions, which shows that they had economic independence. In addition, there were some women who were well-to-do

---

8. François Bérard et al., *Guide de l'épigraphiste: Bibliographie choisie des épigraphies antiques et médiévales*, GIBBENS 7 (Paris: Éditions Rue d'Ulm, Quatrième édition entièrement refondue, 2010), http://www.antiquite.ens.fr/ressources/publications-aux-p-e-n-s/guide-de-l-epigraphiste/article/overview.

9. On the following, and with bibliographic sources, see Eisen, *Women Officeholders*, 15–18.

for other reasons. Both groups also appear in the New Testament. Among women who were employed or had a profession were, for example, Lydia, the purple merchant and head of household in Philippi (Acts 16), the tentmaker Prisca in Corinth (Acts 18:3), and the sewer Tabitha in Joppa (Acts 9:36–41).[10] These women can be considered owners of small businesses. Well-to-do women, who acted independently, are mentioned in Luke 8:3. This probably applies also to the deacon and patron Phoebe of Cenchreae (Rom 16:1–2). These findings clearly contradict the still-prevailing patriarchal model that reduces women to the sphere of home and makes them economically dependent on fathers or husbands. Such a simplistic perspective overlooks the fact that the social reality of ancient women was shaped by the same varied factors as that of men and, for this reason, should be equally nuanced.

The situation is similar in the spheres of politics and religion. Epigraphic, papyrological, and numismatic research has been able to show that women in Asia Minor assumed responsibilities in liturgy and in municipal administration.[11] Inscriptions also offer outstanding proofs that women exercised offices in religious communities. For example, Joan Breton has demonstrated this regarding priestesses in ancient Greece, Bernadette Brooten regarding Jewish women in the ancient synagogue, and Ute E. Eisen regarding Christian women in the first century.[12]

Moreover, women had also other social roles than just that of a virgin daughter, wife, or widow, as the patriarchal theory indicates. Their lives were clearly more varied. The Greek concept χήρα (widow) and its Latin counterpart, *vidua*, already show this, for it designated every "woman living without a man."[13] The concept was not restricted to women who had lost their husbands, as commonly maintained, but all women who were widowed, divorced, or not married could be designated with it. The life of women in antiquity was constructed in a manner similar to that of

---

10. On the women in Acts, see the sociohistorical study by Ivoni Richter-Reimer, *Frauen in der Apostelgeschichte des Lukas: Eine feministisch-theologische Exegese* (Gütersloh: Gütersloher Verlagshaus, 1992).

11. For more information, see Eisen, *Women Officeholders*, 16.

12. See Joan Breton Connelly, *Portrait of a Priestess: Women and Ritual in Ancient Greece* (Princeton: Princeton University Press, 2007); Bernadette Brooten, *Women Leaders in the Ancient Synagogue: Inscriptional Evidence and Background Issues*, BJS 36 (Chico, CA: Scholars Press, 1982); Eisen, *Women Officeholders*.

13. So Gustav Stählin, "χήρα," *TWNT* 9:429; Theodor Mayer-Maly, "vidua," PW 2/16:2098.

men. Thus, women lived with or without children, were unmarried, widowed, divorced (1 Cor 7:8–16, 25–40; cf. Mark 10:2–12 par.), or lived in same-sex partnerships (Phil 4:2–3). They could practice their sexuality or not (1 Cor 7:1–7).[14] The evidence of the inscriptions confirm the diversity of relational configurations and life plans of women.

Women also appear as self-assured protagonists, as shown in the self-representations in the inscriptions. As an example, I would like to cite the inscription of the deaconess Basilissa from Asia Minor. The text of the inscription reads: "The first man of the village, Quintus, the son of Heraclius, with his wife Matrona and his children Anicetus and Catilla, all lie here in this grave. The spouse of Anicetus, the Deaconess Basilissa, has erected this pleasing grave along with her only son Numitorius, who is still an underage child."[15] The deaconess Basilissa behaves self-assuredly by erecting this gravestone for the family of her deceased husband. She mentions first of all the social position of her father-in-law ("the first man of the village"), which has a direct effect on her own self-representation. In addition, she presents her own official title, διάκονος, and immortalizes herself as the mother of an underage child. This also indicates that this woman must still have been relatively young, or at most in middle age. She was evidently the wife of Anicetus, who had died. As a rule, though, the ancient sources do not reveal concretely how individual women and men lived. For example, did the New Testament Lydia live as an unmarried or divorced woman, or had she lost her husband through death? Did she have children? We do not know, but we can see that she was professionally employed and the head of her own household, and thus economically independent, which is certainly also true for Nympha (Col 4:15) and some other New Testament women.

In terms of the self-representation of women in inscriptions, one funerary epigram stands out from the abundance of inscriptions by and for deaconesses in Asia Minor. It also gives some indication of the education of women. The deaconess Paula dedicated an ambitious funerary epigram in hexameter to her brother Helladius: "Paula, the most blessed deaconess of Christ … She built me, this grave for her dear brother Helladius, outside the Fatherland, built of stones as the guardian of the body until the terrible sounding trumpet awakes the mortal beings upon the command

---

14. On this, see Bernadette Brooten, *Love between Women: Early Christian Responses to Female Homoeroticism* (Chicago: University of Chicago Press, 1996).

15. See, in more detail, Eisen, *Women Officeholders*, 167–68.

of God."[16] The deaconess drafted the funerary epigram not only in hexameter but also artistically as the speech of the gravestone itself. She also inserted an allusion to 1 Cor 15:52. Although this inscription stands out clearly from others in this region, it is proof that women could be educated and acted with self-confidence. In the light of such women, it is no longer so surprising that the New Testament Prisca, for example, is mentioned as a rule before her husband Aquila (1 Cor 16:19; Rom 16:3; Acts 18; 1 Tim 4:19). This indicates that the relationship between spouses could be termed individually. The traditions prohibiting women (such as 1 Cor 14:33b–36; 1 Tim 2:11–15) can also be read as evidence for this. Prisca was a tentmaker and worked as such together with her husband and Paul (1 Cor 16:19). In addition to this, Acts speaks about her teaching activity (Acts 18:26).[17]

In sum, speech about "the woman" in antiquity and the monolithic image of women accompanying it should be finally dismissed as an inappropriate reduction of the complex reality. The intersectional approach has made it clear that various intersecting factors mark the reality of individuals, also in the ancient world.[18] The above examples should have sufficiently illuminated this,[19] and also that the inclusion of inscriptions—as well as all other ancient sources that are not counted as literature—seems suitable for demonstrating how incompatible the patriarchal concepts of femininity are with the actual everyday reality of women in antiquity.

2. New Testament Women in the Witness of the Epigraphs

2.1 Method of Procedure: The Intertextuality Paradigm

Intertextuality applies to the study of the reception of the New Testament in epigraphic texts. New Testament references, in the form of citations or

---

16. On this and the following, see Eisen, *Women Officeholders*, **169–70**.

17. On the epigraphical witness of teaching women, see Eisen, *Women Officeholders*, 169–70.

18. See Ute E. Eisen, Christine Gerber, and Angela Standhartinger, "Doing Gender—Doing Religion: Zur Frage nach der Intersektionalität in den Bibelwissenschaften. Eine Einleitung," in *Doing Gender—Doing Religion: Fallstudien zur Intersektionalität im frühen Judentum, Christentum und Islam*, ed. Ute E. Eisen, Christine Gerber, and Angela Standhartinger, WUNT 302 (Tübingen: Mohr Siebeck, 2013), 1–33, and the further essays in the volume.

19. For further reflections, see Ute E. Eisen, "Frauen in leitenden Positionen im Neuen Testament und in der frühen Kirche," *BK* 65 (2010): 207–9.

allusions, can be analyzed, described, and interpreted systematically and most precisely with the instruments developed in intertextuality research. In the following, I refer to the analytical instruments systematized by Gunna Lampe, which she has developed within the framework of her study on the comparison of apocalyptic miracle narratives with those of the New Testament.[20]

Intertextuality can be defined as an analysis of the interaction of texts but also, in the reception-aesthetic perspective, of the interaction between the text and the readers. Thus, the first thing to do is to inquire about the mutual textual reference, and then about the interaction between the text and those reading it. According to Lampe, the recipients together with the potential inherent in the text determine the intertextual constitution of the text.[21]

In intertextual comparison, the first step is to differentiate between the source text and the comparison text. In this essay, the inscriptions form the source text and the New Testament the comparison text. In the following, I will shortly present those steps of the intertextual analysis that Lampe has systematized that are relevant in dealing with the selected inscriptions.

First, one must inquire about the "kind of intertextual marking," that is, whether it is a quotation or an allusion. In the case of quotations, the next step is to examine their intensity, whereby the possibilities are on a scale between "total and unchanged" to "partial and modified." In the case of allusions, it is relevant to analyze to what they refer, for example, to names ("onomastic"), motifs ("motivic"), or distinguishing features that are specific to the text genre and thereby are structurally formative ("structural").[22]

Second, the "degree of intertextual markedness" needs to be addressed, for this can take on different intensities. Lampe names the five basic forms as "unmarked" (zero level), "implicit" (reduction level), "quasi-explicit," "explicit" (full level), and "maximally marked" (potentiation level).[23]

Third, it can be useful to ask about the possible reference points of the source text. Here the fundamental distinction is between a single text

---

20. See Gunna Lampe, "So anders? Die Wundertätigkeit Jesu im Kindheitsevangelium des Thomas: Eine intertextuelle Untersuchung zur Darstellung der Wundertaten und des Wundertäters in den Paidika" (PhD diss., Justus-Liebig-Universität Gießen, 2019), https://tinyurl.com/SBL6010e.
21. Lampe, "So anders?," 118.
22. Lampe, "So anders?," 120–26.
23. Lampe, "So anders?," 126–29.

reference, which merely refers to a single text, and a systematic reference, which bears on one or more text genres, structural similarities, or discourse types.[24]

Fourth, there is the subsequent question about the "impact strategies of intertextuality" and their "functions," which Lampe determines more exactly in her "model of reciprocal determination of the function of intertextual references." She assumes four basic strategies. The functions in the source text and in the comparison text correspond to these strategies. First, the "affirmative" strategy, which accentuates the similarity between the source texts and the comparison texts and, in terms of the source text, fulfills the function of "legitimation" and, in the comparison text, that of "glorification." Second, the "neutral" strategy fulfils the function of "demonstration" in the source text, and in the comparison text that of "verification." The third, "critical" strategy, accentuates controversial aspects, such as contrast, and fulfils the function of "revision" in the source text and that of "degradation" in the comparison text. The fourth one is the "modifying" strategy, which takes over the function of "modification" in the source text and that of "differentiation" in the comparison text.[25]

Finally, the aspect of reception needs to be considered, since there are model readers inherent in texts to whom intertextuality is disclosed. Thus, intertextuality can develop its impact only when the model readers encounter informed readers who are familiar with the encyclopedia of the texts.[26] Reader concepts have been given various names in research. Umberto Eco speaks about the "model reader" and defines them as an "interplay of *fortunate circumstances* that have been laid down in the text and that must be satisfying, so that a text can be actualized completely in its possible content."[27] This reader concept requires a "competence for (recognizing) allusions," as Annette Merz defines it.[28] Without this

---

24. Lampe, "So anders?," 129–33.
25. Lampe, "So anders?," 140–47.
26. Lampe, "So anders?," 147–48.
27. Umberto Eco, *Lector in Fabula: Die Mitarbeit der Interpretation in erzählenden Texten*, trans. Heinz-Georg Held (Munich: Dt. Taschenbuch-Verlag, 1987), 76. Eco's work is not fully available in English translation.
28. Annette Merz, *Die fiktive Selbstauslegung des Paulus: Intertextuelle Studien zur Intention und Rezeption der Pastoralbriefe*, NTOA 52 (Göttingen: Vandenhoeck & Ruprecht, 2004), 64.

competence the horizon of meaning disclosed by intertextuality in the act of reception remains unrecognized.

2.2. The Inscription of the *Diakonos* Sophia from Palestine (Fourth–Seventh Centuries)

A gravestone found on the Mount of Olives in Jerusalem, but transported there probably from Beersheba, speaks of the deaconess Sophia.[29] The gravestone is a marble slab broken into five pieces. The dating given to it in epigraphic research varies between the second half of the fourth century and the seventh century. In the inscription, Sophia is described more exactly as διάκονος and as a "second Phoebe," which is a clear allusion to the New Testament διάκονος Phoebe from Rom 16:7 for informed readers. The text of the preserved part of the inscription runs as follows:[30]

+ ἐνθάδε κῖται ἡ δούλη
καὶ νύμφη τοῦ Χριστοῦ
Σοφία, ἡ διάκονος, ἡ δευ-
τέρα Φοίβη, κοιμηθῖσα
ἐν ἰρήνῃ τῇ κα' τοῦ Μαρ-
τίου μηνὸς Ἰνδ(ικτιῶνος) ια'
[...]θίτω κύριος ὁ Θεός
[- - - - - -]ισων πρεσ-
- - - - - - - - - - - -

Crux immissa Here lies the slave
and bride of Christ,
Sophia, diakonos, the second
Phoebe, who fell asleep
in peace on the 21st of the month of
March during the 11th indication
[...] the Lord God
[- - - - - -]*ison pres-*
- - - - - - - - - - - - - -

The inscription is found, along with others, in a collection of inscriptions from Jerusalem and Palestine (IJerusalem 130). Within this collection, five

---

29. On this and the following inscription, see Eisen, *Women Officeholders*, 158–60.
30. Text and translation by Eisen, *Women Officeholders*, 159. English Bible translations follow the NRSV.

inscriptions witness to six διάκονοι in all (see IJerusalem 119, 130, 147, 166, 167). Three of them are identifiable by name as men, and two as women—the second woman along with Sophia is identifiable by means of the feminine form διακονισ[…], which surely has not been totally preserved (IJerusalem 119) but which is suggested by the preserved sigma. The feminine form διακόνισσα next to διάκονος has not been detected before the fourth century. In the following centuries, though, it did not completely replace the use of διάκονος, but rather both designations are encountered as synonyms.[31] The gender of the sixth person in the collection cannot be determined since only the abbreviation διαx, without the mention of a name, has been preserved (IJerusalem 176a). The functional title διάκονος is abbreviated four times in all of these six inscriptions—three times with διαx (IJerusalem 147, 167) and once with δxo (IJerusalem 166). The titles are (or were) written out only in the inscription for Sophia and in the already mentioned damaged inscription. The inscription for Sophia is the most detailed of the five deaconess inscriptions in this collection.

First, it is important to note that also women were given the title διάκονος, for which Paul is the oldest witness (Rom 16:1–2). This applies also to the further history of Christianity, and women probably exercised the functions related to it. It is essential to bear in mind that this title expressed something else in early Christianity than what we today normally associate with it. In his seminal study *Diakonia*, John N. Collins completely revised the conceptual field.[32] He showed that διακονία describes a communicative and mediatory function that includes a commissioner. Paul's use of this conceptual field shows that these observations correspond to the Pauline letters. Paul frequently uses διάκονος along with ἀπόστολος as a title—above all as a self-designation.[33] Διακονία means in Paul's usage the commissioning of a person with the task of proclaiming the word of reconciliation. The male or female διάκονος is in a way a "bearer

---

31. The oldest instance of *diakonissa* is found in canon 19 of the Acts of the Council of Nicaea. See on this and similar use Eisen, *Officeholders*, 14.

32. John Collins, *Diakonia: Re-interpreting the Ancient Sources* (New York: Oxford University Press, 1990). On the history of research, see Anni Hentschel, *Diakonia im Neuen Testament: Studien zur Semantik unter besonderer Berücksichtigung der Rolle der Frauen*, WUNT 2/226 (Tübingen: Mohr Siebeck, 2007), 11–24.

33. See on this in detail, with necessary nuances, Christine Gerber, *Paulus und seine "Kinder": Studien zur Beziehungsmetaphorik der paulinischen Briefe*, BZNW 136 (Berlin: de Gruyter, 2005), 131–42.

of the offer of reconciliation in the sense of Hellenistic peace diplomacy,"[34] who is dependent on God as the commissioner (2 Cor 5:18-19). Only in the nineteenth century was the conceptual field restricted to charitable activities.[35] The development of an early Christian office of deacon or deaconess had a varied and regionally different history. In many texts, it remains unclear which exact functions related to this office in each case. The same applies to other ecclesiastical offices, as can already be observed in the Pastoral Letters (1 Tim 3:1-13).

Women are clearly documented as deacons in the first Christian centuries in numerous recorded literary and epigraphic witnesses.[36] This fact correlates with attempts to force women out of congregational leadership positions, as already shown in the New Testament in the command directed to women to keep silence in 1 Cor 14:33b-36. Whether this statement originates with Paul or is a later interpolation (for which there is some evidence) cannot be determined.[37] However, it is certain that the authors of the Pastoral Letters wanted to force women out of leadership positions.[38] This becomes especially clear in the categorical prohibition on teaching, with the demand for subordination, in 1 Tim 2:9-15. This authoritarian stance taken by the authors toward women continues in the tendency of the letters to restrict the leadership positions occupied by women and to make them invisible. This becomes especially evident in the

---

34. So Gerber, *Paulus und seine "Kinder,"* 138.

35. See, e.g., Hans-Jürgen Benedict, "Beruht der Anspruch der evangelischen Diakonie auf einer Missinterpretation der antiken Quellen? John N. Collins Untersuchung 'Diakonia,'" in *Studienbuch Diakonik 1: Biblische, historische und theologische Zugänge zur Diakonie*, ed. Volker Herrmann and Martin Horstmann (Neukirchen-Vluyn: Neukirchener Verlag, 2008), 117-33.

36. A detailed discussion of epigraphic sources is offered by Eisen, *Women Officeholders*, 158-98; see also Anne Jensen, *God's Self-Confident Daughters: Early Christianity and the Liberation of Women* (Louisville: John Knox, 1996), 58-80.

37. On the arguments, see Marlene Crüsemann, "Unrettbar frauenfeindlich: Der Kampf um das Wort von Frauen in 1. Kor 14, 34-35 im Spiegel antijudaistischer Elemente der Auslegung," in *Paulus: Umstrittene Traditionen—Lebendige Theologie: Eine feministische Lektüre*, ed. Claudia Janssen, Luise Schottroff, and Beate Wehn (Gütersloh: Gütersloher Verlagshaus, 2001), 23-43.

38. See, in detail, Ulrike Wagener, *Die Ordnung des "Hauses Gottes": Der Ort von Frauen in der Ekklesiologie der Pastoralbriefe*, WUNT 2/65 (Tübingen: Mohr Siebeck, 1994); and Wagener., "(Un-)Ordnung im Haushalt Gottes? Wie Schüler des Paulus die Freiheit ihrer Glaubensschwestern bekämpfen," *BK* 65 (2010): 223-27.

range of offices for the διάκονοι, but also in the case of the office of widow.[39] That women too were active as διάκονοι is disguised almost totally in the roster of deacons and deaconesses (see 1 Tim 3:8–13).[40] Ulrike Wagener comments on this, stating that "the writers for the congregations of the third generation" attempted "to curb the activities of women and to establish a certain image of the Church," namely, the "Church as a patriarchal 'Household of God.'"[41]

But back to the inscription for the deaconess Sophia. She is characterized with two conceptual pairs, "servant and bride of Christ" and "deaconess, the second Phoebe." Both are New Testament allusions.

First, the characterization of Sophia with the expression δούλη ... Χριστοῦ forms a quasi-explicit allusion to the name, frequently imposed by oneself or by others in the New Testament epistolary literature of prominent early Christian missionaries of both sexes as δοῦλοι Χριστοῦ (Rom 1:1; Gal 1:10; Phil 1:1; Col 4:12; Jude 1:1; and others). Paul reserves the metaphor for himself and Timothy and thereby expresses his relationship to God as well as his particular commission.[42] Paul's use is influenced by the Old Testament honorific titles "given to such specially chosen and extraordinary characters as Moses, David, and others.... The designation expresses for Paul not only a relationship of service, but is also a title of office and an honorific description."[43] The interpretation of Sophia's characterization as "servant and bride of Christ" in the same sense seems obvious.

This allusion is amplified through the additional allusion to the Pauline letters: an explicit textual reference to Rom 16:1. Through the characterization as a second Phoebe, Sophia is placed in relation to a prominent woman of the New Testament who occupied a leadership position, namely, the διάκονος Phoebe from Cenchreae praised by Paul. This allusion is explicit insofar as the title διάκονος along with the name Phoebe in combination with the epithet "second" is attached to Sophia, a procedure that clearly refers to the New Testament Phoebe. In Rom 16:1, Paul writes about Phoebe in the following way: "I commend to you our sister Phoebe, a deacon [διάκονος] of the church at Cenchreae, so that you may welcome her in the Lord as is fitting for the saints, and help her in what-

---

39. On the widow's office, see below under 2.3.1.
40. See on this in more detail Hentschel, *Diakonia im Neuen Testament*, 396–404.
41. Wagener, "(Un-)Ordnung im Haushalt Gottes?," 223.
42. See Gerber, *Paulus und seine "Kinder,"* 145–46.
43. Alfons Weiser, "δουλύεω κτλ.," *EDNT* 1:352.

ever she may require from you, for she has been a benefactor [προστάτις] of many and of myself as well."[44] Among informed readers, the allusions evoke a correlation of the inscription with the list of those greeted in the letter to the congregation at Rome (Rom 16:1–16), a list that Paul begins with the recommendation for Phoebe cited above (vv. 1–2). This generates associations between this significant woman in the New Testament and the Jerusalem Sophia of the fourth to the seventh century.[45]

According to Rom 16:1–2, Phoebe is a fellow Christian (ἀδελφή) and a deacon (διάκονος) of the congregation in the Corinthian harbor city of Cenchreae. She has journeyed to Rome, obviously also to deliver Paul's letter to the congregation there. Paul gives Phoebe not only the title of διάκονος, but also that of προστάτις (female benefactor, patron), which indicates that she is a woman of upper social status and of property. The designation προστάτις, as well as πάτρων (Latin *patronus*), has to do with the patronage system of the ancient Mediterranean society and thus points to the social system and its actors.[46] Male and female patrons performed various services in the support of their clientele, such as the provision of legal counsel and of shelter, food, and clothing (social care). Phoebe was a woman with status and property, and she obviously acted solely on her own account, for, in the letter of recommendation, she appears alone. We do not know what exactly made her to take this journey: Was she an envoy from the congregation at Cenchreae? Was she commissioned to deliver Paul's letter? Did she act as a supporter of Paul's mission to Spain? Did she travel out of economic interest? Or did she combine various functions with her trip to Rome? Evident is merely that she possessed a prominent position in the congregation at Cenchreae and its missionary work, and that Paul belonged to her clientele too.

The name Phoebe, originating in Greek mythology, suggests that her origin may have been in the slave class. If so, then she would have accomplished something special in accumulating considerable property and social status. However, Paul not only praises Phoebe but also emphasizes other women in his list of greetings, such as Prisca (Rom 16:3) and the

---

44. All the translations from the Greek in the following are my own, unless otherwise indicated.

45. See Annette Merz, "Phöbe von Kenchreä: Kollegin und Patronin des Paulus," *BK* 65 (2010): 228–32.

46. See on this and on the following, with further bibliography, Eisen, *Women Officeholders*, 160, 187 nn. 13–15.

ἀπόστολος Junia (Rom 16:7).[47] This Pauline list of greetings in the New Testament shows that women in extraordinary abundance occupied leadership positions and were recognized in them, as Paul confirms.

The possible associations that these allusions elicit among informed readers are therefore diverse. The deaconess Sophia is dignified quite especially in that she is linked to the tradition of this famous woman (and these famous women) and companion(s) of Paul. The female and male readers of the inscription are invited to interpret the women reciprocally. The impact strategy of this allusion is affirmative, since the correlation in the inscription with Phoebe in the Pauline letter of recommendation legitimizes Sophia's position. Constructive and legitimizing functions are thereby attributed to this New Testament allusion within the inscription. It augments its reading with positive associations and lends Sophia an outstanding significance with only a few words. Through the reference to this significant woman of the New Testament, Sophia's impact is legitimized and made prominent retrospectively in a special way. However, there is even more; the text of the inscription brings to mind not only Sophia, but also at the same time Phoebe, as an important theologian, contemporary to and companion of Paul. Thus, both women are legitimized and portrayed reciprocally—Phoebe in retrospect and Sophia as her successor. With the affirmative allusion to a female figure of the New Testament, a reciprocal process of emphasis, recognition, and realization occurs in the inscription.

2.3. The Inscription of the Deaconess Maria from Cappadocia (Sixth Century)

A magnificently embellished sepulchral stela in gray marble from the sixth century from Cappadocia in Asia Minor provides evidence for the deacon Maria.[48] The sepulchral stela is made in Provençal style and furnished with a Constantinopolitan ornamentation.[49] In the inscription for Maria there are two citations from the New Testament.

---

47. That Junia is a woman is now accepted in research. See Eldon Jay Epp, *Junia: The First Woman Apostle* (Minneapolis: Fortress, 2005).

48. On this inscription in more detail, see Eisen, *Women Officeholders*, 164–67.

49. Nicole Thierry offers a more detailed description on the basis of the history of art. See Thierry, "Un problème de continuité ou de rupture: La Cappadoce entre Rome, Byzance et les Arabes," *CRAI* (1977): 116.

First of all, it should be noted that the deaconess (διάκονος) Maria mentioned on the sepulchral stela is part of a wealth of epigraphic evidence for female διάκονοι in Asia Minor.[50] Here, too, we encounter διάκονος completely as a matter of course next to the feminine form διακόνισσα. The range of tasks performed by διάκονοι are, as a rule, not enumerated in the inscriptions from Asia Minor. The concrete details of the scope of activities of this deaconess thus form an exception.

The first citation is marked as such and refers to Paul's (pseudepigraphical) first letter to Timothy (1 Tim 5:10b). The second citation comes from Luke 23:42 and is not marked. Both citations are modified. In the following, three texts are offered synoptically: the inscription as source text and the two New Testament texts as comparison texts. Literal agreement between the Greek texts and their translations are underlined:

Inscription	Intertextuality and New Testament Citation
Here lies the deacon [διάκονος] Maria of pious and blessed memory,	
who according to the words of the apostle	explicit marking of intertextuality (full level)
	total, modified citation from 1 Tim 5:10b:
reared children [ἐτεκνοτρόφησεν],	[...] since she reared children [εἰ ἐτεκνοτρόφησεν],
sheltered guests [ἐξενοδόχησεν],	since she sheltered guests [εἰ ἐξενοδόχησεν],
washed the feet of the saints [ἁγίων πόδας ἔνιψε(ν)],	since she washed the feet of the saints [εἰ ἁγίων πόδας ἔνιψεν],
and shared her bread with the needy [θλιβομένοις].	since she cared for the needy [εἰ θλιβομένοις ἐπήρκεσεν],

---

50. On this and the following, see Eisen, *Women Officeholders*, 162–74.

	unmarked (zero-level) total, modified citation from Luke 23:42:
Remember her, Lord, when you come into your kingdom	Jesus, remember me when you come into your kingdom.
[μνήσθητι αὐτῆ[ς], Κύ[ριε], ὅταν ἔρχη ἐν τῇ βασιλίᾳ σου].	[Ἰησοῦ, μνήσθητί μου ὅταν ἔλθῃς εἰς τὴν βασιλείαν σου].

2.3.1. The Citation from 1 Timothy 5:10

The first citation in the inscription is introduced by a direct intertextual link, "according to the words of the apostle," whereby intertextuality is explicitly marked (full level). This citation formula is common in early Christian literature for citations from the Corpus Paulinum. According to Felle, in the inscriptions ascribed to this corpus, the most frequent citations come from the Letter to the Romans and, from the pseudepigraphical Pastoral Letters, especially frequently from 1 Timothy.[51] In this inscription, we find a modified citation from 1 Tim 5:10.

The citation comes from a passage in 1 Timothy that is devoted to widows (1 Tim 5:3–16). In her study on the ecclesiology and ethics in the Pastoral Letters, Ulrike Wagener has demonstrated that the speech about the "widows selected" (χήρα καταλεγέσθω, 1 Tim 5:9) indicates women who exercise a congregational office.[52] Thus, by virtue of the verb "καταλέγειν, a legally binding act of admission to the office of community widow is described," and thus the verse belongs "formally and in content in the genre of lists of offices."[53] Since poverty is not one of the following criteria for registration in the ranks of the widows, this group of women is not characterized as receivers of charitable aid.

As stated above, the Pastoral Letters show a tendency to restrict the existing leadership functions exercised by women. This also appears in the remarks on the community widows (1 Tim 5:9–16). In 1 Tim 5:9, the

---

51. See Felle, *Biblia Epigraphica*, 410.

52. Wagener, *Ordnung*, and, on the widows' office and the group of widows as a whole, also Angela Standhartinger, "'Wie die verehrteste Judith und die besonnenste Hanna': Traditionsgeschichtliche Beobachtungen zur Herkunft der Witwengruppe im entstehenden Christentum," in *Dem Tod nicht glauben: Sozialgeschichte der Bibel, Festschrift für Luise Schottroff*, ed. Frank Crüsemann (Gütersloh: Gütersloher Verlagshaus, 2004), 103–26.

53. Wagener, *Ordnung des "Hauses Gottes,"* 170.

reception into the widow's office is connected with three conditions; first, with age (she should not be younger than sixty years old); second, with marital status (she should be married only once (v. 9); and third, with the demonstration of "good works" (v. 10a). These are defined more precisely as child-rearing, hospitality, washing the feet of the saints, and the care of the needy (v. 10b).

In the inscription, it is exactly these four good works of the community widows that are attributed to the deaconess Maria. This takes place in the form of the literal adoption of four verb forms and two substantive nouns from 1 Tim 5:10b. In contrast to the biblical citation, these are strung together paratactically in the inscription: ἐτεκνοτρόφησεν, ἐξενοδόχησεν, ἁγίων πόδας ἔνιψεν, θλιβομένοις. Only the fourth work is modified. Similarly to the biblical passage, the needy are named as receivers of care, but instead of a general "aiding" (ἐπήρκεσεν), Maria "shared her bread with the needy," that is, Maria took care of feeding them.

The activities of the widows taken up in 1 Tim 5:9–10 and in the inscription correspond "to a great extent to the pattern of Hellenistic doctrines of professional duties that also lie behind the episcopal and diaconal lists (1 Tim 3:1, 13), and are similarly complemented through individual demands connected with social status."[54] The verb τεκνοτροφεῖν is a *hapax legomenon* in the New Testament, but the motif of caring for children appears in the Pastoral Letters in general as a precondition for congregational leadership positions. In the case of ἐπίσκοποι (1 Tim 3:4) and διάκονοι (1 Tim 3:12) and πρεσβύτεροι (Titus 1:6), the focus is on the officeholders' own children; however, πρεσβύτιδας (Titus 2:4) are no longer reminded of taking care of their own children but generally of educating young women. Horsley has pointed out that this verb is related to both men and women in the literary tradition.[55] This is important to notice, since it is customary in the secondary literature to associate the education of children with women only.

The verb ξενοδοχεῖν is likewise a *hapax legomenon* in the New Testament. The virtue of hospitality, however, is also counted among the requirements for the office of the ἐπίσκοπος (1 Tim 3:2; Titus 1:8). It is also emphasized in other New Testament texts (Rom 12:13; Matt 25:35; 3 John 5–8; Heb 13:2). Foot-washing appears in the Pastoral Letters exclusively

---

54. Jürgen Roloff, *Der erste Brief an Timotheus*, EKKNT 15 (Zürich: Benziger, 1988), 284.
55. *NewDocs* 2:194.

in the exhortation to widows (1 Tim 5:10). However, it has a significant place in the New Testament tradition as Jesus's act performed on his disciples in the Gospel of John (John 13:14–17) and as the washing of Jesus's feet by the sinful woman in the house of the Pharisee in the Gospel of Luke (Luke 7:36–50). Foot-washing in antiquity had the function of honoring and receiving guests.[56] In the West, foot-washing also appears as a complementary rite to baptism from the third century onward. Whether the inscription also alludes to this practice must remain an open question.

The support of the needy (θλιβόμενοι) by the widows is circumscribed in 1 Tim 5:10 using the verb ἐπαρκεῖν, which implies various forms of help for the sick, the distressed, and other needy people (1 Thess 3:4; 2 Cor 1:6; 7:7).[57] In the inscription for Maria, this passage is modified and concentrates on the care of the poor in the form of their feeding. This modification at the end of the citation is striking and draws the attention of informed readers. Is this an allusion to a special activity carried out by Maria, as the other activities are listed using Hellenistic topoi? Did she, in fact, share her "own bread"? Was she a well-to-do woman, perhaps a widow, a divorced woman, or a woman living outside marriage who, as a deaconess, shared her goods with the needy? Or does this formulation indicate that Maria, as a deaconess, stood at the head of a community that she led independently?

What is striking about this quote from the instructions aimed at community widows is that it is found in an inscription for a female deacon. The intertextual reading of this inscription with the Pastoral Letters easily evokes the association that the office of deaconess and the widow's office overlap. In research, most diverse hypotheses have been formed concerning the relationship between the two offices.[58] I doubt that a clear answer to this question can ever be found, because the general rule is that the development of the ecclesiastical offices was not as monolithic as has been widely assumed but differed locally. It also proves to be difficult to delimit the tasks of individual offices precisely. This is already shown in the Pastoral Letters, which mainly discuss the requirements and virtues but not the specific activities of the various offices. In this regard, the widow's office stands out, but the works listed as belonging to it also follow the topoi of Hellenistic discourses of professional duties. Thus, they can only be read

---

56. See on this point and on the following Eisen, *Women Officeholders*, 166–67, with further bibliography.

57. Roloff, *Erste Brief an Timotheus*, 295.

58. See Eisen, *Women Officeholders*, 12–14.

to a limited extent as a presentation of concrete actions. They serve above all to upgrade the named officers.

For the interpretation of the inscription for Maria, it follows that the impact strategy of this intertextual reference aims at affirmation. The special accent is on the mutual recognition and emphasis of the virtue of these female ecclesiastical officeholders. However, Maria acted as a deacon, and her activity is legitimized through the explicit reference to the words of the apostle. At the same time, the community widows are remembered and they get their share of glorification, as Lampe emphasizes in her intertextual model. The sixth-century deacon from Asia Minor and the New Testament women are mutually identified, recognized, and valued through intertextuality.

2.3.2. The Citation from Luke 23:42

At the end of the inscription, a request by the unnamed dedicators asks Christ to think of Mary when he comes to his kingdom. The quotation remains unmarked (zero level) and can only be recognized by those who know Luke's text and its potential of meaning. However, Lukan citations obviously enjoyed great popularity in the wording of inscriptions, because according to Felle, this gospel was the most frequently cited in comparison to the other three canonical gospels.[59]

Informed readers recognize that the wording of the inscription comes from the passion narrative, according to which Jesus was crucified together with two criminals. While the narratives in Mark and Matthew only summarily say that they vilified Jesus (ὠνείδιζον αὐτόν; Matt 27:44; Mark 15:32b), this sequence is shaped to a conversation in direct speech in Luke (see 23:39–43). In the Lukan context, only one of the criminals ridicules (ἐβλασφήμει) Jesus by saying: "Are you not the Messiah? Save yourself and us!" (Luke 23:39). The second, on the other hand, confesses his and the other's guilt, likewise in direct speech, and absolves Jesus from guilt (Luke 23:40–41). Then he turns directly to Jesus with the words: "Jesus, remember me when you come into your kingdom" (Ἰησοῦ, μνήσθητί μου ὅταν ἔλθῃς εἰς τὴν βασιλείαν σου; Luke 23:42). Jesus's affirmative answer to this offender's confession follows immediately with the promise that the criminal will be with Jesus "today" in paradise (Luke 23:43).

---

59. See Felle, *Biblia Epigraphica*, 410.

This quotation is taken up and modified in the inscription for Maria. The modifications take place with the personal pronouns, salutations, verb forms, and prepositions, but not in the sense of the speech, which is why the quote, according to Lampe, can be classified as "total and modified" in its degree of intertextuality. It reads: "Remember her, Lord, when you come into your kingdom" (μνήσθητι αὐτῆ[ς], Κύ[ριε], ὅταν ἔρχῃ ἐν τῇ βασιλίᾳ σου).

A change of perspective is carried out in the quotation. The dedicators take over the perspective of the criminal and reformulate the quotation as a recommendation on behalf of Maria. The "remember me"[60] is recast as "remember her"; the direct address "Jesus" is replaced with "Kyrie" and thus transformed and reproduced as a christological confession; the tense of the verb ἔρχομαι is changed from the aorist subjunctive to the present tense, and the preposition εἰς to ἐν. The eschatological horizon of the New Testament text is creatively transferred in the inscription to the dedicators and their current situation in the sixth century.

The dedicators identify themselves with the clairvoyant and finally saved criminal. Nevertheless, they show more humility than he does by asking for salvation not for themselves but for Maria. This intertextuality thus unfolds both an affirmative and a critical impact strategy. The affirmative strategy aims to legitimize the dedicators and to remember the penitent criminal. At the same time, however, the strategy has a critical element. The Christians make use of the criminal's words but adapt them by not praying for themselves, as does the criminal in the gospel story, but for Maria, and thus degrade his speech. The revision of this intertextuality is to surpass the New Testament speaker through Mary's selflessness. At the same time, this allusion sheds new light on the criminal in Luke's narrative, who surely recognizes Jesus as innocent and as the Messiah but is only concerned with his own salvation, not with the salvation of his fellow criminal. In the inscription, the quotation from Luke is skillfully transferred through modification into a new situation with new effects, which also leads to a new perception of the Lukan narrative.

In addition, the "total and modified" citation aims at emphasizing the contrast in the two figures, the nameless and penitent criminal on the cross

---

60. This formulation in the Gospel of Luke is, in turn, a citation from the LXX that prefaces the standardized prayer of the pious to God that saving care might be bestowed on them (e.g., Judg 16:28; Jer 15:15). See Michael Wolter, *Das Lukasevangelium*, HNT 5 (Tübingen: Mohr Siebeck, 2008), 760.

and the true deacon Maria of the inscription, who has acted "according to the words of the Apostle." Informed readers may well make the following association. If the promise of entry into paradise is already given to the criminal (Lampe: verification), how much more appropriate it is for this tried and true deacon Maria (according to Lampe: demonstration). The intertextuality of the inscription and the New Testament text, therefore, also open new perspectives on the latter.

To summarize, the first New Testament quotation of the inscription has an affirmative impact strategy and serves to legitimize Maria by referring to the holders of the widows' office in 1 Tim 5 and thus also calls them to mind. The second New Testament quotation can be interpreted as having both an affirmative and a critical impact strategy. It serves to legitimize Maria and the dedicators of the inscription. The latter are revising the perspective of the New Testament criminal by asking for salvation not for themselves but for another, namely, Maria. How much more willing will Jesus be to accept this woman into his kingdom.

3. Summary

Inscriptions give special information about the diversity of women's lives in antiquity. The two inscriptions discussed document two deacons in the first Christian millennium in Palestine and Asia Minor. In this essay, I have paid particular attention to the reception of New Testament texts in these two exemplary inscriptions. Interestingly, both cite or allude to the generally most popular texts of the New Testament. Using the tools of the methodological analysis developed by Lampe, the special characteristics as well as the impact strategies and functions of the New Testament references can be illuminated. The intertextual analysis shows how reading several texts together opens up new horizons of meaning, both with regard to the inscriptions and the New Testament texts. As can be observed, reciprocal interpretations can begin through intertextuality. The affirmative strategy of intertextuality is particularly dominant in the inscriptions. The reference to New Testament women in them serves to legitimize the later women and, at the same time, reminds of the women in New Testament narratives, who are, likewise, emphasized and acknowledged. Intertextuality fulfills constructive functions. It enriches associative reading and sets in motion a reciprocal process of emphasis, recognition, and awareness.

New Testament quotes and allusions appear only seldom in the grave inscriptions for female officeholders. In the selected examples, they are all the more effective. They connect the deceased female officeholders with the great women of the New Testament. With reference to Christianity's founding period, an authorization and succession are indirectly generated. At the same time, quotes and allusions call the New Testament into the present.

Bibliography

Primary Sources by Author

Achilles Tatius
    Achilles Tatius. *Leucippe and Clitophon*. Translated by Stephen Gaselee. LCL. Cambridge: Harvard University Press, 1969.

Ambrose
    Ambrose. *Saint Ambrose Letters 1–91*. Translated by Mary Melchior Beyenka. FC 26. Washington, DC: Catholic University of America Press, 1954.

Ammianus Marcellinus
    Ammianus Marcellinus. *Books 20–26*. Vol. 2 of *History*. Translated by John C. Rolfe. LCL. Cambridge: Harvard University Press, 1940.

Aristotle
    Aristotle. *The "Art" of Rhetoric*. Translated by John H. Freese. LCL. Cambridge: Harvard University Press, 1926.
    Phillips Simpson, Peter L., trans. *The Politics of Aristotle*. Chapel Hill: North Carolina University Press, 1997.

Clement of Alexandria
    Chadwick, Henry, and John E. L. Oulton, eds. *Alexandrian Christianity: Selected Translations of Clement and Origen*. LCC 2. Repr., Philadelphia: Westminster, 2006.
    Stählin, Otto, and Ludwig Früchtel. *Stromata Buch I–VI*. GCS 52. Berlin: Akademie, 1960.

Cyril of Jerusalem
    Yarnold, Edward J. *Cyril of Jerusalem*. London: Routledge, 2000.

Egeria
    Franceschini, Ezio, and Robert Weber. *Itinerarium Egeriae*. CCSL 175. Turnhout: Brepols, 1981.
    Giannarelli, Elena, ed. *Egeria: Diario di viaggio*. Milan: Edizioni Pauline, 1992.
    Gingras, George E. *Egeria: Diary of a Pilgrimage*. ACW 38. Mahwah, NJ: Newman, 1970.
    Maraval, Pierre, ed. *Égérie: Journal de voyage (Itinéraire)*. SC 296. Paris: Cerf, 1982.
    Pétré, Hélène. *Journal de voyage*. SC 21. Paris: Cerf, 1948.
    Wilkinson, John. *Egeria's Travels to the Holy Land*. Wiltshire: Aris & Phillips, 1999.

Eudocia
    Schembra, Rocco. *Homerocentones*. CCSG 62. Turnhout: Brepols: 2007.
    ———. *La prima redazione dei centoni omerici: Traduzione e commento*. Hellenica 21. Alessandria: Ediciones dell'Orso, 2006.
    Usher, Mark D., ed. *Homerocentones Eudociae Augustae*. BSGRT. Stuttgart: Teubner, 1999.

Gerontius
    Gorce, Denys. *Vie de sainte Mélanie*. SC 90. Paris: Cerf, 1962.

Homer
    Homer. *Iliad*. 2 vols. Translated by Augustus T. Murray. Revised by William F. Wyatt. LCL. Cambridge: Harvard University Press, 1924–1925.

Irenaeus
    Irenaeus. *Contre les hérésies*. Edited by Adelin Rousseau with Bertrand Hemmerdinger, Louis Doutreleau, and Charles Mercier. Vol. 4. SC 100. Paris: Cerf, 1965.

Origen
    Origen. *Homilies in Joshua*. Translated by Barbara J. Bruce. FC. Washington, DC: Catholic University of America Press, 1984.
    Jaubert, Annie. *Origène, Homélies sur Josué*. SC 71. Paris: Cerf, 1960.

Paulinus of Nola
   Hartel, Wilhelm von. *Paulini Nolani Opera 2: Carmina.* CSEL 30. Vienna: Tempsky, 1894.
   Kaptner, Margit. *Paulini Nolani Opera 2: Carmina.* CSEL 30. Vienna: Verlag der Österreichischen Akademie der Wissenschaften, 1999.
   Santaniello, Giovanni, ed. *Paolino de Nola: Le lettere.* Naples: LER, 1992.
   Walsh, Patrick G., trans. *Letters of St. Paulinus of Nola.* 2 vols. ACW 35–36. Westminster, MD: Newman, 1966–1967.
   ———. *The Poems of St. Paulinus of Nola.* ACW 40. New York: Newman, 1975.

Paulus Orosius
   Raymond, Irving W., trans. *Seven Books of History against the Pagans: The Apology of Paulus Orosius.* ACLS. New York: Columbia University Press, 1936.

Proba
   Badini, Antonia, and Antonia Rizzi, trans. *Proba, Il Centone.* BP 47. Bologna: EDB, 2011.
   Clark, Elisabeth A., and Diane F. Hatch, trans. *The Golden Bough, the Oaken Cross: The Virgilian Cento of Faltonia Betita Proba.* AARTTS 5. Chico, CA: Scholars Press, 1981.
   Fassina, Alessia, and Carlo M. Lucarini, trans. *Faltonia Betita Proba: Cento Vergilianus.* BSGRT. Berlin: de Gruyter, 2015.

Pseudo-Cyprian
   Escolà i Tuset, Josep M., trans. *Pseudo-Cebrià, Poemes.* EC. Barcelona: Fundació Bernat Metge, 2007.

Tertullian
   Tertullian. *Adversus Marcionem.* Edited and translated by Ernest Evans. Oxford: Oxford University Press, 1972.
   Quain, Edwin A., trans. *Tertullian, Disciplinary, Moral and Ascetical Works.* FC 40. Washington, DC: Catholic University of America Press, 1959.

Valerius of Bierzo
>Aherne, Consuelo María. *Valerio of Bierzo: An Ascetic of the Late Visigothic Period*. Washington, DC: Catholic University of America Press, 1949.

Other Primary Sources

Attridge, Harold W., and Elaine H. Pagels, trans. "NHC I,5: The Tripartite Tractate." Pages 159–337 in vol. 1 of *Nag Hammadi Codex I (The Jung Codex)*. Edited by Harold W. Attridge. NHS 22. Leiden: Brill, 1985.

Bernard, Odile Bénédicte, Jean Bouvet, and Lucien Regnault, eds. *Vie de sainte Synclétique*. Bégrolles-en-Mauges: Abbaye de Bellefontaine, 1991.

Bonnet, Maximilianus. *Acta Philippi et Acta Thomae: Accedunt acta Barnabae*. AcApAp 2.2. Repr., Darmstadt: Wissenschaftliche Buchgesellschaft, 1959.

Bovon, François, Bertrand Bouvier, and Frédéric Amsler. *Acta Philippi 1: Textus*. CCSA 11. Turnhout: Brepols, 1999.

Bovon, François, and Christopher R. Matthews. *The Acts of Philip: A New Translation*. Waco, TX: Baylor University Press, 2012.

Brashler, James, and Douglas M. Parrott, "The Act of Peter." Pages 473–93 in *Nag Hammadi Codices V,2–5 and VI with Papyrus Berolinensis 8502,1 and 4*. Edited by Douglas M. Parrott. NHMS 11. Leiden: Brill, 1979.

Breytenbach, Cilliers, Klaus Hallof, Ulrich Huttner, Jennifer Krumm, Stephen Mitchell, Julien M. Ogereau, Erkki Sironen, Marina Veksina, and Christiane Zimmermann, eds. Inscriptiones Christianae Graecae (ICG): A Digital Collection of Greek Early Christian Inscriptions from Asia Minor and Greece. Berlin: Edition Topoi, 2016. http://repository.edition-topoi.org/collection/ICG.

Burke, Tony. *De infantia Iesu evangelivm Thomae*. CCSA 17. Turnhout: Brepols, 2010.

Carfora, Anna. *La Passione di Perpetua e Felicita: Donne e martirio nel cristianesimo delle origini*. Palermo: L'Epos, 2007.

Carrasquer Pedrós, Maria Sira, and Araceli de la Red Vega. *Matrología 1: Madres del desierto*. Burgos: Monte Carmelo, 2000.

Detorakis, Theocharis. "ΤΟ ΑΝΕΚΔΟΤΟ ΜΑΡΤΥΡΙΟ ΤΟΥ ΑΠΟΣΤΟΛΟΥ ΑΝΔΡΕΑ." Pages 325–52 in *Acts of the Second International Congress of Peloponnesian Studies 1, Patras 25.–31. Mai*

1980. Peleponnesica: JSPSSup 8. Athens: Hetaireia Peloponnēsiakōn Spudōn, 1981–1982.

Elliott, J. Keith. "The Acts of Peter." Pages 390–428 in vol. 2 of *The Apocryphal New Testament*. Oxford: Clarendon, 1993.

———. *The Apocryphal New Testament: A Collection of Apocryphal Christian Literature in an English Translation*. Oxford: Clarendon, 1993.

Felle, Antonio Enrico. *Biblia Epigraphica: La Sacra Scrittura nella Documentazione Epigrafica dell' Orbis Christianus Antiquus (III–VIII Secolo)*. ICIS 5. Bari: Edipuglia, 2006.

Foster, Paul. *The Gospel of Peter: Introduction, Critical Edition and Commentary*. TENT 4. Leiden: Brill, 2010.

Geffcken, Johannes. *Die Oracula Sibyllina*. GCS 8. Leipzig: Hinrichs, 1902.

Giversen, Søren, and Birger Pearson. "The Thought of Norea." Pages 87–99 in *Nag Hammadi Codices IX and X*. Edited by Birger Pearson. NHMS 15. Leiden: Brill, 1981.

Hennecke, Edgar, and Wilhelm Schneemelcher. *Neutestamentliche Apokryphen in deutscher Übersetzung*. Vol. 1, *Evangelien*. Vol. 2, *Apostolisches, Apokalypsen und Verwandtes*. Tübingen: Mohr Siebeck, 1997.

Hennecke, Edgar, Wilhelm Schneemelcher, and R. McLeod Wilson. *New Testament Apocrypha*. Vol. 1, *Gospels and Related Writings*. Vol. 2, *Writings Relating to the Apostles, Apocalypses and Related Subjects*. Louisville: Westminster John Knox, 2003.

Hock, Ronald F. *The Infancy Gospels of James and Thomas: With Introduction, Notes and Original Text Featuring the New Scholars Version Translation*. Santa Rosa, CA: Polebridge, 1995.

Holmes, Michael W., ed. and trans. *The Apostolic Fathers: Greek Texts and English Translations*. 3rd ed. Grand Rapids: Baker Academic, 2007.

Isenberg, Wesley B., and Bentley Layton. "The Gospel according to Philip, Nag Hammadi Codex II,3." Pages 131–217 in vol. 1 of *Nag Hammadi Codex II,2-7, Together with XIII,2*, Brit.Lib.Or. 4926(1), and P.Oxy. 1,654,655*. Edited by Bentley Layton. NHS 20. Leiden: Brill, 1989.

James, Montague R. "Actae Xanthippae et Polyxenae." Pages 58–85 in *Apocrypha anecdota*. TS 5.1. Cambridge: Cambridge University Press, 1893.

———. *The Apocryphal New Testament Being the Apocryphal Gospels, Acts, Epistles, and Apocalypses, with Other Narratives and Fragments*. Oxford: Clarendon, 1975.

Kaiser, Ursula Ulrike. *Die Hypostase der Archonten (Nag-Hammadi-Codex II,4)*. TU 156. Berlin: De Gruyter, 2006.

———. "Die Hypostase der Archonten (NHC II,4)." Pages 164–74 in *Nag Hammadi Deutsch: Studienausgabe. NHC I-XIII, Codex Berolinensis 1 und 4, Codex Tchacos 3 und 4.* Edited by Hans-Martin Schenke, Ursula Ulrike Kaiser, and Hans-Gebhard Bethge. Berlin: de Gruyter, 2013.

Kaiser, Ursula Ulrike, with Josef Tropper. "Die Kindheitserzählung des Thomas: Einleitung und Übersetzung." Pages 930–59 in vol. 1 of *Antike christliche Apokryphen in deutscher Übersetzung.* Edited by Christoph Markschies and Jens Schröter. Tübingen: Mohr Siebeck, 2012.

Kasser, Rodolpho, Marvin Meyer, and Gregor Wurst, eds. *The Gospel of Judas: From the Codex Tchacos.* Washington, DC: National Geographic, 2006.

Knopf, Rudolf. *Der erste Clemensbrief untersucht und herausgegeben.* TU 20.1, NF 5.1. Leipzig: Hinrichs, 1899.

Köster, Helmut, and Thomas O. Lambdin. "The Gospel according to Thomas." Pages 52–93 in *Nag Hammadi Codex II,2-7, Together with XIII,2*, Brit.Lib.Or. 4926(1), and P.Oxy. 1,654,655.* Vol. 1, *Gospel according to Thomas, Gospel according to Philip, Hypostasis of the Archons, and Indexes.* Edited by Bentley Layton. NHS 20. Leiden: Brill, 1989.

Layton, Bentley. "The Hypostasis of the Archons." Pages 234–59 in *Nag Hammadi Codex II,2-7 Together with XIII,2*, Brit. Lib. Or. 4926(1), and P.Oxy. 1,654,655.* Edited by Bentley Layton. NHS 20. Leiden: Brill, 1989.

———, ed. *Nag Hammadi Codex II,2-7 Together with XIII,2*, Brit. Lib. Or. 4926(1), and P.Oxy. 1,654,655.* NHS 20. Leiden: Brill, 1989.

Leipoldt, Johannes. *Das Evangelium nach Thomas: Koptisch und Deutsch.* TU 101. Berlin: Akademie, 1967.

Lipsius, Richard Adelbert, and Maximilianus Bonnet. *Acta Petri, Acta Pauli, Acta Petri et Pauli, Acta Pauli et Theclae, Acta Thaddei.* Darmstadt: Wissenschaftliche Buchgesellschaft, 1959.

Macdermot, Violet, trans. *The Books of Jeu and the Untitled Text in the Bruce Codex.* NHS 13. Leiden: Brill, 1978.

———, trans. *Pistis Sophia.* NHS 9. Leiden: Brill, 1978.

MacDonald, Dennis R. *The Acts of Andrew.* Santa Rosa, CA: Polebridge, 2005.

MacRae, George W. "The Thunder, Perfect Mind." Pages 231–55 in *Nag Hammadi Codices V,2-5 and VI with Papyrus Berolinensis 8502,1 and 4.* Edited by Douglas M. Parrott. NHMS 11. Leiden: Brill, 1979.

Meyer, Marvin, ed. *The Nag Hammadi Scriptures: The International Edition.* New York: HarperCollins, 2007.

———. "The Nature of the Rulers." Pages 191–98 in *The Nag Hammadi Scriptures: The International Edition.* Edited by Marvin Meyer. New York: HarperCollins, 2007.

Mohlberg, Leo C. *Rerum ecclesiasticarum documenta.* Fontes 1. Rome: Herder, 1960.

Musurillo, Herbert. *The Acts of the Christian Martyrs.* Oxford: Clarendon, 1972.

Parrott, Douglas M., ed. *Nag Hammadi Codices V,2–5 and VI with Papyrus Berolinensis 8502,1 and 4.* NHMS 11. Leiden: Brill, 1979.

———. "Sophia of Jesus Christ." Pages 37–39 in *Nag Hammadi Codices III,3–4 and V,1 with Papyrus Berolinensis 8502,3 and Oxyrhynchus Papyrus 1081: Eugnostos and the Sophia of Jesus Christ.* Edited by Douglas M. Parrott. NHS 27. Leiden: Brill, 1991.

Peel, Malcolm, and Jan Zandee, trans. "The Teachings of Silvanus." Pages 249–369 in *Nag Hammadi Codex VII.* Edited by Birger A. Pearson. NHMS 30. Leiden: Brill, 1996.

Pellegrini, Silvia. "Protevangelium des Jakobus: Einleitung und Übersetzung." Pages 903–29 in *Evangelien und Verwandtes.* Vol. 1.2 of *Antike Christliche Apokryphen in deutscher Übersetzung.* Edited by Christoph Markschies and Jens Schröter with Andreas Heiser. Tübingen: Mohr Siebeck, 2012.

Pervo, Richard I. *The Acts of Paul: A New Translation with Introduction and Commentary.* Eugene, OR: Cascade Books, 2014.

Piñero, Antonio, and Gonzalo del Cerro, eds. *Hechos Apócrifos de los apóstoles.* Vol. 1. BAC 646. Madrid: Biblioteca de Autores Cristianos, 2004.

Pistelli, Ermenegildo. *Il Protevangelo di Jacopo: Prima traduzione italiana con introduzione e note di E. Pistelli; Segue un'appendice dallo Pseudo-Matteo.* Lanciano: Carabba, 1919.

Prieur, Jean-Marc, ed. *Acta Andreae.* CCSA 5. Tournhout: Brepols, 1989.

Robinson, James M., ed. *The Nag Hammadi Library in English.* 4th rev. ed. Leiden: Brill, 1996.

Schmidt, Carl. *Acta Pauli aus der Heidelberger koptischen Papyrushandschrift Nr. 1: Tafelband.* Leipzig: Hinrichs, 1904.

Schneemelcher, Wilhelm. "The Acts of Peter." Pages 270–316 in *Writings Relating to the Apostles, Apocalypses and Related Subjects.* Vol. 2 of *New Testament Apocrypha.* Edited by Wilhelm Schneemelcher and R. McLeod Wilson. Louisville: Westminster John Knox, 2003.

Schoedel, William R. "The (First) Apocalypse of James." Pages 65–109 in *NHC V,2–5 and VI with Papyrus Berolinensis 8502, 1 and 4*. Edited by Douglas M. Parrott. NHS 11. Leiden: Brill, 1979.

Sieber, John H., and Bentley Layton. "NHC VIII,1: Zostrianus." Pages 7–225 in *Nag Hammadi Codex VIII*. Edited by John H. Sieber. NHS 31. Leiden: Brill, 1991.

Steinsaltz, Adin Even-Israel, trans. "Ketubot 7b." William Davidson Talmud. https://tinyurl.com/SBL6010c.

Swan, Laura. *The Forgotten Desert Mothers*. Mahwah, NJ: Paulist, 2001.

Thomsen, Peter. *Die lateinischen und griechischen Inschriften der Stadt Jerusalem und ihrer Umgebung*. Leipzig: Hinrichs, 1922.

Totti, Maria. *Ausgewählte Texte der Isis- und Sarapis-Religion*. SubEp 12. Hildesheim: Olms, 1985.

Treu, Ursula. "Christian Sibyllines." Pages 652–85 in *New Testament Apocrypha*. Vol. 2, *Writings Relating to the Apostles, Apocalypses and Related Subjects*. Edited by Wilhelm Schneemelcher and R. McLeod Wilson. Louisville: Westminster John Knox, 1992.

Turner, John D. "The Trimorphic Protennoia." Pages 371–454 in *Nag Hammadi Codices XI, XII, XIII*. Edited by Charles W. Hedrick. NHMS 28. Leiden: Brill, 1990.

Veilleux, Armand, ed. and trans. *Pachomian Chronicles and Rules*. Vol. 2 of *Pachomian Koinonia: The Lives, Rules and Other Writings of Saint Pachomius and His Disciples*. CS 46. Kalamazoo, MI: Cistercian Publications, 1981.

Waldstein, Michael, and Frederik Wisse. *The Apocryphon of John: Synopsis of Nag Hammadi Codices II,1; III,1 and IV,1 with BG 8502,2*. NHMS 33. Leiden: Brill, 1995.

Secondary Sources

Aageson, James W. *Paul, the Pastoral Epistles, and the Early Church*. Peabody, MA: Hendrickson, 2008.

Aasgaard, Reidar. *The Childhood of Jesus: Decoding the Apocryphal Infancy Gospel of Thomas*. Eugene, OR: Cascade, 2009.

Adelman, Rachel. "Seduction and Recognition in the Story of Judah and Tamar and the Book of Ruth." *Nashim* 23 (2012): 87–109.

Albarrán Martínez, María Jesús. *Ascetismo y monasterios femeninos en el Egipto tardoantiguo: Estudio de papiros y ostraca griegos y coptos*. Barcelona: Abadia de Montserrat, 2011.

———. "Letradas e iletradas en el Egipto bizantino." Pages 29–45 in *Mujer y cultura escrita: Del mito al siglo XXI*. Edited by María del Val González de la Peña. Gijón: Trea, 2005.

Albrecht, Gary L., Katherine D. Seelman, and Michael Bury. "Introduction: The Formation of Disability Studies." Pages 1–8 in *The Handbook of Disability Studies*. Edited by Gary L. Albrecht, Katherine D. Seelman, and Michael Bury. Thousand Oaks, CA: Sage, 2001.

Albrecht, Ruth. *Das Leben der heiligen Makrina auf dem Hintergrund der Thekla-Traditionen: Studien zu dem Ursprüngen des weiblichen Mönchtums im 4. Jahrhundert in Kleinasien*. FKDG 38. Göttingen: Vandenhoeck & Ruprecht, 1986.

Alter, Robert. *The Art of Biblical Narrative*. New York: Basic Books, 1981.

Amat, Jacqueline. *Songes et visions de l'au-dela dans la litterature latine tardive*. Paris: Etudes Augustiniennes, 1985.

Amatucci, Aurelio Giuseppe. *Storia della letteratura latina*. Bari: Laterza, 1929.

Ameling, Walter. "Fermina Liberaliter Instituta: Some Thoughts on a Martyr's Liberal Education." Pages 78–102 in *Perpetua's Passions: Multidisciplinary Approaches to the Passio Perpetuae et Felicitatis*. Edited by Jan N. Bremmer and Marco Formisano. Oxford: Oxford University Press, 2012.

———. "Neues Testament und Epigraphik aus der Perspektive der epigraphischen Forschung." Pages 5–26 in *Epigraphik und Neues Testament*. Edited by Thomas Corsten, Markus Öhler, and Joseph Verheyden. WUNT 365. Tübingen: Mohr Siebeck, 2016.

Anson, John. "The Female Transvestite in Early Monasticism: The Origin and Development of a Motiv." *Viator* 5 (1974): 1–32.

Arbea, Antonio. "El carmen sacrum de Faltonia Betitia Proba, la primera poetisa cristiana." In *Textos del Coloquio Mujeres de la Edad Media: Escritura, Visión, Ciencia*. Santiago de Chile: Facultad de Filosofía y Humanidades, 1999.

———. "El centón homérico de Eudoxia (s. V d. C.)." *TV* 43 (2002): 97–106.

Arzt-Grabner, Peter. "Die Auswertung inschriftlicher Zeugnisse für die neutestamentliche Exegese: Erfahrungen, Chancen und Herausforderungen." Pages 27–44 in *Epigraphik und Neues Testament*. Edited by Thomas Corsten, Markus Öhler, and Joseph Verheyden. WUNT 365. Tübingen: Mohr Siebeck, 2016.

Aspegren, Kerstin. *The Male Woman: A Feminine Ideal in Early Church*. Stockholm: Almqvist & Wiksell International, 1990.

Aune, David. *Prophecy in Early Christianity and the Ancient Mediterranean World*. Grand Rapids: Eerdmans, 1983.

Avalos, Hector, Sarah J. Melcher, and Jeremy Schipper, eds. *This Abled Body: Rethinking Disabilities in Biblical Studies*. SemeiaSt 55. Philadelphia: Fortress, 2007.

Baer, Richard A. *Philo's Use of the Categories Male and Female*. ALGHJ 3. Leiden: Brill, 1970.

Bal, Mieke. Foreword in *On Gendering Texts: Female and Male Voices in the Hebrew Bible*, by Athalya Brenner and Fokkelien van Dijk-Hemmes. Leiden: Brill, 1993.

Baraut, Cipriano. "Bibliografia egeriana." *HispSac* 7 (1954): 203–15.

Bar-Efrat, Shimon. *Narrative Art in the Bible*. JSOTSup 70. Sheffield: Almond, 1989.

Barrier, Jeremy W. *The Acts of Paul and Thecla: A Critical Introduction and Commentary*. WUNT 2/270. Tübingen: Mohr Siebeck, 2009.

Barthes, Roland. "The Death of the Author." Pages 142–48 in *Image—Music—Text*. New York: Hill & Wang, 1977.

Baudry, Gérard-Henry. "La responsabilité d'Eve dans la chute: Analyse d'une tradition." *MScRel* 53 (1996): 293–320.

Baumann, Gerlinde. "Die Weisheitsgestalt: Kontexte, Bedeutungen, Theologie." Pages 57–74 in *Schriften und spätere Weisheitsbücher*. Edited by Christl Maier and Nuria Calduch-Benages. BF 1.3. Stuttgart: Kohlhammer, 2013.

Becker, Adam, and Annette Yoshiko Reed. *The Ways That Never Parted: Jews and Christians in Late Antiquity and the Early Middle Ages*. Tübingen: Mohr Siebeck, 2003.

Becker, Jürgen. "Der Brief an die Galater." Pages 9–103 in *Die Briefe an die Galater, Epheser und Kolosser*, by Ulrich Luz and Jürgen Becker. NTD 8.1. Göttingen: Vandenhoeck & Ruprecht, 1998.

———. *Maria: Mutter Jesu und erwählte Jungfrau*. Leipzig: Evangelische Verlagsanstalt, 2001.

Benedict, Hans-Jürgen. "Beruht der Anspruch der evangelischen Diakonie auf einer Missinterpretation der antiken Quellen? John N. Collins Untersuchung 'Diakonia.'" Pages 117–33 in *Studienbuch Diakonik 1: Biblische, historische und theologische Zugänge zur Diakonie*. Edited by Volker Herrmann and Martin Horstmann. Neukirchen-Vluyn: Neukirchener Verlag, 2008.

Bérard, François, Denis Feissel, Nicholas Laubry, Pierre Petitmengin, Denis Rousset, and Michel Sève, with collaborators. *Guide de l'épigraphiste:*

Bibliographie choisie des épigraphies antiques et médiévales. GIBBENS 7. Paris: Éditions Rue d'Ulm, 2010.
Berlin, Adele. *Poetics and Interpretation of Biblical Narrative.* BLS 9. Sheffield: Almond, 1983.
Berquist, Jon L. *Controlling Corporeality: The Body and the Household in Ancient Israel.* New Brunswick, NJ: Rutgers University Press, 2002.
Bieberstein, Sabine. *Verschwiegene Jüngerinnen—Vergessene Zeuginnen: Gebrochene Konzepte im Lukasevangelium.* NTOA 38. Fribourg: Universitätsverlag, 1998.
Blum, Georg Günther. "Apostel/Apostolat/Apostolizität II." *TRE* 3 (1978): 445–66.
Bolyki, János. "Triangles and What Is beyond Them: Literary, Historical, and Theological Systems of Coordinates in the Acts of Andrew." Pages 70–80 in *The Apocryphal Acts of Andrew.* Edited by Jan N. Bremmer. Leuven: Peeters, 2000.
Børresen, Kari Elisabeth. "Ancient and Medieval Church Mothers." Pages 245–75 in *Women's Studies of the Christian and Islamic Traditions: Ancient, Medieval and Renaissance Foremothers*, by Elisabeth Børresen and Kari Vogt. Dordrecht: Kluwer, 1993.
Børtnes, Jostein. "Schwestern in Jungfräulichkeit: Gorgonia und Makrina in der Erinnerung ihrer Brüder." Pages 100–117 in *Christliche Autoren der Antike.* Edited by Kari Elisabeth Børresen and Emanuela Prinzivalli. BF 5.1. Stuttgart: Kohlhammer, 2015.
Boughton, Lynne C. "From Pious Legend to Feminist Fantasy: Distinguishing Hagiographycal License from Apostolic Practice in the Acts of Paul/Acts of Thecla." *JR* 71 (1991): 362–83.
Bovon, François. "Apocrypha/Pseudepigrapha III: Neues Testament." *RPP* 1:308–9.
———. "Beyond the Canonical and the Apocryphal Books, the Presence of a Third Category: The Books Useful for the Soul." *HTR* 105 (2012): 125–37.
———. "Canonical, Rejected, and Useful Books." Pages 318–23 in *New Testament and Christian Apocrypha: Collected Studies II.* Edited by Glenn E. Snyder. Tübingen: Mohr Siebeck, 2008.
———. *Das Evangelium nach Lukas (Lk 1,1–9,50).* EKKNT 3/1. Neukirchen-Vluyn: Neukirchener Verlag, 1989.
———. "Facing the Scriptures: Mimesis and Intertexuality in the Acts of Philip." Pages 267–80 in *Christian Apocrypha: Receptions of the New Testament in Ancient Christian Apocrypha.* Edited by Jean-Michel

Roessli and Tobias Nicklas. NTP 26. Göttingen: Vandenhoeck & Ruprecht, 2014.

Bowersock, Glenn W. *Julian the Apostate*. London: Duckworth, 1978.

Bowman, Glenn. "Mapping History's Redemption: Eschatology and Topography in the *Itinerarium Burdigalense*." Pages 163–87 in *Jerusalem: Its Sanctity and Centrality to Judaism, Christianity, and Islam*. Edited by Lee I. Levine. New York: Continuum, 1998.

Brakke, David. *The Gnostics: Myth, Ritual, and Diversity in Early Christianity*. Cambridge: Harvard University Press, 2010.

———. "Scriptural Practices in Early Christianity: Towards a New History of the New Testament Canon." Pages 263–80 in *Invention, Rewriting, Usurpation: Discursive Fights over Religious Traditions in Antiquity*. Edited by Jörg Ulrich, Anders-Christian Jacobsen, and David Brakke. ECCA 11. Frankfurt am Main: Lang, 2012.

Bremmer, Jan N. "Aspects of the Acts of Peter: Women, Magic, Place and Date." Pages 1–20 in *The Apocryphal Acts of Peter: Magic, Miracles and Gnosticism*. Edited by Jan N. Bremmer. Leuven: Peeters, 1998.

———. "Drusiana, Cleopatra and Some Other Women in the Acts of John." Pages 77–87 in *A Feminist Companion to the New Testament Apocrypha*. Edited by Amy-Jill Levine with Maria Mayo Robbins. FCNTECW 11. London: T&T Clark, 2006.

———. "Magic, Martyrdom and Women's Liberation in the Acts of Paul and Thecla." Pages 36–59 in *The Apocryphal Acts of Paul and Thecla*. Edited by Jan N. Bremmer. Kampen: Kok Pharos, 1996.

———. "Man, Magic, and Martyrdom in the Acts of Andrew." Pages 15–34 in *The Apocryphal Acts of Andrew*. Edited by Jan N. Bremmer. SECA 5. Leuven: Peeters, 2000.

———. "Women in the Apocryphal Acts of John." Pages 37–56 in *The Apocryphal Acts of John*. Edited by Jan N. Bremmer. Kampen: Kok Pharos, 1995.

Bremmer, Jan N., and Marco Formisano, eds. *Perpetua's Passions: Multidisciplinary Approaches to the Passio Perpetuae et Felicitatis*. Oxford: Oxford University Press, 2012.

Brenner, Athalya, and Fokkelien van Dijk-Hemmes. *On Gendering Texts: Female and Male Voices in the Hebrew Bible*. Leiden: Brill, 1993.

Brooten, Bernadette. *Love between Women: Early Christian Responses to Female Homoeroticism*. Chicago: University of Chicago Press, 1996.

———. *Women Leaders in the Ancient Synagogue: Inscriptional Evidence and Background Issues*. BJS 36. Chico, CA: Scholars Press, 1982.

Buckland, William W. *The Roman Law of Slavery: The Condition of the Slave in Private law from Augustus to Justinian*. Reprint, Holmes Beach, FL: Gaunt, 1994.

Buell, Denise Kimber. "This Changes Everything: Spiritualists, Theosophists, and Rethinking Early Christian Historiography." Pages 345–68 in *Remaking the World: Christianity and Categories*. Edited by Taylor G. Petrey. Tübingen: Mohr Siebeck, 2019.

Burrus, Virginia. *Chastity as Autonomy: Women in the Stories of the Apocryphal Acts*. SWR 23. Lewiston, NY: Mellen, 1987.

———. "Mimicking Virgins: Colonial Ambivalence and the Ancient Romance." *Arethusa* 38 (2005): 49–88.

———. "Women in Apocryphal Acts." *Semeia* 38 (1986): 101–17.

———. "Word and Flesh: The Bodies and Sexuality of Ascetic Women in Christian Antiquity." *JFSR* 10 (1994): 27–51.

Burton-Christie, Douglas. *The Word in the Desert: Scripture and the Quest for Holiness in Early Christian Monasticism*. New York: Oxford University Press, 1993.

Butler, Judith. *Bodies That Matter: On the Discursive Limits of Sex*. New York: Routledge, 1993.

———. *Gender Trouble: Feminism and the Subversion of Identity*. New York: Routledge, 1991.

———. "The Question of Social Transformation." Pages 204–31 in *Undoing Gender*. New York: Routledge, 2004.

Buttarelli, Annarosa. *Sovrane: L'autorità femminile al governo*. Milano: Il Saggiatore, 2013.

Byron, Gay L. *Symbolic Blackness and Ethnic Difference in Early Christian Literature*. London: Routledge, 2002.

Callon, Callie. "Secondary Characters Furthering Characterization: The Depiction of Slaves in the Acts of Peter." *JBL* 131 (2012): 797–818.

Calvert-Koyzis, Nancy, and Heather E. Weir. *Breaking Boundaries: Female Biblical Interpreters Who Challenged the Status Quo*. TTCLBS. New York: T&T Clark, 2010.

Cariddi, Caterina. *Il centone di Proba Petronia: Nobildonna dei IV secolo della lettertura cristiana*. Napoli: Loffredo, 1971.

Carpinello, Mariella. *Données à Dieu: Figures féminines dans les premier siècles chrétiens*. Bégrolles-en-Mauges: Abbaye de Bellefontaine, 2001.

Castelli, Elizabeth. "Heteroglosia, Hermeneutics, and History." *JFSR* 10 (1994): 73–98.

———. "Virginity and Its Meanings for Women's Sexuality in Early Christianity." *JFSR* 2 (1986): 61–88.

Chadwick, Henry. "Enkrateia." *RAC* 5 (1962): 343–65.

Chartrand-Burke, Tony. "Completing the Gospel: The Infancy Gospel of Thomas as a Supplement to the Gospel of Luke." Pages 101–19 in *The Reception and Interpretation of the Bible in Late Antiquity*. Edited by Lorenzo DiTommaso and Lucian Turescu. Leiden: Brill, 2008.

Clark, Elizabeth. "The Celibate Bridegroom and His Virginal Brides: Metaphor and the Marriage of Jesus in Early Christian Ascetic Exegesis." *CH* 77 (2008): 1–25.

———. "From Patristics to Early Christian Studies." Pages 7–41 in *The Oxford Handbook of Early Christian Studies*. Edited by Susan Ashbrook Harvey and David G. Hunter. Oxford: Oxford University Press, 2008.

———. "The Lady Vanishes: Dilemmas of a Feminist Historian after the 'Linguistic Turn.'" *CH* 67 (1998): 1–32.

———. *Reading Renunciation: Asceticism and Scripture in Early Christianity*. Princeton: Princeton University Press, 1999.

Clines, David J. A. "Paul, the Invisible Man." Pages 181–92 in *New Testament Masculinities*. Edited by Stephen D. Moore. SemeiaSt 45. Atlanta: Society of Biblical Literature, 2003.

Collins, John N. *Diakonia: Re-interpreting the Ancient Sources*. New York: Oxford University Press, 1990.

Connelly, Joan Breton. *Portrait of a Priestess: Women and Ritual in Ancient Greece*. Princeton: Princeton University Press, 2007.

Consolino, Franca Ela. "Cristianizzare l'epitalamio: Il carme 25 di Paolino di Nola." *Cassiodorus* 3 (1997): 199–213.

Conway, Colleen M. *Behold the Man: Jesus and Greco-Roman Masculinity*. New York: Oxford University Press, 2008.

Cooper, Kate. *The Virgin and the Bride: Idealized Womanhood in Late Antiquity*. Cambridge: Harvard University Press, 1996.

Corsaro, Francesco. "Memorie bibliche e suggestioni classiche nei sogni della *Passio Perpetuae et Felicitatis*." Pages 261–72 in *Gli imperatori Severi: Storia, archeologia, religione*. Edited by Enrico Dal Covolo and Giancarlo Rinaldi. Rome: LAS, 1999.

Corsini, Eugenio. "Proposte per una lettura della 'Passio Perpetua.'" Pages 480–540 in *Forma Futuri: Studi in onore del card; Michele Pellegrino*. Edited by Maria Bellis. Turin: Bottega d'Erasmo, 1975.

Cox Miller, Patricia. *Dreams in Late Antiquity: Studies in the Imagination of a Culture*. Princeton: Princeton University Press, 1994.

———. *Women in Early Christianity: Translations from Greek Texts*. Washington, DC: Catholic University of America Press, 2005.

Crüsemann, Marlene. "Unrettbar frauenfeindlich: Der Kampf um das Wort von Frauen in 1. Kor 14:34–35 im Spiegel antijudaistischer Elemente der Auslegung." Pages 23–43 in *Paulus: Umstrittene Traditionen—Lebendige Theologie: Eine feministische Lektüre*. Edited by Claudia Janssen, Luise Schottroff, and Beate Wehn. Gütersloh: Gütersloher Verlagshaus, 2001.

Daniel-Hughes, Carly. *The Salvation of the Flesh in Tertullian of Carthage: Dressing for the Resurrection*. New York: Palgrave, 2011.

Daremberg, Charles V., and Edmond Saglio. *Dictionnaire des Antiquités grecques et romaines 1, tome 2*. Paris: Hachette, 1887.

Davies, Stevan L. *The Gospel of Thomas and Christian Wisdom*. New York: Seabury, 1983.

———. *The Revolt of the Widows: The Social World of the Apocryphal Acts*. Carbondale: Southern Illinois University Press, 1980.

Davis, Stephen J. *Christ Child: Cultural Memories of a Young Jesus*. New Haven: Yale University Press, 2014.

———. "Crossed Texts, Crossed Sex: Intertextuality and Gender in Early Christian Legends of Holy Women Disguised as Men." *JECS* 10 (2002): 1–36.

———. *The Cult of Saint Thecla: A Tradition of Women's Piety in Late Antiquity*. Oxford: Oxford University Press, 2001.

———. "From Women's Piety to Male Devotion: Gender Studies, the *Acts of Paul and Thecla*, and the Evidence of an Arabic Manuscript." *HTR* 108 (2015): 579–93.

Deacy, Susan. "The Vulnerability of Athena: *Parthenoi* and Rape in Greek Myth." Pages 43–63 in *Rape in Antiquity: Sexual Violence in the Greek and Roman World*. Edited by Susan Deacy and Karen F. Pierce. London: Duckworth, 1997.

DeConick, April D. "The Great Mystery of Marriage: Sex and Conception in Ancient Valentinian Tradition." *VC* 57 (2003): 307–42.

Deissmann, Adolf. *Bibelstudien: Beiträge, zumeist aus den Papyri und Inschriften zur Geschichte der Sprache, des Schrifttums und der Religion des hellenistischen Judentums und des Urchristentums*. Repr., Hildesheim: Olms, 1977.

———. *Licht vom Osten: Das Neue Testament und die neuentdeckten Texte der hellenistisch-römischen Welt*. 4th rev. ed. Tübingen: Mohr, 1923.

Deissmann-Merten, Marieluise. "Zur Sozialgeschichte des Kindes im antiken Griechenland." Pages 267–316 in *Zur Sozialgeschichte der Kindheit*. Edited by Jochen Martin with Klaus Arnold. Freiburg: Alber, 1986.

Delling, Gerhard. "Geschlechter." *RAC* 10 (1978): 780–803.

Denzey, Nicola. "What Did the Montanists Read?" *HTR* 94 (2001): 427–48.

Destro, Adriana, and Mauro Pesce. "Dentro e fuori le case: Mutamenti del ruolo delle donne dal movimento di Gesù alle prime chiese." Pages 290–309 in *I Vangeli, narrazioni e storia*. Edited by Mercedes Navarro Puerto and Marinella Perroni. Trapani: Il Pozzo di Giacobbe, 2011.

Dietz, Maribel. *Wandering Monks, Virgins and Pilgrims: Ascetic Travel in the Mediterranean World A.D. 300–800*. University Park: Pennsylvania State University Press, 2005.

Dodds, Eric R. *Pagan and Christian in an Age of Anxiety: Some Aspects of Religious Experience from Marcus Aurelius to Constantine*. Cambridge: Cambridge University Press, 1990.

Douglas, Mary. *Implicit Meanings: Selected Essays in Anthropology*. London: Routledge, 1975.

———. *Natural Symbols: Explorations in Cosmology*. London: Cresset, 1970.

———. *Purity and Danger: An Analysis of Concepts of Pollution and Taboo*. London: Routledge, 1966.

Douglass, Laurie. "A New Look at the Itinerarium Burdigalense." *JECS* 4 (1996): 313–33.

Dreyer, Boris. "Ausbildung und Beruf." Pages 157–82 in *Handbuch der Erziehung und Bildung in der Antike*. Edited by Johannes Christes, Richard Klein, and Christoph Lüth. Darmstadt: Wissenschaftliche Buchgesellschaft, 2006.

Dronke, Peter. *Women Writers of the Middle Ages: A Critical Study of Text from Perpetua to Marguerite Porete (1310)*. Cambridge: Cambridge University Press, 1984.

Dulk, Matthijs den. "I Permit No Woman to Teach Except for Thecla: The Curious Case of the Pastoral Epistles and the *Acts of Paul* Reconsidered." *NovT* 54 (2012): 176–203.

Dunn, Peter W. "Women's Liberation, the Acts of Paul, and Other Apocryphal Acts of the Apostles: A Review of Some Recent Interpreters." *Apocrypha* 4 (1993): 245–61.

Dunning, Benjamin H. *Christ without Adam: Subjectivity and Sexual Difference in the Philosophers' Paul*. New York: Columbia University Press, 2014.

Duval, Yves-Marie. *L'affaire Jovinien: D'une crise de la société romaine à une crise de la pensée chrétienne à la fin du IVe et au début du V e siècle*. SEA 83. Rome: Institutum Patristicum Augustinianum, 2003.

Ebel, Eva. "Epigraphik (NT)." WiBiLex. 2009. https://tinyurl.com/SBL6010d.

Ebner, Martin. "Paulinische Seligspreisungen à la Thekla: Narrative Relecture der Makarismenlehre in ActThecl 5f." Pages 64–79 in *Aus Liebe zu Paulus? Die Akte Thekla neu aufgerollt*. Edited by Martin Ebner. Stuttgart: Katholisches Bibelwerk, 2005.

Eco, Umberto. *Lector in Fabula: Die Mitarbeit der Interpretation in erzählenden Texten*. Translated by Heinz-Georg Held. Munich: Dt. Taschenbuch-Verlag, 1987.

Edwards, Mark. *Catholicity and Heresy in the Early Church*. Burlington, VT: Ashgate, 2009.

Eisen, Ute E. "Frauen in leitenden Positionen im Neuen Testament und in der frühen Kirche." *BK* 65 (2010): 205–13.

———. *Die Poetik der Apostelgeschichte: Eine narratologische Studie*. Göttingen: Vandenhoeck & Ruprecht, 2006.

———. *Women Officeholders in Early Christianity: Epigraphical and Literary Studies*. Translated by Linda M. Maloney. Collegeville, MN: Liturgical Press, 2000.

Eisen, Ute E., Christine Gerber, and Angela Standhartinger. "Doing Gender—Doing Religion: Zur Frage nach der Intersektionalität in den Bibelwissenschaften. Eine Einleitung." Pages 1–33 in *Doing Gender—Doing Religion: Fallstudien zur Intersektionalität im frühen Judentum, Christentum und Islam*. Edited by Ute E. Eisen, Christine Gerber, and Angela Standhartinger. WUNT 302. Tübingen: Mohr Siebeck, 2013.

Elm, Susanna. *Virgins of God: The Making of Asceticism in Late Antiquity*. Oxford: Clarendon, 1996.

Elsner, Jas. "The Itinerarium Burdigalense: Politics and Salvation in the Geography of Constantine's Empire." *JRS* 90 (2000): 181–95.

Epp, Eldon Jay. *Junia: The First Women Apostle*. Minneapolis: Fortress, 2005.

Ermann, Joachim. "Folterrung Freier im römischen Srafprozeß der Kaiserzeit bis Antoninus Pius." *ZSS* 117 (2000): 424–31.

Esch-Wermeling, Elisabeth. *Thekla—Paulusschülerin wider Willen? Strategien der Leserlenkung in den Theklaakten.* NTAbh 53. Münster: Aschendorff, 2008.

Estévez López, Elisa. "Breaking or Submitting? Male Control of Female Body in the Apocryphal Acts." Pages 128–60 in *Geschlechterverhältnisse und Macht: Lebensformen in der Zeit des frühen Christentums.* Edited by Irmtraud Fischer and Christoph Heil. EUZ 21. Berlin: LIT, 2010.

———. "Identidades y (de)construcciones socio-religiosas en lso relatos de curación de los Hechos apócrifos de Pedro, Juan Pablo y Tecla." *EstBib* 62 (2004): 205–26.

Evans-Grubbs, Judith. "Abduction Marriage in Antiquity: A Law of Constantine (Cth. Ix. 24. I) and Its Social Context." *JRS* 79 (1989): 59–83.

Faivre, Alexandre. *Ordonner la fraternité: Pouvoir d'innover et retour à l'ordre dans l'église ancienne.* Paris: Cerf, 1992.

Fantham, Elaine, Helene Peet Foley, Natalie Boymel Kampen, Sarah B. Pomeroy, and H. Alan Shapiro. *Women in the Classical World: Image and Text.* New York: Oxford University Press, 1994.

Fernandelli, Marco. "Cultura e significati della praefatio all'Epitamio per le nozze di Onorio e Maria di Claudiano." Pages 75–125 in *Il calamo della memoria V: Riuso di testi e mestiere letterario nella tarda antichità.* Edited by Lucio Cristante and Tommaso Mazzoli. Trieste: Edizioni Università di Trieste, 2012.

Fernández Conde, Francisco Javier. *Prisciliano y el priscilianismo: Historiografía y realidad.* EHO. Gijón: Trea, 2008.

Filosini, Stefania, ed. *Sidonio Apollinare: L'epitalamio di Ruricio e Iberia.* STT 12. Turnhout: Brepols, 2014.

Fischer, Irmtraud. *Gottesstreiterinnen: Biblische Erzählungen über die Anfänge Israels.* Stuttgart: Kohlhammer, 2006.

———. *Gotteslehrerinnen: Weise Frauen und Frau Weisheit im Alten Testament.* Stuttgart: Kohlhammer, 2006.

Forcellini, Egidio, and Vincenzo De Vit. *Totius Latinitatis Lexicon.* Vol. 2. Prati: Aldiniani, 1861.

Formisano, Marco. "Perpetua's Prisons: Notes on the Margins of Literature." Pages 329–47 in *Perpetua's Passions: Multidisciplinary Approaches to the Passio Perpetuae et Felicitatis.* Edited by Jan N. Bremmer and Marco Formisano. Oxford: Oxford University Press, 2012.

Foskett, Mary F. "Virginity as Purity in the Protoevangelium of James." Pages 67–76 in *A Feminist Companion to Mariology.* Edited by Amy-

Jill Levine and Maria Mayo Robbins. FCNTECW. Edinburgh: T&T Clark, 2005.

Foucault, Michel. *The Care of the Self.* Vol. 3 of *The History of Sexuality.* London: Lane, 1988.

———. "What Is an Author?" Pages 101–20 in *The Foucault Reader.* Edited by Paul Rabinow. New York: Pantheon Books, 1984.

Franz, Marie-Louise von. *Passion of Perpetua: A Psychological Interpretation of Her Dreams.* SJPJA 110. Toronto: Inner City Books, 2004.

Gamber, Stanislas. *Le livre de la "Genèse" dans la poésie latine au Ve siècle: Versions françaises et provençales de la Genèse au moyen âge.* Reprint, Geneva: Slatkine, 1977.

García Del Valle, Carmelo. *Jerusalén, la liturgia de la iglesia madre.* Barcelona: CPL, 2001.

Garland, Robert. *The Eye of the Beholder: Deformity and Disability in the Graeco-Roman World.* Ithaca, NY: Cornell University Press, 1995.

Geerard, Maurice. *Clavis apocryphorum Novi Testamenti.* CCSA. Turnhout: Brepols, 1992.

Gelsomino, Remo. "Egeria, 381–384 d.C: dalle radici romane alle radici bibliche." Pages 243–304 in *Atti del Convegno Internazionale sulla Peregrinatio Egeriae: Nel centenario della pubblicazione del "Codex Aretinus 405," già "Aretinut VI,3," Arezzo October 23–25, 1987.* Arezzo: Academia Petrarca, 1990.

Gerber, Christine. *Paulus und seine "Kinder": Studien zur Beziehungsmetaphorik der paulinischen Briefe.* BZNW 136. Berlin: de Gruyter, 2005.

Giannarelli, Elena. "Antiche lettrici della Bibbia: Dame, martiri, pellegrine." Pages 23–48 in *La Bibbia nell'interpretazione delle donne.* Edited by Claudio Leonardi, Francesco Santi, and Adriana Valerio. CSPFF. Napoli: SISMEL edizioni del Galluzzo, 2002.

———. "Il pellegrinaggio al femminile nel cristianesimo antico: fra polemica e esemplarità." Pages 27–54 in *Donne in viaggio. Viaggio religioso, politico, metaforico.* Edited by Maria Luisa Silvester and Adriana Valerio. Rome: Edizioni Laterza, 1999.

———. "Da Tecla a santa Tecla: un caso de nemesi agiografica." *Sanctorum* 4 (2007): 1–16.

———. "Women and Travelling in Early Christian Texts: Some Aspects of a Problem." Pages 155–74 in *Gender and religion.* Edited by Kari Elisabet Børresen, Sara Cabibbo, and Edith Specht. Roma: Viella, 2001.

Glancy, Jennifer A. *Corporal Knowledge: Early Christian Bodies.* New York: Oxford University Press, 2010.

Glancy, Jennifer A., and Stephen D. Moore. "How Typical a Roman Prostitute Is Revelation's 'Great Whore'?" *JBL* 130 (2011): 551–69.
Gleason, Maud W. *Making Men: Sophists and Self-Presentation in Ancient Rome*. Princeton: Princeton University Press, 1995.
González-Haba, Mercedes. "El Itinerarium Egeriae: Un testimonio de la corriente cristiana de oposición a la cultura clásica." *EstCl* 77 (1976): 123–31.
Gorman, Jill C. "Reading and Theorizing Women's Sexuality: The Representation of Women in the Acts of Xanthippe and Polixena." PhD diss., Temple University, 2003.
Green, Roger P. H. "Proba's Cento: Its Date, Purpose and Reception." *ClQ* 45 (1995): 551–63.
Gregory, Andrew, and Christopher Tuckett. *The Oxford Handbook of Early Christian Apocrypha*. Oxford: Oxford University Press, 2015.
Habermehl, Peter. *Perpetua und der Ägypter oder Bilder des Bösen im frühen afrikanischen Christentum: Ein Versuch zur Passio Sanctarum Perpetuae et Felicitatis*. TU 140. Berlin: Akademie, 1992.
Haines-Eitzen, Kim. *The Gendered Palimpsest: Women, Writing, and Representation in Early Christianity*. Oxford: Oxford University Press, 2012.
———. "Women's Literature? The Case of the Apocryphal Acts of the Apostles." Pages 53–64 in *The Gendered Palimpsest: Women, Writing, and Representation in Early Christianity*. Oxford: Oxford University Press, 2012
Haley, Shelley P. "Be Not Afraid of the Dark: Critical Race Theory and Classical Studies." Pages 27–49 in *Prejudice and Christian Beginnings: Investigating Race, Gender and Ethnicity in Early Christian Studies*. Edited by Elisabeth Schüssler Fiorenza and Laura Salah Nasrallah. Minneapolis: Augsburg Fortress, 2009.
Hanson, Ann Ellis. "The Eight Months' Child and the Etiquette of Birth: Obsit Omen!" *BHM* 61 (1987): 589–602.
Harnack, Adolf von. *The History of Dogma*. 4 vols. Translated by Neil Buchanan. New York: Dover, 1961.
———. "Probabilia über die Adresse und den Verfasser des Hebräerbriefs." *ZNW* 1 (1900): 16–41.
Harrill, J. Albert. *Slaves in the New Testament: Literary, Social, and Moral Dimensions*. Minneapolis: Fortress, 2006.
Hartenstein, Judith. "Autoritätskonstellationen in apokryphen und kanonischen Evangelien." Pages 423–44 in *Jesus in apokryphen Evange-*

lienüberlieferungen: Beiträge zu außerkanonischen Jesusüberlieferungen aus verschiedenen Sprach- und Kulturtraditionen. Edited by Jörg Frey and Jens Schröter. WUNT 254. Tübingen: Mohr Siebeck, 2010.

———. *Charakterisierung im Dialog: Maria Magdalena, Petrus, Thomas und die Mutter Jesu im Johannesevangelium im Kontext anderer frühchristlicher Darstellungen.* NTOA 64. Göttingen: Vandenhoeck & Ruprecht, 2007.

———. *Die zweite Lehre: Erscheinungen des Auferstandenen als Rahmenerzählungen frühchristlicher Dialoge.* Berlin: Akademie, 2000.

Hartman, Lars. "Ἱεροσόλυμα, Ἱερουσαλήμ." *EWNT* 2 (1992): 432–39.

Harvey, Susan Ashbrook. "Women and Words: Texts by and about Women." Pages 382–90 in *The Cambridge History of Early Christian Literature.* Edited by Frances Young, Lewis Ayres, and Andrew Louth. Cambridge: Cambridge University Press, 2004.

Hegermann, Harald. "σοφία." *EWNT* 3 (1983): 616–24.

Heininger, Bernhard. *Paulus als Visionär: Eine religionsgeschichtliche Studie.* Freiburg: Herder, 1996.

Hentschel, Anni. *Diakonia im Neuen Testament: Studien zur Semantik unter besonderer Berücksichtigung der Rolle der Frauen.* WUNT 2/226. Tübingen: Mohr Siebeck, 2007.

Hirschmann, Vera. *Horrenda Secta: Untersuchungen zum frühchristlichen Montanismus und seinen Verbindungen zur paganen Religion Phrygiens.* Stuttgart: Steiner, 2005.

Hoklotubbe, T. Christopher. *Civilized Piety: The Rhetoric of Pietas in the Pastoral Epistles and Roman Empire.* Waco, TX: Baylor University Press, 2017.

Holmes, Michael W. "The Biblical Canon." Pages 406–26 in *The Oxford Handbook of Early Christian Studies.* Edited by Susan Ashbrook Harvey and David G. Hunter. Oxford: Oxford University Press, 2008.

Horn, Cornelia B. "Suffering Children, Parental Authority and the Quest for Liberation? A Tale of Three Girls in the Acts of Paul (and Thecla), The Act(s) of Peter, the Acts of Nerseus and Achilleus and the Epistle of Pseudo-Titus." Pages 118–45 in *A Feminist Companion to the New Testament Apocrypha.* Edited by Amy-Jill Levine with Maria Mayo Robbins. FCNTECW 11. London: T&T Clark, 2006.

Horn, Cornelia B., and John Wesley Martens. *"Let the Little Children Come to Me": Childhood and Children in Early Christianity.* Washington, DC: Catholic University of America Press, 2009.

Hunter, David. "Resistance to the Virginal Ideal in Late-Fourth Century Rome: The Case of Jovinian." *TS* 48 (1987): 45–64.
Hylen, Susan E. "The 'Domestication' of Saint Thecla: Characterization of Thecla in the *Life and Miracles of Saint Thecla*." *JFSR* 30 (2014): 5–21.
———. *A Modest Apostle: Thecla and the History of Women in the Early Church*. Oxford: Oxford University Press, 2015.
Ipsen, Avaren. *Sex Working and the Bible*. London: Equinox, 2009.
Irwin, M. Eleanor. "Gender, Status and Identity in a North African Martyrdom." Pages 251–60 in *Gli imperatori Severi: Storia, archeologia, religione*. Edited by Enrico Dal Covolo and Giancarlo Rinaldi. Rome: LAS, 1999.
Ivarsson, Fredrik. "Vice Lists and Deviant Masculinity: The Rhetorical Function of 1 Corinthians 5:10–11 and 6:9–10." Pages 162–84 in *Mapping Gender in Ancient Religious Discourses*. Edited by Todd C. Penner and Caroline Vander Stichele. Leiden: Brill, 2007.
Jacobs, Andrew S. "A Family Affair: Marriage, Class, and Ethics in the Apocryphal Acts of the Apostles." *JECS* 7 (1999): 105–38.
———. "Jews and Christians." Pages 169–85 in *The Oxford Handbook of Early Christian Studies*. Edited by Susan Ashbrook Harvey and David G. Hunter. Oxford: Oxford University Press, 2008.
———. *Remains of the Jews: The Holy Land and Christian Empire in Late Antiquity*. Stanford, CA: Stanford University Press, 2004.
Janeras, Sebastià. "Addenda." *RCT* 28 (2003): 507–10.
———. "Bibliografia egeriana recent." *RCT* 28 (2003): 231–40.
———. "Contributo alla bibliografia egeriana." Pages 355–66 in *Atti del Convegno Internazionale sulla Peregrinatio Egeriae: Nel centenario della pubblicazione del "Codex Aretinus 405," già "Aretinut VI,3," Arezzo October 23–25, 1987*. Arezzo: Academia Petrarca, 1990.
———. "Noves publicacions sobre Egèria." *MLC* 19 (2011): 23–30.
Jensen, Anne. *God's Self-Confident Daughters: Early Christianity and the Liberation of Women*. Louisville: John Knox, 1992.
———. *Thekla—Die Apóstolin: Ein apokrypher Text neu entdeckt*. FKG 3. Gütersloh: Kaiser, 1999.
Jones, Arnold H. M., John R. Martindale, and John Morris. *The Prosopography of the Later Roman Empire. Vol. 1, A.D. 260–395*. Cambridge: Cambridge University Press, 1971.
Kaiser, Ursula Ulrike. "Jesus als enfant terrible in verschiedenen Versionen der apokryphen 'Kindheitserzählung des Thomas'—Ein synoptischer

Vergleich von KThom 4." Uukaiser (blog), March 18, 2011. https://tinyurl.com/SBL6010a.

———. "Jesus als Kind: Neuere Forschungen zur Jesusüberlieferung in den apokryphen 'Kindheitsevangelien.'" Pages 253–69 in *Jesus in apokryphen Evangelienüberlieferungen: Beiträge zu außerkanonischen Jesusüberlieferungen aus verschiedenen Sprach- und Kulturtraditionen*. Edited by Jörg Frey and Jens Schröter. WUNT 254. Tübingen: Mohr Siebeck, 2010.

———. "Die sogenannte 'Kindheitserzählung des Thomas': Überlegungen zur Darstellung Jesu als Kind, deren Intention und Rezeption." Pages 459–81 in *Infancy Gospels: Stories and Identities*. Edited by Claire Clivaz, Andreas Dettwiler, Luc Devillers, and Enrico Norelli. WUNT 281. Tübingen: Mohr Siebeck, 2011.

Kanaan, Marlène. "Jésus et le roi Abgar." *CPE* 94 (2004): 12–20.

Kartzow, Marianne Bjelland. *Destabilizing the Margins: An Intersectional Approach to Early Christian Memory*. Eugene, OR: Pickwick, 2012.

———. *Gossip and Gender: Othering of Speech in the Pastoral Epistles*. BZNW 164. Berlin: de Gruyter, 2009.

King, Karen L. "The Place of the Gospel of Philip in the Context of Early Christian Claims about Jesus's Marital Status." *NTS* 59 (2013): 565–87.

———. "Reading Sex and Gender in the Secret Revelation of John." *JECS* 19 (2011): 519–38.

———. *The Secret Revelation of John*. Cambridge: Harvard University Press, 2006.

———. "Toward a Discussion of the Category 'Gnosis/Gnosticism': The Case of the Epistle of Peter to Philip." Pages 445–65 in *Jesus in apokryphen Evangelienüberlieferungen: Beiträge zu außerkanonischen Jesusüberlieferungen aus verschiedenen Sprach- und Kulturtraditionen*. Edited by Jörg Frey and Jens Schröter. WUNT 254. Tübingen: Mohr Siebeck, 2010.

———. "'What Is an Author?': Ancient Author-Function in the Apocryphon of John and the Apocalypse of John." Pages 15–42 in *Scribal Practices and Social Structures among Jesus Adherents: Essays in Honour of John S. Kloppenborg*. Edited by William E. Arnal, Richard S. Ascough, Robert A. Derrenbacker Jr., and Philip A. Harland. BETL 285. Leuven: Peeters, 2016.

———. *What Is Gnosticism?* Cambridge: Harvard University Press, 2003.

———. "Which Early Christianity?" Pages 66–84 in *The Oxford Handbook of Early Christian Studies*. Edited by Susan Ashbrook Harvey and David G. Hunter. Oxford: Oxford University Press, 2008.

Klauck, Hans-Josef. *The Apocryphal Acts of the Apostles: An Introduction*. Translated by Brian McNeil. Waco, TX: Baylor University Press, 2008.

Klawitter, Frederick C. "The New Prophecy in Early Christianity: The Origin, Nature, and Development of Montanism, A.D. 165–220." PhD diss., University of Chicago, 1975.

Kloppenborg, John S. "Isis and Sophia in the Book of Wisdom." *HTR* 75 (1982): 57–84.

Konstan, David. "Suche und Verwandlung: Transformation von Erzählmustern in den hellenistischen Romanen und den apokryphen Apostelakten." Pages 251–68 in *Askese und Identität in Spätantike, Mittelalter und früher Neuzeit*. Edited by Werner Röcke and Julia Weitbrecht. TA 14. Berlin: de Gruyter, 2010.

Kraemer, Ross Shepard. "The Conversion of Women to Ascetic Forms of Christianity." *Signs* 6 (1980): 298–307.

———. *Unreliable Witnesses: Religion, Gender, and History in the Greco-Roman Mediterranean*. Oxford: Oxford University Press, 2011.

———. "Women's Authorship of Jewish and Christian Literature in the Greco-Roman Period." Pages 221–42 in *"Women like This": New Perspectives on Jewish Women in the Greco-Roman World*. Edited by Amy-Jill Levine. EJL 1. Atlanta: Scholars Press, 1991.

Kudlick, Catherine J. "Disability History: Why We Need Another 'Other.'" *AHR* 108 (2003): 763–93.

Kyriakidis, Stratis. "Eve and Mary: Proba's Technique in the Creation of Two Different Female Figures." *MDATC* 29 (1992): 121–53.

Laes, Christian, Chris F. Goodey, and Martha Lynn Rose, eds. *Disabilities in Roman Antiquity: Disparate Bodies a Capite ad Calcem*. Leiden: Brill, 2013.

Lahe, Jaan. *Gnosis und Judentum*. NHMS 75. Leiden: Brill, 2012.

Lampe, Gunna. "So anders? Die Wundertätigkeit Jesu im Kindheitsevangelium des Thomas: Eine intertextuelle Untersuchung zur Darstellung der Wundertaten und des Wundertäters in den Paidika." PhD diss., Justus-Liebig-Universität Gießen, 2019.

Lampe, Peter, and William Tabbernee. *Pepouza and Tymion: The Discovery and Archeological Exploration of a Lost Ancient City and an Imperial Estate*. Berlin: de Gruyter, 2008.

Lanata, Giuliana. "Sogni di donne nel primo cristianesimo." Pages 77–98 in *Donne sante, sante donne: Esperienza religiosa e storia di genere*. SIDS. Turin: Rosenberg & Sellier, 1996.

Lanzillotta, Lautaro Roig. *Acta Andreae Apocrypha: A New Perspective on the Nature, Intention and Significance of the Primitive Text*. Geneva: Cramer, 2007.

Lapp, Joy L. "Chaste Women: Characterization in the Apocryphal Acts of Apostles and the Greek Romance Novels." PhD diss., University of Denver/Iliff School of Theology, 2002.

Laqueur, Thomas. *Making Sex: Body and Gender from the Greeks to Freud*. Cambridge: Harvard University Press, 1990.

Lawrence, Louise Joy. *Sense and Stigma in the Gospels: Depictions of Sensory-Disabled Characters*. Oxford: Oxford University Press, 2013.

Layton, Bentley. "Prolegomena to the Study of Ancient Gnosticism." Pages 334–50 in *The Social World of the First Christians: Essays in Honor of Wayne A. Meeks*. Edited by L. Michael White and O. Larry Yarbrough. Minneapolis: Fortress, 1995.

———, ed. *The Rediscovery of Gnosticism: Proceedings of the International Conference on Gnosticism at Yale, New Haven, Connecticut, March 28–31, 1978*. 2 vols. Leiden: Brill, 1981.

Lefkowitz, Mary R. "The Motivations for St. Perpetua's Martyrdom." *JAAR* 44 (1976): 417–21.

Lehtipuu, Outi. "Apostolic Authority and Women in Second-Century Christianity." Pages 609–24 in *Receptions of Paul in Early Christianity: The Person of Paul and His Writings through the Eyes of His Early Interpreters*. Edited by Jens Schröter, Simon Butticaz, and Andreas Dettwiler. BZNW 234. Berlin: de Gruyter, 2018.

———. "The Distorters of Resurrection in Apocryphal Acts and Other Early Christian Texts: The Threat of Deviance." Pages 184–98 in *Voces Clamantium in Deserto: Essays in Honor of Kari Syreeni*. SEJ. Åbo: Teologiska fakulteten, 2012.

———. "The Example of Thecla and the Example(s) of Paul: Disputing Women's Role in Early Christianity." Pages 349–78 in *Women and Gender in Ancient Religions: Interdisciplinary Approaches*. Edited by Stephen P. Ahearne-Kroll, Paul A. Holloway, and James A. Kelhofer. WUNT 263. Tübingen: Mohr Siebeck, 2010.

———. "'Flesh and Blood Cannot Inherit the Kingdom of God': The Transformation of the Flesh in Early Christian Debates." Pages 147–68 in *Metamorphoses: Resurrection, Body and Transformative Practices in*

Early Christianity. Edited by Turid Karlsen Seim and Jorunn Økland. Berlin: de Gruyter, 2009.

———. "To Remarry or Not to Remarry: 1 Timothy 5:14 in Early Christian Ascetic Discourse." *ST* 1 (2017): 29–50.

———. "Who Has the Right to Be Called a Christian? Deviance and Christian Identity in Tertullian's *On the Prescription of Heretics*." Pages 80–98 in *Methods, Theories, Imagination: Social Scientific Approaches in Biblical Studies*. Edited by David Chalcraft, Frauke Uhlenbruch, and Rebecca Sally Watson. Sheffield: Sheffield Phoenix, 2014.

Levine, Amy-Jill, with Maria Mayo Robins, eds. *A Feminist Companion to the New Testament Apocrypha*. FCNTECW 11. London: T&T Clark, 2006.

Lieu, Judith M. *Christian Identity in the Jewish and Graeco-Roman World*. Oxford: Oxford University Press, 2004.

Linage Conde, Antonio. *Los orígenes del monacato benedictino en la península ibérica*. Vol. 1. León: Centro de Estudio y de Investigación San Isidoro, 1973.

Lips, Hermann von. "Christus als Sophia? Weisheitliche Traditionen in der urchristlichen Christologie." Pages 75–95 in *Anfänge der Christologie: Festschrift Ferdinand Hahn*. Edited by Cilliers Breytenbach and Henning Paulsen with Christine Gerber. Göttingen: Vandenhoeck & Ruprecht, 1991.

———. *Weisheitliche Traditionen im Neuen Testament*. WMANT 64. Neukirchen-Vluyn: Neukirchener Verlag, 1990.

Loland, Hanne. *Silent or Salient Gender? The Interpretation of Gendered God-Language in the Hebrew Bible, Exemplified in Isaiah 42, 46 and 49*. Tübingen: Mohr Siebeck, 2008.

Lührmann, Dieter. *Die apokryph gewordenen Evangelien. Studien zu neuen Texten und zu neuen Fragen*. NovTSup 112. Leiden: Brill, 2004.

———. *Fragmente apokryph gewordener Evangelien in griechischer und lateinischer Sprache*. MTS 59. Marburg: Elwert, 2000.

Luz, Ulrich. *Das Evangelium nach Matthäus (Mt 8–17)*. EKK 1/2. Neukirchen-Vluyn: Neukirchener Verlag, 1990.

MacDonald, Dennis R. "The Acts of Paul and the Acts of John: Which Came First?" Pages 506–10 in *Society of Biblical Literature 1992 Seminar Papers*. Atlanta: Scholars Press, 1992.

———. "The Acts of Peter and the Acts of John: Which Came First?" Pages 623–33 in *Society of Biblical Literature 1993 Seminar Papers*. Atlanta: Scholars Press, 1993.

———. *Christianizing Homer: The Odyssey, Plato, and the Acts of Andrew.* New York: Oxford University Press, 1994.
———. *The Legend and the Apostle: The Battle for Paul in Story and Canon.* Philadelphia: Westminster, 1983.
MacDonald, Margaret Y. *Early Christian Women and Pagan Opinion: The Power of the Hysterical Woman.* Cambridge: Cambridge University Press, 1996.
———. "Women as Agents of Expansion." Pages 220–43 in *A Woman's Place: House Churches in Earliest Christianity.* Edited by Carolyn Osiek and Margaret Y. MacDonald with Janet H. Tulloch. Minneapolis: Fortress, 2006.
Mack, Burton L. *Logos und Sophia: Untersuchungen zur Weisheitstheologie im hellenistischen Judentum.* SUNT 10. Göttingen: Vandenhoeck & Ruprecht, 1973.
Mader, Heidrun. *Montanistische Orakel und kirchliche Opposition: Der frühe Streit zwischen den phrygischen "neuen Propheten" und dem Autor der vorepiphaninschen Quelle als biblische Wirkungsgeschichte des 2. Jh. n. Chr.* Göttingen: Vandenhoeck & Ruprecht, 2012.
Malick-Prunier, Sophie. "Le corps féminin et ses représentations poétiques dans la latinité tardive." PhD diss., Université Paris-Sorbonne, 2008.
Maraval, Pierre. "Les Catéchèses baptismales de Cyrille de Jérusalem et le témoignage d'Égérie." *CPE* 91 (2003): 29–35.
———. "La découverte de la croix au IVe siècle." *CPE* 89 (2003): 10–14.
———. "Égérie et Grégoire de Nysse." Pages 315–31 in *Atti del Convegno Internazionale sulla Peregrinatio Egeriae: Nel centenario della pubblicazione del "Codex Aretinus 405," già "Aretinut VI,3," Arezzo October 23–25, 1987.* Arezzo: Academia Petrarca, 1990.
Marjanen, Antti. "Female Prophets among Montanists." Pages 127–43 in *Prophets Male and Female: Gender and Prophecy in the Hebrew Bible, the Eastern Mediterranean, and the Ancient Near East.* Edited by Jonathan Stökl and Corrine L. Carvalho. AIL 15. Atlanta: Society of Biblical Literature, 2013.
———. "Gnosticism." Pages 203–20 in *The Oxford Handbook of Early Christian Studies.* Edited by Susan Ashbrook Harvey and David G. Hunter. Oxford: Oxford University Press, 2008.
———. "Male Women Martyrs: The Function of Gender Transformation Language in Early Christian Martyrdom Accounts." Pages 231–47 in *Metamorphoses: Resurrection, Body and Transformative Practices in*

Early Christianity. Edited by Turid Karlsen Seim and Jorunn Økland. Berlin: de Gruyter, 2009.

———. "Rewritten Eve Traditions in the Apocryphon of John." Pages 57–67 in *Bodies, Borders, Believers: Ancient Texts and Present Conversations; Essays in Honor of Turid Karlsen Seim on Her Seventieth Birthday*. Edited by Anne Hege Grung, Marianne Bjelland Kartzow, and Anna Rebecca Solevåg. Eugene, OR: Pickwick, 2015.

———. "The Seven Women Disciples in the Two Versions of the First Apocalypse of James." Pages 535–46 in *The Codex Judas Papers: Proceedings of the International Congress on the Tchacos Codex Held at Rice University, Houston, Texas, March 13–16, 2008*. Edited by April D. DeConick. NHMS 71. Leiden: Brill, 2009.

Markschies, Christoph. "Haupteinleitung." Pages 1–183 in *Evangelien und Verwandtes*. Vol. 1.1 of *Antike christliche Apokryphen in deutscher Übersetzung*. Edited by Christoph Markschies and Jens Schröter. Tübingen: Mohr Siebeck, 2012.

———. "Montanismus." *RGG* 5:1471–73.

———. *Valentinus Gnosticus? Untersuchungen zur valentinianischen Gnosis mit einem Kommentar zu den Fragmenten Valentins*. Tübingen: Mohr Siebeck, 1992.

Markschies, Christoph, and Jens Schröter, eds. *Evangelien und Verwandtes*. Vol. 1.1 of *Antike christliche Apokryphen in deutscher Übersetzung*. Tübingen: Mohr Siebeck, 2012.

Mărmureanu, Cătălina, Gianina Cernescu, and Laura Lixandru. "Early Christian Women Writers: The Interesting Lives and Works of Faltonia Betitia Proba and Athenais Eudocia." Master's thesis, University of Bucharest, 2008.

Martimort, Aimé Georges. *Les diaconesses: Essai historique*. Roma: Edizioni Liturgiche, 1982.

Martos, Ana. *Papisas y teólogas: Mujeres que gobernaron el reino de Dios en la tierra*. HI. Madrid: Nowtilus, 2008.

Matthews, Shelly. "Thinking of Thecla: Issues in Feminist Historiography." *JFSR* 17 (2001): 39–55.

Mayer-Maly, Theodor. "Vidua." PW 2/16:2098–2107.

Mayordomo, Moisés. "Jesu Männlichkeit im Markusevangelium: Eine Spurensuche." Pages 359–79 in *Doing Gender—Doing Religion: Fallstudien zur Intersektionalität im frühen Judentum, Christentum und Islam*. Edited by Ute E. Eisen, Christine Gerber, and Angela Standhartinger. WUNT 302. Tübingen: Mohr Siebeck, 2013.

Mazzucco, Clementina. "*E fui fatta maschio*": *La donna nel cristianesimo primitivo (secoli 1–3)*. Florence: Le Lettere, 1998.

McGinn, Sheila E. "The Acts of Thecla." Pages 800–828 in vol. 2 of *Searching the Scriptures: A Feminist Commentary*. Edited by Elizabeth Schüssler-Fiorenza. New York: Crossroad, 1994.

McGinn, Thomas A. J. *Prostitution, Sexuality, and the Law in Ancient Rome*. New York: Oxford University Press, 1998.

McGuire, Anne. "Virginity and Subversion: Norea against the Powers in the Hypostasis of the Archons." Pages 239–58 in *Images of the Feminine in Gnosticism*. Edited by Karen L. King. SAC. Philadelphia: Fortress, 1988.

Mckechnie, Paul. "St. Perpetua and Roman Education I A.D. 200." *AC* 63 (1994): 279–91.

McRae, George W. "The Jewish Background of the Gnostic Sophia Myth." *NovT* 12 (1970): 86–101.

Merz, Annette. *Die fiktive Selbstauslegung des Paulus: Intertextuelle Studien zur Intention und Rezeption der Pastoralbriefe*. NTOA 52. Göttingen: Vandenhoeck & Ruprecht, 2004.

———. "Phöbe von Kenchreä: Kollegin und Patronin des Paulus." *BK* 65 (2010): 228–32.

Meslin, Michel. "Vases sacres et boisson d'eternité dans les visions des martyrs africains." Pages 139–53 in *Epektasis:* Mélanges patristiques offerts au Cardinal Jean Daniélou. Edited by Jacques Fontaines and Charles Kannengiesser. Paris: Beauchesne, 1972.

Meyer, Marvin W. "Making Mary Male: The Categories 'Male' and 'Female' in the Gospel of Thomas." *NTS* 31 (1985): 554–70.

Milani, Celestina. "Studi sull' Itinerarium Egeriae: L'aspetto classico della lingua di Egeria." *Aev* 43 (1969): 381–452.

Milco, Katherine E. "*Mulieres viriliter vincentes*: Masculine and Feminine Imagery in Augustine's Sermons on Sts. Perpetua and Felicity." *VC* 69 (2015): 276–95.

Militello, Cettina. *Il volto femminile della storia*. Casale Monferrato: Piemme, 1995.

———. "Un'avventura coniugale." Pages 168–90 in *L'amicizia tra uomo e donna nei primi 13 secoli del cristianesimo*. Edited by Clementina Mazzucco, Cettina Militello, and Adriana Valerio. Milan: Paoline, 1990.

Miroshnikov, Ivan. "'For Women Are Not Worthy of Life': Protology and Misogyny in Gospel of Thomas Saying 114." Pages 175–86 in *Women and Knowledge in Early Christianity*. Edited by Ulla Tervahauta, Ivan

Miroshnikov, Outi Lehtipuu, and Ismo Dunderberg. VCSup 144. Leiden: Brill, 2017.

Misset-van de Weg, Magda. "'For the Lord Always Takes Care of His Own': The Purpose of the Wondrous Works and Deeds in the Acts of Peter." Pages 97–110 in *The Apocryphal Acts of Peter: Magic, Miracles and Gnosticism*. Edited by Jan N. Bremmer. Leuven: Peeters, 1998.

Mitchell, David T., and Sharon L. Snyder. *Narrative Prosthesis: Disability and the Dependencies of Discourse*. Ann Arbor: University of Michigan Press, 2001.

Mohrmann, Christine. "Égérie et le monachisme." Pages 163–80 in vol. 1 of *Corona Gratiarum: Miscellanea patristica, historica et liturgica Eligio Dekkers XII lustra complenti oblata*. Bruges: Nijhoff, 1975.

Mommsen, Theodor. *Römisches Strafrecht*. Leipzig: Duncker & Humblot, 1899.

Moore, Stephen D. *God's Beauty Parlor and Other Queer Spaces in and around the Bible*. Stanford, CA: Stanford University Press, 2001.

Moretti, Paola F. "La Bibbia e il discorso dei Padri latini sulle donne: Da Tertullian a Girolamo." Pages 137–73 in *Le donne nello sguardo degli antichi autori cristiani: L'uso dei testi biblici nella costruzione dei modelli femminili*. Edited by Kari E. Børresen and Emanuela Prinzivalli. Trapani: Il pozzo di Giacobbe, 2013.

Moriarty, Rachel. "'Playing the Man': The Courage of Christian Martyrs, Translated and Transposed." Pages 1–10 in *Gender and Christian Religion: Papers Read at the 1996 Summer Meeting and the 1997 Winter Meeting of the Ecclesiastical History Society*. Edited by Robert N. Swanson. Rochester, NY: Boydell, 1998.

Moss, Candida R., and Jeremy Schipper. *Disability Studies and Biblical Literature*. Basingstoke: Palgrave Macmillan, 2011.

Mundó, Anscario. "Il monachesimo nella penisola iberica fino al s. VII. Questioni ideologiche e letterarie." Pages 73–108 in *Il monachesimo nell'alto Medioevo e la formazione della civiltà occidentale: Atti della IV settimana di studio dall'8 al 14 aprile 1956*. Spoleto: CISAM, 1957.

Muraro, Luisa. *Il Dio delle donne*. Milano: Mondadori, 2003.

Nanos, Mark. "Paul's Reversal of Jews Calling Gentiles 'Dogs' (Philippians 3:2): 1600 Years of an Ideological Tail Wagging an Exegetical Dog?" *BibInt* 17 (2009): 448–82.

Nasrallah, Laura S. "'She Became What the Words Signified': The Greek Acts of Andrew's Construction of the Reader-Disciple." Pages 231–58 in *The Apocryphal Acts of the Apostles*. Edited by François Bovon, Ann

Graham Brock, and Christopher R. Matthews. Cambridge: Harvard University Press, 1999.

Ng, Esther Yue L. "Acts of Paul and Thecla: Women's Stories and Precedent?" *JTS* NS 55 (2004): 1–29.

Nielsen, Hanne S. "Vibia Perpetua: An Indecent Woman." Pages 103–17 in *Perpetua's Passions: Multidisciplinary Approaches to the Passio Perpetuae et Felicitatis*. Edited by Jan N. Bremmer and Marco Formisano. Oxford: Oxford University Press, 2012.

Oesterheld, Christian. *Göttliche Botschaften und zweifelnde Menschen: Pragmatik und Orientierungsleistung der Apollon-Orakel von Klaros und Didyma in hellenistisch-römischer Zeit*. Göttingen: Vandenhoeck & Ruprecht, 2008.

Office of the United Nations High Commissioner for Human Rights. "Thematic Study on the Issue of Violence against Women and Girls and Disability." 30 March 2012. https://tinyurl.com/SBL6010b.

Økland, Jorunn. *Women in Their Place: Paul and the Corinthian Discourse of Gender and Sanctuary Space*. JSNTSup 269. London: T&T Clark, 2004.

Olyan, Saul M. *Disability in the Hebrew Bible: Interpreting Mental and Physical Differences*. New York: Cambridge University Press, 2008.

Osiek, Carolyn, and Margaret Y. MacDonald. *A Woman's Place: House Churches in Earliest Christianity*. Minneapolis: Fortress, 2006.

Park, Eung Chun. "ΑΓΝΕΙΑ as a Sublime ΕΡΩΣ in the Acts of Paul and Thecla." Pages 215–26 in *Distant Voices Drawing Near: Essays in Honor of Antoinette Clark Wire*. Edited by Holly E. Hearon. Collegeville, MN: Liturgical Press, 2004.

Parrott, Douglas M. "Gnostic and Orthodox Disciples in the Second and Third Centuries." Pages 193–219 in *Nag Hammadi, Gnosticism, and Early Christianity*. Edited by Charles W. Hedrick. Peabody, MA: Hendrickson, 1986.

Pearson, Birger. "The Figure of Norea in Gnostic Literature." Pages 84–93 in *Gnosticism, Judaism, and Egyptian Christianity*. SAC 5. Minneapolis: Fortress, 1990.

———. "Revisiting Norea." Pages 265–75 in *Images of the Feminine in Gnosticism*. Edited by Karen L. King. SAC. Philadelphia: Fortress, 1988.

Perkins, Judith B. "The Acts of Peter as Intertext: Response to Dennis MacDonald." Pages 627–33 in *Society of Biblical Literature 1993 Seminar Papers*. Atlanta: Scholars Press, 1993.

———. *The Suffering Self: Pain and Narrative Representation in the Early Christian Era*. London: Routledge, 1995.

Perkins, Pheme. "Gnosticism and the Christian Bible." Pages 355–71 in *The Canon Debate*. Edited by Lee Martin McDonald and James A. Sanders. Peabody, MA: Hendrickson, 2002.

Perroni, Marinella. "Disciples, Not Apostles: Luke's Double Message." Pages 173–213 in *The Bible and Women: An Encyclopaedia of Exegesis and Cultural History 4*. Edited by Mercedes Navarro Puerto and Marinella Perroni. Atlanta: SBL Press, 2015.

Pervo, Richard I. *The Making of Paul: Constructions of the Apostle in Early Christianity*. Minneapolis: Fortress, 2010.

———. "Shepherd of the Lamb: Paul as a Christ-Figure in the Acts of Paul." Pages 355–69 in *Portraits of Jesus*. Edited by Susan E. Myers. WUNT 2/321. Tübingen: Mohr Siebeck, 2012.

Pesthy, Monika. "Thecla among the Fathers of the Church." Pages 164–78 in *The Apocryphal Acts of Paul and Thecla*. Edited by Jan N. Bremmer. Kampen: Kok Pharos, 1996.

Petersen, Silke. *Brot Licht und Weinstock: Intertextuelle Analysen johanneischer Ich-bin-Worte*. NovTSup 127. Leiden: Brill, 2008.

———. "Die Evangelienüberschriften und die Entstehung des neutestamentlichen Kanons." *ZNW* 97 (2006): 250–74.

———. "Maria Magdalena wird männlich, oder: Antike Geschlechtertransformationen." Pages 117–39 in *Unbeschreiblich weiblich? Neue Fragestellungen zur Geschlechterdifferenz in den Religionen*. Edited by Christine Gerber, Silke Petersen, and Wolfram Weiße. TFE 26. Berlin: LIT, 2011.

———. "Nicht mehr 'männlich und weiblich' (Gen 1,27). Die Rede von der Aufhebung der Geschlechterdifferenz im frühen Christentum." Pages 78–109 in *Geschlechterverhältnisse und Macht: Lebensformen in der Zeit des frühen Christentums*. Edited by Irmtraud Fischer and Christoph Heil. EUZ 21. Vienna: LIT, 2010.

———. "'Die sieben Frauen—Sieben Geistkräfte sind sie': Frauen und Weiblichkeit in der Schrift 'Jakobus' (CT 2) und der (ersten) Apokalypse des Jakobus (NHC V,3)." Pages 189–211 in *Judasevangelium und Codex Tchacos: Studien zur religionsgeschichtlichen Verortung einer gnostischen Schriftensammlung*. Edited by Enno E. Popkes. WUNT 297. Tübingen: Mohr Siebeck, 2012.

———. "'Wenn ihr Christus anzieht … ' (Gal 3,27). Kleidung, Taufe und Geschlechterdifferenz im frühen Christentum." Pages 157–79 in *Das neue Kleid: Feministisch-theologische Perspektiven auf geistliche und weltliche Gewänder*. Edited by Elisabeth Hartlieb, Jutta Koslowski, and Ulrike Wagner-Rau. Sulzbach: Helmer, 2010.

———. *"Zerstört die Werke der Weiblichkeit!": Maria Magdalena, Salome und andere Jüngerinnen Jesu in christlich-gnostischen Schriften*. NHMS 48. Leiden: Brill, 1999.

Petrey, Taylor G. *Resurrecting Parts: Early Christians on Desire, Reproduction, and Sexual Difference*. New York: Routledge, 2015.

Pfitzner, Victor C. *Paul and the Agon Motif: Traditional Athletic Imagery in the Pauline Literature*. Leiden: Brill, 1967.

Piay Augusto, Diego. "Acercamiento prosopográfico al priscilianismo." Pages 601–26 in *Espacio y tiempo en la percepción de la antigüedad tardía*. Edited by Elena Conde Guerri, Rafael Gonzáles Fernández, and Alejandro Egea Vivancos. AC 23. Murcia: Universidad de Murcia, 2006.

Piscitelli Carpino, M. Teresa. "L'amore coniugale nella poesia cristiana: L'epitalamio di Paolino di Nola." Pages 51–85 in *Carminis incentor Christus*. Edited by Antonio V. Nazzaro and Rosario Scognamiglio. Bari: Ecumenica Editrice, 2012.

Plisch, Uwe-Karsten. "Norea."*RAC* 25 (2013): 1129–33.

———. "'Du zeigst das Übermaß des Erklärers'—Ein Verständnisproblem im Dialog des Erlösers (NHC III,5) und seine Lösung." Pages 233–35 in *Ägypten und der christliche Orient*. Edited by Heike Behlmer, Ute Pietruschka, Frank Feder, and Theresa Kohl. Wiesbaden: Harrassowitz, 2018.

Poirier, John C. "Montanist Pepuza-Jerusalem and the Dwelling Place of Wisdom." *JECS* 7 (1999): 491–507.

Pölönen, Janne. "Plebeians and Repression of Crime in the Roman Empire: From Torture of Convicts to Torture of Suspects." *RIDA* 51 (2004): 217–57.

Potterie, Ignace de la. "Il parto verginale del Verbo incarnato: 'Non ex sanguinibus ... sed ex Deo natus est' (Gv 1,13)." *Marianum* 45 (1983): 127–74.

Powell, Douglas. "Tertullianists and Cataphrygians." *VC* 29 (1975): 33–54.

Price, Simon R. F. "The Future of Dreams: From Freud to Artemidorus." Pages 365–88 in *Before Sexuality: The Construction of Erotic Experience in the Ancient Greek World*. Edited by David M. Halperin. Princeton: Princeton University Press, 1999.

Pricoco, Salvatore. *L'isola dei santi: Il cenobio di Lerino e le origini del monachesimo gallico*. Rome: Edizioni dell'Ateneo & Bizzarri, 1978.

Prinzivalli, Emanuela. "Perpetua, la martire." Pages 153–86 in *Roma al femminile*. Edited by Augusto Fraschetti. Rome: Laterza, 1994.

Raphael, Rebecca. *Biblical Corpora: Representations of Disability in Hebrew Biblical Literature*. LHBOTS. London: Continuum, 2009.

Rasimus, Tuomas. *Paradise Reconsidered in Gnostic Mythmaking: Rethinking Sethianism in Light of the Ophite Evidence*. NHMS 68. Leiden: Brill, 2009.

Reed, Annette Yoshiko. "The Afterlives of New Testament Apocrypha." *JBL* 133 (2015): 401–25.

Reinhartz, Adele. "Women in the Johannine Community: An Exercise in Historical Imagination." Pages 14–33 in vol. 2 of *A Feminist Companion to John*. Edited by Amy-Jill Levine. 2 vols. FCNTECW 4–5. London: Sheffield Academic, 2003.

Reyes, Paulina de los, and Diana Mulinari. *Intersektionalitet: Kritiska reflektioner över (o)jämlikhetens landskap*. Stockholm: Liber, 2005.

Richter-Reimer, Ivoni. *Frauen in der Apostelgeschichte des Lukas: Eine feministisch-theologische Exegese*. Gütersloh: Gütersloher Verlagshaus, 1992.

Roloff, Jürgen. "Apostel/Apostolat/Apostolozität." *TRE* 3 (1978): 440–41.

——. *Der erste Brief an Timotheus*. EKKNT 15. Zürich: Benziger, 1988.

Rose, Martha L. *The Staff of Oedipus: Transforming Disability in Ancient Greece*. Ann Arbor: University of Michigan Press, 2003.

Sack, Robert D. *Human Territoriality: Its Theory and History*. CSHG 7. Cambridge: Cambridge University Press, 1986.

Salisbury, Joyce E. *Perpetua's Passion: The Death and Memory of a Young Roman Woman*. New York: Routledge, 1997.

Salmenkivi, Erja. "Some Remarks on Literate Women in Roman Egypt." Pages 62–72 in *Women and Knowledge in Early Christianity*. Edited by Ulla Tervahauta, Ivan Miroshnikov, Outi Lehtipuu, and Ismo Dunderberg. VCSup 144. Leiden: Brill, 2017.

Salzman, Michele R. "Pagans and Christians." Pages 186–202 in *The Oxford Handbook of Early Christian Studies*. Edited by Susan Ashbrook Harvey and David G. Hunter. Oxford: Oxford University Press, 2008.

Sanders, Gabriel. "Égérie, Saint Jérôme et la Bible: En marge de l'Itin. Eg. 18, 2, 39, 5 et 2, 2." Pages 181–99 in vol. 1 of *Corona Gratiarum: Miscellanea patristica, historica et liturgica Eligio Dekkers XII Lustra Complenti Oblata*. Bruges: Nijhoff, 1975.

Sandnes, Karl Olav. *The Gospel "according to Homer and Vergil."* NovTSup 138. Leiden: Brill, 2011.

Sbrancia, Anna. "L'epitalamio di S. Paolino di Nola (carme 25)." *AFLF* 11 (1978): 83–129.

Schaberg, Jane D., and Sharon H. Ringe. "The Gospel of Luke." Pages 493–511 in *The Women's Bible Commentary*. Edited by Carol A. Newsom, Sharon H. Ringe, and Jacqueline E. Lapsley. Louisville: Westminster John Knox, 2012.

Scheffler, Judith A., ed. *Wall Tappings: An International Anthology of Woman's Prison Writings 200 to the Present*. New York: Feminist, 2002.

Schenke, Hans-Martin. "The Phenomenon and Significance of Gnostic Sethianism." Pages 588–616 in vol. 2 of *The Rediscovery of Gnosticism: Proceedings of the International Conference on Gnosticism at Yale, New Haven, Connecticut, March 28–31, 1978*. Edited by Bentley Layton. Leiden: Brill, 1981.

———. "Das sethianische System nach Nag-Hammadi-Handschriften." Pages 165–73 in *Studia Coptica*. Edited by Peter Nagel. BBA 45. Berlin: Akademie, 1974.

Scheperlen, Wilhelm. *Der Montanismus und die phrygischen Kulte: Eine religionsgeschichtliche Untersuchung*. Tübingen: Mohr, 1929.

Schipper, Jeremy. *Disability and Isaiah's Suffering Servant*. BibRef. Oxford: Oxford University Press, 2011.

———. *Disability Studies and the Hebrew Bible: Figuring Mephibosheth in the David Story*. New York: T&T Clark, 2006.

Schottroff, Luise. "Purity and Holiness of Women and Men in 1 Corinthians and the Consequences for Feminist Hermeneutics." Pages 83–93 in *Distant Voices Drawing Near: Essays in Honor of Antoinette Clark Wire*. Edited by Holly E. Hearon. Collegeville, MN: Liturgical Press, 2004.

Schroer, Silvia. *Die Weisheit hat ihr Haus gebaut: Studien zur Gestalt der Sophia in den biblischen Schriften*. Mainz: Grünewald, 1996.

Schüssler Fiorenza, Elisabeth. *But She Said: Feminist Practices of Biblical Interpretation*. Boston: Beacon, 1992.

———. *In Memory of Her: A Feminist Theological Reconstruction of Christian Origins*. New York: Crossroad, 1983.

———. *Rhetoric and Ethic: The Politics of Biblical Studies*. Minneapolis: Augsburg Fortress, 1999.

———, ed. *Searching the Scriptures: A Feminist Commentary*. 2 vols. New York: Crossroad, 1994.

Schwartz, Saundra. "From Bedroom to Courtroom: The Adultery Type-Scene and the Acts of Andrew." Pages 267–311 in *Mapping Gender in Ancient Religious Discourses*. Edited by Todd C. Penner and Caroline Vander Sitchele. Leiden: Brill, 2007.

Scott, Joan W. "Gender: A Useful Category of Historical Analysis." *AHR* 91 (1986): 1053–75.

Seim, Turid Karlsen. *The Double Message: Patterns of Gender in Luke-Acts*. Translated by Brian McNeil. Edinburgh: T&T Clark, 1994.

Shakespeare, Tom. "The Social Model of Disability." Pages 197–204 in *The Disability Studies Reader*. Edited by Lennard J. Davis. New York: Routledge, 2006.

Shatzmiller, Joseph. "Récits de voyages hébraïques au Moyen-âge." Pages 1281–1374 in *Croisadeset Pélerinage: Récits, chroniques et voages en Terre Sainte*. Edited by Danielle Régnier-Bohler. París: Bouquins, 1997.

Shoemaker, Stephen J. "Early Christian Apocryphal Literature." Pages 521–48 in *The Oxford Handbook of Early Christian Studies*. Edited by Susan Ashbrook Harvey and David G. Hunter. Oxford: Oxford University Press, 2008.

Simon, Marcel. "Les saints d'Israël dans la dévotion de l'Église ancienne." Pages 154–80 in *Recherches d'histoire judéo-chrétienne*. Paris: Mouton, 1962.

Simonelli, Cristina. "Introduzione." Pages 24–29 in *Il Commonitorio*, by Vincenzo di Lérins. Milan: Paoline, 2008.

———. "Il tesoro e la perla: Unificazione e comunione nell'ep.24 di Paolino e Terasia." Pages 31–51 in *Frammentazione dell'esperienza e ricerca di unità*. Edited by Cristina Simonelli, Francesco Botturi, and Patrizio Rota Scalabrini. Milan: Glossa, 2010.

Sivan, Hagith. "Anician Women, the Cento of Proba and the Aristocratic Conversion in the Fourth Century." *VC* 47 (1993): 140–57.

Smith, Jonathan Z. "The Garments of Shame." Pages 1–23 in *Map Is Not Territory: Studies in the History of Religion*. SJLA 23. Leiden: Brill, 1978.

———. *To Take Place: Toward Theory in Ritual*. Chicago: University of Chicago Press, 1987.

Smith, W. Andrew. *A Study of the Gospels in Codex Alexandrinus: Codicology, Palaeography, and Scribal Hands*. Leiden: Brill, 2014.

Snyder, Glenn E. *Acts of Paul: The Formation of a Pauline Corpus*. WUNT 2/352. Tübingen: Mohr Siebeck, 2013.

Solevåg, Rebecca. *Birthing Salvation: Gender and Class in Early Christian Childbearing Discourse*. BibInt 121. Leiden: Brill, 2013.
Sowers, Brian P. *Eudocia: The Making of a Homeric Christian*. Cincinnati: University of Cincinnati Press, 2006.
Späth, Thomas. *Männlichkeit und Weiblichkeit bei Tacitus: Zur Konstruktion der Geschlechter in der römischen Kaiserzeit*. GG 9. Frankfurt: Campus, 1994.
Stählin, Gustav. "χήρα." *TWNT* 9:428–44.
Standhartinger, Angela. "Geschlechterkonstruktionen bei Paulus: Feministische Zugänge zu Gal 3,27f und Röm 7,1–6." *US* 58 (2003): 339–49.
———. "'Wie die verehrteste Judith und die besonnenste Hanna': Traditionsgeschichtliche Beobachtungen zur Herkunft der Witwengruppe im entstehenden Christentum." Pages 103–26 in *Dem Tod nicht glauben: Sozialgeschichte der Bibel, Festschrift für Luise Schottroff*. Edited by Frank Crüsemann. Gütersloh: Gütersloher Verlagshaus, 2004.
Starowieski, Marek. "Bibliografia Egeriana."*Aug* 19 (1979): 297–318.
Stewart, Zeph. "Greek Crowns and Christians Martyrs." Pages 119–24 in *Mémorial André-Jean Festugière: Antiquité païenne et chrétienne*. Edited by Enzo Lucchesi and Henri D. Saffrey. Geneva: Cramer, 1984.
Stichel, Rainer. "Die Einführung Marias in den Tempel: Vorläufige Beobachtungen." Pages 379–406 in *Religionsgeschichte des Neuen Testaments: Festschrift für Klaus Berger zum 60. Geburtstag*. Edited by Axel von Dobbeler, Kurt Erlemann, and Roman Heiligenthal. Tübingen: Francke, 2000.
Stiker, Henri-Jacques. *A History of Disability*. Ann Arbor: University of Michigan Press, 1999.
Stowers, Stanley K. "The Concept of 'Community' and the History of Early Christianity." *MTSR* 23 (2011): 238–56.
Streete, Gail Corrington. *The Strange Woman: Power and Sex in the Bible*. Louisville: Westminster John Knox, 1997.
Tabbernee, William. *Fake Prophecy and Polluted Sacraments: Ecclesiastical and Imperial Reaction to Montanism*. VCSup 84. Leiden: Brill, 2007.
Tafi, Angelo. "Egeria e la Bibbia." Pages 167–76 in *Atti del Convegno Internazionale sulla Peregrinatio Egeriae: Nel centenario della pubblicazione del "Codex Aretinus 405," già "Aretinut VI,3," Arezzo October 23–25, 1987*. Arezzo: Academia Petrarca, 1990.
Taschl-Erber, Andrea. "'Eva wird Apostel!': Rezeptionslinien des Osterapostolats Marias von Magdala in der lateinischen Patristik." Pages 161–96 in *Geschlechterverhältnisse und Macht: Lebensformen in der*

Zeit des frühen Christentums. Edited by Irmtraud Fischer and Christoph Heil. EUZ 21. Münster: LIT, 2010.

Thierry, Nicole. "Un problème de continuité ou de rupture: La Cappadoce entre Rome, Byzance et les Arabes." *CRAI* 121 (1977): 98–145.

Thomas, Christine M. *The Acts of Peter, Gospel Literature, and the Ancient Novel: Rewriting the Past.* Oxford: Oxford University Press, 2003.

Thomassen, Einar. *The Spiritual Seed: The Church of the "Valentinians."* NHMS 60. Leiden: Brill, 2006.

Toepel, Alexander. *Das Protevangelium des Jakobus: Ein Beitrag zur Diskussion um Herkunft, Auslegung und theologische Einordnung.* Münster: Aschendorff, 2014.

Tolmie, François D. "Tendencies in the Interpretation of Gal 3:28 since 1990." *AcT* 34 suppl. 19 (2014): 105–29.

Torjesen, Karen Jo. "Clergy and Laity." Pages 389–405 in *The Oxford Handbook of Early Christian Studies.* Edited by Susan Ashbrook Harvey and David G. Hunter. Oxford: Oxford University Press, 2008.

Trevett, Christine. *Montanism: Gender, Authority and the New Prophecy.* Cambridge: Cambridge University Press, 1996.

Tuckett, Christopher. "Introduction: What Is Early Christian Apocrypha?" Pages 3–12 in *The Oxford Handbook of Early Christian Apocrypha.* Edited by Andrew Gregory and Christopher Tuckett. Oxford: Oxford University Press, 2015.

Turner, Bryan S. *The Body and Society: Explorations in Social Theory.* London: Sage, 1996.

Turner, John D. *Sethian Gnosticism and the Platonic Tradition.* BCNH Section Études 6. Leuven: Peeters, 2001.

Väänänen, Veikko. *Le journal-épitre d'Égérie: Étude linguistique.* Helsinki: Suomalainen Tiedeakatemia, 1987.

Valerio, Adriana. *Cristianesimo al femminile.* Napoli: D'Auria, 1990.

Vander Stichele, Caroline, and Todd Penner. *Contextualizing Gender in Early Christian Discourse: Thinking beyond Thecla.* London: Continuum, 2009.

———. "Gendering Violence: Patterns of Power and Constructs of Masculinity in the Acts of the Apostles." Pages 193–209 in *A Feminist Companion to the Acts of the Apostles.* Edited by Amy-Jill Levine with Marianne Blickenstaff. FCNTECW. London: T&T Clark, 2004.

Vogt, Kari. "'Männlichwerden': Aspekte einer urchristlichen Anthropologie." *Concilium* 21 (1985): 434–42.

Vorster, Johannes N. "Construction of Culture through the Construction of Person: The Construction of Thecla in the Acts of Thecla." Pages 98–117 in *A Feminist Companion to the New Testament Apocrypha*. Edited by Amy-Jill Levine with Maria Mayo Robbins. FCNTECW 11. London: T&T Clark, 2006.

Vuong, Lily C. *Gender and Purity in the Protevangelium of James*. Tübingen: Mohr Siebeck, 2013.

Wagener, Ulrike. *Die Ordnung des "Hauses Gottes": Der Ort von Frauen in der Ekklesiologie der Pastoralbriefe*. WUNT 2/65. Tübingen: Mohr Siebeck, 1994.

———. "(Un-)Ordnung im Haushalt Gottes? Wie Schüler des Paulus die Freiheit ihrer Glaubensschwestern bekämpfen." *BK* 65 (2010): 223–27.

Wehn, Beate. "'Blessed Are the Bodies of Those Who Are Virgins': Reflections on the Image of Paul in the Acts of Thecla." *JSNT* 79 (2000): 149–64.

Weingarten, Susan. "Was the Pilgrim from Bordeaux a Woman? A Reply to Laurie Douglass." *JECS* 7 (1999): 291–97.

Weiser, Alfons. "δουλεύω κτλ." *EWNT* 1 (1980): 844–52.

Welch, Julia L. "Cross-Dressing and Cross-Purposes: Gender Possibilities in the Acts of Thecla." Pages 66–78 in *Gender Reversals and Gender Cultures: Anthropological and Historical Perspectives*. Edited by Sabrina P. Ramet. London: Routledge, 1996.

Wettstein, Johann Jakob. *Prolegomena ad Novi Testamenti editionem accuratissimam*. Amsterdam: Wetstenios & Smith, 1730.

White, Benjamin L. *Remembering Paul: Ancient and Modern Contests over the Image of the Apostle*. Oxford: Oxford University Press, 2014.

Williams, Craig A. *Roman Homosexuality: Ideologies of Masculinity in Classical Antiquity*. Oxford: Oxford University Press, 1999.

Williams, Gareth. "Theorizing Disability." Pages 123–44 in *Handbook of Disability Studies*. Edited by Gary L. Albrecht, Katherine D. Seelman, and Michael Bury. Thousand Oaks, CA: Sage, 2001.

Williams, Michael Allen. *Rethinking "Gnosticism": An Argument for Dismantling a Dubious Category*. Princeton: Princeton University Press, 1996.

———. "Sethianism." Pages 32–63 in *A Companion to Second-Century Christian "Heretics."* Edited by Antti Marjanen and Petri Luomanen. Leiden: Brill, 2005.

Wilson-Kastner, Patricia G. *A Lost Tradition: Women Writers of the Early Church*. Lanham, MD: University Press of America, 1981.

Wisse, Frederik. "Flee Femininity: Antifemininity in Gnostic Texts and the Question of Social Milieu." Pages 297–307 in *Images of the Feminine in Gnosticism*. Edited by Karen L. King. SAC 4. Harrisburg, PA: Trinity Press International, 2000.

Witke, Charles. *Numen Litterarum: The Old and the New in Latin Poetry from Constantine to Gregory the Great*. MST 5. Leiden: Brill, 1971.

Wittig, Monique. "The Point of View: Universal or Particular." Pages 59–67 in *The Straight Mind and Other Essays*. Boston: Beacon, 1992.

Wolter, Michael. *Das Lukasevangelium*. HNT 5. Tübingen: Mohr Siebeck, 2008.

Ziegler, Joseph. "Die Peregrinatio Aetheriae und das Onomastikon des Eusebius." *Bib* 12 (1931): 70–84.

———. "Die Peregrinatio Aetheriae und die hl. Schrift." *Bib* 12 (1931): 163–64.

Contributors

Carmen Bernabé Ubieta holds a doctorate in theology from the University of Deusto and serves currently as an extraordinary professor of biblical studies at the same university. She specializes in the study of the historical Jesus and the origins of Christianity, based on social-scientific analysis of texts.

Bernadette J. Brooten, who holds a doctorate from Harvard University, is Robert and Myra Kraft and Jacob Hiatt Professor Emerita at Brandeis University. Her research areas include Jewish and Christian women's history in the Roman period, slavery in early Christianity, and religion and law.

María José Cabezas Cabello holds a doctorate from the University of Sevilla. She works currently at Almenara High School in Vélez-Málaga as a teacher of Latin and classical culture.

Anna Carfora is Associate Professor of Church History at San Luigi Papal Theological Seminary of Southern Italy in Naples, where she is director of the "Cataldo Naro" Institute of Research on Christian History. She specializes in ancient martyrdom.

Ute E. Eisen, who holds a doctorate from the University of Hamburg, is Professor of Old and New Testament at the Institute of Protestant Theology, University of Giessen. Her research interests include feminist and gender studies, narratology, and emotion research.

Judith Hartenstein holds a doctorate from the Humboldt University of Berlin. She is Professor of Protestant theology with a focus on the New Testament and religious education at the University of Koblenz-Landau. She specializes in noncanonical gospels, especially from Nag Hammadi and related documents, the Gospel of John, the characterization of disciples, and questions of hermeneutics.

Ursula Ulrike Kaiser holds a doctorate from the Humboldt-University of Berlin and is Professor of Biblical Theology and Its Didactics at the Seminary of Protestant Theology and Religious Education, University of Braunschweig. Her main fields of research include the interpretation of metaphors in early Christian literature, the Nag Hammadi writings, and the apocryphal infancy gospels.

Karen L. King received a Ph.D. from Brown University and is currently the Hollis Professor of Divinity at Harvard University. Her research areas focus on women and gender studies, Nag Hammadi and related literature, and early Christian martyrdom.

Outi Lehtipuu holds a doctorate from the University of Helsinki. She works currently as Senior Lecturer at the Department of Biblical Studies at the same university. She specializes in New Testament gospels, apocryphal acts, and other early Christian literature, together with the reception history of biblical texts.

Heidrun Mader holds a doctorate from the University of Heidelberg. She works currently as an extraordinary professor at the Department of New Testament Studies at the same university. She specializes in prophecy in early Christianity, comparative studies on Mark and Paul, emotions in biblical narratives, and gender aspects in Galatians.

Antti Marjanen holds a doctorate from the University of Helsinki. He is Professor Emeritus of Gnostic Studies of the same University. He specializes in Nag Hammadi texts, early Christian texts dealing with women, and Christian apocryphal literature.

Silvia Pellegrini holds a doctorate in classical philology from the Catholic University of the Sacred Heart in Milan and in theology from the Humboldt University of Berlin. She works currently as Professor at the Institute of Catholic Theology of the Vechta University and at the Institute of Catholic Theology of the Osnabrück University. Her research interests include methodology for New Testament exegesis, semiotics, the

Gospel of Mark and the Gospel of John, 1 Thessalonians, the Nag Hammadi codices, and the New Testament apocrypha.

Silke Petersen holds a doctorate from the University of Hamburg. She is extraordinary professor in New Testament Studies at the same university. Her publications focus on Mary of Magdala, the Gospel of John, questions related to gender, and early Christian literature that became apocryphal.

Uwe-Karsten Plisch received a doctorate from the Humboldt University of Berlin and works as Senior Researcher in the project "Digital Edition of the Coptic Old Testament" at the University of Göttingen. His research interests include ancient Christian apocryphal texts, particularly the Nag Hammadi manuscripts.

Cristina Simonelli holds a doctorate in theology and patristics from the Institutum Patristicum Augustinianum in Rome. She works currently as Lecturer at the Theological Faculty of Northern Italy in Milan, teaching early Christian literature, church history, and ancient theology.

Anna Rebecca Solevåg has a PhD from the University of Oslo and is Professor of New Testament Studies at VID Specialized University in Stavanger, Norway. In her research, she studies the intersections of gender, class, dis/ability, age, ethnicity, and other forms of marginalization, exploring the complexities of identity and negotiations of power taking place at these crossroads.

Maria Dolores Martin Trutet is a Benedictine who has completed a degree in theology at the University of Paris and in philosophy at the University of Strasbourg. She teaches at the Theological School of the Abbey of Montserrat.

Ancient Sources Index

Hebrew Bible/Septuagint

Genesis
1	221–236
1–2	232
1–4	224–228, 230–234
1–6	45, 48
1–12	48
1:1–4	223–224
1:11–31	224–225
1:16	232
1:21	232
1:24–25	232
1:26	233
1:27	233
1:28	49, 71, 72, 87, 225
2	91, 108
2:4–25	236
2:7	224, 225–228
2:8	47, 73, 225
2:10	225
2:15	233
2:21–23	225
2:21–24	86, 87
2:23	253
3	227
3:5	228–230
3:7	229
3:15	229
3:16	212
3:20	91, 229
4:22	49
4:25	60
6:18	60
16:1	60
	100
16:2–3	174
16:6	176
17:17	100
18:11–15	100
19:26	248
22:18	107
25:21	100
28:12–17	211
29:31	100
30:1	100
30:3–4	174
30:6	100
30:9	174
30:22	100
31:1	100
38	174
38:14	177

Exodus
	223
13:15	102
25:29	215

Leviticus
12	91

Numbers
23:5	292
23:16	292

Judges
16:28	314

Ruth
	174
4:11	107

1 Samuel		**Sirach**	
1	102	24	293
1:6	100	26:14	5
2:22	102	46:17	66
1 Kings		**New Testament**	
14:21	60		
21:25–26	197	Matthew	2, 10, 25
		1–2	92, 115
2 Kings		1:18	106
24	102	1:19	116
		1:20	105, 106
Psalms		1:20–24	116
16:5	215	2	105
22:10	97	2:11	121
23 [LXX 22]	214	2:13	116
29:3	66	2:19–23	116
		5:4–9	159
Proverbs		7:15	283
1:20	60	11:25–30	64
8	9	13:55	119
8:21–30	57–58	20:20–23	215
9:1	60	23:37	290
		25:35	311
Job		27:44	313
9:9	232	27:55	35
38:31	232	27:57	37
		28	41
		28:16–20	39
Isaiah			
2:3	291	Mark	2, 43, 112
42:13–14	289	2:14	42
46:3–4	289	6:2–3	115
49:14–15	289	6:3	106, 119
51:53	292	10:2–12	299
65:23	107	10:35–40	215
		15:32	313
Jeremiah		15:40	35, 76
15:15	314	16:1	76
25:30	66	16:17–18	140
Hosea			
3:1–4	197	Luke	2, 43, 280
		1–2	92
Zechariah		1:3	168
9:15	215	1:7	100

Ancient Sources Index 363

1:27	106	20:29	283
1:42	83	21:9	277
1:48	286	24:25	153
2	115		
2:3	105	Romans	
2:17–20	121	1:1	306
2:22	91	5:12–21	92
2:22–24	102	12:13	311
2:28	121	15:19	291
2:36–38	102	16:1–2	298, 304, 306–307
2:38	121	16:1–16	307
2:41–52	115, 116, 121, 123	16:3	300, 307
2:49	114	16:7	284, 303, 308
2:50	125		
3:31	105	1 Corinthians	10, 153, 159–161
7:35	292	1–2	292
7:36–50	312	2:4	283
8:1–3	34	3:16–17	159
8:2	35	5:10–11	200
8:3	298	6:16–19	159
12:50	215	7	156, 160–62
20:36	160	7:1–7	299
23:39–43	309, 313	7:2–5	160
23:42	310, 313	7:8–16	299
		7:9	156
John	2, 20, 34, 42–44	7:10–16	160
1:1–14	64	7:25–40	299
1:45	115	7:29	159
2:1–11	271	7:29–31	161
6:42	115	7:36–38	160
8:44	228	9:16–17	284
8:58	114	9:24–26	217
12:28	66	9:25	156
13:14–17	312	11:8	91
20	43	11:11	92
		11:11–12	91
Acts	156	12	292
1–2	291	12:8	292
5:7–11	203	12:13	72, 275
9:36	36	12:27	275
9:36–41	298	14:33–36	5, 197, 278, 300, 305
16	298	14:34	278
18	300	14:35	149
18:3	298	14:36	291
18:26	300	15:28	275

364 Ancient Sources Index

1 Corinthians (cont.)		2:11–15	75, 278–279, 259
15:45	92	2:12	5
15:52	300	2:15	26, 153
16:19	300	3:1	311
		3:1–13	305
2 Corinthians		3:2	26, 164, 311
1:6	312	3:4	311
5:18–19	305	3:8–13	306
6:16	159	3:12	311
7:7	312	3:13	311
		4:1–5	26, 154
Galatians		4:19	300
1:10	306	5	315
3:26–28	72, 79	5:3–16	310
3:28	72–73, 274–275	5:9	310
4:4	95	5:9–10	311
4:26	291	5:9–16	310
5:11	284	5:10	309, 310–312
5:23	156	5:14	160
Ephesians	26	2 Timothy	25, 155
1:17–21	155	2:16–19	154, 155
2:5–7	155		
4:1–16	275	Titus	153
5:22–33	26, 275	1:6	311
		1:8	156, 311
Philippians		2:4	311
1:1	306		
3:12–14	218	Hebrews	280
4:2–3	299	13:2	311
Colossians		2 Peter	
3:1–4	155	1:6	156
3:9–11	72		
4:12	306	2 John	200
4:15	299		
		3 John	
1 Thessalonians		5–8	311
3:4	312		
4:3–5	26	Jude	
		1:1	306
1 Timothy	28		
2	15	Revelation	200, 218, 258
2:9–15	305	2:20	286
2:11–12	197	2:20–23	277

Ancient Sources Index   365

5:8	215	9	134
7:4–17	213–214	27	134
12	212, 291	29.2	140
14:2	66	76–78	140–141
14:4	162		
14:8	199	Acts of Paul	127, 138, 147
16:19	199		
17:5	199	Acts of Paul and Thecla. *See* Acts of Thecla	
18:2	199		
19:2	199	Acts of Peter	10, 127, 137, 138–40, 187–204
19:6	66		
21:9–10	291		

Other Ancient Texts

Achilles Tatius, *Leucippe and Clitophon*	
5.20.2	94
8.6.12–14	94
Act of Peter (BG 4)	189–90
128.4–6	191
128.10–19	191
129.4–5	195
129.10–12	191
129.10–17	201–2
129.14–19	191
131.13–14	191
132.14–15	196
135.10–13	192
139.19–140.4	193
Acts of Andrew	10, 127, 137, 142, 162, 165–186. *See also* Passion of Andrew
14	135
14.2	134, 135, 141
17–22	131, 162
23.2	135
39 (7)	134
48.8	134
Acts of the Council of Nicaea	
Canon 19	304
Acts of John	127, 137, 140–141
2	134

Acts of Peter, Actus Vercellenses	189–90, 192
2	192
7	200
9	200
10	200
12	200, 201
13	201
14	200
17	201, 203
20–21	201
21–22	191
22	192–193, 198
23	201
25	203
28	200
29	191, 201
Acts of Philip	83–84, 127
8.3	83
8.4	83
Mart. 20.25.32 (A)	84
Acts of Thecla	10, 11, 82–83, 137–38, 144, 147–164, 259, 261
1	154
5	153, 154
5–6	158–162
7	154
9	154, 155, 162
12	153, 160, 162
14	154–155
15	152

Ancient Sources Index

Acts of Thecla (cont.)
21	152, 163
25	82
29	159
37	152
40	82, 152, 154, 163
41	138, 152
42	154
43	138
48	138

Acts of Thomas 127, 137, 142, 258
56	179
82	142
87	142
93	142
102	142

Acts of Xanthippe and Polyxena 82, 127, 144
33	82–83
36	82–83

Allogenes (NHC XI 3) 24

Ambrose, *Epistulae*
19	272
27.1–2	265
42	269

Ambrose, *De virginibus*
1.2–11	209
1.3.10	209
3.3.11	5

Ammianus Marcellinus, *Res Gestae*
22.10.7	222

Apocalypse of Peter (Akhmim)
29	179

Apocalypse of Peter (Ethiopic)
9	179

Apocryphon of James. *See* Secret Book of James

Apocryphon of John. *See* Secret Book of John

Apophthegmata Patrum (et Matrum)
81–82, 253–54, 263

Aristotle, *Nikomachean Ethics*
7,1145a–1154b	155

Aristotle, *Politcs*
I,5,1254b 13–14	73

Aristotle, *Rhetoric*
I 1366b	134, 135

Ascension of Isaiah
11.7–10	97, 98

Athanasius, *Festal Letter* 39   3, 18

Augustine, *Epistulae*
30–31	265–66
31.6	266
186	267

Augustine, *Against the Two Letters of the Pelagians*
4.2.2	268–69

Augustine, *Sermo* 280   219

b. Gittin 23a	172
b. Ketubbot 7b	272

Barnabas
2.2	156

Basil of Seleucia, *Life and Miracles of Saint Thecla*   261

Ancient Sources Index

Bernard of Clairvaux, *In assumptione B.V.Mariae sermo* 4.5   107

Boccaccio, *De mulieribus claris*   238

1 Book of Jeu   35

2 Book of Jeu   35, 39, 40
- 42   36
- 45   36

Book of Thomas (NHC II 7)   35, 42
- 139.33   78
- 140.32   78
- 141.34   78
- 143.28   78
- 145.9   78

Celsus, *True Doctrine*   144
- 1.28   95

1 Clement   6
- 21.6–7   157
- 21.7   5
- 35.2   156
- 38.2   156
- 62.2   156
- 64   156

2 Clement   6
- 4.3   156
- 5.2–4   283
- 12.2   72
- 14.2   291

Clement of Alexandria, *Excerpts from Theodotus*
- 67   35

Clement of Alexandria, *Paedagogus*
- 2.7.58   5

Clement of Alexandria, *Stromata*
- 3.1.1   26, 86
- 3.4.29   86
- 3.14.94.3   227
- 3.45   35
- 3.58   26
- 3.63   35
- 3.63.1   76
- 3.66   35
- 3.66.1–2   77
- 3.92   35
- 3.92.2–93.1   77
- 3.93.1   2
- 4.17.108   5
- 6.100.3   285

Codex Theodosianus
- 9.24.1   196

Corpus Hermeticum *Poimandres*   214

Corpus iuris civilis
- Digesta 23.2.24   181
- Digesta 24.2   185
- Digesta 48.5.2.2   181
- Digesta 48.5.6   181
- Digesta 48.18   178
- Digesta 48.18.1.1   178
- Digesta 48.18.12   178
- Digesta 48.19.29   178
- Institutiones 1.5.3   173
- Institutiones 1.9   185
- Institutiones 2.12–13   185

Cyprian, *Letters*
- 75.10   291

Cyprian, *The Dress of Virgins*
- 22   163

Cyril of Jerusalem, *Catechetical Lectures*
- Prolog 14–15   257
- 4.33–36   258
- 16.8.6   279

Dialogue of the Savior (NHC III 5)   35, 38, 41, 42, 43, 44
- 144.19   76

Dialogue of a Montanist with an Orthodox	280	20.11	249
		20.13	244, 252
		21.1	249–250
Didache		21.4	250
16.3	283	23.3	260
		23.5	259
Didascalia apostolorum		23.7	261
25	145	24.1	256
		25.9	261
Didymus the Blind, *De trinitate*		29.4	256
3.18.23	279	46.2	257
3.41	280	47.2	257
3.41.3	15–16	48.2	244

Egeria, *Itinerarium*	7, 11, 16, 145, 239–62, 281	Epiphanius of Salamis, *Panarion*	3
		26.1.3	60, 61
1.1	239	26.1.4–9	61
1.4	252	39.5.2	60
2.5	244	48–49	277
4.1–3	245	48.1.4	278, 282
4.2	244	48.1.4–13.8	278, 292
4.7	244	48.2.1	279
5.1	244	48.2.1–2	288
5.6	244	48.2.4	282, 284, 293
5.8	244	48.2.8	278
5.12	243, 244	48.3.1	278
6.3	244	48.3.2	283
7.1	245	48.8.7–9	278
7.5	244	48.9.10	278
9.2	252	48.10.4	278
10.1	244	48.11.1	293
10.3	244	48.11.7	278
10.7	245–246	48.11.9	293
12	248	48.11.10	278
12.2	244	48.12.4	284, 287
12.6–7	248	48.12.5	278
14.1	245	48.12.12	278
14.2	252	48.13.1	277, 282, 284, 285, 292
16.6	252	49.1.1	288
18.1–2	243	49.1.3	289
19.2	258	49.2.2	279, 291
19.16–19	258–259		
20–21	248		
20.4	249		
20.10	244, 258		

Ancient Sources Index

Epistle of the Apostles	35, 40, 42	5.16.13–15	281
		5.16.17	279, 281, 283, 285, 286
Epistle of Christ and Abgar	258, 260	5.17.3	279
		5.17.4	278, 288
4 Ezra		5.18.2	293
9	291	5.18.3–14	281
		6.12.3–6	2

Eudocia, *Homerocentones* 230–237
- 1–7: 230–231
- 8–10: 231–232
- 8–13: 232
- 8–33: 231–234
- 16–17: 232
- 18–20: 233
- 21–22: 233
- 25: 233
- 29–32: 233
- 33: 233
- 34–38: 234
- 34–91: 231, 234–236
- 47–57: 234–235
- 67: 235
- 77: 236
- 78–80: 236
- 82: 236
- 85–87: 236–237
- 92–2354: 231
- 157–169: 235

Eudocia, *The Martyrdom of Saint Cyprian*
238

Euripides, *Ion*
- 454: 92

Eusebius, *Historia ecclesiastica*
- 3.25.6: 165
- 3.31.4–5: 277
- 3.37.1: 277
- 5.1.41: 290
- 5.13.4: 283
- 5.16–18: 277, 278
- 5.16.6: 279
- 5.16.9: 281
- 5.16.10: 279

Eusebius, *Onomasticon* 246

Eusebius, *Vita Constantini* 261

Exegesis on the Soul (NHC II 6)
- 133.1–10: 45

Gerontius, *Vita Sanctae Melaniae*
- 2.34: 242

Ginza (Mandean)
- Rba 2.1.121: 60

Gospel of the Egyptians (Greek) 2, 35, 38, 41, 72, 75–79

Gospel of the Egyptians (NHC III 2, IV 2) 52

Gospel of Judas (CT 3) 4, 35
- 52: 45

Gospel of Mary 4, 16, 27, 35, 38, 43

Gospel of Peter 2, 35, 37
- 12.50: 36

Gospel of Philip (NHC II 3) 25, 26, 28, 38, 42, 86
- 60.34–61.12: 45
- 61.5–12: 86
- 68.17–22: 86
- 68.22–26: 45, 85
- 70.9–17: 87
- 70.9–22: 45
- 71.16–21: 97
- 78.12–79.13: 86

Gospel of Thomas (NHC II 2)   4, 9, 35, 40, 42, 43, 69–75, 77
- 22   70–72, 75, 87
- 61   36
- 90   64
- 99   70–71
- 114   41, 69–70, 73–75, 285

Gregory of Nyssa, *On the Soul and the Resurrection*   263

Gregory of Nyssa, *Life of Saint Macrina*   253, 258, 263

Heliodorus, *Aethiopica*
- 1.11.15–17   174

Homer, *Iliad*
- 14.347–348   233
- 18.481–486   232
- 23.107   233
- 23.536   233

Homer, *Odyssey*
- 4.565–567   235
- 5.70–71   233
- 5.136   235
- 6.181–185   235
- 13.221–440   289–290
- 17.287   236

Hypostasis of the Archons. *See* Nature of the Rulers

Ignatius, *To the Ephesians*
- 19.1   96

Ignatius, *To the Philadelphians*
- 2.2   283

Ignatius, *To the Smyrnaeans*
- 1.1–2   96

Ignatius, *To the Trallians*
- 9.1–2   95–96

Infancy Gospel of Thomas   10, 111–126
- 2   116, 117, 121–122
- 2.5   121
- 3   117, 122, 124
- 4   117, 122, 124
- 4.1   121
- 5   121, 122
- 5.1   117
- 5.2   117
- 5.3   115, 117, 118
- 6   118
- 6–8   119, 122
- 6.1   118
- 6.2   114, 118, 121
- 7   120
- 7.3   122
- 9   122
- 9.3   121
- 10   125
- 11[12]   120
- 12[13]   119, 121
- 13[14]   119, 122
- 13[14].3   119
- 14[15]   119
- 14[15].2   125
- 17[19]   115
- 17[19].3   114

Inscriptions   295–300
- Honorary, from Miletus   286–87
- Deaconess Basilissa   299
- Deaconess Maria   308–15
- Deaconess Paula   299–300
- Deaconess Sophia   303–8
- Grave   295–316
- Isis aretalogy of Cumae   86

Irenaeus of Lyon, *Adversus haereses*   2, 14, 21, 28, 31, 96, 226
- 1.6.4   26
- 1.30.9   60
- 3.11.8–9   2
- 3.22.4   227
- 4.31.3   248
- 4.33.11   96

5.1.2	28	m. Gittin 7:4	184
5.31.2	237		
		Marsanes (NHC X)	24
Itinerarium Burdigalense	250–251		
		Martial, *Epigrams*	
Jerome, *Adversus Helvidium de Mariae virginitate perpetua*		11.2.4	172
		11.104.5	172
20	97	12.43.10	172
Jerome, *Adversus Pelagianos dialogi III*		Martyrdom of Peter	189–190
2.4	97	1	197
		2	191, 193
Jerome, *Epistulae*		3	193
54.15	163		
		Melchizedek (NHC IX 1)	
John Chrysostomos, *De non iterando coniugo*		9.28–10.11	45
5	163	Nature of the Rulers (NHC II 4)	
		9, 45–55	
John Chrysostom, *De virginitate*		87.1	47
11.1	26	87.7–8	47
13.4	26	88.4–5	49
		88.10–16	47
Justin Martyr, *First Apology*		89.7–11	48–49
16.13	283	89.11–13	49–50
		89.23–28	52
Justin Martyr, *Dialogue with Trypho*		90.6–12	51
35.3	283	90.8–9	51
81.2	283	90.15–16	51
		90.34–91.3	51–52
Letter of Peter to Philip (NHC VIII 2)	28, 35	91.2	52
		91.3–7	51
139.15–30	28	91.11–12	51
		91.12	52
Life of Syncletica	253, 261	91.13–14	51
		91.30–92.2	53
Livy, *Ab urbe condita*	195, 199	91.30–33	51
3.44–48	195	91.35–92.2	53, 61
		92	62
Longus, *Daphnis and Chloe*	93	92.2	61
3.25.2	94	92.3–18	61
4.28.2	94	92.14	60
		92.21	60
Lysias, *On the Murder of Eratosthenes*		92.32	60
15–17	175	92.18–21	53

Ancient Sources Index

Nature of the Rulers (cont.)
93.2–97.21	61
93.6	60
94	59–60
96.19–35	53
97.4	61
97.18	47

Nonnus of Panopolis, *Paraphrasis S. secundum Ioannem euangelii*
1.76	234

Odes of Solomon
19.6–9	97–98
19.11	108

On the Origin of the World (NHC II 5)   52, 54, 55, 58
102.10–11	53
102.11	60
102.24–25	53
102.25	60
106.34	78
112.25–121.27	45
117.15–18	55

Origen, *Cantanae in sancti Pauli epistolas ad Corinthios*
14.36	280

Origen, *Contra Celsum*
1.28	95

Origen, *Fragmenta in Psalmos 1–150*
21	97

Origen, *Homiliae in Josuam*
9.9	75, 285

Origen, *Homiliae in Lucam*
14	97

Ovid, *Amores*
1.5.7–8	192

Ovid, *Ars amatoria*
2.619–620	192

Ovid, *Metamorphoses*
9.666–797	290
12.170–209	290

Pachomius, *Koinonia*
139–140	254

Paraphrase of Shem (NHC VII 1)
37.34	7

Passio Perpetuae et Felcitatis   84, 207–19, 280, 287
2.1	208
3.5	208
4.3	211
4.4	212
4.7	212
4.8–9	213
7.4	215
7.9	215
8.3–4	215
10.1–14	217
10.7	85, 287

Passion of Andrew
1–16	165–186
5	169–170
17–18	168
18	170–172
19	172–176
19–21	175
22	176–179
23	179–180
24–25	180–181
25	169
25–65	181–182
28	181
37	169
37.26–27	183
39	183
39.2–4	183
40	183

Ancient Sources Index

64–65	168	Philo, *De congressu eruditionis gratia*	
64.6	185	7	99

Paulinus (and Therasia) of Nola, *Carmina*

5.31	273
10.190	267
21	266
21.281	267
25	269–273
25.15–17	271
25.15–27	273
25.31	271
25.151–153	271
25.175–176	275
25.180–183	274
25.195–199	275
25.199–202	272
25.240	267
31.626	267

Paulinus (and Therasia) of Nola, *Epistulae*

3.4	265
6.1–3	265
13.3–5	267
24.2	275
24.15	274
28.2	275
32.6	267
42	267
45	267
51.1	266
51.3	266–267
51.4	267
80	267
149	267

Paulus Orosius, *Historiae adversus Paganos*

7.30	222

Philo, *De cherubim*

42–50	99

Philo, *Quaestiones et solutiones in Exodum*

1.18	73, 285

Pindar, *Olympic Odes*

7.35	92

Pistis Sophia 35, 38, 39, 40, 41, 43, 44, 47

7	39
136	36, 40
Book 4	40

Plutarch, *De curiositate*

519F	175

Plutarch, *De garrulitate*

507B–F	175

Polycarp, *To the Philippians* 157

4.2	157
5.2	156
5.3	163

Proba, *Cento Vergilianus* 11, 221–238, 280–281, 286

1–55	223
10	286
56–171	224–228
56–332	223
134–135	227
136–277	228–230
157–169	235
333–688	223
689–694	223

Protevangelium of James 10, 91–109

1–17	92
1.2	100
1.4	100
2.2	101
2.4	94
4.1	101, 102
4.4	101

Protevangelium of James (cont.)		Revelation of Adam (NHC V 5)	52
5.1	100		
5.2	101	1 Revelation of James	27, 35, 39, 42, 43
6.1	103, 104	NHC V, 3 38.16–18	36
6.3	101	CT 2, 25.18–25	37
7.1	103		
7.3	93, 292	2 Revelation of James (NHC V 4)	42
8.1	102, 104, 109		
8.2	94, 105	Salvian (and Palladia) of Marseille, *Epistulae*	
9.1–3	106		
9.2	106	4	266
9.3	106		
10.1	104, 105	Secret Book of James (NHC I 2)	35, 42
11.2	94, 104		
12.2	104	Secret Book of John (NHC II 1)	35, 42,
13.2	105, 106	46, 47, 49, 52, 54, 58, 66, 78, 290	
13.3	104, 106	18.28	78
14.1	106	19.18–33	47
14.2	94	20–25	45
15.2	107	24.8–18	50
15.3	105	24.24–25	50
15.4	94, 105, 106	24.28–29	50
16.1	106		
16.2	94	Secret Book of John (NHC III 1)	
17.1	94	27.5–14	78
17.2	106	31.21–32.3	50
18	106		
18–21	93	Secret Book of John (BG 2)	
18.1	94	21.19–21	290
18.2–3	94, 99	26–27	58
19.3–20.4	93	30	59
22	94	36–37	59
22–24	93	51.8–52.1	47
		55–64	45
Prudentius, *Hamartigenia*	249	63.1–9	50
Prudentius, *Peristephanon*		Sentences of Paul	
14	209	2.26	180–181
(Pseudo-)Aristotle, *De virtutibus et vitiis*		Shepherd of Hermas, Mandates	
155		1.26.2	156
		8.38.3	156
Pseudo-Cyprian, *De Sodoma*			
125–126	249	Shepherd of Hermas, Visions	
		1.2.4	156

3.8.4	155	45.23–47.14	45
2.1.1–4	291		
2.4.1	291	Theophilus of Antioch, *Ad Autolycum*	
		2.25	227
Sibylline Oracles			
2.313–321	214	Therasia (and Paulinus) of Nola	263–76
2.339–345	286		
		Thought of Norea (NHC IX 2)	53
Siricius, *Letter to Himerius*	272	27–29	62–63
		27.21	60
Siricius, *Optarem*	269	29.3	60
Sophia of Jesus Christ. *See* Wisdom of Jesus Christ		Three Forms of First Thought (NHC XIII 1)	64–66
		47	65–66
Tacitus, *Annales*			
2.85.1–3	181	Thunder: Perfect Mind (NHC VI 2)	66–68
15.37	172		
		13–14	67–68
Teachings of Silvanus (NHC VII 4)	81–82	16.3–4	67
93.3–13	81	Tripartite Tractate (NHC I 5)	25, 79
102.15	81	78.11–13	80
104.28	78	94.16–20	80
		132.16–28	79–80
Tertullian, *De anima*			
9.4	287	Valerius of Bierzo, *Epistula Beatissime Egerie laude*	241–242, 262
55	207		
Tertullian, *De cultu feminarum*		Virgil, *Aeneid*	
1.1.1–2	218–219	1.652	226–227
		6.405	226
Tertullian, *Adversus Marcionem*			
3.11	96	Virgil, *Eclogues*	
		9.37	226
Tertullian, *De baptismo*			
17.4–5	144, 149, 164	Vision of Paul	
		39	179
Testament of Abraham			
4.8 A	293	Wisdom of Jesus Christ (BG 3)	16, 27, 35, 38, 39, 41–43
Testimony of Truth (NHC IX 3)	14	77–78	37
3.56–58	26	100.3	39
30.28–30	26	102.7	39
44.2–19	27	107.14	39

Wisdom of Jesus Christ (cont.)
   114.12   39
   127.6   39

Xenophon, *Ephesian Tale*   94

www.ingramcontent.com/pod-product-compliance
Lightning Source LLC
Chambersburg PA
CBHW032147010526
44111CB00035B/1240